Emotion–Focused Couples Therapy

Emotion–Focused Couples Therapy

The DYNAMICS *of* EMOTION, LOVE, *and* POWER

Leslie S. Greenberg
Rhonda N. Goldman

AMERICAN PSYCHOLOGICAL ASSOCIATION
WASHINGTON, DC

Published by
American Psychological Association
750 First Street, NE
Washington, DC 20002
www.apa.org

To order
APA Order Department
P.O. Box 92984
Washington, DC 20090-2984
Tel: (800) 374-2721; Direct: (202) 336-5510
Fax: (202) 336-5502; TDD/TTY: (202) 336-6123
Online: www.apa.org/books/
E-mail: order@apa.org

In the U.K., Europe, Africa, and the Middle East, copies may be ordered from
American Psychological Association
3 Henrietta Street
Covent Garden, London
WC2E 8LU England

Typeset in Goudy by Stephen McDougal, Mechanicsville, MD

Printer: Maple-Vail Book Manufacturing Group, Binghamton, NY
Cover Designer: Berg Design, Albany, NY
Technical/Production Editor: Devon Bourexis

The opinions and statements published are the responsibility of the authors, and such opinions and statements do not necessarily represent the policies of the American Psychological Association.

Library of Congress Cataloging-in-Publication Data

Greenberg, Leslie S.
  Emotion-focused couples therapy : the dynamics of emotion, love, and power /
Leslie S. Greenberg and Rhonda N. Goldman.
    p. cm.
  Includes bibliographical references and index.
  ISBN-13: 978-1-4338-0316-1
  ISBN-10: 1-4338-0316-X
  1. Emotions. 2. Self. 3. Marital psychotherapy. I. Goldman, Rhonda N. II. Title.

  BF531.G74 2008
  362.82'86—dc22   2007031800

British Library Cataloguing-in-Publication Data
A CIP record is available from the British Library.

Printed in the United States of America
First Edition

CONTENTS

PREFACE

Two major events have influenced the explosion of interest in emotion-focused couples therapy (EFT-C) over the past decades. First, EFT-C has had sufficient research to be viewed as an evidence-based approach to the treatment of marital distress, and this has promoted its recognition. Second, a paradigm shift has been spurred by (a) psychological research on the critical role of attachment processes in adults and couples and, possibly even more important, (b) the more basic research on emotion, attachment, and the brain. Emotional and relational processes now are seen as central in development and change from infancy to adulthood (Schore, 1994, 2003). These are the processes at the heart of EFT-C, and they are seen as what needs to be addressed in psychotherapy if enduring change is to be effected. Emotion is no longer seen as the result of cognitive change alone but rather as the raw material that needs to be accessed and changed, and attachment is seen as a key affect regulating process. Finally, by working with such powerful experiences as attachment, dominance, and emotions ranging from love to hate, EFT-C has a human quality to it that appeals to clients and therapists alike by getting to the heart of the matter. Whatever the theoretical persuasion of therapists, most agree that for real change to happen the process must be "hot," meaning emotion must be activated for transformation to occur. The authors of this book argue that it is emotion that fuels couples conflict and that access to alternative emotion is the ultimate antidote to those conflicts.

This book addresses how to help couples identify negative emotional interactional cycles, how to get underneath them to the primary emotions that both produce and are produced by them, and how to work to transform these emotions into adaptive, more functional ones, thereby changing interactions. The authors explicate how to work with both the couple and the individuals in couples therapy, to focus on and shift underlying core processes related to both attachment and identity so that couples may form healthier relationships and become more self- and other-regulating.

This book has grown out of Leslie S. Greenberg's desire to integrate his experience at York University, Toronto, Ontario, Canada, over the past 20 years of working with both individuals and couples using an emotion-focused approach to therapy. Prior to his return in 1986 to York University, from which he graduated with a PhD in 1975, he had been working intensively for a number of years with couples and families at the University of British Columbia (UBC). During that time, in collaboration with his graduate student Sue Johnson, he developed a promising integrated experiential systemic approach to couples therapy. On returning to York University, Greenberg decided to refocus his efforts on developing and studying an experiential approach to individual therapy, an enterprise in which he had been engaged with his mentor, Laura Rice, since he was a doctoral student. At that point, Johnson and Greenberg agreed that she would continue to promote and develop the couples approach, which she has done admirably.

At York University with Rice, where Greenberg received a major National Institute of Mental Health grant to study the experiential change processes in the individual therapy of depression (R. Goldman, Greenberg, & Angus, 2006; Greenberg, Rice, & Elliott, 1993; Greenberg & Watson, 1998), he thus refocused on individual therapy. Although he continued to practice and teach couples therapy, it was only in 2002 that Greenberg turned back, with the help of a grant from the Templeton Foundation's Campaign for Forgiveness Research, to actively study the process of forgiveness in both individual and couples therapy. This project afforded him the opportunity to begin more explicitly integrating his approach to couples and individuals.

Greenberg trained initially at York University in the 1970s in individual therapy (as both a client-centered and a gestalt therapist) and there was exposed to a systems approach; he also did some training with Virginia Satir. Greenberg grew more involved in systems therapy when he went to UBC, where he worked for a number of years with couples and families. Structural and systemic therapies were becoming very popular; after further training with Satir in 1980, on his first sabbatical from 1981 to 1982, he completed an externship in systemic approaches at the Mental Research Institute (MRI) in Palo Alto, California, under Carlos Sluzki. It was there that Greenberg began integrating the emotion-focused perspective that he had been developing for individual therapy (Greenberg & Safran, 1981, 1984, 1987; L. Rice & Greenberg, 1984) with a systemic interactional perspective. Greenberg became particularly impressed with the importance of interactional cycles and hierarchy in systems but also saw how much the systemic approaches ignored affect and internal experience. He returned from the externship at MRI to UBC with the intention of integrating humanistic–

experiential and systemic interactional perspectives, to which he had been recently exposed. It was out of this context, in collaboration with Johnson, that EFT-C was developed (Greenberg & Johnson, 1986a, 1986b, 1988).

Rhonda N. Goldman's interest in EFT-C dates back to graduate school, where she worked under the tutelage of Greenberg. Her primary focus during graduate school was on individual EFT therapy. Early on, she was strongly attracted to social constructionist views of human nature (Averill, 1980; Gergen, 2001; Harré, 1984) and saw emotions as largely cultural constructions shaped by social context and learning. As she studied and worked in the field, she became more convinced of the universality of emotion and the strength of the biological components of emotion (Ekman, 1984; Frijda, 1986; Izard, 1991). On witnessing what a brilliant therapist Greenberg was and seeing the powerful effects of both the client-centered relationship and gestalt therapy techniques to address people's core pain, Goldman thought it most important to be involved in the articulation of the EFT model. Specifically, she wanted to break down and spell out the behaviors and actions of the EFT therapist. She thus endeavored to create and validate the Experiential Therapy Adherence Measure (R. Goldman, 1992) for her master's thesis. It was in this project with Greenberg that she developed a measure for rating the varieties of empathic responses, such as explorations and conjectures, along with other responses, such as exploratory questions and immediate feedback that the EFT therapist uses in working to facilitate change in emotional processes during therapy. As her interest in couples therapy grew, it became clear to her that the therapeutic techniques that she saw as so effective in individual therapy were not sufficient by themselves for couples. Although the individuals themselves were distressed, one needed a model that accounted for the interaction that was often bigger than the couple itself. Goldman then began to study systems theory and how it could be integrated with individual models in work with couples. She was particularly impressed by the work of Satir, who skillfully integrated systemic principles with interpersonal warmth. Goldman, in working with Greenberg, was impressed with the power and simplicity of the EFT-C model to bring about change and finally felt she was able to bring her thinking full circle by integrating the social context with the individual focus.

The purpose of writing this book is to bring together the authors' learning in both individual and couples therapy that has occurred over the past 20 years since the seminal presentation of EFT-C and to expand the EFT-C framework into an even more integrative approach by further focusing on working with self and system, by promoting both other- and self-soothing, and by dealing with both adult and childhood unmet needs. In addition, Greenberg and Goldman focus more explicitly on how to work with emotion, which they see as the bedrock of the therapeutic process. This effort brings the authors full circle, back to the 1980s, to the first efforts of EFT-C to integrate individual and systemic perspectives.

A COMMENT ON THE NAME OF THE APPROACH

The term *emotionally focused therapy* first appeared in the original couples book in 1988 and was used by Greenberg and Johnson to describe the couples approach. Why have we now adopted the term *emotion-focused therapy*? Greenberg, Rice, and Elliott (1993), in their efforts to develop an integrative experiential approach to individual therapy—and being opposed to the development of new schools of individual psychotherapy, to add to the over 500 hundred existing named approaches—referred to their manualized experiential approach to the treatment of depression as process experiential to clearly identify it as belonging to the existing major school of experiential–humanistic therapy. Subsequently, Greenberg (2002a) decided that on the basis of the developments in emotion theory that treatments such as the process experiential approach, as well as some other approaches that emphasized emotion as the target of change, were sufficiently similar to each other and different from existing approaches to merit being grouped under the general title of emotion-focused approaches. Encouraged by publishers, and on the basis of this being the term gaining use in general psychological research, we decided to use the more American phrasing of *emotion-focused* to refer to therapeutic approaches that focused on emotion, rather than the original, possibly more English term (reflecting both Greenberg's and Johnson's backgrounds) *emotionally focused*. We have thus used this term throughout the volume rather than the more English phrase *emotionally focused* that we used initially to describe the couple therapy approach.

The subtitle *The Dynamics of Emotion, Love, and Power* reflects our efforts in this book to discuss how to work with the major emotions of anger, sadness, fear, and shame, as well as the positive emotions, and to focus on both the affiliation and influencing motivations that govern interaction. *Love* and *power* are the two most potent terms to describe the motivational, emotional, and interactional issues that pervade couples' relationships. This book focuses on how to work with the flow of these ever-changing emotions and motivations that so influence couples' moment-by-moment interactions. Hence the subtitle—*The Dynamics of Emotion, Love, and Power*.

Emotion–Focused
Couples Therapy

1

INTRODUCTION

Marriage will never be given new life except by that out of which true marriage always arises, the revealing of two people of the Thou to one another.

—Buber (1958, p. 51)

On the basis of developments in research on emotion over the past decades, in this book we expand the original theory of emotion-focused couples therapy (EFT-C) to view affect regulation as a core motive that organizes attachment, identity, and attraction. In this view, affect regulation does not mean control of emotion but the process of having the emotion one wants and not having those emotions one does not want. We argue that adopting an affect regulation lens helps us understand human behavior and couples interaction in more observable and concrete terms. We thus offer that couples conflict results from breakdowns in both other- and self-regulation of affect, and we look at ways to work in couples therapy to help the couple, and each individual, regulate the emotions of anger, sadness, fear, and shame, as well as love and other positive emotions. We thus expand the initial EFT-C framework of promoting other-regulation of affect to include work on increasing self-regulation of affect. This then adds work on the transformation of the pain of unmet childhood needs that often organizes responses in the present to the encouragement of the expression of adult unmet needs for closeness and validation, which has been the hallmark of our approach to couples therapy. We see this addition as an explication of what has always been implicit in this approach but now is spelled out more clearly in this book.

In our efforts over the past decades to develop a comprehensive emotion-focused therapy approach to human functioning (R. N. Goldman & Greenberg, 1995, 1997; Greenberg, 2002a; Greenberg & Johnson, 1986a, 1988; Greenberg & Paivio, 1997a; Greenberg, Rice, & Elliott, 1993; Greenberg & Safran, 1986; Greenberg & Watson, 2006), we found that the ability for depressed, anxious, and traumatized individuals to access core maladaptive emotion schemes and learn how to self-soothe and regulate their own deepest core fears, shame, and anger—plus their ability to transform these, by accessing internal resources—was central to individual change. We have come to see that in couples therapy, dealing with the pain of unmet needs from the past and learning to self-soothe can at times be as important in developing relationship satisfaction as it is in alleviating individual distress. In the quest to alleviate couples distress, we have found that revealing underlying feelings based on adult unmet needs for closeness and recognition to the responsiveness and soothing by an intimate partner is crucial to restructuring the emotional bond (Greenberg, Ford, Alden, & Johnson, 1993; Greenberg & Johnson, 1986a, 1986b, 1988). The ability to deal with past, often childhood, wounds and self-soothe some of the pain from them (Greenberg & Paivio, 1997a, 1997b; Greenberg, 2002a, 2002b), however, also can be important in couples work, especially to ensure enduring change. This is a finding that has been well borne out in research by Gottman (1999), who found self-soothing to be an important element of what makes marriage work. We thus propose combining work on self-soothing with work on other-soothing to form a more comprehensive approach.

AFFECT REGULATION AND THREE MAJOR MOTIVATIONS

In this book, we discuss the affect regulation involved in three major motivational systems central in couples therapy—attachment, identity, and attraction. We suggest that the centrality of these relational needs in marital conflict leads to therapeutic work that emphasizes focusing on the three related sets of emotions of fear–anxiety, shame–powerlessness, and joy–love, plus promoting three associated relational response forms: nurture–comfort, empathy–validation, and warmth–liking.

Attachment and Connection

Johnson (e.g., see Johnson, 2004) has written extensively on the importance of attachment and on its role in EFT-C, and we fully endorse its importance in couples therapy. Although we still view the attachment bond and the security it provides as a central concern in most couples, we see this bond as a key form of affect regulation governing emotional arousal and approach and avoidance rather than as a set of styles of interaction or as love.

We will not further discuss attachment here, as it has been so clearly explicated in prior work on EFT-C (Johnson, 2004), but rather we will focus more on how to work with identity issues and dominance. This in no way implies that these latter issues are more important than attachment. Clearly, an individual needs to be close and involved with a partner before issues of dominance and validation become an issue, but we do feel that we need more than attachment to explain human and couple functioning and will elaborate on this in the next section.

Identity Influence

Although the original theoretical presentations of EFT-C (Greenberg & Johnson, 1986a, 1986b, 1988, 1990) focused on both pursue–distance and dominance–submission cycles, the vulnerable feelings underlying dominance cycles and how to work with them were never clearly delineated. In our view, understanding the emotional processes in the formation and maintenance of identity and the dominance–submission cycle, as well as working with issues of influence, power, and control, although not nearly as heartwarming as working with comfort and security in the attachment domain, are crucial pieces of the puzzle of how to resolve couples' conflicts. We propose that self-soothing, as well as other-soothing, is important in resolving dominance cycles. Although self-soothing in the attachment domain—when one feels lonely or abandoned—is important, the ability to self-soothe is more important in the identity domain. A partner truly can provide a corrective emotional experience in the attachment domain by responding to the other's feelings of loneliness or abandonment and need for closeness with the partner. In the identity domain however, although the partner's responses can soothe the vulnerable fear and shame underlying dominance, they often are less able to convince the partner of his or her self-worth. In addition, in a struggle of identity-related differences, having the submissive partner respond to the dominant partner's needs for influence perpetuates the cycle, and change requires the dominant partner to let go of some of the need for control requires the submissive partner to assert. We thus elaborate an emotion-focused perspective on how to work with dominance and control in couples therapy.

Hierarchy and issues of influence, dominance, and control are significant issues in couples' functioning. Couples struggle over the definition of reality, and issues of power and control are often the most difficult interactions to deal with in therapy. When identity is threatened, people act and interact to protect their identities. People exert influence and control to regulate their affect (i.e., to not feel shame of diminishment and fear of loss of control and to feel the pride of recognition and the joy of efficacy). We thus propose a model that explicates the specific emotions involved in conflicts centered on influence, power, and control and how to work with them.

A primary aim of this book is to add to the EFT-C framework a clearer description of how to work with the emotions that underlie issues of identity and dominance in influence cycles and to provide an explication of how to promote self-soothing. We elaborate on the original EFT-C theory of disclosing underlying vulnerability by discussing how couples conflict occurs in the identity–dominance domain, as well as in the attachment domain, and we show how dominance struggles exert a strong influence on the attachment bond. We argue that in dominance conflicts it is each partner's concern with how they are being viewed (their *identity*) by the other and whether their needs for agency and recognition are being met, rather than concerns with closeness and connection, that become primary. In these conflicts partners argue not about being close or needing distance but about being seen and validated or being diminished—they argue to maintain their identities. It is important to note we are not suggesting dominance is more central than attachment. Far from it! If the connection were not important, validation would not be as much of a concern, and feeling invalidated in a relationship directly impacts the affiliation domain showing the interdependence of these forces and how affiliation is always of concern in couples.

In identity struggles, the central concern is whose definition of "self" and "reality" is right, who has the right to define what's right, and whose agentic needs are more important. Partners then fight to defend the view of reality important to their identity, and they defend themselves against the humiliation of being found wrong or lacking because it makes them feel unworthy, inferior, deficient, or incompetent. Partners also control, in efforts to stave off possible imagined catastrophes and feelings of loss of control. They also fight to influence decisions and courses of action in order to feel recognized, maintain status, confirm their identities, and operate by choice under their own volition rather than feeling coerced. When partners' identities are threatened, they are most concerned about whether they are being valued and respected and whether their influence and right to choose is recognized, and they argue passionately to try to change their partners' view of them or what they did in order to regulate their self-esteem, maintain their identities and their sense of agency. Alternatively, couples give up their identity needs and become fused to avoid conflict, but excitement and positive feelings are the victims.

Attraction and Liking

We also argue that a third motivational system, attraction and liking, is an important additional factor that needs to be considered in promoting bonding in couples therapy. The positive feelings that are generated when partners are interested in, like, and feel attracted to each other are important maintainers of intimate bonds. Feeling excited by, and enjoying, each other helps couples stay together. Feeling warmth and appreciation and cherishing and valuing the other, as other, leads, in our view, to both pleasure in and compassion toward the partner. Without these positive feelings, the relationship may be functional but it will not flourish and therefore may not last. We thus emphasize this third motivation and the related set of feelings of attraction to, caring for, and liking of the other as a very important ingredient in what makes a relationship work.

A CONCEPTUAL HISTORY OF EMOTION-FOCUSED COUPLES THERAPY

EFT-C was developed initially on the major premise that disclosing underlying vulnerable, adaptive feelings related to unmet adult needs leads to strengthening the emotional bond in couples. EFT-C was an integration of experiential–humanistic and systemic approaches. Work with emotion was combined with work with interaction (Greenberg & Johnson, 1986a, 1986b, 1988). The treatment approach was an attempt to integrate a growing understanding of the role of emotion in therapy (Greenberg & Safran, 1984, 1986) with an understanding of the role of interaction and communication (Fisch, Weakland, & Segal, 1984; Watzlawick, Beavin, & Jackson, 1967). EFT-C took from systems theory the importance of a focus in therapy on interactional cycles that occur between members of a relational system. In addition, Minuchin's methods of enactment to produce change in interaction (Minuchin & Fishman, 1981) plus Gestalt therapy techniques (Perls, 1969) of heightening experience in enactments were also incorporated in this integration.

Structural and strategic approaches emphasized changing hierarchies, boundaries, and interactional positions by working with people's ways of viewing and doing. Systemic therapies mainly used reframing, prescriptions, and restructuring to change both how people viewed things and how they interacted with each other. There was not a strong focus on affect. Communication was of central concern, and the focus was on how messages and metamessages defined interactional positions. EFT-C, however, added that it is through affect and affective tone that intimate partners primarily convey their interactional positions and communicate their views of each other. It is therefore affective tone and what partners feel in response to it that primarily influences their viewing and doing.

The original unique contribution of EFT-C to a systemic view thus involved putting the self back in the system by highlighting the role emotion plays in maintaining negative cycles and the use of emotion to break negative interactional cycles to create new patterns of interaction (Greenberg & Johnson, 1986a, 1986b). This assimilation of systemic perspectives into an experiential approach resulted in an approach that emphasized the importance of focusing on present experience and present interaction. It added both reframing and the promotion of enactments to the humanistic therapy tradition of using empathy and an emotion focus as a basic therapeutic style, and it adopted a growth-oriented and nonpathologizing view of human functioning. Conflict also was seen as being a function of unmet adult needs rather than infantile neurotic needs.

Notions of adult attachment had also just begun to be presented at this time (Weiss, 1982), and they offered a highly compatible framework for understanding marriage and marital conflict (Greenberg & Johnson, 1986a, 1988). Johnson (1986), in her seminal theoretical contribution, began to stress the importance of attachment in the emotional bond and contrasted this with a view of marriage as a social reinforcement bargain. The importance of accessibility and responsiveness of caretakers, so central in an attachment perspective, was readily integrated with humanistic views of the importance of acknowledging and revealing underlying vulnerable emotions in promoting intimacy. This integrated well with the early humanistic underpinning of EFT-C captured by L'Abate (1977) in the title of his article "Intimacy Is Sharing Hurt Feelings" and with Buber's (1958) existential view of the importance of revealing authentic feelings, which is captured in the quote at the beginning of this chapter.

Greenberg's initial motivation in developing EFT-C came from an interest in studying couples to see whether their conflict resolution paralleled the process of intrapsychic conflict resolution that he had found in his individual therapy research (Greenberg, 1979). In this research, using a task-analytic approach to the study of change processes (Greenberg, 1980, 1984, 1986, 2007; Greenberg, Heatherington, & Friedlander, 1996; Heatherington, Friedlander, & Greenberg, 2005), he found that clients resolved self-critical conflict by deepening the experience of the self and by softening the internal critic (Greenberg, 1979, 1984). He thus developed a research program at the University of British Columbia to see whether couples resolved conflict in a similar fashion. EFT as an overall approach had been guided by the fundamental idea that therapy could best be understood by being seen as a set of marker-guided, task-focused interventions embedded in an empathic relationship (Greenberg, 1983; Greenberg & Safran, 1986; L. Rice & Greenberg, 1984). This approach to therapy led to empirically based specification of different tasks, each focused on dealing with particular in-session problem states and the specification of interventions and processes of change most effective for those problem states. EFT-C, drawing on this basic approach, thus identified blamer softening and withdrawer reengagement as basic tasks in couples therapy (Greenberg, Ford, et al., 1993; Johnson & Greenberg, 1988; Plysiuk, 1985). This task-analytic approach to the study of how therapy works also has been recently applied to describe the intervention processes in EFT-C that help promote these couples processes (Bradley & Furrow, 2004).

To facilitate the study of the process of change in resolving couples conflict, Greenberg and Johnson (1986a, 1988) developed an EFT-C manual that assimilated the systemic perspectives into an experiential approach. The first evaluation of the effectiveness of an emotion-focused approach to couples treatment found it to be superior to a problem-solving approach (Johnson & Greenberg, 1985a, 1985b). A later study compared EFT-C with a systemic interactional therapy for which a manual was also devised (A. Goldman & Greenberg, 1992). In this second trial, EFT-C was compared with a systemic–interactional approach with more severely distressed couples, whom it was believed might be less accessible to emotion-focused intervention, because of their high emotional reactivity (A. Goldman & Greenberg, 1992). The EFT-C and the systemic treatments, however, were not found to be significantly different, but, it is important to note, EFT-C was found to have less relapse at 1-year follow-up. In a third evaluation, another dissertation (P. James, 1991) of one of Greenberg's students developed a communication-based psychoeducation training component, based on EFT-C principles, that emphasized disclosure and expression of underlying feelings, as well as empathic responding by the partners. The effects of a treatment that combined 4 sessions of psychoeducation with 8 sessions of therapy were compared with the effects of 12 sessions of EFT-C; no significant differences were found between the two treatments, but the psychoeducation training appeared to be promising (P. James, 1991).

As part of the overall initial research program to study conflict resolution in couples, an intensive task analysis of couples conflict resolution was completed in a master's thesis (Greenberg & Johnson, 1988; Plysiuk, 1985). From this intensive analysis, it emerged that accessing underlying self-experience and softening the critic, so important in intrapsychic conflict resolution, were also important in interactional conflict resolution. However, with two people in a live interaction, it was clear that there was more to couples conflict resolution than to intrapsychic conflict resolution. Research was therefore undertaken to try to study the unique elements of conflict resolution in couples, and it was found that good sessions were characterized by deeper experience and more affiliative responses and that these in-session processes predicted outcome (Greenberg, Ford, et al., 1993; Johnson & Greenberg, 1988). Posttherapy interviews done as part of another master's thesis (James, 1985) also revealed that the expression of new feelings by one partner led the other to change his or her perception of the partner (Greenberg, James, & Conry, 1988). These findings, in different ways, confirmed the importance of revealing underlying feelings in couples conflict resolution.

Further studies by Johnson and colleagues (Johnson, 2002; Johnson, Hunsley, Greenberg, & Schindler, 1999) subsequently found that EFT-C was an effective treatment for a variety of types of marital distress, including trauma. Johnson further articulated the importance of revealing underlying attachment-oriented feelings to restructure bonds and developed and promoted this aspect of EFT-C as she applied it to different populations, and this has become a central, identifying feature of her approach to EFT-C (Johnson, 2004; Johnson & Whiffen, 2003). Working with sadness, loneliness, and the need for security in the attachment cycle thus has become a central organizing principle of treatment. Over the ensuing years, a tremendous amount of work has been done at the Ottawa Couple and Family Institute in refining the approach and applying it to different populations. Johnson went on to compassionately illuminate and develop an adult attachment theory of love as a base for EFT-C (Johnson, 2004; Johnson & Whiffen, 2003).

DEVELOPMENTS IN EMOTION-FOCUSED COUPLES THERAPY AT YORK UNIVERSITY

On Greenberg's return to York University, he began to focus his research and theoretical efforts on articulating the basic principles of an overarching emotion-focused approach to functioning. The importance in determining psychological distress of an individual's core maladaptive emotion schemes, based often on fear of abandonment and/or on shame at diminishment, and the associated unmet childhood needs, was established, and the central role of affect regulation in human functioning (Greenberg, Rice, & Elliott, 1993) was clarified. A dialectical–constructivist perspective on functioning, based on the interaction of emotion schemes and narrative, was developed (Greenberg & Pascual-Leone, 1995, 1997, 2001). As well, a dynamic-systems theory of self-functioning, in which people were seen as living in a constant process of making sense of their emotional experience, was developed (Greenberg & Watson, 2006; Whelton & Greenberg, 2004). This constructivist perspective on the self bridged realist and constructionist perspectives by recognizing that experience results from a synthesis of biology and culture and an integration of bodily felt emotion and more culturally derived language-based symbolization and narrative (Greenberg & Angus, 2004).

Research on individual therapy for depression at the York Psychotherapy Research Center also emphasized the importance of intrapsychic affect regulation (self-soothing), affect transformation (changing emotion with emotion), and the resolution of unfinished business (Greenberg, 2002a, 2002b). The significance of shame in the protection of personal identity, as well as fear in maintaining relational attachment (R. N. Goldman & Greenberg, 1997; Greenberg & Goldman, 2007), was observed to be of crucial importance in human distress. These elements began to be added more explicitly to our couples work so that more recently, in addition to focusing on revealing underlying vulnerable feelings to promote relational soothing, we also have focused on transformation and regulation of the core emotion schemes of fear and shame, on which these vulnerabilities are based. Thus an approach emerged that not only prioritized the expression of underlying vulnerable feelings and healthy adult met needs, to promote bonding, but also focused on promoting each individual's capacity to self-soothe and to transform his or her core maladaptive emotion schemes based on childhood unmet needs. This resulted in an approach in which partners first are encouraged to identify and express their unexpressed adult attachment- and identity-related feelings and ask for what they need. The change process here is seen as one of turning vicious cycles into virtuous ones by way of partners' ability to be empathic and compassionately responsive when they see their partners as truly vulnerable and more in need than deserving blame. When partners can reveal and be responsive, the focus expands to include working with partners on self-regulation of their own affects and dealing with their own unfinished business from past wounds that makes them vulnerable to their partners' nonresponsiveness. Self-regulation and self-soothing is especially useful for the times when partners are unable to respond compassionately to each other. The importance of healing emotional injuries and unfinished business from people's past, so central in individual therapy, thus has begun to play a more clearly conceptualized and prominent role in our couples work, especially with longer term couples therapy.

Self-Regulation of Affect

When Greenberg and Johnson (1988) developed EFT-C, in the aftermath of the 1960s, a view of health as independence, autonomous functioning, and self-actualizing prevailed. EFT-C was offered as an antidote to an independence view. From this perspective, the acknowledgement and sharing of human weakness and vulnerability and support seeking were at the center of health and healthy relationships; an adult attachment perspective, which was just beginning to develop, provided an excellent framework for this view. Since then, however, it has become clearer that self-regulation of affect is a key process involved in motivation and that a therapy with a dual focus on self and other is important. We thus focus on both other-soothing and self-soothing of affect and on both the expression of adult unmet needs and the transformation of childhood unmet needs. We have a dual purpose in our couples work: (a) to have partners both reveal and become responsive to each other's underlying vulnerabilities based on healthy adult needs for closeness and recognition and (b) to enhance partners' expression and self-regulation of underlying painful affect, based on unmet childhood needs and unfinished business.

Agency and Communion

David Bakan, one of our mentors at York University, early on argued persuasively in *The Duality of Human Existence* (Bakan, 1966) for the fundamental role of both agency and communion in human experience. He stated,

> I have adopted the terms "agency" and "communion" to characterize two fundamental modalities in the existence of living forms, agency for the existence of an organism as an individual, and communion for the participation of the individual in some larger organism of which the individual is a part. Agency manifests itself in self-protection, self-assertion, and self-expansion; communion manifests itself in the sense of being at one with other organisms. (p. 14)

We believe that a comprehensive view of human functioning needs to address both a fundamental tendency to connect to others and a fundamental tendency to agentically self-organize to maintain self-coherence and grow. We see the development of the self as a coherent, agentic, affective, and continuous system (Stern, 1985) that is independent of, but dialectically interactive with, the development of secure attachment. This is the crucial point. The self has a self-organizing tendency (Tronick, 2006). A crucial aspect of this tendency is to relate to others because this regulates affect and promotes survival. The two drives, to self-regulate and to relate to others, are highly intertwined but separate. This view leads us to see *empathic attunement* to the other's self-feelings and needs as well as *nurturing responsiveness* to others' needs for closeness (often viewed as synonymous) as two different forms of relational responses that both serve important, but different, functions in couples interaction. Empathic attunement, we argue, is important in validation of the other's identity, and nurturing and caregiving are important in promoting attachment security.

Therapist as Coach

In our approach, therapists are viewed as facilitative emotion coaches (Greenberg, 2002a) who work directly with emotions to help people improve relationships. They guide partners to become more aware of primary anger and sadness, fear and shame, and the attendant needs and to regulate, make sense of, and communicate these in nondemanding ways to promote security, validation, and warmth. In addition, coaches help partners reveal their most vulnerable feelings to each other to promote bonding and validation and help couples learn to soothe and transform emotions that are maladaptive. To do this, they need a good understanding of how to work differentially with the different emotions.

In this book we thus discuss how to regulate and transform the different emotions related to attachment, identity, and liking in couples and, by extension, family systems. We discuss the role of both negative emotions such as anger, sadness, fear, and shame and positive emotions such as joy, excitement, and love in coupling. We also demonstrate how work with these emotions forms the foundation of facilitating change in couples and by extension in all types of interacting emotional systems where people may be in conflict. This work is thus seen as informative for work with families, organizations, and groups.

OVERVIEW OF THE BOOK

Part I of this volume lays out the theoretical background for our approach to EFT-C. In the first chapter of Part I, chapter 2, we explore the role of emotion in the interactional life of couples. The evolution of emotion and how emotions are generated are explored. We distinguish the biological, social, and cultural elements of emotion and also identify the different types of dominance- versus attachment-related emotions that lead to negative interaction cycles. In chapter 3, a case is made that affect regulation is a primary motive in marriage and conversely that marital breakdown is a breakdown in affect regulation. We then call for a balance between self- and other-soothing as equally important pieces in the healing process with couples.

In chapter 4, we identify and discuss the three proposed relational motives, or core drives: the need for attachment, identity recognition, and attraction. We explore how these systems function. In particular, we trace the evolution of the identity system and the importance of the mutual regulation of identity in relationships. We also discuss the development of the attachment system as well as the limitations of the attachment system alone in explaining relational motivation. In chapter 5, we explore how interaction combines with emotional, motivational, and cognitive processes to produce couples conflict. Interactions, particularly negative escalatory ones, are conceptualized as mutual threats to attachment and identity. Relationships are seen as regular, repeating cycles of interaction produced and maintained by affect regulation and dysregulation.

In chapter 6, we explore the role that culture plays in determining emotional awareness and expression in couples. We review research that points to cross-cultural examples of identity being an important relational motive in many cultures. We point to research that suggests that gender may to some extent determine emotional expression in relationships and discuss whether the same principles from heterosexual relationships may be applied to same-sex relationships.

Part II lays out our intervention framework. In chapter 7, we present an expanded 5-stage, 14-step framework that builds on the original 9-step model laid out by Greenberg and Johnson (1988). More steps have been added that focus on self-process, and guidelines are provided for how to work with the self at various stages in the model. This chapter serves as a manual for treatment. In chapter 8, we identify therapeutic tasks related to negative interactional cycles that emerge from the basic dimensions of interaction— affiliation and influence. We discuss differences between pursue–distance cycles and dominance–submission cycles. We discuss the structure and dimensions of the cycles and how to work with them. We provide guidelines for how to both work with negative interactional cycles and engender positive cycles. In chapter 9, on intrapsychic therapeutic tasks, we delineate some of the specific tasks that can be transported from individual therapy to work with couples process. We point out how to recognize markers for tasks and delineate the steps involved in seeing tasks through to resolution.

In Part III, we change our focus again to explore work with specific emotions in EFT-C. Chapters 10 through 14 focus on, respectively, working with anger, sadness, fear, shame, and positive emotions that emerge regularly in EFT-C. In each chapter, we discuss how the particular emotion functions in the context of interactional positions within affiliation and influence cycles. Many examples are given that explicate how EFT-C approaches the particular emotion in the different negative interaction cycles. Illustrations are provided that guide the reader in how to identify, increase awareness of, regulate, transform, and express more emotions in relationships.

CONCLUSION

In this book, we thus discuss how to work with affect in couples, with both the regulation and the communication of emotions. We differentiate among three central groups of emotions: those primarily related to connection and attachment, those primarily related to identity and self-esteem, and those related to liking and warmth. It is problems with emotions related to these sets of needs that are most important in marital difficulty. Emotions, we suggest, are more fundamental, more concrete, and more differentiated than motivation, and they allow us as therapists to work with them in a more direct manner. Emotions present themselves more experientially than motives and are thus more accessible and provide us with a map of how to work with couples. We thus focus on how to work with the different sets of felt emotions, especially fear, shame, contempt, anger, and sadness, related to perceived threats to attachment and identity, as well as on the role of positive emotions, such as joy and excitement, related to attraction.

In our view, the emotional bond between partners is constituted by a host of emotions such as sadness at loss, loneliness, fear of abandonment, fear of rejection, fear of annihilation, shame at diminishment, and anger at violation, as well as joy and pleasure in contact and interest and excitement in one's partner's unique qualities. We argue here that it is helpful to understand and work differentially with different emotions. Finally, in line with developments in affective neuroscience, we view intimate relating as a primary means of affect regulation in couples and view other-soothing and self-soothing as important processes in couples therapy.

I

THEORY OF EMOTION-FOCUSED COUPLES THERAPY

2

EMOTION

Emotional occasions . . . are extremely potent in precipitating mental rearrangements. The sudden and explosive ways in which love, jealousy, guilt, fear, remorse, or anger can seize upon one are known to everybody. Hope, happiness, security, resolve . . . can be equally explosive. And emotions that come in this explosive way seldom leave things as they found them.

—W. James (1902, p. 198)

If we are to work with accessing, expressing, and regulating emotion, we need to understand its nature and function. Affect at its base is neurochemical and physiological. People feel it in their bodies. Conscious articulation of feelings and thoughts come only later. As humans develop, affect is organized into discrete emotions. Emotion is above all a relational action tendency. It occurs at the boundary between organism and environment and provides a rapid-action adaptive tendency. People feel threatened when attacked, and fear motivates them to flee or defend themselves. People feel angry when unfairly treated and assert themselves to protect their boundaries.

Emotion also is communication. Emotion is people's primary signaling system and forms the most crucial component of an interactive relationship. As the emotions that humans come into the world with become used for interacting with others, vital changes begin to occur. Emotions become signals and the basis of people's first interactions. Signals are different from action. As more intense emotions become soothed and modulated, their activation no longer leads to direct motor action and they become signals. Original basic emotions thus, with development and interactive experience, rapidly turn into emotional signals that become part of a pattern of interaction.

In couples, emotional communication between partners occurs not only at a conscious, verbal level but also nonverbally and is strongly affected by physiology. Partners affect each other's heart rate, breathing, perspiration, and physical well-being. When two people connect intimately, all kinds of neurochemical reactions occur. Unbeknownst to intimate partners, they produce little squirts of neurotransmitters in each other that send messages pouring through their partner's body. Affection is associated with pleasure, and the look or touch of a loved one sends endorphins on a complex journey through one's body. This is an especially pleasurable journey because endorphins are natural opiates that kill pain and produce pleasure. However, when people assert themselves or express hostility, testosterone, adrenaline, and cortisol all increase; muscles tense; and hearts beat faster. A relationship clearly is a marriage of chemicals and receptor sites (Ackerman, 1995).

In addition to providing an action tendency and communication, emotion provides meaning—it evaluates the significance of situations to one's well-being. In psychological terms, emotions are generated by the automatic appraisals of situations in relation to one's needs, goals, and concerns (Frijda, 1986; Greenberg, 2002a). In simple terms, emotions tell people whether things are good or bad for them and whether things are going their way. Emotion is the fundamental datum of relational existence, and, as we have said, in this book we focus on how to work with different emotions to improve relationships and resolve conflict.

Emotions, once in awareness, give people information about the state of their intimate bonds, telling them whether their bonds are in good condition, whether they have been disrupted, or whether they need maintenance. The self, when seen and confirmed by the other, feels vital and strong, but by contrast it feels depleted and weak when diminished or neglected. People are calm and feel good when all is going well between them and their intimate partners. They feel bad, however, and upset when their relationship is disturbed, thereby signaling that action is needed to repair the tear in the relational fabric. Emotion binds couples together, but it also is what rips them apart.

Emotion influences what people pay attention to and how they interpret what they see. Because emotions involve both appraisal and arousal in both the right and left hemispheres, they influence many aspects of cognition, from perception to decision making. Emotion has a direct impact on the entire mind. The limbic brain has neural connections to every part of the neocortex and is more interconnected to more parts of the brain than is any other part (Tucker et al., 2003). In addition, there are more connections from the emotional brain to the rational prefrontal cortex than vice versa. All this attests to the influence of emotion on consciousness. The amygdala, at the center of the emotional brain, acts like a guard, constantly alert and scanning every experience for signs of danger. It scans faces for signs of anger or fear and basically evaluates situations in terms such as "Is this bad for me?

Could it hurt me?" If the information is threatening enough, the amygdala broadcasts a distress signal to the entire brain, which in turn activates a cascade of physiological and neurochemical responses. Muscles tense; breathing is affected; the heart speeds up; arousal and desires increase; and the fight–flight hormones, adrenaline and noradrenaline, flow. The amygdala's extensive web of neural connections allows it to activate much of the rest of the brain, including the centers for decision making and rational thought (Damasio, 1994, 1999). Thus, in couples conflict, partners rapidly explode with rage or freeze in fear well before they have any conscious sense of what is happening or can regulate their emotional response.

The emotional brain constantly compares emotionally charged events with memories of prior emotionally charged experiences. The more active the amygdala and the limbic system at the time of learning, the more it enhances the storage of those memories that had emotional content. So people are vulnerable to interpret the present in terms of past traumatic experience. If any key aspects of the present are similar to the past, the sounds of a voice or the expression on a face, the amygdala automatically sends out an alarm signal to the rest of the brain organizing the self to feel such things as "My partner doesn't love me"; "I am being diminished"; "I am in danger of being trapped or destroyed"; or "My partner may leave me." When the amygdala judges that a situation is an emotional threat, it mobilizes the entire brain and body long before the prefrontal cortex and thought ever begin to influence decisions (LeDoux, 1996). It is precisely these kinds of emotionally activated states that couples therapy needs to address. It is here that therapies dealing only with cognition, behavior, or interaction without attending to their emotional origins may miss the central determinant of the problem and the central ingredient of change—emotion.

When a person perceives a threat, this activates in-wired, basic evaluations and fixed physiological and motor sequences. In response to danger, the startle reflex and various expressions of the fight, flight, or freeze response are activated (Cacioppo, 2002). In response to such things as loss, danger, humiliation, or entrapment, in-wired affective psychomotor programs of mourning, escape, withdrawal, and defeat are activated (Greenberg & Watson, 2006). Panksepp (2002) suggested that the most basic tendencies for which in-wired evaluations and affective motor programs exist in animals are those for seeking, rage, fear, lust, care, panic, and play. Other affect theorists propose six to nine basic affective programs including anger, sadness, fear, disgust, surprise or interest, and excitement or joy (Ekman & Friesen, 1975; Tomkins, 1962). Love, the most complex emotion of all, has only recently been recognized as possibly a basic emotion, although it is probably a blend of different neuromotor systems, and it is possible that romantic passion is a drive more than an emotion (Fisher, 2004). This small group of affects, then, is the basic force that drives people. The degree to which these automatic, basic responses can be inhibited depends in part on a person's relative level of emotional arousal, which in turn depends on the activation of brain stem arousal centers. Under ordinary conditions, people can regulate their anger or irritation or ignore the sensation of hunger or tiredness, even while the physiological processes associated with these states, such as increased blood pressure, the secretion of saliva, and contraction of stomach muscles, continue. Higher (neocortical) top-down levels of processing can, and often do, override, steer, or interrupt the lower levels, or interfere with emotional and sensorimotor processing. But when emotional arousal increases, it interrupts other mental functioning and draws attention to the goals it embodies.

Reviews of affective neuroscience show that emotions and feelings of closeness and empathy, as well as awareness, labeling, reappraisal, and meaning making, can all help modulate amygdala arousal (Greenberg, 2002a, 2002b; Greenberg & Watson, 2006). Amygdala-generated experience of withdrawal generated by one side of the brain can be transformed by the activation of alternate hemispheric processes that promote approach or positive feelings (Davidson, 2000a, 2000b; Frederickson, 1998). Thus, one of the best ways of transforming aroused emotional states is by generating other feeling states. In our approach to couples therapy, we focus on generating new emotional states by helping the couple create an emotional bond in which each partner feels secure and validated and by helping each partner learn to self-soothe painful feelings and access new feelings. A comforting and empathic relationship helps partners regulate their anxieties and feel safe, secure, validated, and worthy. Corrective emotional experiences with partners also help transform maladaptive emotional states by the provision of new experience that disconfirms pathogenic expectations based on past emotional–relational experience. In addition, taking a self-focus helps partners learn to tolerate, regulate, and make sense of their emotions as well as learn to access alternate emotions to change their own states. Thus, anger at a partner can be transformed by accessing and focusing on feelings of compassion or love for them, or anger can be transformed by accessing one's own sadness. Fear can be transformed by accessing anger, and shame can be transformed by accessing anger, sadness, or pride (Greenberg, 2002a, 2002b).

LeDoux (1996) suggested that new neural networks that were not previously associated can be associated to create new levels of neural integration in the brain. New levels of neural integration can be created by promoting the growth of new neurons, the expansion of existing ones, and changes in the connections between existing neurons (Cozolino, 2002). Having new experience is what brings this about. Therapy therefore is about providing new experience, not new explanations. In individuals, problems generally arise because parts of the brain are not communicating well with each other. When they are calm, partners often acknowledge that certain maladaptive reactions need to change, but as soon as they get upset, another organization takes over, and this new self-organization governs their reactions and leads these reactions to escalate.

Couples therapy needs to help clients activate more adaptive emotions that provide access to new interactional responses to their partners. Access to new experience needs to occur while the old response is still up and running. People then transition from one emotional state to another and thereby, over time, transform one emotional response into another (Greenberg, 2002a, 2002b). This is done, for example, by activating sadness at feeling unloved by one's partner to undo anger at feeling wronged, or by accessing anger at a partner's judgmentalness to undo the shame of feeling worthless. As this experience of transition from one emotion to another is repeated over time, again and again over the course of therapy new pathways begin to be laid down, enabling partners to respond in new ways when in conflict. To interact, think, and perceive in a new way, clients must develop the ability to feel and act differently in the moments when the emotional state they want to change has been activated. Thus, emotion is best changed by emotion (Greenberg, 2002a), and the relationship is a primary source of new emotion.

In our experience and observations of couples, the emotions of fear, sadness, and shame often are at the core of experiences of poor relational connections, and they prevent interdependence. Either a partner is unable to express his or her fear, sadness, and shame when he or she feels it, and the other partner is not able to tolerate and respond to these feelings, if expressed, or a partner's fear or shame becomes so dysregulated that the self and possibly the other partner is overwhelmed. When these feelings are not dealt with adequately, they generally result in withdrawal or reactive attack. Fear–anxiety, a core relational feeling related to separation, is generated when one is cut off from, or left, by loved ones. Sadness at loss soon follows. These feelings are calmed by connection (Bowlby, 1962). Attachment-related fears are about loss of the other or loss of the other's love. Separation anxiety and the fears of abandonment that plague unhappy relationships are soothed by relational security. The reliable and soothing presence of the other helps one feel safe and secure and develop trust. Shame, however, is a core feeling related to one's identity; to feeling not validated or recognized; and to feeling disapproved of, humiliated, or diminished in the eyes of others (Kohut, 1977; Tomkins, 1963). Shame also occurs when one feels powerless or trapped and is unable to be an agent and assert one's self to maintain one's dignity. The loss of control from entrapment over which people experience shame and humiliation is best overcome by experiencing one's self as an agent, able to act or control one's environment (Gilbert, 2003).

Shame is always about the adequacy of the self and diminishment of self-esteem, and most often is overcome best by a combination of relational and self-processes. Validation of one's identity by another—the other's empathy and recognition—are important in developing and maintaining one's self-coherence and self-esteem. It is both by being seen and validated by another and by facing one's own shame in a confirming environment that shame is overcome. People need to be able to face their shame, rather than avoid it, and to be able to receive empathy and self-soothe. Being able to receive empathy and self-soothe is done by accessing one's own sense of compassion for one's self and by accessing a sense of strength, pride, and self-worth.

Shame and fear often intermingle in relational experience. There is much anxiety about being shamed and much shame about being anxious or afraid, and these emotions feed each other and prevent people in relationships from revealing themselves to each other. Anger and contempt, the more overt relationship destructive emotions, often are the consequence of underlying fear and shame. Efforts to regulate painful affect, to minimize the possibility of feeling shame, for example, leads to much controlling behavior; efforts to minimize the feeling of being afraid and alone motivate much blaming or clinging behavior. The two painful emotions of fear and shame thus are at the core of much marital and couples distress and lead to much of the anger and associated sadness that couples feel. This also relates to the contempt so destructive to marriage. Thus, fear, anger, sadness, shame, and disgust are forces to be reckoned with in relationships. Emotions such as these in response to partners and to loss and humiliation can be overwhelming and therefore need soothing (Gottman, 1994). Dysregulated emotions that are not processed do not inform action or purpose, and their action tendencies do not get translated into adaptive action.

Adaptive and positive emotions help regulate both self and interaction. Adaptive sadness and anger can be seen as serving a positive relational function. These emotions inform partners that their basic needs are not being met. Sadness leads to crying out for the missed other, and anger leads to protecting boundaries. These two emotions often emerge when love fades or respect has died. People are sad for the closeness or validation they miss or have lost, and they are angry when their goals for these have been thwarted and they are not getting what they want or need from their partners. The more nurturing emotions of sharing and caring, and giving as well as receiving love, are also important in creating calmness and regulating anxiety. The pleasant emotions of enjoyment, pleasure, interest, excitement, and other positive emotions related to love and attraction are important emotions that regulate and are regulated by marriage.

Emotions in intimate relationships thus are responses to the brain's rapid response to the meaning of changes in relations between self and other, and lead to modifying (or maintaining) those relations. From this perspective, quarrels can be seen as neurochemicals in combat, backed up by physiological resources. The sensory experience of emotion, such as a tightness in the belly or a shallowness of breath, are internal signals representing the significance of relational events to one's well-being. The action tendency associated with one's emotional reaction to one's partner provides inclinations to act to change or maintain the relationship. Partners who wish to maintain healthy relationships ignore these signals and action tendencies at their peril.

Emotions thus tell people the state of one's intimate bonds. They tell people whether these bonds are in good condition, whether they have been disrupted, or whether they need maintenance.

THE EVOLUTION OF EMOTIONS

The human emotion system evolved to aid survival-related goals, and affect regulation was the means by which this was achieved. If we take six of the most basic emotions central in intimate relationships—sad, happy, angry, fear, shame, and liking or loving—we can see that each evolved over time by being triggered by a particular kind of event in relation to a need or goal. Each kind of event recurred in the evolutionary history of the species and shaped humans' repertoire of responses to it. Sadness occurs in response to loss and leads to withdrawal or a tendency to cry out for the lost object. Happiness occurs when a need is satisfied or a goal is achieved and leads to approach and continued engagement. Anger arises in response to goal frustration or boundary violation and leads to trying harder and striving forcefully, and fear arises at danger or conflict and leads to freezing, vigilance, or escape. Shame occurs in response to being diminished in the eyes of the other and involves needing to belong, whereas liking comes from interest, attraction, and excitement and involves approach exploration and involvement and loving from a combination of these. The emotion system thus evolved primarily to deal with the attainment and frustration of survival-related goals.

The origin of the system of human emotions can be traced to the asocial prereptilian and reptilian brain, which is related mainly to territoriality. With the development of the limbic system in mammals, however, the emotions began to serve the relational goals of mammals, as well as the territorial ones. Horses, for example, show sadness at loss. The emotion system then was enhanced further by the neocortex of primates, which grew to allow people to engage with ever-greater complexity in a world of others. Humans came to recognize and know others as unique individuals, and as social relations became a more central concern in survival, they became a major concern of human emotions (Oatley, 2004). Happiness then resulted when the need to be with others was met and led to cooperation and showing affection. Sadness resulted from the loss of close relationships and led to seeking help and forming new relationships. Anger came from insult, and loss of respect or status and led to retaliation and fighting. Fear resulted from separation or social rejection and led to submitting or withdrawing. More complex social emotions also evolved. Love came from attraction and physical and mental closeness and led to support, help seeking, giving, and nurture, whereas shame came from feeling exposed and diminished and led to trying to disappear from others' gazes and to deferring to dominants. Contempt came from threat from an outgroup person and led to treating the other as a nonperson. Even disgust, a primal emotion toward things, was extended from the rejection of toxic substances to apply to people. With this basic wiring in place, humans then became beings who sought out the more pleasant emotions and avoided the unpleasant ones. Relationships were sought because of the affects they provided, and so humans became sensitive relational beings.

Basic emotions serve two general purposes: They organize the self, and they organize interaction. First, basic emotions signal to the self that action is necessary to maintain, repair, or enhance the emotional bond, either because of a deviation from an ideal state of the relationship or because an opportunity presents itself. These basic emotional responses involve perceptual, mostly automatic, appraisal, and experiential processes that monitor the conditions of ongoing relations, detecting disturbances (e.g., a spouse's tone of voice) or opportunities for connection (e.g., an intimate look or touch). Once activated, emotion-related perception and experience interrupt any ongoing cognitive processes and direct information processing to features of the relationship that allow for the continuation, restoration, or establishment of a desirable connection. Basic emotions thus motivate behavior that establishes or reestablishes more ideal relational conditions. These emotions involve autonomic, hormonal, and central nervous system activities that are tailored to specific actions, such as offering comfort, asserting one's self, or inviting play (LeDoux, 1996; Panksepp, 2002; Porges, 1995).

Primordial emotions also involve biologically based vocal, facial, and postural communication that provides quick and reliably identified information to others (Ekman, 1984, 1993; Izard, 1991), which shapes interactions. Emotional communication in couples conveys information about the sender's mental states, intentions, and dispositions, which are critical to marriage. The nonverbal level of communication of emotion thus is crucial in regulating couples interaction. Emotion then is as much "out there" in the "in-between" of the relationship as it is inside the individual. Communication proceeds in two simultaneous streams, verbal symbolic communication associated with the "high road" of rational cognition, and spontaneous nonverbal communication with the emotional "low road" (with no implication that one is "higher" than the other in anything but a descriptive sense). Spontaneous communication is biologically based and direct in both its sending and its receiving aspects, and through it, partners act as bioregulators of one another. In a very real sense, partners know each other directly and immediately through the nonverbal communication of emotion. *Empathy* is when one's emotion is sensed and understood by another; when empathy is reciprocated, a special form of psychological intimacy occurs, that of feeling mutually known by each other.

Emotion produces action tendencies and information; these tendencies and implicit meaning, when coupled with higher order reflexive cognition, produce the final expression and behavior to one's partner. The partner then reacts to the behavioral expressions of emotion, and thus interaction is produced. Emotion also influences decision making and thereby influences the way partners decide to respond to each other. Emotions in relationship thus generally became coupled in an interactional system. Different emotions beget specific other emotions. Anger begets fear; contempt begets shame; and love begets love.

EMOTION GENERATION

LeDoux (1996) showed that there are two roads to emotion. One is the rapid low road, through the amygdala, the center of the emotional brain (limbic system), which produces people's gut feelings that influence how they think, plan, and behave. The other is the slower high road, which, through the influence of the cerebral cortex on the amygdala and other parts of the limbic system, influences how people feel. On the basis of this conceptualization, emotions essentially involve two moments.

The first moment generated by the limbic system organizes people into one of a few coordinated states of readiness: either to continue with what one is doing (happiness), to try harder (anger), to freeze or escape (fear), or to give up or withdraw (sadness; Oatley, 2004; Oatley, Keltner, & Jenkins, 2006). Emotion orients people to what is of concern, and it poses problems to be solved. The second moment in the emotional process is one of explicit reflection and consideration and includes working out what caused the emotion and deciding what to do about it. This helps solve the problems set by emotion. People live in a constant dialectical process of explaining their experience to make sense of it (Greenberg & Pascual-Leone, 1995, 2001; Greenberg & Watson, 2006; J. Watson & Greenberg, 1996). The first moment sets the limbic system in motion to generate the emotion (Oatley, 2004). In fear, for instance, the brain becomes specialized for dealing with dangers, and the feeling is that familiar sense of anxious dread that signals something bad might happen. In anger, the brain scans for violation, unfairness, and boundary or territorial invasion and signals that one is being wronged. Emotion, as we have discussed, is people's primary signaling system. As part of the first moment, it also sends out signals to others about one's state of preparedness for different types of action. Beyond signaling to the self and other that something important to one's well-being has happened and setting the brain rapidly into a state of preparedness for the general kind of occurrence that has been detected, the first moment does not give much detailed information beyond this. It is more like an alarm system going off. Coarse distinctions are made, but exactly what caused the emotion and what to do to cope with the particular circumstance may not be clear.

The second moment, however, which typically extends in time, involves an elaborated process of evaluation and reevaluation that helps solve the problems set by the first moment (Oatley, 2004). It is by reflecting on, understanding, and explaining what one is experiencing and what triggered it that one begins to create meaning and to make sense of what is happening. It is important to note, however, that the first-moment emotional experience constrains the explanations but does not fully determine it (Greenberg & Pascual-Leone, 1995). Thus an automatically generated feeling of depletion can be explained in the second moment as tired, depressed, or abandoned, but not as joyful or excited. A real bodily felt referent of experience is generated in the first moment, but how it is then symbolized and what people make of it makes people who they are. People's explanations of their primary experience thus influence the construction of the self they are about to become. However, they cannot just make up any meaning. Their emotions tell people how their bodies are reacting. To maintain coherence, people need to incorporate this information into their meaning construction. How one explains one's experience to one's self in the final analysis also influences the next moment of experience. It is quite different to explain one's experience as tired and depleted because of jet lag than as depressed because of the emptiness of one's relationship. Emotion is thus an important part of a self-organizing process that provides the basis for the meanings people create, and it organizes people for action and coping.

Usually, one's first emotional response to an event in the world comes from the earliest, nonspecific, internal, affective signals from one's body in response to some activating stimulus. People are organized to respond in a certain way: to flee, to attack, to approach, or to withdraw. They simultaneously begin to perceive the internal affective signal and to be able to use it as information. For example, a husband automatically feels anxious and sad when his wife leaves him alone at home to go out for the evening with her friends. He is organized by his limbic system's primary emotional reaction of sadness and loneliness to feel abandoned and has a tendency to cry out for the lost object and to search for security. Note that this is an action tendency, not yet an actual behavior. Thus he is organized to cry out and scan for protection but does not unless this tendency is further processed to turn it into behavior. In the second moment, some complex symbolization, evaluation, and explanation of what has occurred takes place, as he works to make sense of his experience. How the husband analyzes the situation, his reaction, and his explanation will influence what he experiences next. If, for example, he automatically avoids his fear and/or sadness and misguidedly symbolizes his internal experience as one of anger, he will react angrily; if he does symbolize his fear of abandonment and sadness accurately but then cannot tolerate it, he will evaluate his wife's going out as an unfair violation rather than loss, and he will construe the situation as "she is treating me unfairly," and this will strongly influence what he says and does next. Rather than feel his anxiety and sadness, he will get angry. Either way, if anger dominates his self-organization when his wife comes home, he will not be able to share his more vulnerable feeling of anxiety and sadness at loss but will, for example, accuse her of being too flighty or will blame her for not having paid a bill. She immediately will feel threatened and, depending on what she attends to and how she understands and explains her own emotional experience, she will attack, defend, or apologize. The negative dance of attack–defend or the positive one of disclose–listen will begin, generated by the dialectical interaction of the first and second moments of emotional experience in each partner and the partner's reactions to each other. Automatically generated, limbic-system–based, emergency emotions thus are at the core of the perception of threat and are key generators of couples conflict.

EMOTIONS: BIOLOGY OR CULTURE?

Emotion theorists, although they disagree in many ways about the functions of emotions, all share the assumption that emotions help people solve many of the basic problems of social living and relationships. Evolutionary theorists see emotions as universal, hardwired psychoaffective motor programs that solved ancient, recurrent threats to survival (Ekman, 1992; Panksepp, 1998, 2002; Plutchik, 1980; Porges, 1995; Tomkins, 1984; Tooby & Cosmides, 1990). Social constructionists, however, view emotions as socially learned responses constructed in the process of social discourse governed by culturally relevant concerns about identity, morality, and social structure (Averill, 1980; Harré, 1984; Lutz & White, 1986). They also view human culture as loosening the in-wired connections between emotions and problem solutions in that cultures over time find new ways to solve those problems for which emotions evolved. Cultures also find ways of using existing emotions for new purposes. Although these contrasting biological and social approaches conceive of the source of emotions in markedly different ways, both ascribe important relational functions to emotion.

The Evolutionary View of Social Emotions

In the bioevolutionary view, emotions developed in the course of evolution to solve many problems of living. In this view, different emotions are seen as having distinct psychoaffective motor programs, each forming a specific emotion, and emotions are viewed as occurring in discrete categories. Different basic emotion systems evolved to handle different problems and have different brain systems devoted to them. Activation of any one of these special-purpose affective–motivational states will automatically produce motivation and behavior to accomplish critical tasks necessary for survival, such as escaping from danger, learning from novelty, eagerness to approach, directed purposefulness, taking care of another, or moving closer to others for protection or warmth. When these neural systems are operating freely, feelings of all sorts such as tenderness, the longing for emotional contact, hostility, pushing away, or the desire for joyful interaction with others emerge. In this view, different emotions have developed evolutionarily to help solve two different major social problems—those of affiliation and dominance.

Evolution of Affiliative Emotions

Fear is the primordial emotion at the heart of the fight–flight system (Öhman, 1986). Fear helps individuals avoid danger and is at the center of an attachment system. It is now known that the amygdala contains specialized areas that scan incoming sensory information for patterns that have been associated with danger. The amygdala can trigger a fear response even before the incoming information has been sent to the visual cortex, where it is seen, or before it has been fully consciously processed (LeDoux, 1996).

Social species have evolved attachment and caregiving-related emotions, which facilitate protective relations between parent and offspring (Bowlby, 1973; Shaver & Hazan, 1988). The care-seeking system involves anxiety, protest, separation, and running to parents for protection. The caregiving system involves perceptions and experiences that sensitize parents to infantile dependence cues (such as baby-faced features, infants' vocal and visual cues of distress). In addition, love and compassion in these primary care bonds are characterized by experiences of warmth and expressive behavior such as mutual smiles and gaze patterns. These are elements of interactions that strengthen both protective and loving bonds and physiological responses that help caretakers respond to the other's distress.

The experience and display of emotions of distress–sadness related to the absence of a loved one provokes succorance in others and eventually helps individuals establish bonds with other people. Emotions of love and desire facilitate the identification, establishment, and maintenance of pair bonds and reproductive relations. These emotions involve appraisals and perceptions that are sensitive to cues related to potential mate value. These include beauty, fertility, chastity, social status, and character (Buss, 1992; Ellis, 1992); expressive behaviors that signal interest and commitment (Frank, 1988) and evoke desire and love; and hormonal and autonomic responses that facilitate sexual behavior. The protection of potential mates from competitors is equally critical. Jealousy relates to mate protection and is triggered by cues that signal potential threats to the relationship, such as possible sexual involvement of the mate with others (Buss, 1992). Jealousy motivates possessive and threat behaviors that discourage competitors and prevent sexual opportunities for the mate (Wilson & Daly, 1996).

Evolution of Dominance-Related Emotions

Emotions also evolved to help solve relational problems related to hierarchy and organization. Issues of status, identity, and agency and associated concerns with power, influence, and control are central in social interaction.

Status hierarchies provided heuristic solutions to the problems of distributing resources, such as mates, food, and social attention, and the labor required of collective endeavors (de Waal, 1986; Fiske, 1991). Hierarchies that defined people on an up–down dimension involved dynamic processes and required continual negotiation and redefinition to maximize the probabilities of surviving and thriving. The establishment, maintenance, and preservation of status hierarchies was in part accomplished by emotions related to dominance and submission (de Waal, 1996; Öhman, 1986). For example embarrassment and shame appeased dominant individuals and signaled submissiveness, appeasement, or placating (Keltner & Buswell, 1996; R. Miller & Leary, 1992). This led to the self feeling inferior. Contempt was the feeling of superiority and dominance vis-à-vis inferior others. The primordial form of shame involved submissive-related behavior much akin to the appeasement displays of other species (e.g., gaze aversion, head movements down, controlled smiles) and submissive experience (e.g., feelings of smallness and weakness). In these dominant–submissive relationships, awe tended to be felt by those in the submissive role and was associated with the experience of being in the presence of an entity greater than the self.

Early in evolution, to encourage cooperation and avoid the problems of cheating and defection, in particular among nonkin, humans reciprocated cooperative and noncooperative acts toward one another (Trivers, 1971). Several emotions signaled when reciprocity had been violated and motivated reparative behavior in the form of assertion and appeasement (de Waal, 1996; Frank, 1988; Nesse, 1990; Trivers, 1971). Guilt occurred following violations of reciprocity and was expressed in apologetic, remedial behavior that reestablished reciprocity (Keltner & Buswell, 1996; Tangney, 1991). Moral anger motivated the punishment of individuals who had violated rules of reciprocity and was defined by a sensitivity to issues of justice and unfairness (Keltner, Ellsworth, & Edwards, 1993). Gratitude at others' altruistic acts was a reward for reciprocity (Trivers, 1971). Envy motivated individuals to derogate others whose favorable status was unjustified, thus preserving equal relations (Fiske, 1991).

Dimensional Approaches

In addition to the categorical approach, in which emotions are seen as discrete psychoaffective motor programs, such as anger and sadness, a biologically based dimensional approach has been proposed as an alternative way of measuring emotions (Russell & Mehrabian, 1977). In this approach, a two-factor model of emotion proposes that emotions can be best understood as combinations of the two fundamental dimensions of arousal and valence. In this view, fear, for example, involves high arousal and high negative valence, whereas contentment is low arousal and high positive valence. The most commonly proffered alternative to a two-dimensional view is a three-factor model in which the third dimension is "dominance," "potency," or "aggression" (Mehrabian, 1995; Morgan & Heise, 1988; Russell & Mehrabian, 1977). This three-dimensional model helps resolve the acknowledged limitation of the two-dimensional circumplex model, based on arousal and valence, that cannot differentiate between anger and fear (Larsen & Diener, 1992; D. Watson, 2000). In two-dimensional models, both anger and fear are unpleasant, activated emotions (in other words, high negative valence and arousal). However, anger and fear are quite distinct experientially, behaviorally, and expressively. It is difficult to reconcile the distinct subjective experiences and motivational properties of these two emotions with their coincidence in a two-dimensional model of emotion. The introduction of a third dimension of affect helps differentiate anger and fear in emotion factor space.

Ethologists have long identified dominance as an important affective aspect of social behavior beyond the approach–avoid dimensions represented by positive and negative arousal (Eibl-Eibesfeldt & Sütterlin, 1990). The ethological construct of dominance, representing control in a social hierarchy, is related to emotional dominance. Emotional dominance is related to the perceived controllability of the emotion-eliciting situation (Mehrabian, 1995). Dominance appears to be independent of positive and negative arousal and may be more related to serotonin and to androgen functions than positive, and possibly negative, arousal. Testosterone, adrenaline, and cortisol all increase, muscles tense, and hearts beat faster when a person asserts dominance. Fear and shame related to loss of control, diminishment, and humiliation send neurochemicals speeding through the brain and bodies, and these are powerful motivators of submission. (Cloninger, Svrakic, & Przybeck, 1993). This third dimension, dominance, is important in couples therapy because investigations of dyadic interactions have demonstrated the uniquely toxic effects of expressions of contempt and overbearing dominance in couples relationships (Gottman, 1994; Holtzworth-Munroe, Smutzler, & Stuart, 1998). Couples can express a variety of other negative emotions, including sadness, fear, and guilt, without any clear association with dissolution or divorce. Conversely, contempt and domineering behavior are associated with increased risk of divorce or violence. It appears useful, then, in understanding couples emotional cycles to introduce a three-dimensional view of emotion that takes into account not only valence and arousal but also dominance. In classifying emotions on three dimensions, sadness, shyness, shame, guilt, fear, and self-directed hostility load on a factor of negative emotions. Surprise, enjoyment, and excitement consistently load on a general positive affect factor. Contempt, anger, and disgust toward others can be thought of as a hostile triad that is high on the dominance dimension.

The Cultural Development of Social Emotions

Culture clearly has elaborated on the evolutionary aspects of basic emotion. Thus, in addition to the biologically provided function of universal human emotions, culture modulates both inputs (e.g., what counts as an insult or a loss) and outputs (e.g., which emotional displays can be expressed in which circumstances). Elaborated emotions such as envy and pride clearly are shaped by culture and interaction and by concepts of the self, morality, and social order (Markus & Kitayama, 1991; Shweder & Haidt, 2000). Love and other feelings are expressed according to cultural rules and, equally important, according to subculture and family rules. For example, is a gift a sign of love in a given family? Is respect for elders a primary form of devotion in a given culture? Is the acknowledgement of birthdays or anniversaries to be done with words or actions, or is true caring shown by expensive gifts or with handmade signs of care?

Culturally elaborated emotions and their causes vary across cultures and cannot be experienced by infants. Clearly, all emotions are not evolutionarily primed. Showing the underside of one's feet, for example, is insulting in some cultures; as another example, pride for a national flag is clearly not inborn. Elaborated emotions can last for years or centuries and be handed on for generations. For example, the hatred felt toward a member of another family who has been an historical enemy can last for centuries. Although at any moment in time this hatred is composed of brief emotional experiences, it is made up of values, beliefs, images, action tendencies, and affective dispositions or sentiments that can pass from one generation to the next or one group to another and last for extended periods of time. Witness the enactment of familial and societal prejudices by the Montagues and the Capulets in *Romeo and Juliet*.

Culture and the elaboration process also can loosen the link between a basic emotion and the relational problem it was designed to solve. Culture does this in two ways. First, cultures find new solutions to the ancient problems that emotions were designed to solve. Second, cultures find new uses for old emotions that have little to do with their original function. For example, marriage can be built on sexual-, romantic-, and attachment-related emotions in cultures that practice love-based marriage, to create stable environments for child rearing. Or marriage can be built on the emotions of the reciprocal status or altruism system in cultures that practice arranged marriages or bind families together by trading daughters.

Culture has put disgust to a variety of new uses. The eliciting conditions of disgust have expanded so much that disgust may now be seen to be a social emotion whose function is to guard against certain forms of deviance and debasement (Rozin, Haidt, & McCauley, 2000). Disgust and its associated cognitions about contamination and purity are recruited into child rearing in place of physical punishment and into the maintenance of social groups with distinct boundaries (e.g., the Indian caste system, upper class attitudes toward the lower class). Shame, too, has been similarly culturally adapted and is now the primary means of child rearing in Western cultures (Stearns & Stearns, 1988). In many Hindu and Islamic cultures, the expression of submissive emotions such as shame demonstrates feminine virtue (Abu-Lughod, 1986; Menon & Shweder, 1994). Flirtation and courtship involve submissive similes of embarrassment (Eibl-Eibesfeldt, 1980) and submissive–dominant displays (Fisher, 1992). In Japanese and other Eastern cultures, greetings involve the junior person bowing the head in submissive, shame-like gestures.

Once this loosening of emotion from its biological base is recognized, it becomes easier to reconcile evolutionary approaches (which focus on basic emotions and therefore find universality) and social constructionist approaches (which focus on elaborated emotions and therefore find cultural variation). Elaborated emotions thus combine biology and culture, and the total package provides meanings, behaviors, and social practices. An integration of evolutionary and social constructivist approaches illuminates the central role of emotion in relationships and helps researchers understand the biological and cultural aspects of emotion in intimate relationships.

A Dialectical Constructivist View

We have attempted to capture this dialectic between biology and culture in our dialectical constructivist view of the self-in-relation (Greenberg & Pascual-Leone, 1995, 2001; Greenberg, Rice, & Elliot, 1993; Guidano, 1991; Mahoney, 1991; Neimeyer & Mahoney, 1995; Pascual-Leone, 1987, 1990a, 1990b, 1991; J. Watson & Greenberg, 1996; J. Watson & Rennie, 1994). This view encompasses the biological and social constructive aspects of emotion in a dynamic-systems view of functioning. In this view, we see that as well as having emotion in relationships, people also live in a constant process of making sense of these emotions. The self-in-relation is seen as a multiprocess, multilevel organization emerging from the dialectical interaction of many component elements within the self and between selves. The highest level dialectic within the self is the dialectic that generates meaning from emotion. The highest level dialectic in the relationship is the interaction between self and other that regulates emotion.

The most important process that people attend to in the self is the interaction between ongoing, moment-by-moment *implicit experience* (the first moment of bodily felt experience) and higher level *explicit reflexive processes* (the second moment) that interpret, order, and explain elementary experiential processes. This process of self-formation, however, always also is in the process of being regulated by an ongoing interaction with others. Thus the most important interpersonal process people attend to is the interactional position taken by each partner that acts to evoke an affective reaction in the partner. Partners in interaction thus are viewed both as self-organizing and as mutually regulating each other's self-organization or emotional states.

Partners thus function as dynamic emotion systems in interaction. They constantly create the selves they are about to become by synthesizing biologically based information, culturally acquired learning, and social context. This results in affect, cognition, and interaction being inextricably intertwined. Important in this view is that at any point in time more experience is always available to an individual than is being symbolized in conscious awareness and that what is available is highly context dependent (Greenberg, 2002a; Greenberg & Watson, 2006). If the interaction changes, emotion and self-organization change in harmony. If emotion changes, the self-organization and the interaction changes.

Emotion Schematic Processing and Scripts

In this dialectical constructivist view, an emotion scheme is the central structure that generates an individual's experience (Greenberg, 2002a, 2002b; Greenberg, Rice, & Elliott, 1993; Greenberg & Watson, 2006). An *emotion scheme* is an integrative internal organization that integrates emotion with cognition, motivation, action, and interaction; was developed through lived experience; and when activated, produces lived experience. An emotion scheme for love of a partner is an encoding of a pattern of complex emotional interactions that captures many aspects of the experience of love: the feeling; the tone; the memories of the relationship's physical sensations and accompanying interactions; the associated sensory, motor, and language experiences and the context in which they occur and will come to involve feelings of devotion, caring, anger, and ambivalence; and the many other complex characteristics based on the unique experience of a person. Or a person may have an emotion scheme of shame that will contain all the sensations, feelings, memories, and interactions related to experiences of failing to live up to expectations of a parent, or a scheme of joy at particular smiling faces. At the level of the brain, schemes can be thought of as a network of neuronal connections or a neural operating system (Atkinson, 2005). At the level of behavior, they can be thought of as a script for action. People have many emotion schemes that store their affective experience and, when activated, produce that experience. Learning and experience are organized into schemes based on emotions experienced in situations. These become the primary generators of future experience. At any one time, a set of schemes is activated by both self- and interactional processes, and the person is organized by a tacit synthesis of a number of these emotion schemes into one of many possible self-organizations such as vulnerable, withdrawn, approaching, or good humored. The emotion schematic response system thus is seen as the central catalyst of self-organization, and therefore the central catalyst of dysfunctional or hypersensitive reactions in partners.

The fact that many of one's thoughts and decisions are influenced by automatic emotion schematic processes that operate outside of one's awareness is to one's benefit most of the time. The emotion schematic neural operating systems are activated automatically at the right time to provide emotionally adaptive responses. People thus automatically experience affection for loved ones, compassion when others are in pain, anger when someone is treating them unfairly, and sadness at loss. People also automatically experience empathy when others share their inner world, and they simply sense what it's like to be them with the help of "mirror" neurons (Gallese, Fadiga, Fogassi, & Rizzolatti, 1996; J. Watson & Greenberg, in press), the matching neurons that fire in the observer when observing a person engaged in actions or expressions.

When individuals or relationships are distressed, however, there nearly always are problems with the automatic activation and suppression of the adaptive internal states necessary to maintain one's emotional bonds. When maladaptive emotion schemes and self-organizations are activated, emotions are no longer a reliable guide. People then find themselves repeatedly doing things in relationships that they know are not helpful, such as getting angry at loved ones, and they fail to do the things they know would be helpful, such as feeling concerned. This occurs because their automatically activated emotion schematic system that governs their functioning does not produce the required adaptive relational feeling. For example, being unable to respond to a partner's conciliatory gesture in kind or being unable to assert when intimidated are all problems of lack of adaptive emotional responsiveness. When relationships are distressed, positive feelings toward one's partner are inaccessible and intimate bonds become dormant, leaving partners without the emotional connection that once sustained them. Partners may try to be positive to resolve a conflict or engage a learned skill, but without the powerful emotionally driven states that promote affiliation, or assertion, the words of love or limits a partner utters may be right but the emotional tone, facial expression, and manner will not be convincing. No relational healing will occur from these interactions (Atkinson, 2005). Alternatively, a partner's words can be apologetic, but there will be no experienced remorse unless the words comes from an emotionally based self-organization of authentic apology (Malcolm, Warwar, & Greenberg, 2005). If inside a partner's brain, the internal state that produces intimacy or assertion is not activated, conflict will not be resolved. With the activation of any particular state, the types of feeling, thinking, and acting associated with it will dominate, and it is nearly impossible to engage in other ways of seeing things without a switch in emotional organization.

Emotions, once evoked, thus set up basic modes of processing, and these outline scripts of commitment to particular ways of relating to others. Happiness sets up scripts of cooperation; anger sets up scripts of conflict or boundary setting; fear sets up scripts of defense; sadness sets up seeking comfort; shame sets up deference; and liking sets up involvement. These commitments enable a certain mode of processing and relating to the other to take precedence over anything else for certain periods of time. Activation of emotions in couples thus sets up interactional scripts for how to address basic concerns, and any new emotionally important situations that occur are likely to be processed according to the scripts they activate. Emotion schemes thus shape interactional scripts between partners, and it is these schemes that need to be accessed in couples therapy, as they are the generators of interaction and conflict. Once accessed in therapy, the distressed attachment- and identity-related feelings embedded in schemes and organized into scripts are to be understood, communicated, soothed, and transformed by self and partners.

Core Schemes

Couples conflict results most when maladaptive schemes based on attachment fear and identity shame are activated. With these, the self is organized experientially to feel abandoned and unlovable or as humiliated and worthless. These self-organizations are strongly influenced by the automatic activation of core emotion schematic memories of earlier abandonment and neglect, or humiliation or failure, and partners often find it difficult to regulate these emotions. When emotion memories of prior abandonments and diminishments are evoked in response to current rejections, losses, or diminishments in the relationship, these cause the self to lose resilience, to collapse into powerlessness, to withdraw, or to attack to defend the self against further injury.

It is important to note that memories are stored at emotion addresses. Thus sad memories are all stored under the common characteristics of "sadness," and all fear memories are organized together under "fearfulness." Thus when people feel sad, other sad memories are more likely to be evoked; when they feel shame, other memories of humiliation will be evoked; and when they feel fear, fear memories are more likely to be evoked. It is these core maladaptive feelings and all the attendant unresolved emotions and thoughts that then govern functioning.

The maladaptive emotion schematic memory system thus produces the maladaptive emotions of shame, fear, and anxiety that are at the core of much problematic individual distress within couples. Thus, feeling sad or distressed in response to a rejection or invalidation often ends up evoking states of core shame and fear and a weak, bad, defeated sense of self, formed from the person's previous life experiences (Greenberg & Watson, 2006). Once these organizations are activated, the person feels worthless, unloved, abandoned, alone, and empty and withdraws, feeling powerless and defeated. The partner, not being privy to the withdrawing partner's internal feelings of unworthiness, experiences his or her reaction as rejection, as "you are unlovable" rather than one of "I am afraid to fail." A criticism by one partner based on feeling abandoned is experienced by the other partner as being attacked rather than as being needed, as "you are bad" rather than "I am lonely."

The Unbearable Complexity of Being

It also is important to recognize that because people are dynamic systems, they do not simply feel only one thing at one time. Rather, there are many possibilities and levels of feeling and meaning, especially in interactional situations. The therapist's goal is to access the relationally healing adaptive emotions. Thus, when a wife informs her husband that she has just been offered a new job, the husband might feel very happy that she is so successful but disappointed that she now will have to travel more and sad that he will have to miss a recently planned outing to see his family. At the same time, he himself, feeling very tired from a stressful day at work, might react to her promotion with relief at the prospect of having to work less now that her salary will increase. The husband thus may be aware of having a very complex mixture of feelings. It probably would be most accurate to say that he rapidly cycles through a number of different emotional states rather than feeling a complex blend of emotions, but he will organize and form a narrative around one dominant feeling: either happy, sad, or relief. In this case, which feeling is accessed will determine the interaction with his wife.

Talented novelists are often able to represent the subtleties of these complex states of being in which often enduring states interact strongly and occur almost simultaneously with more fleeting reactions. They describe these states because they observe that human experience allows for such complex interacting feelings and processes. These complex states often are good reflections of the processes that occur in the lived human experience in partners in therapy. It is the therapist's job to catch which are the more enduring core states that influence the relationship.

A good theory of functioning needs to explain how all these states are possible. This is what we attempt to do in our dialectical constructivist, dynamic-systems view of functioning. It helps explain the very fluid states we see in therapy, which sometimes last only moments. As we have discussed, according to the dialectical constructivist model, people construct meanings that permit the coexistence of multiple, enduring, and partially interacting states of many kinds. Individuals are multivocal, and the organization that results is a function of dialogue between their many voices (Smith & Greenberg, 2007). Thus, from a dynamic-systems perspective, instead of seeing partners in therapy as just feeling one emotion, say, anger, therapists need to understand that experience is a product of many physiological, behavioral, and/or neural processes and that people are multileveled, with many types of feelings at one time. It is the subtle variations in the different states of anger, fear, hope, joy, dismay, surprise, pride, jealousy, infatuation, schadenfreude (i.e., pleasure in another's pain), and so on, and interactions between them, that we need to capture in describing a partner's feelings. Partners' experiences thus often are more complex and nuanced than simply experiencing something that is easily represented as a single emotion, such as anger.

Bearing in mind this complexity, therapists still need to work with identifying categorical emotions such as anger, sadness, fear, and shame but must remember that this categorization is a simplification or reification of a dynamic process. It produces clarity, but it also is simplified. There is always more there. So even if at any one moment, the partner is organized as angry, sad, or afraid, this is not all they are feeling. They are complex dynamic systems in interaction, and at any moment how they are organized is only one of many possible self-in-relation organizations. The possibilities of changing from one state to another then are enormous, and this fluidity is a resource, because couples therapy is about changing these states to change interactions. Our job as therapists is therefore to focus at particular moments on feelings, and to amplify those feelings, among the varied possibilities that are being felt and could be voiced, that will help the couple resolve conflict and promote harmony.

Narrative

The dialectical constructivist model recognizes that in addition to possessing biologically based, in-wired meaning and expressive systems, individuals also are active agents, constantly constructing meaning and creating the self they are about to become. A level of organization of self, higher than the schematically based self-organization that generates the feeling of who one is can be referred to as a person's *narrative identity* (Angus & McLeod, 2004; Greenberg & Angus, 2004; Whelton & Greenberg, 2001). This identity involves the integration of accumulated experience and of various self-representations into some sort of coherent story or narrative. Identity narratives influence couples interaction. Human lives, to assume coherence and meaning, are "emplotted" in a story, and events within the relationship are organized by narrative discourse such that disparate actions and experiences of the couple's life are formed into a coherent narrative. Thus, relationship narratives emerge as well as identity narratives.

What our dialectical constructivist view suggests, then, is that the many voices that compose the self are given coherence in the stories that people tell to account for themselves and their relationships. It is these stories that provide the connective thread that weaves together disparate experiences and events to create a meaningful and coherent whole—a storied experience of what is occurring in self and in the relationship. All emotions thus are storied and all relational stories are shaped by—emplotted within—the trajectory of emergent emotion themes (Greenberg & Angus, 2004). Changing both identity and couples narratives thus helps consolidate changes in experiential organizations and helps solidify new interactional patterns.

CONCLUSION

Over evolutionary time, the goals and the plans in emotion evolved to become explicitly social and to help people deal adaptively with relating. The effect of an emotion is to set the framework for a mode of processing and relating: for affectionate cooperation; for solicitation of help; for aggressive conflict, dominance, or submissive fear; or for the grieving of loss, abandonment, or rejection. The more humans evolved, the more social emotions came to include specific types of attributions. People not only reacted with fear or anger but they also came to explain their reactions often as being caused by another person. Blame was born. Modern-day marriage and other intimate relationships are filled with negative attributions to the other with resulting blame. Although people may often be wrong about their partners' intentions, they tend to attribute to them the cause of their own feelings and then direct their emotions toward them.

Emotion and its communication are at the heart of marriage and marital therapy. Sadness and fear prototypically relate to attachment, security, and connection; joy and excitement prototypically relate to love, which appears to combine many emotions into a unique and mysterious blend; contempt, disgust, and anger—the hostile triad—relate to dominance and threats to identity. In addition, sadness and anger relate to frustration of both attachment and love needs. The hostile triad is often the most direct target of intervention in couples therapy. Contempt and disgust may be signs of the dissolution of marriage, whereas anger is often a sign of the frustration of underlying needs and is more a symptom of distress than a cause of it.

3

AFFECT REGULATION

People seek to maximize the experience of positive emotions and minimize the experience of negative emotions.
—Ekman & Davidson (1994, p. 412)

As the above quotation indicates, people are motivated by the affects they seek (Greenberg, 2002a). Generally, they seek to feel calm, feel joy, pleasure, pride, excitement, and interest; equally, they seek to not feel pain, shame, and fear, as these feelings all have survival-related value. They do this because emotions promote survival. Most of what people think and do is motivated by their affective goals. People primarily organize within themselves and their relationships to regulate their affect. In large part, people relate to others to help regulate their affect. People seek connection because it helps them feel secure, and they seek understanding or empathic mirroring from others because it makes them feel seen or special. The security and validation provided by others is a major source of affect regulation for most people.

We are proposing that marriage and interpersonal connection, one of the major sources of human emotion, is sought after because it helps partners regulate their affect. Relationships help people feel joyful, secure, excited, and confident and in this way are primary regulators of affect. In addition to emotion being motivational, by virtue of people's desire to have or not have certain affective experience, feeling emotion also is motivation enhancing (Tomkins, 1962). Feelings strengthen and help desires seek their aim. Excitement promotes seeking sexual union; fear promotes escape; and anger promotes attack or defense. People would not flee from danger unless they felt afraid and would not bond unless they felt love. Emotions, by enhancing motivation, amplify goal-oriented behavior. Marriage and intimate coupling thus is motivated by the affects it gives people, and the affects it produces further promotes coupling.

Emotion and motivation are intrinsically linked, and without emotions, there would be no motivations. Affect is intricately intertwined with motive such that motives are dependent on affective building blocks, whereas affects result from need and goal satisfaction and gratification. Emotions are signals about need or goal satisfaction, whereas needs are motivated by efforts to attain or regulate affect. It is important to understand that the relational needs so important in intimate relationships, such as needs for attachment and identity-validation or self-esteem, are most fundamentally based on affect. Without anxiety and calm, there could be no attachment seeking or soothing, and without fear, there would be no harm avoidance. Without interest, there would be no involvement and agency; without anger, no assertion; without pride and shame, no identity; and without joy and excitement, no pleasure in connection. Without emotions, people would not seek out the other. Human connection would not be satisfying, and people would not bond. Emotion is a fundamental element of these relational tendencies and is the means by which motivation works. As this becomes clear, we understand that people seek supportive and loving relationships because these make them feel good, and they extricate themselves from unsupportive, judgmental, relationships because these make them feel bad. People's emotions thus regulate coupling, and coupling regulates emotions.

Partners affect regulation, and their related affective communications thus are at the core of intimate relationships and couples therapy. The dyadic regulation of affect, by means of affect attunement and affect communication, begins and is most crucial in infancy. It carries through to adulthood and is as important, if not as crucial, in adult intimate relationships. The dyadic regulation of affect occurs mainly through nonverbal channels and through implicit meanings and communication. Partners attend and respond to the affective tone of each other's messages far more than they do to the content of what the partner is saying, and it is this that most affects them and their sense of security and well-being. Partners read each other's emotional signals with great care, and this reading dominates their interactions. What they see on their partners' faces, hear in their partners' voices, and feel in their partners' touch is worth a thousand words. Explicit emotional expression of course also influences how others respond. Connection and closeness to one's partner, empathic validation of the self by one's partner, as well as the freedom to express and assert one's identity and competence, are all important elements in affect regulation in marriage. Taking care of others also regulates one's own, as well as the other's, feelings, while liking and being liked by others elevates one's sense of vitality and purpose. All these relational experiences help people to feel good, thereby regulating their affective states of being in the world.

Marital breakdown, in turn, is a breakdown in affect regulation and affective responsiveness and communication. When one no longer feels understood, soothed, joyful, validated, and secure but instead feels anger, shame, boredom, and anxiety in one's marriages, the relationship is in trouble. Intimate relationships and marriages, so centrally fueled by affect, with time, become patterned around particular emotions or combinations of affect. Marital satisfaction depends on the patterns of emotion experienced and expressed in the relationship. People seek marital therapy when affect regulation and communication in the marriage is failing and the relationship becomes patterned around distressing affects. Difficulties in intimate relationships, then, are most centrally about problems in the regulation, communication, and patterning of affect. It is important to note that although people primarily seek to feel positive emotions, negative emotions are highly functional, and people self-regulate emotions with the aim of achieving their goals. If people's goals consist of more than "feeling good," which they often do, then people also sometimes will seek negative emotions under certain circumstances. Thus, we are not proposing simply that the seeking of pleasure and the avoidance of pain motivate people. Rather, we are proposing that people are motivated to regulate their affect. In thinking about whether people seek negative emotions, it is important to distinguish between long-term and short-term goals in the affect regulation process. People may well seek negative emotions in the short term as a means of achieving the happiness and contentment of meeting their goals in the long term. In addition, people are motivated to seek meaning, and this brings pleasure; affect is people's primary meaning system. People are born into meaning, and ultimately making meaning from affect is highly regulating.

DYADIC AND SELF-REGULATION OF AFFECT

The dyadic regulation of affect starts at birth and grows more and more complex as people develop an identity. In infancy, the other person is the primary affect regulator. With development, the responsive soothing of the (m)other is internalized over time into a capacity for self-soothing. In addition, as the brain and the self develop, capacities for self-regulation of affect grow. Adults thus become capable of regulating their own affect. The role of the other as a soothing agent is, however, never dispensed with in human life (Fosha, 2001). Through the dyadic process, individuals often are able to emotionally process what they are not able to process alone.

People need connection and closeness to feel secure (Bowlby, 1973). In the face of threat, the toddler runs and clings to the caretaker. This is done because contact and comfort soothe anxiety. Similarly, in the face of threat, adults turn to their intimate others for comfort and soothing. At the same time, people also develop a sense of identity by configuring their self-experience with others' views of the self into a coherent self narrative. As Stern (1985) showed, the infant self in the 1st years of life rapidly develops a sense of coherence, affectivity, agency, and continuity. This is greatly facilitated by the caretaker's affect attunement and mirroring. The self strengthens as its affects and intentions are recognized, and it begins to be able to self-regulate. Self- and other-regulation are two separate but interconnected strands of affect regulation that develop simultaneously.

As adults, people seek connection to feel secure and they seek validation to feel esteem. Being close and connected to one's partner helps one to regulate one's anxiety and feel secure. In addition, people seek empathy, validation, confirmation, and acknowledgment from others to maintain a sense of identity and self-coherence, and this regulates people's self-esteem and shame and strengthens agency. The self needs empathic attunement to regulate self-esteem, like the body needs oxygen (Kohut, 1984). The self grows stronger, and a coherent identity develops when its agentic strivings are recognized and through validation and empathy. When a partner's identity is threatened or self-esteem is damaged, say at work or with associates, support and validation from an intimate partner, who knows one best, is good medicine. When, however, invalidation comes from one's intimate other, on whom one relies for validation, the threat to one's identity is great and the shame can be devastating. In our view, two important needs, one for security and the other for validation, are present from birth to death, and both contribute in adulthood to the creation and maintenance of well-being.

In an environment in which one's emotions are affirmed—and even better, shared—by the other, it becomes safe to be one's self and to disclose and explore all sorts of intense, difficult feelings, without fear of being overwhelmed (the other is there to hold and support) or of being shamed (the other is there understanding and validating). With safety, and without the dysfunctional inhibiting impact of fear and shame, partners can own and explore their reactions and the partners' responsiveness can become actively healing and bonding. Thus, emotional connection occurs in optimal fashion in an emotionally engaged dyad within which the individual feels secure (attachment) and validated (identity).

In adults, the self-regulation of affect is as important as the dyadic regulation of affect. Partners' inability to regulate their own affects, especially when the other is unavailable, can be a major source of marital difficulty. When partners are unable to regulate their own distress, they cope with it by attacking or withdrawing. This means that couples therapists, as well as focusing on other responsiveness and blocks to it, also need to focus on enhancing partners' ability to regulate their own affect and not turn their distress into attack or withdrawal. Partners thus need to develop the ability to soothe their own anxiety and shame when their partners disappoint them or are not able to be there for them. When normally responsive partners cannot be responsive, because they are stressed and are concerned with regulating their own affective states, or simply because they find the demands of the other partner too intense, the dysregulated partners need to be able to soothe themselves. So a balance needs to be struck in all relationships between good enough responsiveness and good enough self-regulation. All partners need good enough warm responsiveness from each other to feel loved and cherished.

Individuals with past relational disappointments or difficulties, or with traumatic histories, benefit greatly from their partner's ability to be responsive and understanding of their vulnerabilities, and this gives the vulnerable partners an experience that their feelings and needs can be responded to by a loving partner, that is, it provides a corrective emotional experience. Over time, in good enough relationships, some partners who are vulnerable, as a function of past wounds, and become desperate and anxious about separation or invalidation, or those who find need frustration dysregulating, have to learn to tolerate when the other is not available or confirming or does not give them what they want. They have to develop the ability to soothe themselves and to tolerate need frustration, rather than to fly into a rage or withdraw for days. People need to be able to curtail negative absorbing states in which feeling bad builds on itself and leads them to feeling worse (Gottman, Gortner, Berns, & Jacobson, 1997). Partners thus need to be helped in couples therapy not only to reveal themselves and to receive the others' responsiveness but also to face their own painful emotions, tolerate them, and soothe them, and rather than becoming dysregulated, to feel worthy and lovable even when they experience relational disappointments and disruptions.

Although it is important to first promote other-soothing and responsiveness, as that is what is most lacking when a couple enters therapy, we have found, especially in longer term couples therapy, that the focus often needs to shift from responsive attunement of the other or the inability to reveal the self, to the inability of one or both partners to affectively self-regulate. Harmony requires both mutual accessibility and responsiveness and that partners be able to regulate their own affect rather than explode, withdraw, self-harm, or self-medicate when the other is unable to be available and responsive. The ability for partners to tolerate need frustration and regulate their own affects is thus as important to the long-term stability of a marriage as is the responsive soothing from, and emotional availability of, the other. The ability to reveal one's underlying feelings and needs and the other's ability to respond in a nurturing and validating manner are crucial in producing intimacy. These abilities help couples who were previously alienated to connect and bond and sets more positive interactions in motion that help sustain the bond. This, however, may still not be enough for the bond to endure. Lasting change also often requires change in the partners' abilities to regulate their own affect. The ability to take responsibility and to be able to respond to one's self in a self-soothing and self-caring manner, when necessary, is as important to the maintenance of intimacy as is responsive attunement by the other.

Thus, in couples, the blaming partners' abilities to regulate their abandonment anxiety will dramatically influence whether they disclose or attack. A dominant partner's ability to tolerate shame, anxiety, or need frustration will influence how much control is felt to be necessary. A withdrawing or submitting partner's sense of adequacy (based on his or her ability to soothe fears of inadequacy or to cope with shame), will influence how much he or she withdraws or approaches. In our couples therapy practice, we now put a focus both on what the partners need to do to help regulate each other's affect and on what the individuals in the couple need to do to regulate their own affect. Self-soothing thus becomes an important focus as well as relational soothing. In a mutually regulating system, we always have to work with what both the partner and the self need to do differently to help deal with painful affect. Thus therapists' empathic responses at the right time to a very fragile partner, which focus on the self's difficulty in regulating affect, such as "At times like this, you just feel so desperately alone like he'll never ever be there for you again, and you feel like a flower in the desert that you'll wither and die without water. It's so hard to hold on to his love for you when he isn't responsive in the right way" are as important as the more standard emotion-focused couples therapy (EFT-C) empathic responses captured in the first sentence. A more standard response would only help to reveal the person's underlying vulnerability so the partner can respond to it; it would not reflect the self's difficulty in maintaining what can be thought of as object constancy in the affective domain.

We are not suggesting that affective self-regulation is more important than other-regulation by contact, comfort, and validation. Rather, both self- and other-regulation are necessary for enduring change. This emphasis on self-focus is not intended to deemphasize the importance of soothing through the attachment relationship, especially as a way of initially restructuring negative cycles, but we have observed that enduring change requires the development of both self- and other-soothing. There thus are two broad domains of affect regulation that need to be worked with in couples therapy: relational or dyadic regulation of affect and self-regulation of affect. In relational regulation of affect, the partners reveal themselves to each other and provide each other with soothing and with joy, pleasure, security, excitement, and validation and they do not trigger too much anger, sadness, fear, and shame. They also help each other to accept, tolerate, manage, and make sense of their feelings. In self-regulation of affect, partners are able to calm and soothe themselves by accepting, tolerating, and managing the intensity of their own emotions. They also orient to their own emotions as information and are able to make sense of them and use them to help identify and solve problems (Greenberg, 2002a). Marital harmony thus has to do with both (a) greater accessibility and responsiveness and (b) greater ability to tolerate some disappointment, separation, criticisms, and disagreement and still respond nondefensively and compassionately to one's partner's needs. In fact, too great a sense of entitlement that one's partner has to be there for you exactly in the right way, when and how you need them, is a source of much marital disharmony. Therefore, if we are to achieve change in therapy, partners who previously became, upset, angry, and emotionally dysregulated and escalated their demands to get their needs met when they perceived their partners as even slightly not caring, need to be able to respond to frustration in a new way. If after communicating their feelings and needs, they find their partners are unable to respond, instead of escalating demands or withdrawing, they need to take a step back and work on regulating their own emotions. They need to be able to soothe their own anxiety, tolerate the frustration of their needs, and respond constructively to minor need frustration and criticism. This ability to calm one's self in turn will help their partners to respond in more caring ways. It also will allow the self-soothed partners to respond more compassionately and empathically to their spouses.

IMPLICATIONS FOR TREATMENT

In EFT-C, as we now see it, it is best to think about how to work with both the relationship and the self in terms of both affect regulation and affect communication. At any one time, there may be more focus on working with the system or with the self, and we continually are aware of how they mutually regulate each other. Thus at one time, we may be working on changing the relationship by revealing underlying feelings and promoting responsiveness. At another time, we may be working on helping the self regulate itself, to become more self-soothing and resilient or more responsive to the other. The focus thus is on both self and system.

We differ from, for example, Bowenian approaches to couples therapy (Kerr & Bowen, 1988; Schnarch, 1991, 1997) and ego psychological approaches (Blank & Blank, 1974), which, seeing fusion and entitlement as the main source of couples problems, emphasize differentiation or separation of self from other. Their focus in therapy is self-development, and they see the self as needing to become more autonomous. We, however, see self-regulation of affect, rather than differentiation, as the key process and affect dysregulation as the main source of couples problems. As we see it, it is mutual regulation of affects such as anxiety, shame, and anger that is the key task for couples. The ability to be emotionally accessible and responsive brings the couple together while the ability to self-soothe allows a partner not to become overreactive when disagreements or conflict arise. Both are crucial in promoting marital satisfaction and intimacy. This differs from a point of view that promotes differentiation, autonomy, and dependence.

EFT-C, rather, emphasizes fostering interdependence, which involves mutual caring, validation, and concern for the needs of self and other. A healthy intimate relationship is seen as involving a balance between needing the other (including being able to receive nurture), and being able to affirm and soothe the self and being truly appreciative of the other, as an "other," separate from the self. Interdependence, which involves a balance of emotional accessibility and responsiveness plus the ability to regulate one's own affects rather than independence or dependence, then, is our view of the goal of intimate relationships. This involves being able to be vulnerable and need others and to tolerate need frustration and regulate one's own emotions.

We have also found that couples differ in what needs therapeutic work. In some couples, one or both partners need more of a focus on developing other responsiveness, whereas in other couples, partners may need more focus on regulating themselves. In couples who enter therapy with a more individualistic view of self as indicated by expressing views such as "I am responsible for myself and am not responsible for your happiness. Only you can make yourself happy," other responsiveness is the needed first step. Other couples or partners, who have a more collectivist or self-sacrificing view of relationships, may be overresponsive to their partners' needs. They have to find their own voices, focus on their own feelings, and/or assert their own needs. However, some highly dependent or emotionally demanding partners need to learn how to soothe themselves and be aware of the other as another person in his or her own right, rather than expect the other always to meet their needs. Cultural backgrounds are important in people's different views of relationships and need to be taken into account here. It thus seems important that the therapist initially assess and differentiate between different types of couples and different cultural influences.

Initially, problems may arise in relationships because people do not say what they feel or need, or when they try to explain to their partners what they need, their partner does not understand. At the first level, this is a communication problem, and some couples early in a relationship can be helped by improved communication and understanding. Many therapists have talked about teaching the skills of good communication, such as making "I" statements, being nonblaming, listening, and so on. All are correct. All these skills will help people break the cycle that maintains the conflict. The problem, however, as we see it, is dealing with what organizes people to adopt more hostile or conciliatory stances. In our view, it is emotion that organizes how partners perceive, think, and act. Partners' compassion, caring, love, and interest organize them to attend and listen. Their unexpressed fear, shame, and anger organize them to be defensive and far less conciliatory. In addition, over time, people may succeed in communicating their needs to their partner but still have problems. It becomes clear that no longer is it lack of communication or misunderstandings that leads to problems, it is their undisclosed and unresponded to emotions that are at the source of problems.

We do not see couples problems as resulting from a lack of communication skills alone. We see problems mainly as resulting from a fear of opening the self and being seen by the other and fear of one's own and one's partner's emotions. Thus, fear of abandonment and rejection and anticipation of shame at diminishment are major problems, and overcoming these is the work of therapy. No longer is couples therapy a simple problem of communication, but rather it is a more complex one of dealing with experiential avoidance and of accessing, regulating, and transforming painful affect. As relationships develop, spouses often understand only too well what their partners need, but they simply are unable or unwilling to give them the response they are looking for. Because partners differ, because each is a unique person with his or her own needs, they are unable to respond to each other always in the right way at the right time. Often one partner just does not feel the way the other wants him or her to feel. Partners do not always feel giving or concerned at the exact same time the other needs them to, nor do they do what one wants in just the right way. Then people begin to feel that their partner is cold or uncaring. This is when conflict further entrenches. People then begin trying to change their partners. Powerful struggles begin.

When partners' needs are not being met, either through an inability to reveal or through an inability to respond, they begin to blame or to withdraw in service of these efforts. One of them may end up screaming, "Give me, give me! You're so closed; you are afraid of intimacy!", while the other may be screaming, "Leave me alone! You're so demanding [or needy]!". This is when the real problems begin. Each one's response just further invalidates the other, exacerbates the emotional distress felt, and escalates the cycles of attack and defense. Cycles such as these often emerge because of people's inability to express their most intimate feelings.

How can they resolve these conflicts? They need to be able to step out of the vicious cycle of attack and defend, pursue and withdraw, or dominate and submit and truly accept and validate themselves and their partners. To do this, they need to feel something different. Partners need to change their interactions by going to a place inside and feel and express their primary attachment- and identity-related feelings—their needs for closeness and for validation. Partners also need to be able to regulate their own feelings when partners are unable to respond. To do this, they often need ultimately to change themselves rather than their partner.

We found in our research on how couples change in short-term couples therapy that the single most effective way of resolving couples conflict is for partners to reveal and respond to each other's underlying vulnerable feelings and needs (Greenberg, Ford, Alden, & Johnson, 1993; Greenberg, James, & Conry, 1988; Greenberg & Johnson, 1988; Johnson & Greenberg, 1988). Sharing core feelings nondefensively and without complaint helps create intimacy. Sharing underlying hurt feelings in a regulated manner can be the antidote to acrimonious relating. This is the type of change we are seeking to facilitate. We are not suggesting this method, however, when violence is present or rage is too strong. Partners in moderate conflict who shifted to reveal and express their previously unexpressed emotions of sadness at loss, or fear at threat and anger at offense, instead of attack or demand had a magical effect on each other. When partners actually saw each other's tears or heard their fear or unexpressed anger, they snapped out of the trance of stating or defending their position over and over again. Instead they became more alive, compassionate, softer, interested, and concerned. Couples can be coached quite quickly to realize that because emotions form the basis of relating, expressing genuine feelings has incredible powers to change interactions. Authentic vulnerability evokes compassion and disarms, while nonmanipulative anger sets a limit and evokes respect and attention.

IDENTIFYING TYPES OF EMOTION

Couple therapists need a guide to help assess which emotions to access to change the self and interactions. Not all emotions are the same, and simply helping partners in therapy get in touch with all feelings or encouraging the expression of any emotion will not resolve conflict. Rather, it is important to distinguish between different types of emotions and to decide which emotions need to be acknowledged and expressed; which need to be bypassed, contained, or soothed; and which need to be explored. Our approach to treatment is based on the idea that some emotions are adaptive and some are maladaptive and that some are primary, some are secondary, and some are instrumental (Greenberg, 2002a; Greenberg, Rice, & Elliott, 1993). The most important skill of the EFT-C therapist is to be able to make accurate process diagnoses of what emotions at any one time are secondary, primary, or maladaptive; what underlying emotions are being obscured; and what new emotions need to be accessed. If a therapist can do this, then he or she is in a better position to know which emotions to bypass and which to attempt to access.

Primary emotions are the person's most fundamental, original reactions to a situation. They include sadness in relation to loss, anger in response to violation, and fear in response to threat. These emotions are attachment- and identity-oriented, and they enhance the self and intimate bonds. These are the emotions we want to help our clients access, symbolize, and express. We want to help them express the adaptive vulnerable feelings of hurt, fear, and shame related to their unmet adult needs for closeness and recognition rather than the secondary emotions, blame and anger.

Secondary emotions are those responses that are secondary to other more primary internal processes and may be defenses against these processes. Examples include feeling anger in response to feeling hurt, crying when angry, or feeling afraid of, or guilty about, feeling angry. They are not people's responses to a situation but responses to their own feelings. Secondary emotions, if too intense, need to be down-regulated and explored, and the sequence of generators unraveled, to get at the more primary emotions that were not expressed. The key here is that it is the awareness of primary adaptive emotions that promotes attachment and identity. Thus accessing primary anger at unfairness promotes empowerment. Expressing secondary anger that obscures hurt and vulnerability does not dissipate anger, provide relief, or promote listening. We have to get past the secondary anger to explore the underlying hurt.

Instrumental emotions are those feelings that are expressed to influence others. They are strategic and are conscious or unconscious efforts to get people to respond in desired ways, such as crying crocodile tears to get sympathy. These emotional expressions are attempts to achieve an aim, and partners need rather to learn to communicate their needs and wishes more directly without the fear of nonresponsiveness that leads to instrumental expression.

Maladaptive emotions are those old, familiar bad feelings that occur repeatedly and do not change. They come most often from past trauma, wounds from unmet childhood needs, or unfinished business with significant others. These are feelings such as a core sense of loneliness, abandonment, shame, worthlessness, explosive anger that destroys relationships, or recurrent feelings of anxious inadequacy that lead to clinging. These feelings do not change in response to partner soothing, to changing circumstance, or with expression; they do not provide adaptive directions and do not promote bonding or enhance identity. Rather, they leave people feeling stuck, overwhelmed, and out of control emotionally, and they generally need to be down-regulated and transformed. These emotions lead people to problems in relationship and are the emotions we want to help partners transform. Maladaptive responses such as hypersensitivity to abandonment, rejection, slights, criticism, or control are best transformed first by awareness and symbolization of these tendencies, by exposing them to corrective emotional experience with a partner, and then by bringing them into contact with people's own adaptive emotions and internal resources so that the maladaptive can be changed by the adaptive.

When both partners enter maladaptive emotional states, the escalating interactions intensify these states and lead them to say and do things that later often are seen as not representative or not real, or as having gone a bit "crazy." People will later say that what was felt and what was said in these states was untrue, it was really "not them." These "not me" states seem to have a mind of their own. These "not me" states are states of dysregulation that are self-reinforcing. Once in these states, people may begin to yell at each other rather than speak to each other, or they may cut off and not listen. They think they have heard it all before. They probably have repeated these fights before and have resolved them or understood and forgiven each other many times. But it just happens all over again. They can even see it coming, but once they enter these unhealthy emotional states of threat, violation, or humiliation, they are transformed into their other maladaptive selves. For example, in one of these dances of maladaptive states, a husband sensing some abandonment may experience a physical longing, and he may yearn for something from his partner, from deep within his body, but he sees her as cold, rejecting, and impenetrable. Or the wife, on hearing a hint of anger or demand, automatically may feel a desperate need to protect herself from destruction. She fears becoming overwhelmed by her partner; she sees him as intrusively powerful and closes up, becoming rigid, feeling icy, and walling out any contact. These extreme states generally reflect that each partner has entered a maladaptive emotional state, often based on past wounds. These states also often are not partners' initial, primary responses to their partners. Rather, they result from unhealthy internal affective–cognitive sequences and from escalating interactional sequences. Therapists need to help people develop the ability to soothe their own maladaptive emotional states and insecurities and also to soothe these states in their partner. One of the best antidotes to negative escalation is the ability to soothe vulnerability in the self and other.

PRINCIPLES OF EMOTIONAL CHANGE IN THERAPY

From an EFT-C perspective, a significant issue in relationships is that emotions that are experienced may not be the emotions that are expressed, whereas those that are expressed may not be the ones that are being experienced at the core. Thus, fear may be a partner's core experience, but anger may be what is expressed, or sadness may be expressed when anger may be more core. Which emotions are experienced and which are expressed strongly influence couples interaction, partner's self-organization and sense of self, and marital satisfaction. EFT-C helps guide partners to express their deeper experience related to core needs for connection and security and for identity-validation and self-esteem. In turn, couples interactions strongly affect each partner's affect regulation and which emotions are being experienced and expressed. EFT-C guides interactions to be more affiliative, comforting, and validating.

A set of empirically grounded principles of EFT-C has been proposed as a guide for therapists in working with emotion to help understand differential intervention with emotion. The four principles of dealing with emotions drawn from individual therapy (Greenberg, 2002a; Greenberg & Watson, 2006) are increasing awareness of emotion, regulating emotion, reflecting on emotion to make sense of it, and transforming emotion with emotion, and all are important in couples work. These, however, have been supplemented by a fifth principle important in interactional therapy—that of expressing emotion to a partner to change interaction. These principles are described in the sections that follow.

Increasing Awareness of Emotion

Increasing emotional awareness involves helping partners to symbolize emotions in words as well as perceiving emotional expressions in others. A number of problems arise from the inability to detect one's own emotions or correctly recognize emotions in the displays of others. Putting emotion into words can be curative in and of itself. In couples therapy, this helps partners reveal their inner worlds both to themselves and to partners in a manner that has not previously occurred. This type of emotional awareness is not just talking about feelings; it involves experiencing the feeling in awareness, and this allows the partner to perceive it. Accessing and experiencing emotions are important in that this also involves overcoming avoidance. Partners learn that by facing and acknowledging their most dreaded feelings and painful emotions and surviving, they are more able to cope (Greenberg & Bolger, 2001). Recognizing the other's emotion is another important aspect of emotional awareness and this allows one to respond appropriately to the other and thereby better cope with interpersonal problems.

There are three ways in which awareness of one's own emotion operates within EFT-C. First, helping individuals gain emotional awareness of softer underlying attachment and identity-oriented emotions such as fear and shame underneath their anger or contempt, and the anger under withdrawal, is key to interactional change. In couples, secondary emotions such as angry, blaming responses tend to fuel conflict. They are in fact attempted solutions to the problem of not getting needs met for closeness and validation, but these solutions become the problem. These responses tend to focus on the other and involve attack and attempts to destroy. In these states, people use "you" language, for instance, "You are bad [or wrong, or to blame]." Expressing secondary anger that obscures hurt and vulnerability does not dissipate the anger or enhance communication but rather just tends to lead couples into further negative cycles, and the therapy process goes in circles. Acknowledgement of the more vulnerable emotions of sadness, fear, and shame changes both the person's self-organization and his or her interactional position. The person then moves from blaming and complaining to disclosing and revealing. Being aware of, and getting in touch with, core feelings as they arise are key ways to prevent the development of destructive rage.

Second, awareness of the role of emotional responses in driving interactions leads to the possibility of developing new patterns. By bringing partners' attention to the role of their emotions in perpetuating negative cycles, they can choose to change their interactions and engender new patterns. Third, helping partners explicate beliefs and past experiences around emotional expression helps partners to reframe each other's emotional behavior. Thus, hearing that anger was expressed freely in one's partner's family and did not mean people did not love each other helps contextualize one's partner's expression of anger. Awareness of past socialization around emotional expression thus can help partners to depersonalize negative emotional expression. Couples then have a choice about how to create new, more positive emotional interactions. Finally, the ability to read emotions from partners' expressions allows for recognition of when ruptures in the intimate bond are occurring and also is the basis for empathic understanding of the other.

Regulating Emotion

It is important to distinguish between problems of overregulation and underregulation of emotion. The overregulated person is highly constricted and avoids feelings, intellectualizes, interrupts any emergent expression, or avoids situations that might evoke feeling. Within couples therapy, the overregulated partner who is highly constricted or overly rational and avoidant requires help in increasing emotional awareness and expression. Accentuating pleasant experience as well as accessing suppressed, unpleasant, or negative emotional experience is important. For example, a person who has become overly rational will not be able to express warmth and love and help a partner feel loved.

By contrast, partners who struggle with underregulated emotions describe emotions as overwhelming, getting the better of them, and making them feel out of control. They may explode in rage, be overwhelmed by tears, or shrink away in shame. Emotions that require down-regulation in couples generally are either secondary emotions such as anger or resignation, or primary maladaptive emotions such as the shame of being worthless, the anxiety of basic insecurity, panic, or rage. Overwhelming grief or sudden anger may also need to be regulated.

Therapeutic skills useful in down-regulation with couples involve such things as helping individuals establish a working distance from feelings of hopelessness or worthlessness; increase positive emotions such as joy, hope, or caring; reduce vulnerability to overwhelming fear, shame, and hopelessness; engage in self-soothing, time-outs, relaxation, development of self-empathy and compassion, and self-talk. The ability to regulate breathing, as well as the ability to observe emotions and let them come and go, are important processes to help regulate many types of emotional distress. Skills useful in helping couples down-regulate escalating interactions involve such things as the underregulated person taking a focus on self rather than other, the partner learning about and avoiding things that provoke partner escalation, both partners being able to step back or to see the humor in conflict situations, the partner being soothing to his or her underregulated partner, and soft start-ups in conflict situations (Gottman, 1999).

Two of the most important skills for individuals to master in regulating fears of abandonment and feelings of shame are taking an observer's stance to get a working distance from overwhelming despair and hopelessness and developing self-soothing capacities to calm and comfort core anxieties and humiliation. Often, these emotions are not the result of irrational thoughts or misappraisals; it is the intensity, rather than accuracy, of the response that is problematic. Physiological soothing involves activation of the parasympathetic nervous system to regulate heart rate, breathing, and other sympathetic functions that speed up under stress. At the more deliberate behavioral and cognitive levels, promoting people's abilities to recognize and be compassionate to their emerging painful emotional experience is the first step toward teaching them to tolerate their own emotion and self-soothing. Soothing also comes interpersonally in the form of empathic attunement to affect and through acceptance and validation by the partner.

Expressing Emotion

Expressing emotion changes the self and interactions both by revealing and by mobilizing the self. New lived experience with another, especially one's intimate partner, provides a corrective emotional experience. Having positive experiences where negative ones were expected helps disconfirm pathogenic beliefs. Expressing one's vulnerable feelings and having them received and understood provides interpersonal soothing. New success experience changes emotion, and thus any disclosure that meets with acceptance will help partners learn new ways of behaving. Emotional expression also changes interaction. Anger creates distance, pushing the other away, whereas expressions of vulnerability generally produce affiliative responses in the other. Expressions of the more vulnerable emotions of sadness, fear, and shame allow partners to draw closer. Thus, if a partner feels secondary rage, he or she needs to learn how to regulate the rage and become aware of what is at the bottom of it. If one often gets very angry, one needs not only to control one's anger but also to learn to experience and express more vulnerable feelings beneath the anger. Usually, this involves feelings of shame, powerlessness, vulnerability, or helplessness or feeling sad, lonely, or abandoned. Expressing underlying fear, shame, or hurt will have a very different impact on one's partner than expressing destructive rage. Expression also involves overcoming self-inhibition and can lead to enhanced processing and completion of the emotional experience. Expression helps overcome overcontrol and inhibition of emotion and results in neurochemical changes in the body that change self-organizations.

Reflecting on Emotion

In addition to recognizing emotions, promoting further reflection on emotional experiences to make sense of them allows partners to integrate their emotions into their own stories. Reflection helps to create new meaning and develop new narratives to explain experience (Greenberg & Pascual-Leone, 1997). Reflection also allows both partners to reframe emotions and take a new position vis-à-vis their partner. Thus, rather than one feeling "I can't survive; I need you," a person, after creating a working distance from the feeling of desperation and reflecting on it may be able to say, "I need you but I see that you have needs too." Similarly, reflecting on anger may allow one to change one's position from "I am angry. I hate you, and it is all your fault that I feel so alone and abandoned," to "Yes, I do feel angry at you, but it is not all your fault. I realize some of my anger belongs to the way I was treated by my mother."

In couples, understanding one's own vulnerabilities to abandonment, rejection, slights, criticism, and control is very important. Once one recognizes these as one's own and acknowledges their possible origins, one may be able to deblame partners and begin the process of taking a self-focus on how better to deal with these emotions and how to transform them.

Transforming Emotion

The final, and probably most fundamental, change principle in working with emotion involves the changing of emotion with emotion. Change, from this perspective, involves helping partners access the maladaptive emotions at the core of their vulnerabilities and then transforming them by accessing more attachment- and identity-related adaptive emotions. In other words, once the evaluation is made that a person's response in an interactional cycle is maladaptive and needs to be changed, the maladaptive emotion needs to be aroused and another more adaptive feeling that will help undo or replace the maladaptive state needs to be evoked. Reason alone or insight into patterns or origins of emotion is seldom sufficient to alter the thoughts and feelings associated with these maladaptive states. Similarly, exposure to these emotions alone is not enough to change these maladaptive states. The maladaptive feeling does not simply attenuate by the person feeling it. Rather, a new corrective emotional experience either with one's partner or from within the self that will generate an alternative feeling is necessary to transform or undo the maladaptive emotion.

Much couples work involves exposing the partner's maladaptive states to responsive attunement and validation by a partner. This helps create a new experience and an alternative healing emotion, which helps transform the maladaptive emotion. Thus, having one's fear of rejection or unworthiness responded to with caring and appreciation of one's worth creates a feeling of being loved and valuable. In EFT-C, we also help partners transform their own maladaptive states that stem from their history. Thus maladaptive states from the past, such as fears of rejection and shame from not fitting in or from body image, can be transformed first by activating the maladaptive feelings in the session and then by accessing alternative feelings of worth and experiences of adult self-love and having these flood shame and fear with self-compassion and possibly even adult empowered anger. Alternative action tendencies, feelings, and meanings from the new emotions, along with new meaning creation, help to transform the fear and shame. In a further example, accessing empowering anger at prior maltreatment by a parent helps the self feel more deserving. Pathogenic beliefs about one's defectiveness embedded within the maladaptive emotions then are addressed, and corrective emotional experiences with partners are provided. In the case of partners who have been sexually abused as children, they may have learned to associate physical closeness with fear. Therapy can then focus on evoking the maladaptive emotional response from the abuse situation, then evoking both the person's feeling of anger at violation and the positive and nurturing response in the other partner. The anger strengthens the self, and the partner's attuned responsiveness provides feelings of safety and validation. This provision of feelings of safety and comfort in the abused partner helps him or her to overcome fear and shame and leads to a restructuring of the interaction. The partner coming from the abuse situation feels stronger and can now see that the partner is caring, and he or she can feel that overtures of physical closeness do not necessarily indicate attack but rather indicate a move toward closeness, love, or security. The process of resolving unfinished business has been explicated elsewhere (Elliott, Watson, Goldman, & Greenberg, 2004; Greenberg, Rice, & Elliot, 1993; Greenberg & Watson, 2006), as have specific methods for evoking alternative feelings including such interventions as shifting the focus of attention to subdominant emotions, accessing needs to get to other emotions, self-soothing, and remembering feeling adaptive emotions in the past (Greenberg, 2002a).

CONCLUSION

Relationship formation, then, in our view, is most profitably dealt with as a process of affect regulation and communication. Attachment theory and object relations theory (Bowlby, 1962; Fairbairn, 1954; Winnicott, 1965) have led us to think of connecting with another as regulating emotion, especially as regulating anxiety; self theory (Kohut, 1977; Rogers, 1951) has led us to think that empathy and validation from another regulates self-esteem and shame. It is important, however, to see that the inverse is even truer, that it is the need to regulate affect that produces both human attachment and validation seeking. People form attachments because attachments make them feel good, and they need recognition because recognition makes them feel good. Thus, people seek others for the feelings they give them. Affect regulation is therefore the fundamental mechanism of relationship, and mutual regulation is the goal. EFT-C aims not at developing a more differentiated self, not at training partners in communication skills, but at the self and the other developing the capacity to regulate their own and their partners' affect.

Problems arise in couples when emotionally based interactional scripts become so highly reactive that unregulated escalation in both affect and interaction occur. *Emotional reactivity* in couples can be defined as the frequency with which affect becomes dysregulated. This occurs as individuals experience a feeling of threat to their security or their identity and engage in a protective and/or defensive action. Alternatively, when individuals are able to soothe themselves and regulate their own affective responses or when they are responsive to their partner's need for connection and validation and when they feel joy with, interest in, and warmth toward their partners, an interaction is activated wherein attributions are made that reestablish a positive affective balance in the relationship.

One of the most universal problems in couples is that when one partner feels primarily hurt, rejected, or diminished, this vulnerable feeling is expressed as secondary anger at the other for doing this to him or her, and then the accused partner feels attacked and feels fear but defends and ends up expressing secondary anger as well. Couples therapy is about helping partners change the way they respond emotionally to each other, which changes the interaction that ensues. The hurt parties need to become aware of and express the hurt in a regulated manner without anger; the accused partners, if they do have anger directed at them, need to be able not to react with anger to the attack and either to hear the partners' underlying feelings or to express their fear in a regulated manner. This means that each partner is able to tolerate and regulate his or her own vulnerable feeling so as to express it in a nondemanding manner and then be able to respond in a soothing manner to his or her partners. Over time, partners too need to reflect on their emotions and transform them when they are maladaptive.

4

MOTIVATION

Nature, to be commanded, must be obeyed.

—Francis Bacon

The goal of life is living in agreement with nature.

—Zeno

In developing the humanistic views on the growth tendency motivation, Greenberg, Rice, and Elliott (1993) suggested that a basic principle of all life is to maintain coherence and adaptive viability in the environment in which it finds itself and that affect is information about how well this process is proceeding. In this view, affect tells the organism what is good or bad for it and thus is the source that informs this tendency. All emotional reactions are aimed, in one way or another, directly or indirectly, at regulating the life process and promoting survival. Emotions provide a natural means for the brain and mind to evaluate the environment within and around the organism and to respond accordingly and adaptively. Feelings, in the final analysis, are the mental manifestations of balance and harmony, or of disharmony and discord (Damasio, 2003). The organism, as soon as it detects change in relation to the environment, acts to create the most beneficial situation for its own self-preservation and efficient functioning. People's behavior guided by affect in this sense is exquisitely rational, moving with subtle and ordered complexity toward the goals the organism is endeavouring to achieve.

As Johnson and Whiffen (2003) argued, attachment is a fundamental motivation, and it is highly relevant to couples therapy. There is a basic need in intimate relationships for proximity and security with loved ones to buffer against the stresses of life. We suggest that another basic need important in relationships emanates from the growth tendency. This is the need to be recognized for who one is, to have one's identity confirmed, and to be accepted. Being affirmed and valued by one's intimate other enhances one's sense of agency and self-esteem. Our framework thus recognizes that there are two fundamental tendencies important in relationships—to attach and to maintain identity. These are adult needs, and a lot of marital conflict emanates from the partners' being unable or unwilling to express their unmet adaptive needs for connection and validation. It is only when partners are able to express and respond to adult unmet needs that one can begin to work with childhood unmet needs that may be affecting the relationship.

The self, in our view, thus is constantly striving to feel safe and secure and to have its agency and identity validated. This leads to two sets of core emotions when these needs are not met in relationships—fear and shame. The core fears in relationships are fears of abandonment and of rejection, whereas the core shames in relationships are shame at the humiliation of not being seen, being diminished, or feeling powerless. A multimotivational perspective such as this helps therapists understand the important role of shame that comes from identity diminishment rather than abandonment anxiety.

We have also come to view an attraction–affection system as constituting another important drive. This tendency to feel affection for, and like or dislike, transcends both a drive toward relatedness and a drive toward self-maintenance and is a third motivational system important in intimate relationships and coupling. This is a system that is more concerned with positive than with distressing emotion and is therefore less central in conflict but more important in relationship maintenance, enhancement, and sustenance. It inoculates couples against conflict and at times may be an antidote to couples conflict. In the face of conflict and distress, this is a system that can be activated to jump-start the positive systems in the relationship. According to Maslow (1958), both relational connection and self-development are fundamental survival-oriented tendencies or deficiency needs, whereas attraction and the actual feeling of love is a more positive "being" need, important to maintaining a happy and successful marriage. Whereas attachment and self-development are more related to organization and regulation of the self, attraction–affection is more a feeling for the other. The attraction–affection system thus is responsible for some of the positive feelings in relationships such as love, joy, pleasure in the other, and cherishing of the other.

In this chapter, we discuss the three adult relational motivations of identity, attachment, and attraction important in emotion-focused couples therapy and illuminate how they function by means of affect and its regulation. The development of a more differentiated affect regulation process theory of adult intimate relationships, and how it works, helps provide a more differentiated base for interventions with couples. A more differentiated theory of attachment and identity should be based on an understanding of the function of different emotions and their regulation in the attachment and identity process at different times, rather than global concepts such as security, self-esteem, different attachment styles, or types of selves. We need to focus on, and intervene with, the emotions that result from ruptures to secure attachment and deflation of self-esteem. The process of distress in attachment ruptures involves a sequence of angry protest, anxious clinging, depression, sadness, hopelessness, despair, and finally, alienated detachment; it is these emotions we need to focus on in intervention. This is one of the scripts, and often the most fundamental script, in marital distress. It, however, also differs from scripts of affection, involving pleasure, compassion, love, and warmth, and from scripts related to identity and agency, which involve emotions of interest, curiosity, pride, and anger; and yet again from scripts of threats to dominance, which involve shame, rage, and guilt. We need to attend to all these emotions in couples therapy.

THE THREE RELATIONAL MOTIVES

The three motives are described in order of their evolutionary development. First came the forerunner of identity, the assertion of organisms against others to define boundaries in conflict over territory, status, and position. Next came attachment to others on whom people depended and trusted for protection from danger. Third and only more recently came attraction to others whom people recognized as subjects just like themselves and whom they liked, appreciated, and felt compassion for and to whom they wished to give of themselves. In our view, people are fundamentally relational beings. As Kohut (1984) offered, people do not grow from dependence to independence any more than they can grow to be independent of a need for oxygen or free of other biological needs. People need contact and comfort for security, and they need empathic affirmation to have confidence in who they are. Couples problems then do not arise from a conflict between people's need for connection and need for separateness, nor a struggle between dependence and independence, or intimacy and autonomy, as so often has been suggested in the family therapy field. Rather, in our view, couples conflict is an issue of threats to attachment and threats to identity, and it is fears of annihilation and fears of abandonment that govern conflict. In intimate relationships, people protect their identities as though it is life itself. After people move on from their earliest attachments, they generally resist letting anyone again have that much power to define them and determine what they do and how they will feel and see themselves. This is so until they fall in love and form a new attachment. Then, once more, they let someone be important enough to them to influence what they do and how they see themselves.

Both attachment and identity are highly relational and involve the other person. The process of relating and of self-maintenance and self-development thus is a dialectical one of achieving interdependence between the self and other. Self-regulation and mutual regulation emerge simultaneously rather than people growing from dependence to independence. People are interdependent and mutually regulating beings, and mutual regulation facilitates both self-regulation and connection (Beebe & Lachmann, 1998; Stern, 1985). Attachment and identity thus are dialectically related rather than independent strands of development. The relational dialectic means that people need others to confirm their selves because they come into existence only by being seen in the eyes of others (Sullivan, 1955). This is captured in the Zulu form of the greeting *Sawabone*, "I see you," and answered with *Sikhona*, "I am here," and by the Zulu saying, "A person is a person through other people." Buber (1958) described this process of I–Thou confirmation, saying that it is only when people hear coming back from the silence a response to their cry that they are absolutely sure that their cry has truly happened. This highlights that it is only when people are seen and confirmed as such by the other's response that they are sure that they really exist as such.

It is important to note, parenthetically, that people are also motivated by some important nonrelational motivations, such as achievement motives of mastery and efficacy in relation to the environment and curiosity and interest in the workings of the nonhuman world. These, however, are less important in intimate relations, unless they are part of an identity need that is threatened, and they will not be discussed further here.

The Importance of the Identity System

Following Bakan (1966), Kohut (1984), Rogers (1959), and others, we postulate a psychological need for self-coherence, self-esteem, and mastery based on the self's need for survival and well-being. This is a complex and not clearly conceptualized dimension of human relatedness. It is difficult to identify this motivation with a single name. It can be called a need for a coherent identity, agency, self-esteem, mastery, or control. It also can be seen more as a need for status, power, control, or influence, although these, we argue, seem to be more a manifestation of the need to maintain identity than a fundamental motivation. Identity encompasses the assertion of preferences or agency and includes an exploratory and mastery motivation but differs from Freud's (1923/1961) aggressive drive or a need for autonomy (H. A. Murray, 1938), if this is interpreted as a need for separateness or independence, in that identity requires the other. The opposite pole of this dimension has been variedly called dependence, enmeshment, undifferentiated, powerlessness, low self-esteem, annihilation, disintegration, or invalidation. We call this complexly evolved human tendency a "need for identity," as we feel this best captures how it functions in intimate relationship. Out of the need to maintain the coherence of the organism against threats to its physical integrity grew a self that needs to maintain its coherence and needs to control and master the environment so as to survive and not damage its identity or disrupt its coherence. This is a relational need in that to maintain its identity, the self requires recognition from others, needs to have its feelings, and needs its competence, validated and its agency supported. Failure to satisfy this need for validation of identity will inevitably result in difficulties or even damage to the self and will produce relational distress. People are social and highly concerned about how others see them and whether they are understood and respected. Much marital conflict involves issues of not being seen or appreciated, not having one's needs seen or responded to, being defined by the other in ways that are identity damaging, or feeling controlled. For example, one woman's deep hurt in therapy was that she had worked alongside her husband on the farm for 20 years, and when finally the farm was sold, the husband acted as though it was his money to control and never recognized her contribution to what they accrued.

What Is Identity?

Identity is the conscious experience of a unique and unfolding self, coupled with a distinctive internal relationship within the self that evolves internally. At its most basic level, identity is how people make sense of their experiences. In part, people discover who they are from the very unfolding within them, and in part they invent who they are. This internal dialectical process, however implicit it may be, gives shape to an individual's identity and is both genetically and historically influenced as well as socially and individually created. Identity unites who people were in the past with who they are becoming in the present, and it also shapes who they will become in the future.

The inner experience of one's self over time is both continuous and discontinuous; at any one time, a person, in important ways, is still very much the person he or she always was, but in other significant ways, he or she is now distinctly different. Identity, in addition to involving a person's current view of him- or herself, also involves characteristic and patterned expressions of attitudes and feelings toward one's self. All relationships, be they between self and other or between self and self are governed by affect: How one feels toward one's self, however, often is less visible than how one feels toward others. People's changing relationships with their intimate partners over time are central to their well-being, but the inner relationship with themselves forms the other inexplicable core of their well-being. This self–self relationship also influences and is influenced by how others see them.

The core affects underlying the identity motivational system are interest, pride–shame, fear, powerlessness, and anger. Interest motivates exploration and agency, whereas pride–shame motivates status seeking and self-expression. Shame promotes efforts at protection of identity and is the core response to one's self-expressions not being seen or to being invalidated. Shame places a distinctive stamp on identity, thereby exercising a powerful force in guiding how people feel about themselves. The fear of loss of control, and the powerlessness and diminishment that result from threats to identity, promotes efforts at control, and anger promotes the assertion of preference.

Ultimately, adults, to give meaning and purpose to their lives, create certain identities. The "who I am" that one forms is important to a person and wants to be seen, validated in the eyes of others, and have its preferences recognized. A person's preferences need to be recognized for the person to feel valued and important. And if a person's identity is not validated, then the person will begin to seek out ways to get validation, wanting or needing certain outcomes to validate its existence. Partners who suffer invalidation from their spouses often compensate by finding intimate relationships with others who confirm them as valued and enjoy the same things as them. When a person's identity is not validated by a partner, the attainment of validation becomes the focus, and the partner may become intent on getting things externally through the attainment of objects and material success. The "who I am" then begins to measure itself in terms of others' perceptions of "my" achievements and by the acquiring of objects. However, when image management through external means becomes the sole focus of identity maintenance, inner needs for validation do not get met. Although the striving to maintain an image in other people's eyes is initially an attempt to survive socially, it does not satisfy the inner self's need to be validated. Eventually, the core self's voice breaks through, saying, "I want to be recognized for who I am." In couples therapy, we need to help partners to "show up" in the relationship, to express what they feel and become who they really are so they can be validated at their core.

Validation of identity by a partner ranges from the validation of a person's core feelings to validation of all that makes up the person's sense of self. This includes validating the characteristics of partners' personalities—whether they are warm, generous, or humorous; validating their preferences by agreeing to do what they like (e.g., going on camping holidays or seeing particular types of movies); or validating their competence or achievements. Finally, the validation of their roles as a good wife, husband, or parent is also important. Those aspects of identity that need to be validated are highly culturally dependent. In one culture, being an obedient wife or a sensitive man might be an important part of a positive identity; in another cultural context, it might be seen as a negative quality. What is seen as a positive identity thus is not biologically or evolutionarily determined, but the need to be valued and respected and to have one's preferences recognized and the emotions this engenders does seem to be more in-wired.

Self theory (Rogers, 1959; Stern, 1985), while recognizing the importance of the other in the formation of the self, posits a separate line of development for a self-regulating system of self-organization that is independent of, but interacts with, attachment. In this view, the self is seen as an independent source of affect and motivation, striving toward a sense of control of its environment, mastery, and competence. This tendency is driven by, among other things, affects of curiosity and interest. The self, in our view, is motivated toward autonomy, meaning volitional control, rather than separateness or independence, and by mastery or competence, as well as by connection. A sense of well-being occurs when all these needs are satisfied (Ryan & Deci, 2000). In addition, as mastery and self-confidence are built, the self develops growing capacities to self-regulate and to self-soothe. This process of self-organization and identity formation, however, interacts with and is positively influenced by attuned responsiveness from others. Identity requires mirroring and validation, and this differs from attachment, which requires proximity and availability. What we are suggesting here is that attachment, which is primarily formed by proximity and availability, has come to include notions of mirroring and validation. All these dyadic processes are part of maternal infant bonding and language development and important to adults, but the latter, we are suggesting, are important to identity formation and maintenance and the former to security.

Basic Research Support for an Identity System

Animal research that supports the existence of an independent line of development of an agentic, exploratory system, separate from an attachment system, comes from a series of interesting studies on the effects of handling of mice and rat pups (Denenberg, 1999, 2000). Handling of infant rats in an initial set of experiments was found to result in animals that were behaviorally less stressed and had a lesser corticosterone response to novel stimuli, as compared with controls. In a further set of experiments, shock, handling, or exposure to a rich environment, as well as increased maternal care, were all shown to independently produce lasting brain effects resulting in improved learning. Summarizing this line of research, Denenberg (1999, 2000) concluded that the same underlying mechanism is involved whether the pups are stimulated by shock, handling, exposure to a novel environment, or maternal care. He suggested that maternal affection or secure attachment is much too limited to explain all development and has proposed, rather, that stimulus variation is a key dimension of early experience. He also suggested that the wider the range of variation the pup is exposed to in early life, the better it will be able to adapt to events in later life. Recently, Tang (2001, 2003) found that pups exposed to novel environments later were more active and exploratory in an open field, had better learning scores, lower corticosterone levels, and greater social memory. In this line of investigation, maternal behavior and an experimenter-imposed manipulation (handling and exposure to a novel environment) each independently reduced emotional reactivity, both behaviorally and physiologically, and modified other behavioral and biological processes.

We thus believe that confidence and agency can derive from sources of experience other than attachment and that it is helpful to treat the development and maintenance of identity, agency, and self-esteem as separate from attachment and security. To understand how partners behave in couples, we thus need more than an attachment motivation perspective. The practical relevance of this to couples therapy is that struggles related to identity involve different emotions and require significantly different therapeutic responses than do struggles related to attachment. The adult attachment literature has treated identity and self-esteem as a component of attachment, noting that secure attachment produces feelings of positive self-worth and confidence and has held that a secure attachment inevitably results in good self-esteem. Although it is certainly true that a history of secure attachment usually produces a feeling of being loved and lovable, self-esteem in people with a history of secure attachment still fluctuates as a function of being validated or invalidated by success with peers and achievement. This often has an impact back on the attachment relationships they form as adults. Similarly resilient people with poor attachment histories have still been found to develop strengths, competence, and self-esteem (Masten, 2001).

Development of the Self

Stern (1985) demonstrated that self-development in infancy involves the construction of agency, affectivity, coherence, and continuity. He believed that infants do not begin life in a state of merger with the mother, out of which they must differentiate themselves in form a sense of a separate, unique self. According to him, infants come into the world with capacities that actively impact their caretaking environment. These capacities include a *preverbal sense of self*—the sense of agency, physical cohesion, continuity in time, and intention. Capacities for self-reflection and language, which develop later, eventually come to work on these preverbal experiences of self, and both reveal their existence and transform them into new experiences. Organizational change within the infant and the interpretation of the change by the parents are mutually facilitative of the new integrations of an infant's sense of self and identity. Stern noted that although no one can agree on exactly what the self is, adults still have a very real sense of self that permeates their daily social experience. This self arises in many forms: as a single, distinct, integrated body; as an agent of actions; as an experiencer of feelings; as the maker of intentions; as the symbolizer of experience in language; and as the communicator of personal knowledge. People instinctively process their experiences in such a way that the experiences appear to belong to some kind of unique subjective organization that we commonly call the "sense of self." It is this sense of one's self as a coherent whole that lays the foundation for developing an identity to define who this "me" is.

This sense of self, according to Stern (1985), thus includes the sense of agency, the sense of physical cohesion, the sense of continuity, the sense of affectivity, the sense of a subjective self that can achieve intersubjectivity with another, the sense of creating organization, and the sense of transmitting meaning. These senses of self develop through life, and in adolescence an identity is formed; this identity, plus its more basic substrate, needs attunement, recognition, and validation from others throughout life. Stern's concept of "a need for affect attunement," an essential part of developing of a sense of a subjective self, becomes particularly significant in marital relationships in the validation of identity. Attunement to all affect, then, is essential in the validation of identity, whereas it is only attunement to distress, separation anxiety, and needs for comfort that is essential in attachment. The invalidation of any of one's feelings growing up as a child, or as a partner in an intimate relationship, results in a core injury to identity. People's affects need mirroring and validation to help people develop clear and confident identities.

Identity is primarily formed later in life than attachment styles and crystallizes in adolescence. A sense of self and of agency forms early in childhood, but a sense of identity is crystallized more fully in adolescence. As people develop and differentiate, survival and assertion of identity becomes of paramount importance to most people. In development, children differentiate from their parents and they become more different to parents and more similar to others like them. As well as adolescents, even toddlers are soon drawn to their own kind. Gender identity, and translation of how one interprets one's gender identity, is crucial in determining with whom one is in a relationship. In some lesbian relationships, for example, being butch or femme is an important part of an identity and influences with whom one will partner and what role one will play in the relationship. Being gay or transsexual is a crucial part of identity development, which until achieved, precludes adult attachment and then requires this attachment to confirm identity. Identity thus becomes a central concern of most adults, and relationships that confirm identity become a central concern.

Adults develop far greater capacities than do infants for regulating their own affective disturbances, as well as greater capacities to attain joy, excitement, and satisfaction through their own agency. Adults develop identities, the validation of which is experienced as almost as important to them as a close bond and sometimes as more important. This is witnessed by relationship ruptures that stem from fears of loss of identity, from damage to self-esteem, or from a feeling that one's preferences are not being valued or respected. Ultimately, threats to identity can prevent adult attachment. To protect their identities, partners in conflict often hold on to attacking, controlling, or submissively yielding stances rather than risking change. "Stuckness," or impasse, often is based on preservation of the integrity of the self's identity. Resistance to change may be based in fear sensed as "what will happen to who I am if I change"; hostility, "Don't try to change me"; or shame, "If I change then how will all the times I've refused to in the past be viewed?"

Evolutionary Development of Identity, Status, and Rank

Assertion of identity is an evolutionarily developed, relational motive that derives from what observers of animal behavior have called the dominance hierarchy, referred to more popularly as the "pecking order." Sociologists refer to position in such a hierarchy as *status*, and they refer to any moves to assert or improve one's status in relation to others as the *exercise of power*. Observations of chimpanzees have revealed many displays of dominance and deference (de Waal, 1986, 1996). Quite typically, the leader of the group, an alpha male, asserts his power by shows of anger, bullying, and threats. The power is social. Other members of the community acknowledge it in recognizable ways, such as by the display of fear (preparing to flee, screaming) and by deference (paying homage). When signaling power, the individual making the display expects to get his own way and will use force to prevail, perhaps in a sexual matter or in obtaining some resource such as food. The other members of the community accept this entitlement. The alpha chimpanzee looks bigger than others because in his displays his hair stands on end, while the hair of those who defer to him does not stand on end. These others offer submissive greetings. They bow, sometimes make offerings such as a leaf or stick, and sometimes give a kiss on the feet or neck.

Animals who are not acutely aware of their rank endanger themselves, miss opportunities for acquiring resources (food, mates, allies), and could be put down vigorously by more powerful dominants for inappropriate resource seeking. Animals behave differently if they are in high-rank than low-rank positions, and they change their behavior when they change their rank. This status-related behavior is not learned but an innate complex affective, cognitive, motivational, behavioral system just like an attachment system. People, too, are primed by evolution to be concerned about social rank and identity and to compete for resources, just as they are primed to give and receive care by an evolutionarily developed attachment system (Gilbert, 2003; Gilbert & McGuire, 1998).

Aggressive dominance, power, and control can be used as a means of maintaining one's identity, self-esteem, or status. In both human and animal groups, aggressive dominants try to control subordinates. This is seen in extreme forms in humans such as in bullying and in violence in couples and families. In less obvious ways, humans compete for position and resources in a manner that does not involve aggression. It is not necessary to think of the needs for identity, self-esteem, and status as only engendering hostility (Gilbert, 2001). The way humans compete for recognition can be aggressive, but more often involve attempts to attract others. People strive to have status, value, and position given to them, and they benefit greatly from recognition and validation. People strive to be seen as desirable lovers and friends, and as team players, by being attractive and lovable. In this context, for many people the central concern is about avoiding low rank, being controlled by others, and/or being excluded or missing opportunities. To be seen as attractive to others one must stimulate positive affect in the mind of others, not fear or fearful submission with aggression (Gilbert, 1997, 2001; Gilbert & McGuire, 1998). Partners, too, need to be valued by their mates. People in more stable and satisfying relationships see strengths in their partners that they do not see in the partners of others (Rusbult, Van Lange, Wildschut, Yovetich, & Verette, 2000). People also are most likely to see the best in others when they see the best in them (S. L. Murray, Holmes, & Griffin, 2000). Cooperation and belonging thus have become more important than dominance for survival and reproductive success (Gilbert, 1989). These skills sometimes are lacking in some marital partners who equate dominance or forced recognition of status with respect or love.

Concerns about identity and ranking involve tracking other people's views of one's self and responding to potential threats to recognition of one's identity. Gauging the reactions of others and being able to distinguish when people can trust and who truly values them is thought to be one of the more daunting evolutionary challenges humans had to solve (Tooby & Cosmides, 1990). Nonverbal communication, which often is automatic, evaluating trustworthiness, identity concerns, and behaviors, is as important in social rank, as it is in attachment. Partners in loving relationships gaze into the eyes of each other, and this is a clear signal of desire and affection, of both wanting to look at and wanting to be looked at. However, in conflict situations, dominant partners stare but submissive partners do not. For subordinates to engage in eye gaze would almost certainly increase arousal in both dominant and subordinates and increase the chances of fighting. A partner's signal of shame will have an impact on the other's anger. People who are in high states of shame commonly adopt submissive postures, have low eye gaze, feel inhibited, and are unable to express themselves. This is a highly defensive position, quite different from a caregiving or a cooperative one, for example. A submissive, defensive position can click in even when a person consciously does not want it to. People have been primed by evolution with emotions such as embarrassment, shame, and humiliation to adopt these roles. These are the emotions that are particularly sensitive to how people see themselves through others' eyes and come when their identities are being threatened or vulnerable feelings are being invalidated. When this type of shame occurs in intimate relationships, it cannot but lead to troubles in intimacy.

Emotions and Identity Assertion in Relationships

Shame, and the anxiety involved in protecting against it, is a master emotion in interpersonal relations. When evoked, it becomes the individual's highest priority and will take over from whatever else may be occurring, except fear. Shame and its lesser version, embarrassment, operate in important ways in marriage. Shame arises most centrally in response to contempt, humiliation, or invalidation by one's partner. When partners are feeling vulnerable, insult or lack of support from their spouses can lead to deep narcissistic injuries that take a long time to heal. Kicking partners while they are down will not easily be forgotten. Reciprocally, when a partner is feeling shamed or humiliated, the ability to share this, rather than hide, although probably one of the most difficult of human experiences, will help bring the soothing and affirmation needed from a loving partner. To wish for, but not be able to ask for, the support or affirmation one needs is one of the greatest problems in preventing people from getting what they need from their partners. To protect an identity as being strong and self-sufficient, many people have great difficulty revealing weakness and asking for support. In fact, the lower one's self-esteem, the less likely one is to reveal one's self for fear of rejection (S. L. Murray et al., 2000). When people believe their partners see them more positively on specific interpersonal qualities, they feel more valued and accepted (S. L. Murray, Holmes, Griffin, Belavia, & Rose, 2001). A partner needs to perceive that the other sees positive qualities in him or her to feel loved and valued, and if the partner has trouble pinpointing specific qualities that are valued, especially those not easily found in others, it is not likely that the partner will feel loved. People need to feel special to, and appreciated by, their partners.

The primary vulnerable emotions underlying the experience of not being valued and threats to identity are shame at diminishment or invalidation, fear from threat to one's standing or control, and the complex feelings of powerlessness. Dominating anger often is a secondary response to challenge to identity or to need frustration. Contempt is a response of superiority to disliked difference. When either of these emotions occurs in response to threats to identity and status, essentially they are efforts to regulate a person's affect by protecting self-esteem and position in the eyes of both self and other. Contempt emerges as more extreme than anger and as the most destructive form of attempting to maintain identity by establishing a superior position and looking down on one's partner (Gottman, Coan, Carrère, & Swanson, 1998). The healthy primary assertive emotion at violations of identity often is empowering anger, which promotes boundary setting.

In an important dynamic sequence in couples, shame is often followed by rage. Shame followed by anger or rage, and then often later by sadness and guilt about the anger, appears to be a fundamental affective sequence. Feelings of powerlessness in relation to a partner's actions that are experienced as challenging or decreasing one's status are frequently followed by the rage of retaliation and often lead to marital violence, particularly in men. Here, rage is a secondary emotion and a misguided means of avoiding the intolerable feelings of shame. Powerlessness is a more complex state than shame at humiliation, although it may include it. Powerlessness includes feeling helpless and trapped without the ability to stand up for one's self, as well as shame at being so powerless, and possibly includes the fear of what may happen because one is helpless. Too many experiences of powerlessness in a relationship can poison the relationship and lead to passivity, withdrawal, giving up, and turning away.

Another significant response to threats to identity is to withdraw to protect identity rather than try to dominate. Here, rather than reacting with anger and rage, people react by putting up a protective wall and withdrawing behind it to protect themselves. The dangers of opening up and getting close outweigh the benefits. Lack of trust becomes a major concern that organizes their interactions. Partners adopt a position of self-protective hiding for fear that if they came out they would be invalidated, judged, and criticized. The attempted solution then becomes the problem, contact is lost, and the relationship becomes functional rather than emotionally connected.

The Function of Identity Assertion in Intimate Relationships

Power, hierarchy, and boundaries have been emphasized by systemic and interactional views, which although they do not posit a motive for identity, power, or dominance, focus on analyzing communication and interaction in terms of degree of influence and their influencing effects. Sluzki (1983), for example, defined *communication and interaction* as continuous proposals and counterproposals about position and status. From an emotion theory point of view, which sees emotion as a central organizing force, acts of power, control, and influence are seen as being engaged in because of the feelings they produce. Emotionally controlling behaviors are essentially attempts to regulate the controlling person's own affect. Men, who possibly are more sensitive than women to their own affective arousal and less tolerant of affective dysregulation (Gottman, 1999), are typically socialized to not show weakness. They often became dominant or controlling to regulate their own affect. The emotions they are usually trying to regulate are their own fear or shame, although sometimes it is anger. Their deepest fears are those of humiliation, powerlessness, and loss of control. The deepest shames are those of feeling invisible or unworthy and defective, or feeling invalidated. From these come efforts to bolster and defend their identities. Control therefore becomes an effort to stave off fear and shame.

Exacerbating men's fear of vulnerability, society often rewards dominance and competitiveness in the market place or on the sports field. Men thus bring this mentality home in their briefcases or kit bags. Competition and dominance, however, are not the best strategies for intimacy, connection, and validation. Control and dominance thus need to be understood in terms of both their affect regulation functions and their social learning roots. Regardless of gender, emotional reactions of powerlessness and diminishment activate the need for identity-validation, efforts to regain position, and emotion regulation strategies that often end up being attempts to control others.

Thus in a marital relationship, if a partner's sense of worth, self-esteem, hierarchical position, or status is challenged, the person's identity is threatened. When identity is threatened, issues of power and control raise their ugly heads. Control, as we have said, is an effort to regulate affect, maintain identity, and protect position in the couples hierarchy. Partners generally perceive their behavior as their attempts to simply maintain equal status in the eyes of the other—not to dominate the other. Assertive behaviors in relationships are not inherently pathological responses but are the ways people are programmed to react to challenges to their identities. These responses only become unhealthy if threats to identity lead to coercive dominance. Healthy dominance involved in the need for identity leads to appropriate assertion, boundary setting, and working for recognition. Maladaptive dominance involves trying to coerce or change the other and prove that one is right such as when there is disagreement and the dominant partner uses force to show who's right.

This tendency to coercively dominate often comes from not currently receiving sufficient relational validation. When their status is challenged, some people can become particularly coercive in their attempts to stave off the shame at invalidation or the fear of loss of control. This is usually based on a history of having been rendered powerless or shamed and feelings of a sense of loss of control earlier in life. When these dominant partners feel threatened, they attempt to coerce their spouses into behaving and being the way that suits their needs, demanding, for example, that the partner "do as I say" or "respond to my need." Other problematic behaviors in response to identity threats are based on having learned a number of other dysfunctional ways to respond to these threats. Some people turn away, saying, for example, "I don't need you, I'll handle it myself," and proceed to become pathologically independent. However, others give up their identity and submit, allowing their needs to become subsumed by those of their partners. The submissive partner in these instances will do anything to please, seeks approval, and will sacrifice him- or herself.

Roles, Rights, and Who's Right?

Establishing identities within relationships is an ongoing task for both partners in a couple, and agreement on roles consistent with one's identity is a prerequisite to the performance of many cooperative tasks in marriage. Often, in couples' daily life, the tasks are figural and the partners' identities that facilitate the tasks are background. This is true until a critical incident occurs in which a role is not respected or appreciated, such as when determining whose job it is to clean the house, arrange for babysitters, or go to work when a child is sick, or when determining how money should be spent, or when calling into question the working arrangement on which identities are based. When the implicit or explicit role agreements on marital or family tasks are violated, marital conflict results until roles and identities are restored or renegotiated. Arriving at definitions of situations settles identity definition for the moment, but this is an ongoing process. If either partner acts out of character, the identity of the other will be threatened, and restorative measures validating identity will be required. Each partner monitors the implications of his or her behavior so as not to contradict his or her partner's image of self or other. If identities are contradicted, this must be explained away or there will be a permanent injury and the working agreement will erode.

Partners who feel that their contributions have been taken for granted begin to feel very resentful, and unless recognized, this will become a significant identity injury in the relationship. Most of the time, most partners in well-functioning couples relationships more or less accept their position in the established hierarchy, and as long as their status is respected, there is no conflict. But people in most social contexts resist being moved downward or diminished. So too in intimate relationships, the most characteristic reactive emotion to threats to status is anger, and it is a person's culture that often provides the outline of scripts for what is a threat to status and for how to handle conflict and competition. Much marital conflict involves confrontations about rules and arrangements, which bear on identity and self-esteem. In male-dominant cultures, the privileges associated with male status and challenges to these are central in conflict. When the resource structure is asymmetrical, the control of the marital process lies in the hands of the powerful spouse. Because both partners are aware of this, threats and promises can be used strategically. Conflicts over financial support, neglect or indifference, extramarital affairs, physical abuse, child rearing, and extended family relationships are all influenced by status and identity concerns.

In an intimate relationship, the dominance struggle is not only over resources and decisions but also about who has the right to define reality. The fight about the definition of reality is a source of major concern in couples. Often, one partner makes more decisions, is more dominant, needs to be right, and gets angry when challenged. In addition, in many couples, what also is important is not only how one's partner sees one but how other people see them and their partner relating on the identity–dominance dimension. Status in most societies is expressed by ideas of respect and even honor, and this involves maintaining not just one's own respect but a cultural view of what will maintain the respect of one's family or friends. This goal of being respected in society and of being seen to be respected by one's partner is very important for some couples in some cultures. What is perceived as respect is dependent on the particular cultural model of marriage. In Western culture, under the influence of the feminist era, how the woman is seen is very important to some couples. Often, one or both partners are very concerned that they be seen as being in an egalitarian relationship. It has become the case for many couples that being seen that way can be as important as being that way.

In contrast with Western individualistic identities, Asian couples are said to have a more "contextualizing self," a form of personal identity in which the self is experienced as being a facet of a collective whole comprising their marriage, extended family, and community. Their sense of themselves is more connected with being a member of the collective than with being independent. Hence, to understand coupling in these cultures, one needs to understand identity within the context of the extended family and/or community. An important part of a marital partner's identity is that of fitting in to the larger whole. The self is individual yet, at the same time, complementary in the marriage. This organic sense of an "us" identity can be contrasted with a Western notion of self and marital identity as two separate people interconnecting. For South Asian couples, the "we" or "us" identity involves a high degree of involvement with extended family, and this is seen as an important aspect of their marriage (Ahmed, 2006). Romance and love are viewed as more transient emotions that do not hold a marriage together; rather, a sense of "being" with each other, being part of each other's world, and working toward collective goals is more central. Couples work together in a way that is accommodating as opposed to negotiating, to achieve complementarity, as opposed to equality, in relationship. Accommodating is about achieving balance and unity, through adjusting one's self and accepting each other, a sense of embracing each other without trying to change each other. Identities fostered in the West often promote more independence, whereas those in Asian cultures promote more communality. It is important to see that identity is thus a high-level construct that subsumes under it different degrees of independence and agency.

Identity and Mutuality in Couples

In intimate relationships, regardless of the culture, a tension rapidly develops between assertion of self-identity and recognition of the identity of the other. In trying to successfully establish one's identity within a relationship, the self has to recognize that the other is a "subject" like one's self. Recent relational and intersubjective views (J. Benjamin, 1988, 1990) suggest that although the self requires identity-validation, being dependent on another for one's identity creates a struggle. Often, to break this dependence on the other, one frequently stops seeing the other as a subject, just like one's self, and attempts to have an independent existence by treating the other as an object, a nonperson. This is done under the assumption that to the degree that one can objectify the other, one will not need them to confirm one's identity. The paradox of existence thus is that "If I need you to confirm that I exist as a person, my existence is predicated on your confirmation. But being dependent on you for my existence is so insecure that I cease to see you as a person." When, after the blissful honeymoon period, a relationship begins to establish itself, and when romantic passion subsides, each partner's wish to meet his or her own needs emerges more strongly, and this sometimes conflicts with the self's need for recognition and validation from the other.

Partners thus rapidly have to be able to set clear boundaries and simultaneously recognize each other's independent will. They need to balance their own identity assertion with recognition of the other's identity. If they cannot do this, one partner grows to dominate and mutual recognition is not achieved. The ideal resolution to the problem of establishing mutuality is that there remains a constant conscious tension between recognizing the other and asserting the self (J. Benjamin, 1988). The core feature of the development of intersubjective relatedness in couples, then, is recognizing similarity in tandem with acknowledging difference. Recognition of similarity involves knowing that the other is separate, has another mind, and can share the same feelings, values, and attitudes. This requires empathy and compassion. If this exists, the experience of sharing occurs and the bond is strengthened. However, a crisis occurs as the couple begins to confront difference and realize, "You and I don't want [or feel] the same thing." The couple's response to this realization is crucial in defining how control will be handled in the relationship. Either the partners will both accept difference and respect each other or there will be a breakdown of recognition between self and other. One partner will adopt a position of "I insist on my way; I refuse to recognize you; I begin to try to coerce you, and I experience your refusal as you coerce me." For resolution of this conflict, the capacity for mutual recognition must stretch to accommodate the tension of difference, and this requires empathy and compassion. When this accommodation is not achieved, the relationship is not balanced by mutual recognition, and a struggle for control emerges.

The upshot of failures of confirmation of identity and recognition of the self by one's significant other in healthy adult relationships is assertion of agency. This assertion moves into the unhealthy domain when attempts at domination or control of the other, to ensure validation, predominate. Partners' recognition of both their own and the other's subjectivity is necessary for noncoercive, mutual recognition and validation. It is important to note, however, that full mutual recognition is very difficult to achieve and is most meaningful as an ideal. The striving for mutual recognition in couples needs to be understood as the basis for struggle and negotiation. The impossibility of reaching complete recognition and validation of each other's needs always to be held in mind in conjunction with the idea of the striving to attain it. People need to understand that the struggle to recognize another as different from themselves has many difficulties and impediments. We thus need to recognize the difficulty of achieving full mutuality in couples without losing sight of the possibility that sometimes mutual recognition and respect for difference between partners can be fully realized.

The breakdown in the recognition between self and other in favor of relating coercively or as subject and object is a common fact of couples life. Breakdown of mutuality is a common fallout of relatedness—what matters is the ability to restore or repair recognition of each other. People need to communicate, not coerce, in the face of difference. Relatedness in intimate relationship is characterized not by continuous harmony but rather by continuous disruption and repair. In marriage, the continual struggle is thus one of acknowledging difference while recognizing likeness. The difficulty, however, lies in assimilating difference without repudiating likeness. It is easy to accept the other as different and to reject the other as "not like me." What is difficult to attain is the recognition of difference, being unlike the other, without giving up a sense of mutuality. It is important to note that the recognition of difference and otherness also brings novelty and mystery to relationship, and it is this that brings some of the excitement to the relationship and to sexual intimacy. This, of course, needs to be counterbalanced with recognition of similarity, which brings with it safety and a sense of belonging.

For the partner who enters a marriage hoping to be perfectly understood and responded to, difference, however, is disillusionment. The fantasy of the perfect partner is that one's partner would want what one wants and do what one wants to do. This fantasy inevitably is shattered. In facing difference, partners must also relinquish their fantasies that they can be perfect and provide a perfect world for their partners. Couples have to develop the ability to tolerate both frustration of their needs and a loss of control as a step on the road to recognition of the other as a subject just like one's self. Partners need to help each other fully realize that each is a person in his or her own right, with his or her own feelings and wishes. This process allows an internal shift so that the confrontation with one partner's inner world of feelings and wishes can result in a greater appreciation of the other's unique subjectivity.

A problem that often prevents the forming of a differentiated identity of other and self within a couple is that if one or another partner either dominates or submits, the partners do not really experience each other as separate. Rather than differentiating and becoming real, the partners become objects to each other. The outcome is a relational cycle of "doer" and "done-to." A pattern is established in which there is no real other subject, and no real feeling for the other. As an example, let us imagine a wife who gives in to her husband and never challenges his identity or definition of reality and never asserts her need. The husband feels he has succeeded in controlling his wife, and this means "Now she is my fantasy wife." Thus, as the husband loses contact with the real wife, the perfect fantasy wife fills the space. The husband now is no longer able to develop either his sense of self or his abilities to soothe himself. Rather, he feels his wife must literally be there constantly to soothe him and provide for his emotional needs. If she is not, he experiences his fear and anger as if in reaction to a real, outside danger. If, alternatively, his wife initially frustrates him but then under coercion gratifies him, the husband feels he has controlled her but still has not learned to soothe himself to increase his sense of agency and responsibility for his own affect regulation.

As Buber (1958) suggested, it is the revealing of the "I" to the "Thou" that allows partners to appreciate each other's subjectivity and to tolerate conflict and disruption without withdrawing from a sense of mutuality. This is the healthy alternative to dominating, punishing the other, or withholding to maintain a sense of control. Levinas (1998) went even further than Buber, to emphasize that the self is possible only with its recognition of the "other," a recognition that carries responsibility toward what is irreducibly different. For Levinas, the face-to-face encounter with another is a privileged phenomenon in which the other person's proximity and distance are both strongly felt, and seeing the face of the other not only evokes experience but also calls a person to be there for the other. He puts the emphasis on a relationship of respect and responsibility for the other person, rather than a relationship of mutuality and dialogue, as proposed by Buber. This has important implications for relationships, suggesting that seeing the other's humanness compels one to care for that other.

The process of revealing one's self to the other, listening, and negotiating conflict to establish a shared reality, that is, a sense of "we-ness" in which both partners have a sense of agency and impact, helps to establish identity and has people taking greater responsibility for themselves. Couples' satisfaction has been found to correlate with their sense of "we-ness" (Fergus & Reid, 2001; Reid, Dalton, Laderoute, Doell, & Nguyen, 2006). The breakdown into the complementarity of doer and done-to reflects the inability to sustain the necessary contradiction of differentiation, in which partners both recognize each other and continue to assert themselves.

The Need for and Development of Attachment

Attachment to others and the need for contact and comfort have been established clearly as central primate and human motivations (Bowlby, 1962; Harlow, 1958). From infancy through adolescence and adulthood to old age, people need connection to survive and thrive. Harlow demonstrated that contact and comfort was a primary drive in monkeys, who chose cloth mother surrogates over food. During World War II, Bowlby began making observations of children who, in the course of the war, had been separated from their parents. He noticed the children's emotions in such separations: at first, noisy protest; then, sadness; finally, apathy and despair. Attachment theory (Bowlby, 1969, 1973), which emphasizes the emotional nature of close bonds between two people, grew out of these observations. Bowlby (1973) defined *attachment bonds* in terms of four classes of behavior: proximity maintenance, safe haven, separation distress, and secure base. His original theory focused only on understanding the close enduring bonds between infants and caregivers. The attachment system was thought to serve survival by keeping infants close to their caregivers. Infants were seen seeking out caregivers in the face of threat, and caretakers' responsiveness was seen to reduce distress. Attachment behavior in infants, such as seeking or crying out, primarily occurs when the child feels internal discomfort or perceives danger (Bowlby, 1969; Cassidy, 1999). If the child's distress is moderate, the mother's soothing sounds may suffice. With greater distress, more contact comfort may be needed to regulate distress. The infant tracks at least three aspects of care crucial to survival: the proximity, availability, and responsiveness of the caregiver. In the attachment system, the set goal is physical or psychological proximity to a caregiver. When a child perceives an attachment figure to be nearby and responsive, he or she feels safe, secure, and confident and behaves in a generally playful, exploration-oriented, and sociable manner. When the child perceives a threat to the relationship or to the self (e.g., illness, fear, separation), however, he or she feels anxious or frightened and seeks the attention and support of the primary caregiver. Attachment behavior is terminated by conditions indicative of safety, comfort, and security, such as reestablishing proximity to the caregiver.

A great deal of research has shown that animals, such as monkeys, raised without mothers have very problematic relationships with other animals (Harlow, 1958). This work reinforces the idea that the genetically inherited programs of attachment and maternal care in humans are derived from evolution and that they provide components for experience-based building of relationships. More recently, research has shown that the neurochemicals oxytocin (OXY) and vasopressin (VP) have been found to play a crucial role in promoting attachment in voles. OXY has been linked with nurturance in (particularly female) mammals and VP with protectiveness in (particularly male) mammals. For instance, some species of voles are monogamous—mating for life—with strong bonds underlying a rich family life, while others are solitary and independent. The monogamous voles were found to differ from the solitary nonattaching males by the amount of VP in the males and OXY in females. Injection of the VP receptor gene into the same area of the brain, which researchers in an fMRI study found was activated by the image of the lover in humans, however, caused the profligate, licentious, and ruggedly individualistic male voles to act like monogamous dads. Other studies have shown the importance of OXY in nurturing, and this link between neurochemicals and trust in humans is truly remarkable and potentially significant.

Bowlby (1969) also proposed that early emotional relationships were the foundations for later ones. He suggested that if one's personal history is that of having received security, one will be able to form secure attachments. If one's early relationships were experiences of having been separated, let down, or disappointed, one faces a harder task in forming trusting relationships with others in adulthood. What Bowlby called "maternal deprivation," a lack of a continuous nurturing relationship in the first 3 years of life, would make it difficult, sometimes impossible, for a person to form trusting intimate relationships in adulthood. According to Bowlby's view of attachment, over the course of repeated intervals, children develop knowledge or an internal working model about the other's responsiveness and their own lovableness. These models then are viewed as guiding feelings, thoughts, and behaviors in subsequent situations and relationships.

Hazan and Shaver (1987), extending infant attachment theory to adult romantic relationships, argued that adults appear to experience bonds of attachment toward romantic partners that have some of the same characteristics as infant caretaker bonds. They proposed that the emotional and behavioral dynamics of infant–caregiver relationships and adult romantic relationships are governed by the same biological system (Hazan & Shaver, 1987, 1990; Shaver & Hazan, 1988). The infant's tendency to monitor the caregiver's proximity, availability, and responsiveness is present in adults in close relationships. Partners become distressed when loved ones leave or are unavailable for any length of time. When an individual is feeling distressed, sick, or threatened, the partner is used as a source of safety, comfort, and protection. Touch, contact, and comfort regulates physiology, and protest, anxiety, withdrawal, and depression result from loss. Adults' basic concerns in intimate relationships thus involve the same affect regulation needs as infants': (a) a need for proximity ("Are you there when I need you?"), (b) a need for availability ("Do you give me the things I need, such as support and care?"), and (c) a need for responsive receptiveness ("Do you respond when I need you to?"). These all help adults regulate their affect and feel secure. For the young child, these are mostly automatic responses, but adults often (although not always) are able to articulate their felt needs and beliefs in regard to their needs for care. This need for attachment is an adult, not an infantile, need and becomes unhealthy only if a person cannot tolerate need frustration and flies into a rage or becomes depressed at loss, separation, distance, or nonresponsiveness. Thus, the emotions and behaviors that characterize romantic relationships and infant–parent relationships share similar activating and terminating conditions and appear to exhibit the same latent dynamics (Shaver, Hazan, & Bradshaw, 1988).

Adults also appear to share the same attachment styles as toddlers. Initially, three adult attachment patterns were postulated: a secure pattern and two insecure patterns. These were later expanded to four patterns: secure, anxious–ambivalent, fearful avoidant, and dismissive avoidant. These attachment styles have been used in an effort to clarify a person's motives in interpersonal relationships: Does the person want closeness, or does the person prefer distance? Does the person feel in control of the relationship, or does the person feel helplessly vulnerable to rejection and abandonment? Some people routinely avoid closeness to protect themselves from rejection. Partners who are avoidant feel uncomfortable being close to others and find it difficult to trust them completely and difficult to depend on them. They get nervous when a partner gets too close, and often feel their partner wants them to be more intimate than they feel comfortable being. Partners who are anxiously attached find that others are reluctant to get as close as they would like. They often worry that their partners do not really love them or will not want to stay with them. They often want to get very close to their partners, and this sometimes scares their partners away. Spouses who are fearfully avoidant adopt an avoidant orientation toward attachment relationships to prevent being hurt or rejected by partners. Dismissing partners adopt an avoidant orientation as a way to maintain a defensive sense of self-reliance and independence.

It appears, however, that individual differences in romantic attachment are best organized within a two-dimensional framework rather than by the type of attachment patterns previously mentioned (Mikulincer & Goodman, 2006). One dimension, *anxiety*, relates to the degree of anxiety and vigilance concerning rejection and abandonment. The other dimension, *avoidance*, relates to the degree of discomfort with closeness and the dependence or a reluctance to be intimate with others. People are thus seen as monitoring and appraising events for their relevance to attachment-related goals, such as the attachment figure's physical or psychological proximity, availability, and responsiveness, and then regulating their attachment behavior. For example, to regulate attachment-related anxiety, people can orient their behavior toward the attachment figure or withdraw and attempt to handle the threat alone.

A Revised Theory of Attachment in Intimate Relationships

Attachment theory, in our view, too often is overapplied to explain all relating and is used as an all-encompassing theory to explain not only security seeking and comfort but also love, warmth, emotion regulation, and even agency, exploration, and self-esteem. Attachment also conflates closeness and nurturing with validation, which we see as separate phenomena. It is important to see that a partner can be close and caretaking but not necessarily validating. A partner can be close and caretaking and also be invalidating by giving advice or being critical or controlling. In addition, to believe that the agentic, curiosity, mastery, and efficacy system is totally dependent on secure attachment is questionable. Although facilitated by it, it appears, according to the work of Stern (1985), that the infant possesses a self-organizing capacity that operates to some degree independently of the attachment system, or at most, interdependent with it. Also, it is important to note that although certain attachment styles may be learned early in life, people do not always have to go back to early childhood to explain all adult development (Harris, 1999). In addition, attachment styles often are multiple and dynamic. People have more than one style, and these can change depending on the context and can transform over time.

People clearly are relational, but what they need from connecting with others is more than only security and proximity, as suggested by attachment theory. The relational need has to be differentiated into its different aspects. Attachment has come to be seen as the master motive by many theorists and practitioners, and in our view now has been overapplied to explain almost all of human functioning, even to explain love itself. Adult love seems to be more than, but includes, attachment. We also should not assume that all romantic or couples relationships always are attachment relationships. In addition, in a long-term adult relationship, as opposed to in an infant–caregiver relationship, the attachment and caregiving roles are interchangeable, making adult attachment quite different from infant attachment. Adults also are able to self-soothe and need to develop this ability if they cannot. What is important and unique about attachment figures is that people internalize their functions, so they feel their soothing effects without their physical presence. Anticipating their soothing responses thus regulates emotions. To assume, however, that adult attachment parallels infant–caregiver bonding is a stretch, and to call this "love" is also a problem. The similarities are called into question simply by thinking about the differences in the development of these bonds. It takes a minimum of 6 months for infants to become fully attached with the primary caregiver, and this occurs within a context of almost total dependence and constant physical contact. It is clear that adult attachment relationships are formed in a different manner. In addition, infants also have secondary attachment figures who can soothe them. So do adults. However, it would be unwise to assume that adults are in love with secondary attachment figures, such as parents, friends, or mentors, in the same way they love their partners. Sex is one big difference in the relationships with secondary attachment figures, but so is the degree of nonsexual physical and emotional intimacy. Changes in the traditional model of adult attachment are needed.

Bowlby and Beyond: Emotions in the Adult Attachment System

Emotion-based theory has posited the emotion scheme or emotion script as the core organizing structure of experience (Greenberg & Safran, 1986; Oatley, 1992; Tomkins, 1963). An *emotion scheme*, as we have said, is an integrated emotional, motivational, cognitive, interactional, behavioral, internal organization that is based on the emotional experience that it serves to organize (Greenberg, 2002a). The loss of, for example, an attachment figure is the loss of someone who is an important source of the positive affective stimulation of joy and comfort to which the emotion system is sensitive and whose loss produces the negative stimulation of sadness and anger. It is difficult to conceive how a purely cognitive model of human relationships would result in such a sense of loss and the production of so much affect in an infant or adult. In adults, loss is a highly emotional experience.

Perhaps because Bowlby (1973) lacked an adequate theory of both the positive and the negative emotions involved in intimate relationships, he proposed a more cognitive mechanism, the working model, as the structure underlying the long-term continuity of attachment. His internal working model is essentially a cognitive model of expectations regarding the behavior of others. Most attachment researchers have assumed, sometimes implicitly, that mental representations of the self in relation to others, or internal working models, trigger the experience and regulation of emotion. However, as Pietromonaco and Feldman Barrett (2000) pointed out, to serve as a vehicle of continuity, the working model must be self-sustaining and enduring, properties that suggest some sort of affective process. In our view, a biological–emotional explanation of the working of attachment, its description, and continuity in patterns of attachment thus is more accurate and representative than a model based on beliefs and expectations.

Some individuals become literally addicted to the positive stimulation provided by others, so that the loss or rejection is experienced as a highly charged negative event. Indeed, Panksepp, Siviy, and Normansell (1985) likened the social dependence characteristic of attachment to opioid dependence. The administration of opioids is intrinsically rewarding to humans and animals, and their withdrawal results in severe distress. Working models, in our view, then, are better seen as part of a dynamic system that is organized by both the experience and the regulation of emotion (Pietromonaco & Feldman Barrett, 2000; Reis & Patrick, 1996).

In our view, attachment, however, serves a role even more profound than that of only regulating security—it serves the role of promoting the coregulation of affective signaling, which is at the base of much development, including the development of symbolic communication and social negotiation (Greenspan & Shanker, 2004). Not only did attachment evolutionarily serve protective functions, but it also served to help transform emotions from intense levels to more regulated and differentiated affect expressions, which allowed emotions to act as communicative signals and promoted the development of communication. As caretaker and infant developed a variety of patterns of coregulation of affect, this promoted the ability to develop differentiated communication and the dual coding of objects by infants, as entities that had certain feeling effects. Evolutionarily, attachment, by promoting the beginning of affective communication, promoted the capacity for the complex social negotiation of subtle affects that facilitated living in groups and this promoted survival. Attachment thus primarily serves the purpose of affect regulation, and it becomes the arena in which affective communication is first learned.

Viewing attachment (and the other major relational motives) as most fundamentally governed by affect regulation (rather than as producing it) allows us to ask which emotions to access in therapy and which to regulate or transform to create attachment or attain other goals. An affect regulation model also provides more of a process than a structural, or trait, model of relational functioning. What constitutes attachment between adults can be subtle, complex, and dynamic and involves more than is captured by secure, anxious, or dismissive styles. Attachment, in our view, is better worked with as a process, governed by anxiety and avoidance and not something that is categorically present or absent. Soothing happens in small pieces and in steps that together combine to create the felt sense of security. Researchers and therapists need to understand the component pieces and steps of this emotional process.

Understanding of, and working with, individual adults and couples will benefit from a more differentiated, dynamic, affect regulation process view of attachment functioning and relatedness. Once we see attachment as affect regulation, both *emotional reactivity*, the degree to which people feel threat activating a need for security, and *emotion regulation*, the relational behaviors enacted to maintain or restore security, become the key concerns in attachment. Attachment thus functions by means of the emotions it produces far more than by any form of conscious expectations or implicit cognitive model of self- and other relationships. Emotion thus is an organizing force in working models rather than an outcome of them, and emotion regulation strategies are formative in the development and maintenance of any internal models that may exist. The precise role of emotion in the attachment process, however, remains to be articulated.

Rather than emphasizing the patterns of attachment as central, we emphasize emotions and emotion regulation as the central organizing principle of attachment. Emotional reactivity is the process that activates the need for felt security, and emotion regulation strategies are the processes that maintain or restore felt security. Security is the ability to regulate affect. Reactivity and regulation are the two affect-based processes that underlie the operation of the attachment system. So in our view, it is emotional reactivity and regulation, not internal working models and attachment styles, that generate people's attachment-related perceptions, motivations, and behaviors. Thus we focus on how anger, sadness, fear, shame, compassion, and love, as well as other emotions, are activated and regulated and how to work with these processes in therapy.

The prototypical emotion of attachment is a feeling of trusting security when the attachment partner is present. This presence sets up the emotion script of being contentedly present with a caregiver and of having courage to explore the world from the secure base of the caregiver's presence. When the caregiver is absent or is leaving, there is anxiety of the most intense kind, and this results in a draining away of confidence. With the loss of a caregiver, or in adult life, an attachment partner such as a spouse, the processes of bereavement offers scripts for mourning and for disengaging the self from the lost partner that involves angry protest, sadness, and grief. Many of people's most intense emotions arise during the formation, maintenance, disruption, and renewal of attachment relationships.

As Bowlby (1973) suggested, attachment falls essentially into a category "under the general rubric of fear behavior" (p. 90). A problem thus arises if we use attachment only as a base for a theory of intimacy and love as we are left without an analysis of the positive emotions involved in intimate relationships. Romantic love, as commonly conceived in an attachment view, involves the interplay of attachment with caregiving and sex. Although romantic love is partly an attachment phenomenon, it is recognized that love involves additional behavioral systems, at least including caregiving and a sexual system, and it is useful to separate these from the need for security when doing couples therapy. As Fisher (2004) showed, love seems to include romantic passion and lust, as well as attachment. In our view, attachment, which has more to do with security and anxiety, is not love, although it is an aspect of love.

The Attachment System and Its Parameters in Adult Intimate Relationships

The concept of an "attachment bond" does, however, help describe the behavior of adults in relationships. When we say that an adult is attached to a romantic partner, we mean that the person feels secure and trusts the partner and the partner is able to comfort the person at times of stress. In addition to the need to be connected, people also are primed by evolution with both care-eliciting and caregiving capacities. As adults, people have evolved potential abilities to be highly competent caregivers. People have developed capacities for caretaking, concern, sympathy, and compassion. Although some theorists see people as fundamentally selfish, and although there may be all kinds of other nonaltruistic reasons for wanting to care for others, the fact is that people also have an in-wired feelings of compassion that motivate caretaking. People have tendencies to help those in distress and to take care of them if they are suffering. This is a very important component of the adult bond in intimate relationships.

In emphasizing the importance of attachment, we are not, however, advocating fusion, enmeshment, lack of independence, wallowing in emotion, or encouraging dependency. Some have suggested that a focus on attachment does not save marriages—and that it's bad for sex (Schnarch, 1991, 1997). We disagree. Needing and receiving closeness and support is the essence of being human. Our competitive Western society has emphasized individuality, differentiation, and self-esteem to the detriment of nurture and support. It makes little sense to work in therapy exclusively on strengthening identity, differentiation, and independence when the whole purpose of an intimate relationship is mutuality and interdependence. Problems arise in relationships when one partner does not respond to a need urgently felt by the other partner. It is important, too, that when one partner wishes, the other is responsive and that the partner be able to not only express the need without shame but also regulate it if the partner is unresponsive.

Partners need to be able to express their needs for care and support, but too often people are unable to express their adult unmet needs for fear of being too dependent or not being responded to or from shame of appearing weak. Alternatively, it is also true that fusion of identities can destroy intimacy and negatively affect attachment. Recognizing difference creates excitement both sexually and in the affectional bond. The capacity to self-regulate when the other is unavailable is also important. A balance is thus needed between self and other support.

Attachment in adults, however, has undifferentiatedly come to mean that the bond not only is comforting at times of stress but also is affectional and is love. This serves to blur an important distinction. It is important to distinguish between the security aspects of attachment and the warmth or affectional aspects (MacDonald, 1992). The feelings of caring for the other, warmth, and additional aspects of attachment are not related to a need for security, as we discuss in the next section. Panksepp (1998), in his treatment of attachment, made an important distinction between attachment to nests versus attachment to the caretaker, pointing out that rat pups feel secure at nest sites even without the mother being in it. They would not feel affection for the nest. This finding suggests that attachment and affection are separate and serve different functions in relationships. We now discuss the attraction and affection system.

AFFECTION, LOVE, WARMTH, COMPASSION, AND ATTRACTION

MacDonald (1992) cogently argued that "the systems underlying warmth and intimacy in human relationships must be distinguished from the systems underlying the propensity for fear in the absence of an attachment object" (p. 754). In line with this distinction, Fox and Davidson (1987) showed that infants, on the approach of their mother with open arms, showed joy and activation of the left side of the cortex, whereas with the approach of a stranger, they showed fear and activation of the right side of the cortex showing that joy is not the calming of fear.

The overall goal and concern of separation anxiety is protection and security. Originally, during the many millions of years of mammalian evolution, this protected infants from predation and from aggression from other members of their own species. More recently, protection has been from whatever might make a child feel fearful. The attachment need for protection is fundamentally organized by separation anxiety, and the primary emotions motivating attachment therefore are fear and anxiety. Attachment based on a need for security and for protection, however, is not love and does not fully explain affection, warmth, attraction, liking, and intimacy. Affection, warmth, and liking seems to be another important but distinct aspect of the bonding or affiliation system (MacDonald, 1992). The function of attachment is to remove the negative emotion of fear. The function of affection is to be attracted to another person and to feel liking.

Data from the study of attachment in other cultures support the possible separation of the reward system that undergirds warmth and affection, and the fear system that undergirds security of attachment. For instance,

Ainsworth's (1967) study of Ugandan mothers and infants showed that securely attached infants were cared for by mothers who showed sensitivity and responsivity but did not demonstrate warmth and affection. The babies showed attachment behaviors at levels that were higher than found in American samples, despite this lack of affectionate behavior and that the majority of the babies studied were considered securely attached. Similarly, LeVine and LeVine (1967) reported that among the Gusii of Kenya, "It is rare to see a mother kissing, cuddling, hugging, or cooing at her child" (p. 126) and that mothers nursed their infants "mechanically, without looking at the child or fondling him" (p. 122). A warmth and affection system that thrives on social stimulation thus can be differentiated from the secure attachment phenomena. Parent–child warmth also has emerged as a factor independent of attachment in several factor-analytic studies of parenting (MacDonald, 1992). Maternal affection and secure attachment therefore are not synonymous.

Attachment is commonly found among a wide range of primates and other mammals, and a similar system occurs in birds; it functions to keep the animal close to the mother, especially in threatening situations. However, for the great majority of these species, there is no warmth and no reason to suppose that there has been an evolution of intimate relationships or affection. A system that evolved for the purpose of protecting the young need not also function to produce affectional bonding and intimacy (MacDonald, 1992). The implication is that the conceptualization of the biology of the human affectional system must go beyond merely viewing it as attachment and as a means of protection in the face of threat, toward a positive conceptualization of the nature of positive affective interchanges and pair bonding.

Another reason for distinguishing between attachment and warmth and liking is that attachment appears to be compatible with lack of warmth and even maltreatment. Rajecki, Lamb, and Obsmacher (1978) reviewed data from several species indicating that attachment occurs even in the face of punitive and abusive behavior by the caregiver. Despite rather harsh treatment, infants were observed to persist in their attempts to cling to the mother (Seay, Alexander, & Harlow, 1964). The primitive function of attachment is indeed protection, and the animal appears to seek out the attachment object even under negative conditions. This has been observed clinically in humans who demonstrate strong attachment behaviors to abusive caregivers (J. Benjamin, 1988).

A further reason for distinguishing security in the presence of threat from warmth and affection is that security is a more crucial issue in infancy than in the romantic relationships of adults. In couples relationships, partners affiliate with each other because they like and are attracted to each other. Reciprocal positive social interaction is most important. The precise role of different emotions in the adult bonding processes, important in maintaining intimate relationships, thus needs clarification. Loving and liking and excitement are not the same as the calming of fear. An affectional, affiliative system thus differs from an attachment system. Fisher (2004) suggested that lust and romantic passion are independent neurochemical systems from companionate attachment and offered all as components of love.

Because the development of a good bond depends on the experience and expression of positive emotions of warmth, liking, and loving, as well as feeling secure and validated, individuals need to develop and exercise their ability to appreciate the other as "other." The following quote, attributed to author Iris Murdoch, captures that love is about recognizing the other as other: "Love is the extremely difficult realization that something other than one's self is real." The ability to see the other, as a person, as an "other," who just like one's self wants happiness, coupled with warmth and liking for this "other," constitutes what is called love and affection, and this differs from feeling securely attached by virtue of the others accessibility and reliable responsiveness. Love leads to the other feeling cherished in addition to feeling secure. The affectionate system, involving needs for intimacy and feelings of warmth and love, thus appears to be different from the attachment need for safety and security and clearly differs from identity needs for recognition, mastery, validation, and self-esteem. Affection and love involves having feelings for the other as well as receiving feelings from the other. This system is important in the development of positive feelings in marriage. Conflict in couples, then, comes from failures to resolve struggles around adult needs for security and identity and is exacerbated by lack of liking, warmth, and feelings of good will.

Finally, according to MacDonald (1992), the momentous evolutionary development of play in mammals depends on the affection system. In mammals other than humans, play is of the rough-and-tumble kind. In it, assertion is contained within an envelope of affection. In addition, in humans, starting in what Winnicott (1965) called the "space in-between mother and infant," there grows the discovery of objects and activities of shared interest. This space is the space of play. Affection-based play is both laboratory and proving ground for the skills, the mental resources, and the creativity, of the human social world. As Frederickson (1998) showed, the positive emotion system leads to the broadening and building of skills that enhance survival. In couples, laughter and sense of humor is important and promotes affection and liking. Laughing at one's partner's jokes and enjoying their mannerism and idiosyncrasies is an important source of positive feeling in relationship. Laughter has been shown to reduce heart rate and to deescalate conflict (Levenson, 1992).

The emotion of affiliation is happiness, which again is not the same as the calm and security offered by attachment; its extended feelings are affection, enjoyment, and warmth toward others. Happiness is the script of continuing to do what one is doing, of broadening one's concerns, and of building one's resources (Fredrickson, 1998). Most important, happiness is the emotion of cooperation. The most intense sentiment of affiliation is love, a script of being united with another person and making that person's concerns one's own. The emotions of lack of affection are coldness and disdain. Affection varies then from cold contempt and unhappiness to warmth, pleasure, and happiness. Attachment varies from fear and anxiety to security and calmness. Positive feelings of affection and warmth result from a different biological system than do negative emotions such as fear, distress, and anxiety, which are central to attachment research. Of interest too is the finding already mentioned that the joy elicited by a mother approaching and reaching for her infant was associated with left frontal EEG activation (Fox & Davidson, 1987). Separation protest, however, was associated with right frontal activation, showing that joy is not the calming of fear and that different systems are involved in warmth and attachment.

It appears that millions of years ago, human ancestors combined sex and affection into something people now recognize as love, or pair bonding. Each person inherits from his or her ancestors a tendency to bond with another over a long period in a more-or-less exclusive sexual union. This has been transformed into an aspect of being human that people value highly, the ability to love. These considerations suggest that it is important to work with warmth and affection as emotions independent of the calm and security of attachment and to explore the relations between these two sets of phenomena. The essential proposal, then, is that the human affectional system be conceptualized as an evolved reward system (Porges, 1995, 1996). The stimuli that activate this system act as natural clues for pleasurable affective response. Intimate relationships are thus pleasurable to the participants and are actively sought after. Their termination is met with disappointment and grief, and there is eager anticipation of reunion with a loved one.

CONCLUSION

In this chapter, we have made the case for the importance of the three major affective–motivational systems that affect intimate relationships, in preparation for discussion of how to deal with these therapeutically. Relationships are a natural arena for the gratification of basic human needs for connectedness and for identity and are a source of intimacy and positive feelings, which involve the giving and receiving of love and appreciation. Needs for both emotional connectedness and identity-validation have been viewed as universal factors operating in couples systems. We have suggested that this duality of human nature, the basic need for connection and the need for identity and agency, provides the optimal framework for understanding couples and conflict and that it is the warmth and affection system that produces feelings of joy and pleasure. We also have suggested that conflict in intimate relationships emerges most fundamentally from unmet adult needs for attachment and identity, not because of infantile or pathological needs, and that emotional accessibility and responsiveness, empathy, validation, and respect can be seen as the antidotes to conflict.

5

INTERACTION

Symptoms are answers, given by the modified organism, to definite demands: they are attempted solutions to problems derived on the one hand from the demands of the natural environment and on the other from the special tasks imposed on the organism in the course of the examination.
—Goldstein, (1995, p. 35)

In working to resolve conflict in couples, it is important now to look at interaction and to combine this with emotion, motivation, and cognition to get an integrated perspective on couples functioning. Interaction is best viewed as occurring on two orthogonal axes of affiliation and influence (Leary, 1957). Concerns about love and power that dominate couples interactions are acted on along these dimensions. Couples conflict involves escalating interactions on these dimensions, which rigidify into negative interactional cycles. We argue that interactions both influence emotional states and are reciprocally influenced by emotion. People's responses in interactional conflict are attempts at coping with and protecting against two fundamental threats to their basic survival—threats to attachment and threats to identity. These threats are perceived rapidly by the amygdala and produce basic modes of processing such as processing for danger or loss and appropriate action tendencies designed to protect. The emotionally based action tendencies prepare people for basic survival actions such as fight, flight, crying out, or withdrawing. Once these tendencies are further processed cognitively, they manifest as conscious meaning, as willed behavior, and, ultimately, as interaction, to promote affiliation or influence. On the basis of the fundamental mode of processing set in motion by affect, attributions of responsibility or cause are made to the partner, and the partner often is blamed for the threat or distress experienced. Now cognition has come into play, and thoughts begin to cloud one's consciousness, and this further influences emotion and interaction. Emotion, motivation, cognition, and interaction thus are all linked intimately. Ultimately, it is an understanding of how to work with all of these together that helps facilitate conflict resolution.

THE EXPERIENTIAL–SYSTEMIC SYNTHESIS: INTEGRATING AFFECT AND INTERACTION

Emotion, as we have said, occurs at the organism environment boundary in the form of a readiness to act and thus influences the other. In emotion-focused couples therapy (EFT-C), therapists therefore can help couples change negative interactions by accessing and expressing adaptive attachment emotions and needs and adaptive identity-enhancing emotions and needs. Interactions also are changed by regulating dysregulated emotion and by transforming maladaptive emotions into more adaptive ones. In EFT-C, action by one partner is not seen as causing a reaction by the other partner, but rather the couple is seen as in mutual regulation and partners' actions are seen as maintaining each other's experience and reactions. We thus adopt a circular view of mutual regulation. For example, in distressed couples, demand by one partner for closeness is seen as contributing to and maintaining, rather than causing, anxiety and withdrawal in the other, whereas withdrawal is seen as pulling for, and maintaining, feelings of abandonment and demand rather than causing them. Similarly, dominance by one partner contributes to and maintains the other's feelings of inadequacy and submission, whereas submission pulls for and maintains feelings of adequacy and dominance. Both partners' responses are shaped by each other, and an interactional cycle emerges. Experience and behavior are considered as dependent on both self and context. The organization of the self and the organization of the system are both viewed as the problem, as opposed to viewing either the experience, behavior, or personality of the partners alone, or the interaction alone, as the cause of the problem. To understand the behavior of one partner, the therapist thus must always consider couples behavior in the context of both intrapsychic experience and the behavior of the other partner.

Couples relationships, then, in our view, are characterized by the presence of regular, repeating cycles of interaction that are circularly produced and maintained by affect regulation and dysregulation. The more negative, narrow, and rigid these cycles, the more affect is dysregulated and the more likely the relationship is to be distressed; vice versa, the more affect is dysregulated, the more narrow and rigid are the interactional cycles. When threats to attachment or identity are perceived, partners no longer feel safe; affect becomes dysregulated; meanings become governed by affect rather than by the situation; behavior changes; and conflict, wariness, or distance result. If the therapist can recognize the perceived threat and maintain a focus on the automatically activated underlying emotions related to safety, rather than focus on the content of the conflict, interaction will change.

Within this view, all of a person's behavior is seen as communication that influences his or her partner's self-organization. Turning away and not saying anything is communication, and it leads to changes in a partner's experience and self-organization. In addition, what is said and how it is said, especially its affective tone, define the role of both the speaker and the listener. In other words, each communication is a proposal about an interactional position and a role relationship, and each response is a counterproposal, accepting or rejecting the prior offer (Sluzki, 1983). When a husband asks his wife in an accusing manner why she came home so late or why she did not want to make love, he is proposing that he be the prosecutor and that the wife be the defendant. When she answers and gives reasons, she is accepting the proposal that he be the prosecutor and that she be the accused and defend herself. The task of the therapist is to interrupt negative cycles of interaction like these by helping people self-organize in terms of their underlying more vulnerable feelings and concerns, thereby changing their interactional positions so that new, more adaptive interactional patterns can begin to emerge and partners can develop alternative ways to relate to each other.

Although we adopt a process view of functioning, we also recognize that each partner has more enduring, underlying vulnerabilities in which both the couple and the self are dynamic self-organizing systems. Sensitivities and maladaptive emotional responses from past injuries that act as attractor states in the self exert a pull on the self-organizing process, and particular cycles rapidly emerge, resulting in repetitive or consistent ways of responding (Whelton & Greenberg, 2004). Any emotion can become so magnified that it begins to dominate and monopolize that person's entire affective life. Relational patterns result largely from partners' responses to each other's predominant emotions. Some partners seem dominated by one particular emotion—for example, someone who is always annoyed and complaining (anger), or a partner whose face and voice are sad regardless of the interaction. It is the repeated coactivation of maladaptive emotional states by minor cues of abandonment or insult, often based on the partner's own traumatic learning histories, that is the source of much of the more destructive conflict in couples. Changing these repeated, vulnerable forms of self-organization often becomes the major focus in the later part of couples treatments, especially in longer term couples treatments. In this chapter, we focus on understanding the nature of interaction in the context of emotion, motivation, and cognition. In chapter 8, "Therapeutic Tasks: Focusing on Interactional Cycles," we again take up interaction with regard to developing interventions to change them.

Interaction, Emotion, Motivation, and Cognition

In our view, to best understand interactional conflict, it is helpful to deconstruct interaction into its essential emotional, motivational, and cognitive processes. In any interaction, emotions and associated needs or goals in one partner (Partner A) influence overt action in that partner, which in turn leads to covert processes in the other partner (Partner B). These processes include emotional reactions, perceptions, attributions, explanations, need satisfaction–frustration, intentions and other subjective events, and they then influence Partner B's overt reactions. As a result of the complexity and subjectivity of this process, partners often react emotionally to their partners, on the basis of their unfulfilled needs, and they perceive or explain each other's behaviors in different ways than intended by the other. Thus, in a relationship, one partner's intention and action and the other partner's reaction to or perception of that intention and action may be very different. For example, a husband may wish to get support from his wife and attempt to communicate this to her, but she may rather feel pressured or criticized or may not recognize that he needs support, or she may recognize his need and try to respond, but the husband may react to her response as insufficient or smothering or may not perceive the wife's reaction as support at all. If the wife's response does not satisfy the husband's need, goal, or concern, then he would feel frustrated. If that concern was important to the husband's sense of well-being, then he would experience negative affect, and the negative emotion would be a signal that a need has not been met.

Simple cases of couples distress often result from this type of mismatched communications and misinterpretations of, or responses to, intentions or needs. Improved communication of the intentions, thoughts, feelings, and needs are then the appropriate treatment. A wife, for example, may want compassion, but her husband may offer advice. Wives who express sadness or vulnerability frequently receive unwanted advice from well-meaning "fix-it" husbands who tell them to look on the bright side or propose solutions rather than empathize with the sadness. Getting partners to clearly express what they need and having the other understand this can clearly help. In other instances, when one partner says, "You must be feeling very sad," the other partner may experience this as compassionate support or as patronizing condescension, depending on his or her perception and construal. As a result, the very same message may be interpreted differently by two people. An empathic remark such as "It must have left you feeling so lonely" may seem supportive to a person seeking connection but judgmental to a person seeking status. Therefore, opportunities for miscommunication, for misinterpretation, and for misunderstanding abound.

However, in our view, marital distress is not based primarily on either lack of communication, skill deficits, or misinterpretation. Often, after a number of years, partners have clearly communicated their feelings and needs only too well. They perceive what the other is communicating. The problem is the partners are unable or unwilling to give each other what they so desperately feel they need or want from each other. At this point, as the partners become more frustrated, rather than express core feelings related to threats to their unmet adult attachment and identity needs, they attack or withdraw, and their core maladaptive emotions, related to core vulnerabilities, begin to be activated. When the partners' deeper insecurities or feelings of inadequacy become activated, the partners often are unable to regulate these feelings, and they begin to enter those dysregulated states in which they say and do things they later regret, and later also disclaim as not really representative of what they truly feel toward their partners. It is this dysregulated affect that is the source of much more severe marital distress and conflict.

Dimensions of Interaction

The empirical study of interaction has found that interpersonal behavior is best represented along two orthogonal axes that mirror the major dimensions of motivation (Leary, 1957). These axes have been referred to by many names, but basically one axis has to do with attachment, or what Bakan (1966) called "communion." This dimension is anchored by the polar opposite terms of *closeness* and *distance*, or *love* and *hate*. The superordinate term *agency* has been used to describe the other axis (Bakan, 1966; Horowitz, 2004). This axis has been more difficult to name and has to do with identity, differentiation, control, or influence and is anchored by the polar opposite terms of *dominance* and *submission*, or *freedom* and *control*.

Researchers who have developed circumplex models of interaction (L. S. Benjamin, 1993; Leary, 1957; Wiggins, 1973) have referred to the attachment-related *x*-axis alternatively as *connectedness, affiliation, love, warmth,* and *nurturance* and the identity-related *y*-axis as *interdependence, influence, control,* or *dominance.* Thus, the horizontal dimension of communion could be labeled *connected, loving, or close* to *disconnected, indifferent, hateful, or distant.* We refer to this axis as the *affiliation axis.* Agency, as the vertical dimension, ranges in meaning from "differentiating, influencing, controlling, or dominating" to "enmeshing, yielding, relinquishing control, or submitting." We refer to this axis as the *influence axis.* All interactional behaviors can be described by a combination of these two dimensions. Of all the circumplex models, L. S. Benjamin's (1993, 1996) structural analysis of social behavior is the most helpful to us in coding actual interactions in therapy. Her measure is based on a model of interpersonal behavior with the two underlying dimensions that run from *hate* to *love* (related to attachment and affection) and *enmeshment* to *differentiation* (related to identity). Any couple's interaction, verbal or nonverbal, can be described on these axes. It is important to note that in circumplex models, interpersonal behavior is generally understood as acting in a reciprocal fashion, and each class of actions is seen as evoking a particular class of reactions from the partner. For example, according to this system, if a person blames his or her partner, he or she is focusing on the other in a manner that is both somewhat hostile and somewhat controlling, and the partner is likely to react by acting put upon, which is somewhat hostile and somewhat submissive. Thus, attack begets defend or reciprocal attack, depending on whether the response is a complementary or symmetrical one, whereas love is reciprocated by love and pulls for openness in the other. The evoked reaction is most generally a complementary behavior (Kiesler, 1996; Leary, 1957) that it is assumed will satisfy the person's goal, motive, or desire.

L. S. Benjamin proposed that although both the affiliative and the influencing dimensions of interaction have been seen as equally important, resulting in a circumplex model (represented by a circle), there is no a priori reason for the affiliation, or love–hate, dimension to have equal weighting to the influence dimension in interpersonal discourse. She argued that behaviors having to do with attachment and affection may be more important in interpersonal space than differentiation, control, or dominance (see L. S. Benjamin, Rothweiler, & Critchfield, 2006). Interaction is thus best thought of as falling on an oval as shown in Figure 5.1 rather than on a circle, indicating that the affiliation dimension has a stronger influence on interaction, especially intimate relationships. L. S. Benjamin suggested that it is reasonable to argue that the attachment-related affiliation axis is a major dimension because the human is a herd animal (L. S. Benjamin et al., 2006). Also, as we discussed in the previous chapter, two motives, one for security and another for affection, underlie the affiliation dimension, whereas only one motive, for identity, underlies the influence dimension. As we have seen, attachment behaviors ensure connection to the caretaker, and this ensures survival, whereas affection produces pair bonding. The affiliative–interactional dimension, therefore, often is more important in intimate relationships. Behaviors to protect identity and status, as represented on the vertical influence axis, although also important to survival, arguably are less important than attachment and affection in intimate relationships. In addition, there has to be proximity before there can be validation, so this alone gives attachment primacy. Although interpersonal interaction can be described along two dimensions, the affiliation dimension may count more heavily in intimate relationships than the influence dimension. However, we discuss dominance in this and later chapters more than affiliation, not because we see it as more important but because we want to add to prior work on attachment to achieve a more comprehensive description of couples conflict.

It also is important to note that in L. S. Benjamin's (1993) interactional model, hostility, which is a central component of marital distress, lies on the horizontal axis and has to do with not getting the love or security one needs, not with influence. Hostile behavior in marriage, although it often begets hostility, is more of an indication of feeling that a central motive or

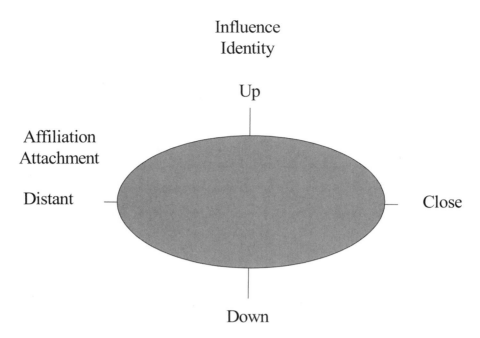

Figure 5.1. Two-dimensional oval model of interaction. The horizontal affiliation dimension is weighted more strongly than the vertical influence dimension, resulting in an oval to represent the space of interaction.

goal for affiliation has been frustrated than it is a desire to destroy or to evoke counter hostility. Note also that the negative end of the closeness dimension sometimes is marked by some other investigators as detached or disengaged, rather than as hostile. Sometimes the opposite of love is withdrawal or indifference. From this model, we also see that the influence dimension is not related to love, hate, or hostility but rather is related to being in control, feeling powerless, or feeling validated or being free to be one's self.

LOVE AND POWER

The concepts of "love" and "power" are often seen as major forces in intimate relationships and marriage and are the key dimensions on which interactions are often understood. Love, as we have said, is a complex emotion, but its interactional elements are clear. It moves people closer to the ones they love. Love is many different things to different people, but it refers to all human ways of being united, connected, joining, and open to one another. No one, scientist or layperson alike, however, is clear on what love really is. Clients report feeling loved when someone is interested in them, desires them, respects them, values them as a human being, and admires the way they are or what they have done, and they wish to be loved for every single aspect of themselves forever. Some theorists see it as a blend of other emotions: pleasure, compassion, interest, and joy. Some define different kinds of love such as compassionate love, romantic love, filial love (Singer, 1984), and others break it down on the basis of different physiological and/or biological system responses (Fisher, 2004). Historically, love has often been seen as involving sexual desire, and the Egyptians saw it as a disease, the only cure for which was a dose of the beloved. Love also brings the possibility of suffering and feeling exposed, vulnerable, or intimately fallible. People can hate the one they love and fear the one they trust.

Love, of course, also brings positive emotions. Positive emotions in couples, such as joy, excitement, and the feeling of being valued and cherished, which in intimate relationships come greatly from attraction and love, help engender positive interaction. Gottman (1999) suggested that a ratio of five positive to one negative interactions are necessary to maintain a happy marriage, whereas Frederickson and Losada (2005) reported that probably a ratio of three positives to one negative are important on a more universal basis to help people and systems flourish. Love, whatever it is, and positive emotions of attraction and liking clearly involve a phenomenological experience—a feeling—and one that moves people closer to the loved one. In attempting to understand love, it is helpful to remember the following phrase on love attributed to Chaucer: "The life so short, the craft so long to learn."

Power and influence, however, are not so much emotions as complex relational concepts. Power is not in itself a feeling. We do not feel power in the same way we feel anger, sadness, or love. *Power* is an interactional term describing relations between people rather than an emotion or even a motivation. Although one can refer to feeling powerful or powerless or to having a need for power, power fundamentally is a highly interactional concept. Even feeling powerless, which seems more like an actual experience, is the description of an interactional position. The feeling of power or powerlessness is based on more basic feelings, such as pride, excitement, shame, fear, and helplessness.

Power is best defined interactionally as the ability to influence others. Power can determine which partner's interests are met and, in a sense, who gets a better deal out of the relationship. Egalitarian relationships exist where responsibilities, decisions, and attention are distributed equally between both partners. However, some relationships are moderately or extremely imbalanced when it comes to power. Power is exercised to have one's will prevail, to get what one wants. What people want most is to have their identities confirmed, to maintain their position, and to have their status confirmed. Power manifests most visibly when these are threatened.

Love, then, is first and foremost an intrapsychic, emotional experience, whereas power is most fundamentally a relational concept. A problem arises theoretically when we mix intrapsychic and interpersonal frameworks and try to compare concepts such as "love" and "power" in these different frameworks. Phenomenologically experienced and interactionally observed phenomena occur at different levels of analysis. In work with couples, however, we need to think at both levels and understand the significance of internal experience and observed interactional influence. The ability to simultaneously think interactionally and phenomenologically is most necessary in the identity–influence domain, where power, dominance, and control manifest. In the final analysis, in our view, power or control is not a need—it is a strategy for dealing with a situation, an attempted solution. People therefore do not have a basic need to control the other or a need for power, as some theorists have suggested. The terms *dominance* and *control* are observers' descriptions of an interactional position or influence strategy rather than a need. If one asks dominant controlling people if they are trying to dominate or control, generally they will deny it, not because they are deceiving themselves but because it's neither their deliberate intention nor a need. What they are doing is trying to get what is important to them to feel good. The need is to maintain identity, coherence, self-esteem, and/or a sense of agency. Acts of dominance or control thus are engaged to ensure that people get what they feel they need to maintain and protect their identities and their associated positions in a hierarchy.

Power and Dominance

Power and dominance, however, are not the same thing. Although power and dominance are often used interchangeably, it is helpful to see *dominance* as referring to the actual control attempts made by a partner within in an interaction. Power exists in all close relationships. Within these close relationships, decisions regarding who spends money, initiates sex, takes out the garbage, makes dinner, determines leisure activities, and so on, all bring power into the picture. Power also is involved in the construction of reality and whose views of what is right and wrong prevail and in determining who has the right to set the rules of relating.

Power often comes from unrealized, unsaid, and even socially determined rules that were not necessarily overtly agreed on by either partner. Thus, a powerful position is often preserved through the self-maintenance of fear by the less powerful partner or by social norms and not by overt expressions of how things are going to be. Unlike power, dominance is overt, whether it is expressed verbally or nonverbally. Exhibiting dominant behavior, however, does not necessarily equate to being powerful. Often, people who have less power exhibit dominance in an attempt to attain power. Powerful people may exhibit very little dominance, because they are already powerful (Burgoon & Dunbar, 2000, 2005).

To identify dominance, which often appears in much more subtle forms than in overt controlling behaviors, we look at how dominance has been measured. First, in any conversation, the form of the message can be coded as exerting dominance and control (a *one-up message*), as submissiveness (a *one-down message*), or as neutral (a *one-across message*; Rogers-Millar & Millar, 1979). Transactions in which both parties simultaneously make one-up utterances or one-down utterances are called *symmetrical transactions*. Dominance-attempt strategies have been conceptualized as either indirect, for instance, using negative affect, pouting, or hinting, or direct, consisting of more open communication such as debate or negotiation (Falbo & Peplau, 1980). Women tend to use more unilateral or indirect strategies, whereas men tend to use more direct or bilateral strategies, although relative power, as opposed to gender, most determines which dominance strategy a person uses (Cowan, Drinkard, & MacGavin, 1984). Dominance strategies can include, for instance, talking more often or for longer periods of time, thereby restricting others from talking. Dominating is also done through topic control and by control of the direction of the interaction through initiations that are met with compliant responses. Determining the content of conversations can become especially important in maintaining power.

Jacobson and Whisman (1990) found that both dominance through talking and dominance through listening were inversely related to marital satisfaction. This latter pattern was characterized by the listener, rather than the speaker, dominating the conversation with his or her lack of interest in what the other spouse is saying and by concurrently withholding information. In this form of interaction, dominant spouses disengage themselves from conversations, asking no questions, not responding, or giving short answers to questions.

Dominance can be expressed nonverbally through spatial behavior, body movements, the instigation of touch, and close interactional distance; facial expressions such as a deep frown or a sneer are seen as highly dominant (Leach, 1972; Schwartz, Tesser, & Powell, 1982; Spiegel & Machotka, 1974). In addition to spatial presence, elevation also has been shown to be related to dominance. Smiling, however, is seen as submissive (Guerrero, Andersen, & Afifi, 2001). Finally, eye contact is an extremely powerful strategy and measure of dominance. People who use high levels of gaze while speaking and low levels of gaze while listening usually are very dominant (Guerrero et al., 2001).

Felmlee (1994) argued that withdrawing was a way of asserting dominance. A wife-demand/husband-withdraw pattern has been found to be especially present when the topic was of importance to the wife and pertained to the husband's lack of involvement in closeness or housework (Christensen & Heavey, 1990). In this case, husbands had nothing to gain from discussing these problems, so minimizing discussion preserved the status quo as well as their dominant position. Minimizing communication tends to elicit pursuit from the partner with questions such as "What's wrong?" or "Can we talk about this?"; Felmlee's studies demonstrate that the less emotionally attached partner (usually the man) is perceived to have more power.

Power and dominance can become problematic in romantic relationships when excessive, and to the degree that there is a submissive partner whose interests, needs, and wishes are not being met. In these relationships, the submissive partner often meets control attempts with acceptance. Power imbalances such as these have been shown to lead to unhappiness, depression, and decreased marital satisfaction (Halloran, 1998; Jacobson & Whisman, 1990). Dominant behavior reduced trust, reduced perspective taking, and increased conflict. Stets and Burke (1994) looked at how a person's view of their actual versus their ideal control identity (the perceived level of control over others) led to overly dominant behavior with their partner. Identity theory, they suggested, holds that people have "personal identities" that are control systems that act to maintain congruency between identity ideals and perceptions of identity-relevant information. Identity-influenced behavior, then, is enacted to bring the identity perception in line with the persons' identity standard (Stets & Burke, 1994). The person then often becomes controlling.

The importance of emphasizing the influence dimension in interaction, in addition to the affiliation dimension, has been brought home to us by our clinical experience with couples. Couples often reach impasses in therapy that appear to be related more to their identity and the resulting issues of power and control than to connection. Sessions often are filled with arguments about who is right, who wronged whom, whose needs are more important, and whose version of reality is the correct one. Each partner tries to correct the way that he or she is being portrayed by the other. In these couples, partners respond defensively: "I didn't say it like that"; "So you're saying it's really my fault"; "Let me speak"; "You're not listening to me"; or "You're the one who started this." Although these arguments can be due to unmet desires for closeness, they often are about not feeling valued, responded to, or confirmed. The underlying problem that fuels the recurring conflict is how partners are seen and valued by each other and the feeling that one's needs are not important to the other. The conflict is about diminishment of their self-esteem and their identity, which is deeply threatened when their needs, wants, and desires are not met.

In these conflicts, arguments often erupt when partners react to how they feel they are being portrayed or viewed by their partners. Of course, if partners' self-esteem is strong enough and/or their sense of self is sufficiently developed, they may be able to tolerate frustration or withstand criticisms and not have this deflate their self-esteem. In general, however, when invalidated, partners generally react so as to refute the way they are being negatively portrayed in their partners' mind. People cannot easily hold on to their positive view of themselves in the face of disconfirmation by their partners. Thus, when these identities, felt to be so crucial to psychological survival, are threatened, people mobilize all their resources to protect them and fight to defend themselves against disconfirmation of their reality and against any perceived losses of esteem.

Feelings Involved in Dominance

In working with dominance issues, we have found that the basic EFT-C method of accessing underlying feelings has helped resolve conflict but that the set of feelings that were accessed differed from those involved in attachment conflicts. We found that it was feelings of shame at diminishment and fear of loss of control that had to be accessed in the dominant partner and shame of inadequacy and fear of abuse in the submitter. These feelings were more than the feelings of loneliness in the pursuer or fears of closeness and engulfment in the distancer in attachment-related struggles. We also found that in these influence cycles, these feelings of shame and fear often were more difficult to access than the feelings of fear and sadness related to needs to be close. The process involved in resolving dominance struggles often required helping the dominant partner to tolerate and regulate the more dreaded affects of shame and fear. Dominant people appear to resort to control of others with secondary and instrumental expressions in efforts to regulate their own fear of loss of control, shame at losing face, or powerlessness. Struggles for dominance often do not seem to emanate from threats to connection but rather from threats to identity, but they clearly damage connection. There seems to be an attack system that is activated when identity is threatened, and this differs from the "attach" system when closeness is threatened and has different implications for intervention. The attack system originally was related to boundary violation and maintenance of territory rather than to connection. Conflict in couples thus sometimes is more about who is right, or has rights, than who is close or distant. Attack and control thus often are related more to threats to identity, status, and self-esteem than to attachment and abandonment. Intervention in this domain thus involves helping dominant partners take more of a self-focus and regulate their own fear and shame rather than demanding that others be responsive and soothe them to resolve the conflict.

In a recent task analysis of the resolution of dominance interactions in couples therapy, all of the dominant partners in the resolved cases were able to examine their dominance in a self-reflective, emotion-focused way, whereas none of the dominant partners in the unresolved cases did so. The dominant partners connected their interactional stances of dominance during moments of vulnerability to early experiences in the family of origin, recognized their dominance as a stance that was problematic to the relationship, and most important, experienced and acknowledged a primary emotion of fear or shame related to their sense of identity (Sharma, 2007).

Thus the dominant partners needed to express a genuinely felt account of what underlay this particular interactional stance, and unlike those in the unresolved group, they were able to let down their self-protective guard and be authentic with themselves, their partners, and the therapist. They allowed themselves to truly feel the fear that drives their destructive interpersonal behavior and, in doing so, provided their partners with a "softer" glimpse of themselves and their motivation to look strong and in control of the relationship. The submissive partner, who has a new view into what the other partner is truly experiencing underneath the façade of dominance now is able to be more responsive to the fear and shame. Why the dominant has to be able to self-soothe as well as receive other validation is that the submissive partner, however responsive, cannot heal the dominant partner's self-esteem wound from the past. Some of the affect regulation of the fear and shame of being wrong or defective needs to come from the dominant partners themselves.

Dominance conflicts are not about feeling abandoned or alone, or about anxiety about loss or separation, that are so important in attachment related conflict. Rather, dominance struggles are about who makes decisions, whose needs are met, who determines reality, and who has "the right" to do so. For example, a husband may criticize his wife for being too sensitive when they are engaged in solving problems in living. When they tackle projects together, such as rearranging furniture, and they hit any kind of a snag, the husband analyzes what went wrong that got them into the situation, and in this points a finger at her. The wife, feeling put down by the analysis, reacts and says this is not helping them solve the problem and starts defending why they were doing it the way they were. They then begin to argue about whose way of doing it is better. Or the husband makes suggestions or proposes ideas and the wife takes the position of approving or vetoing his suggestions. He then says, "You always put up constraints," and she says, "You always criticize me." He then says, "The problem with you is I can never criticize you. You are far too sensitive." And then they fight about who is too controlling and who is too sensitive. He says he needs to be able to criticize her and the problem is that she always points out what is wrong with him, or his suggestions, but does not take any responsibility or initiative in making suggestions, such as how to change the furniture, for example. In these fights, he also sometimes says she does not trust him or respect him, because if she did, she would just allow him to do things the way he wants. She says this is not true, that sometimes they just disagree and that's okay. Then they fight about whether or not it is okay to disagree.

These are the prototypical fights about who is right, who is too controlling, who is too sensitive, or who is respected or takes initiative. In these fights, it is the regulation of self-esteem and validation of identity and the affects associated with them that are of central importance. It is also important to see that the partners are struggling with words to feel good inside, that is, to regulate their affect. They need to feel they are right and be recognized, validated, and respected by the other to feel good. Once struggles like these that are fundamentally about identity and self-esteem dominate, intimacy soon suffers. These fights often are managed either by one party giving in—in this case the wife, who, to avoid further conflict, goes along with the husband but resents him and over time withdraws—or by neither party yielding, so that they walk away from the argument, and another brick in the wall that separates them is built.

A particular intervention, that of identifying the dangers of improvement (Fisch, Weakland, & Segal, 1984), often highlights the importance of identity. When a couple is in high conflict or stuck at an impasse, helping them to identify the dangers of improvement or the dangers of change, that is, of changing one's interactional position in the cycle, often leads them to articulate a fear of loss of identity. Some partners may fear that if they stop blaming or pursuing, they will be unable to tolerate and regulate their anxiety; others fear that if they come out of withdrawal, they will be annihilated by the other. Others feel that if they admit to being wrong, they will be worthless; yet others feel that if they stand up and assert themselves, they may fail. Partners fear change because change threatens the sameness of identity with which they are most familiar. The attempted solutions to their differences, which are causing the negative interaction, are all efforts to protect their identities and to avoid a danger they see as worse than resolving the problem. The danger often is some type of threat to the self and identity. People strive to have their identities validated because invalidation leads to feelings of not being accepted and valued and ultimately loved because "if I don't feel like you truly see me and respond to my needs, you cannot love me because you do not see me and treat me as important."

The Dominance Process

Struggles for dominance arise when partners begin to feel that their efforts to get their needs met are being thwarted and goal attainment and identity is threatened. They then often resort to influence, to attempt to control or dominate the other to get needs met, rather than focus on what they themselves are feeling. When partners restrict in awareness the feeling of diminishment or lack, which is arising within them, they do not simply eliminate the feeling of unease, threat, or vulnerability. Instead, they start attending to something in the environment and focus on it as a cause of the disease, thereby transforming their internal experience into a perception or construction of reality. Thus, dominant people, whose identities demand strength and who dread feelings of weakness, focus outward rather than inward as soon as they begin to feel the slightest bit vulnerable or not in control. They either attribute blame to their partners or project their weakness onto them. If they perceive or promote weakness in their partner, they then respond with either disdain or protection to their projected weakness. Those who adopt a dominant position thus tend to disown their own vulnerability and powerlessness, and either blame their partners or project these feelings onto their partners, to protect their own identity and sense of control.

The first step in this process is that partners deny their own interior feelings of fear or shame. The second is that they focus outward and blame or project. The third step is that often they succeed in producing these disowned feelings of weakness in others. However, the wish to submit or to be protected by the submissive partner is a reciprocal response to the pull from the dominant partner to be weak or to be taken care of and controlled. Submitters often give up their strengths and look for them in their partners.

To change, the task for the dominant partners is to experience and acknowledge their own vulnerabilities and powerlessness, rather than resort to control. The task for submitters is to feel worthy and stand up and assert themselves. Both dominant and submissive partners need also to be able to own their own strengths alongside their felt weakness. It takes strength to be able to acknowledge weakness. It is important, however, to note that when a person openly admits his or her vulnerability, that person can either put that out with quiet assurance or with an expression of weakness that can involve pleading and its implied demand. To be weak is not to be without resources. People need to learn that they can be weak and strong, vulnerable and assertive, all at the same time. It is the ability to integrate strength and weakness that is so important an antidote to dreaded feelings of powerlessness. To acknowledge felt vulnerability and to continue to be present and to be in touch with one's resources requires strength.

When a person reveals weakness in a helpless manner, without this accompanying attitude of assuredness, that person is coming from a submissive mode and giving away power to the other. This weak-only presentation is most frequently instrumental in that the individual is seeking to have the other take responsibility for making one feel better. It thus is important when dealing with weakness to distinguish between a person's healthy need for support from a partner and a coercive demand for the other to take care of the vulnerability. To be vulnerable is lonely and scary, and all people need a holding environment in which to be open about their vulnerability. The support that is required from another to help handle one's weakness is the support of helping one to stay with one's feeling of weakness; for the other to commit to being, and staying, with one during this; and encouragement from the other to find one's own power. Partners or therapists need to convey "I understand you feel powerless, but I have faith in your ability, and I will be here with you." This is not taking control or saving the person but offering support to help him or her face his or her own doubts and vulnerabilities.

As therapists, then, we need to support people in acknowledging and owning their weakness, and we need to coach partners to encourage each other in admitting weakness and in finding strength. We must facilitate the expression of powerlessness rather than facilitate attempts at dominance. This can be done by noticing that the dominant partner tries so hard to manage because it is hard to feel powerless or out of control and by commenting, "It's so hard when you feel diminished. Of course you feel a need to assert or define to maintain your position." This validates the effort to maintain control but reframes it as a protection against vulnerable feelings that are hard to face. When encouraging contact with, and expression of, powerlessness and shame, we must be careful not to leave people with only that message; their strengths also need to be brought into play alongside their felt limitations. This validates their sense of self. However, it is only by openly owning felt vulnerability that a person can begin to differentiate what it is he or she really needs and needs to do. Once weakness is in awareness, people can begin to look at their vulnerabilities in terms of past and present precipitators.

It also is helpful for therapists to point out that some of human vulnerability is biological and existential in that all people are mortal and vulnerable and that all experience the biological weakness of illness and loss and all are ultimately alone and small in a large world. In addition, it is important to recognize that vulnerabilities often are derived from people's past, because everyone has been wounded or subjugated at one time or another—as children at home and in school, and/or as adults in relations with friends, bosses, and partners.

Primary and Secondary Emotions and Interaction

When affiliative and identity needs are not being met in couples, their interactions evolve rapidly into organized negative cycles, which are described in detail in chapter 8, "Therapeutic Tasks: Focusing on Interactional Cycles." Here we want to stress the importance of primary and secondary emotions in generating these cycles. For example, when primary attachment-related emotions, such as fears of abandonment, are activated but cannot be tolerated, they are often transformed into secondary emotions such as anger. When primary identity-related emotions, such as shame, are activated but cannot be tolerated, they are often transformed into secondary emotions such as contempt.

Because partners are unable to tolerate their primary emotions, they protect against experiencing and acknowledging them and instead resort to expressions of secondary emotions, such as blame and resentment, superiority and contempt, and indifference. These secondary emotions maintain negative interactional cycles and govern communications between the partners. Communication driven by secondary emotions generally results in negative attributions about the partner and subsequent blame and invalidation of the partner. The other reacts defensively with secondary emotions, leading to mutual blame and invalidation that intensifies the cycle. For example, Partner A feels lonely and abandoned when his wife, Partner B, works late. However, unable to tolerate these primary feelings, Partner A instead feels anger, construes Partner B as not caring, and then invalidates Partner B by saying, "You should be able to finish your work on time and then leave it at the

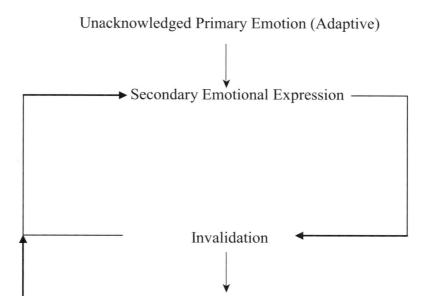

Unacknowledged Primary Emotion (Adaptive)

Secondary Emotional Expression

Invalidation

Maladaptive Primary Emotion

Figure 5.2. Escalating cycles of invalidation. Unacknowledged primary emotion leads to the expression of secondary emotion and invalidation with the other partner, which leads to secondary emotion in the invalidated partner and a repetitive cycle. In addition, invalidation may lead to activation of maladaptive emotion, and this will intensify the cycle.

office." Partner B feels hurt and invalidated, construes Partner A as seeing her as defective, but protects against this feeling by saying, "What difference does it make? All you do is watch TV at night," thereby invalidating Partner A. This escalating negative process is depicted in Figure 5.2 by the feedback loop between secondary emotional expressions and invalidation.

This cycle leads to high emotional and behavioral reactivity, to dysregulation of emotion in both partners, and to further invalidation. Therapy needs to counteract this cycle by promoting awareness and expression of primary emotional experience. This, in turn, will lead to reduction in blame and invalidation, to nonjudgmental acceptance of self and other, and to reduction in emotional arousal. This enhances the possibility of validation, closeness, intimacy, empathy, and compassion for each other, which will lead to positive interactional cycles.

Invalidation and validation appear to be core processes in generating negative and positive interaction cycles, respectively. In a qualitative analysis of change processes in EFT-C, from couples retrospective reports, nonjudgmentalness or reduction of criticisms or blame seemed to be a core factor in producing change in couples therapy (Greenberg, James, & Conry,

1988; Wile, 1993). One of the key issues in all couples conflict, therefore, is reducing criticism, blame, and invalidation. Thus, one of the key ways to reduce couples conflict is to do just that: reduce criticism, blame, and invalidation.

As shown in Figure 5.2, if invalidation from the secondary emotions involved in blaming leads to the activation of maladaptive emotions, the escalatory process is exacerbated, and the cycle becomes more rigid and destructive and leads to greater dysregulation of affect in both partners. Thus, if loneliness or making mistakes is not responded to empathically but is rather invalidated, then core maladaptive emotions of fear or shame may be evoked, leading to more intense distressing emotions and more negative interaction.

We might, for example, see the following negative processes involved in setting up a negative affiliative cycle. Beginning with the automatic activation of a primary emotion, say, loneliness, the person scans for abandonment threat and, rather than acknowledging the primary emotion, engages automatically in a defensive attribution and construes the other as not caring, feels angry, and begins to criticize. The partner may feel shame, scan for humiliation, and think the other will see him or her as defective, and he or she then protects the self by dominance, thereby evoking the other partner's shame or fear. In another couple, one partner may feel afraid, scan for danger, and think, "I can't survive without the other," and feel anxious and distant. This distance then may lead the other partner into maladaptive fear of abandonment.

To help therapists identify degrees of validation and invalidation in couples, Greenberg and Mateu-Marques (1997) developed an 8-point scale, presented in Exhibit 5.1, that describes the processes involved and provides exemplary statements a partner might make. Although the scale has not been subjected to a full-scale study, it has shown preliminary reliability, based on a sample of 55 two-statement interactions during couples therapy.

CONCLUSION

Interaction is best understood on the two dimensions of affiliation and influence. Love and power have been seen as major themes in relationship and are best understood as involving interactions occurring along these dimensions. Problems in couples occur predominantly around struggles for closeness and feeling lonely and abandoned and struggles around identity and feeling invalidated, controlled, or diminished. In these struggles, partners need and want support, availability, and accessibility of their partners, as well as validation, understanding, and acceptance. Interactions can be viewed as the patterns of relationship behavior that individuals enact in an attempt to maintain or restore feelings of security, self-esteem, and intimacy. Expres-

EXHIBIT 5.1
Couples Validation System: 8-Point Scale

Validation is the communication to the other that his or her experience or response makes sense and is understandable. This is done by making sense of the other's experience in terms of the person's perceptions of his or her current or past situation or life context. Validation involves accepting and respecting the other and communicating this, thereby demonstrating a true valuing of the other.

INVALIDATION

1. Ignoring. The partner ignores the internal experience of the other. The partner does not hear what the other is telling him or her or does not recognize that the other is experiencing something. For example, in response to "I'm feeling really tired," the partner says, "Let's go for an ice cream."

2. Criticizing. The partner criticizes the internal experience, actions, or identity of the other, showing a lack of acceptance. The manner and/or content are contemptuous, critical, or diminishing. Examples of criticizing statements include "You are wrong"; "You are stupid"; "You don't know what you are talking about."

3. Dominant defining. The partner defines the other's reality in an imposing manner, explaining the other's experience or behavior in a negative or controlling way that does not recognize or fit the other's view or experience. This disqualifies the other and conveys an authoritarian or paternalistic attitude, telling the discloser that his or her experience is wrong or that the discloser should not be having this experience or that the partner knows best what is going on for the spouse. An example of this is a partner saying, "You have no reason to cry. It's silly."

4. Misunderstanding. The understanding that is conveyed is inaccurate or only captures the most obvious aspect, and one partner may misunderstand much of what the other is saying. The speaker does not recognize the meaning of the other's experience and in addition may be unaware that he or she is not recognizing the others experience. An example of misunderstanding is when a partner provides an inaccurate or reassuring statement that misses the other's experience.

VALIDATING

5. Understanding. The partner conveys both verbal and nonverbal understanding to the speaker. The partner conveys that he or she is listening and understands the discloser using at least minimal responses. There is no criticism. There is no attempt to change, interpret, or criticize the partner's experience. The understanding is to a large degree accurate or captures some important aspect of the other's experience, resulting in the other feeling understood. An example of this is when a partner nods and looks at the discloser while saying, "I hear how sad you are feeling."

6. Confirming. The partner conveys an acceptance of the other's experience, communicating that the other's feelings, needs, and behaviors are valid and make sense. This is done verbally as well as emotionally, with face, eyes, and voice. Verbally, the partner understands the other's feeling either in terms of the current context or in terms of historical context. This confirmation helps to coconstruct a stronger sense of identity by confirming the reality of the other's experience, thereby validating them. For example, a partner may say, "I hear how sad my not calling left you feeling and how it felt like I was not thinking about you" (current context) or "I hear how sad my not calling left you feeling, because it reminded you of your father never calling" (historical context).

continues

EXHIBIT 5.1
(Continued)

7. Respect. The partner expresses respect for, and valuing of, the other and his or her experience and a deep interest and concern for the welfare of the other. The partner shows genuine involvement in what the other is saying, caring, and warmth to the other. An example of this is a partner saying, "I do care about what you need, and I want you to tell me when you feel I am neglecting you. When I get stressed, I can neglect your feelings, but I'm only too happy for you to tell me because I really don't want to do that."

8. Attunement. The partner confirms the other's emotional experience by being highly emotionally attuned nonverbally, sensitively following the other's moment-by-moment experience. The partner shows a full and elaborated understanding and may add to or build on what the other has said such that the partner elaborates his or understanding and focuses on and confirms possibilities for contact and intimacy implicit in what the partner said but was not yet stated. For example, the partner's rhythm and tempo match that of the discloser's, and he or she elaborates and conveys value. He or she might say, "I hear how sad my not calling left you feeling, and how it felt like I was not thinking about you" (current context) or "I hear how sad my not calling left you feeling, because it reminded you of your father never calling" (historical context); then, "I know how awful it is to feel unimportant or abandoned like that, and I'm really concerned." In addition, the partner might say, "I see how that led you to withdraw and be silent. I guess you were saying, 'I feel too unsafe to reach out unless I get the message that you really do care,' and I want you to know I really do."

sion of certain underlying emotions and needs leads to change in partners' perceptions of each other and to changes in interaction.

Helping couples resolve difference and come to terms with dilemmas about differences in the domains of love and power is at the heart of couples therapy. Assessing where interaction lies on the two dimensions of affiliation and influence and what emotions underlie each partner's interactional position allows us to intervene in ways that will change the negative interactional cycle. We describe in detail some of the major cycles and discuss how to work with them in chapter 8.

6

CULTURE AND GENDER

No culture can live, if it attempts to be exclusive.

—Mahatma Gandhi

Pair bonding itself began early in human history and, influenced by culture, it has evolved into many forms. Marriage in Western culture has evolved over the past centuries, from a more utilitarian political and economic arrangement into the 20th-century view of marriage as based on romantic love. In the last part of the 20th century, however, marriage again has been transforming, with divorce being increasingly more common and acceptable (Pinsof, 2002). By 1985, more than 50% of all marriages in the United States ended in divorce, and many more people than previously chose not to marry (Cherlin, 1992). As Coontz (2005) highlighted in *Marriage, a History: How Love Conquered Marriage*, the Western move to egalitarian love marriage possibly had in it the seeds of its own demise. She contested that, following on the ethic of "better single than miserably married," if people cannot find the love and respect they desire, they do not get married or they end unsatisfactory marriages. The radical idea of love marriage, inconceivable for most of human history, requires a therapy such as emotion-focused couples therapy (EFT-C) that helps people develop intimacy by caring and validation.

With the feminist revolution, a Western egalitarian view of relationships also has come to dominate many people's view of urban marriage, at least theoretically. It now is more acceptable than it was 50 years ago for women to be in the workforce, and child care and household duties now are more often seen as shared responsibilities. Heterosexual couples still, however, and perhaps unwittingly, fall into traditional gender roles, so that women more often take on the role of managing the household, whereas men often manage the finances and are the primary breadwinners. Although there is no longer a singular view of marriage in Western culture, especially on the dimensions of identity, power, and role, most view marriage as based on love. Not all cultures, however, value love-based marriage, nor do they necessarily possess the egalitarian model that is more generally espoused in the West. But as the quote in the beginning of this chapter suggests, no viable culture remains exclusive for long, so we need to understand each couple's unique blend of emotional and cultural assumptions.

In this chapter, we explore how love, power, and emotion are conceived of in marriage outside of Western culture and the implication this has for an intimacy and emotion-focused approach to couples therapy. First, we explore how culture affects emotional arousal and expression in non-Western couples relationships, as well as the impact of cultural norms on the role of affection in the formation of the marital bond. Second, we consider the themes of attachment and identity in non-Western marital relationships. Research suggests that identity strongly affects mate selection and informs the basis of couples relationships in non-Western culture. We thus speculate that the influence axis of the interactional cycle is of primary importance in non-Western relationships that are based on identity and status. The chapter then turns to a discussion of how race and culture may determine the nature of issues that face interracial couples. We then focus on gender and how emotions may be experienced differently by gender. We speculate that shame and identity-based emotions may be more difficult for men to allow and express. Further, status and the need for respect may be more important for men than for women, whereas role may be important for women. Finally, we explore attachment and identity themes in same-sex relationships and how this might affect work within the EFT-C model. It is possible that shame may be a more prevalent emotion in same-sex relationships, given the societal messages regarding identity that may have been internalized.

EMOTIONAL AROUSAL AND EXPRESSION
IN RELATIONSHIPS ACROSS CULTURES

In chapter 2, we explored the relative impact of both culture and biology on the formation of emotional experience. It is important here to consider how culture may alter how emotion is expressed in relationships. It appears to take different forms across different cultures. In some cultures, emotionality may indirectly be shown through somatic means. For example, a common somatic expression of emotion among Puerto Ricans is *ataque*.

Ataques appear as dissociative states in which the person falls on the floor and flails his or her limbs. This has been interpreted as a culturally acceptable means of affective expression in a culture that places a strong value on self-control (Searight, 1997). Mesquita (2000) demonstrated that people may experience emotions differently across cultures. This is seen as a function of either an individualist or a collectivist context. In Mesquita's work, emotions experienced by people in a collectivist cultural context were more grounded in assessments of social worth, taken to reflect "reality," rather than in the inner world of the individual, and appeared to belong to the self–other relationship rather than to be confined to the subjectivity of the self. Thus, it seems that culture impacts emotion at the level of what objects and actions are schematically associated with particular emotions.

Emotions may also have different meanings and functions across culture. Culture has a strong impact on emotional expression, and the structure of values in a society may in turn influence whether secondary, instrumental, or maladaptive emotions are experienced or expressed. Kitayama, Markus, and Matsumoto (1995) showed that emotions vary across culture in the degree to which they engage or connect the self in ongoing relationships or disengage or separate the self. Certain cultures (e.g., Asian, Latino) value cultural tasks related to interdependence, whereas others (e.g., Anglo) value cultural tasks related to independence more highly. Furthermore, some negative emotions result from threats to an independent sense of self, such as anger (e.g., "I am treated unfairly") in response to the blocking of goals, desires, or rights. Other negative emotions result from threats to interdependence. Examples are guilt and feelings of indebtedness that result from the failure to participate fully in an ongoing relationship (e.g., "I caused trouble for him") or to live up to the expectations of others (e.g., "People expected me to do that, but I couldn't"). Thus, cultural and social orientation must be taken into account in considering how emotional experience is organized, as well as the social function of emotions. Emotions that threaten independence in a culture that values it (e.g., Western) may not be as easily tolerated. For example, vulnerability, which is characterized by a loss of personal control, may be so uncomfortable for those raised in a Western culture that it is quickly redirected outward (in the form of secondary anger) so as to produce a more self-affirming state. Alternatively, in other cultures (e.g., Asian, Latino), emotions such as anger or pride that pose a threat to social engagement may be more dangerous and may thus need to be transformed. In shame-based cultures such as in Japan and China, expressing emotions that will shame a partner or even expressing shame in therapy may be very difficult.

The implication for the EFT-C therapist working with multicultural or interracial couples is that it is important to understand what happens when individuals experience emotions, how they feel about their partners expressing certain emotions, and what they are likely to do with them. Culture may inform the sequence of emotions (e.g., primary, secondary). For example, if shame or vulnerability is difficult to tolerate, is it quickly transformed into anger, or if anger is difficult to tolerate, is it quickly transformed into guilt? Certain emotions are likely to be expressed with greater or lesser ease, even with therapeutic support, depending on whether they are culturally sanctioned and their contextual meaning. For example, anger may be particularly difficult to experience, let alone express, if it threatens social engagement. What is the affect on one's partner and what cultural lens does he or she need to adopt to understand the expression of a socially unacceptable emotion?

CULTURE AND ROMANTIC LOVE

Cultural norms seem to have a strong impact on the role of affection in the formation of marital bonds in some non-Western cultures. Chinese couples are viewed as having what Westerners might characterize as a relatively unromantic vision of love. In a study using focus groups, the words most often found accompanying remarks about love were *respect, mutual understanding,* and *support* (Shen, 1996). With respect to the process of mate choice, expressions of passion, of "sparks flying," or similar discussions were not present. Research by Pimentel (2000) showed similar findings with urban marital couples in China. The marital relationship was hardly the focus of romantic expectations. Marriage was considered universal and utilitarian, conducted for the purposes of having children and furthering the larger family group.

According to Yelsma and Athappilly (1988), in India, love marriages, as compared with arranged or companionate marriages, generally create turmoil at all points of the hierarchical, segmenting caste society, but they particularly affect members of the couple's household and kin groups, because love marriages breach caste and kinship principles. Chinese couples commonly avoid open communication, both positive and negative, following the Chinese emphases on implicit communication and the avoidance of open conflict in interpersonal relationships (Gao, Ting-Toomey, & Gudykunst, 1996). In Japan, direct communication is seen as problematic, especially in close relationships (Iwao, 1993). Putting feelings into words is a sign that they are not deep or sincere and that the listener's ability to infer feelings is limited (Clancy, 1986). It may also suggest that the relationship is not close. In Japan, expressions of appreciation can be seen as signs of interpersonal distance because the absence of verbalization signals appreciation (Iwao, 1993). Self-assertion brings with it the possibility of offending others and causes feelings of guilt in close relationships (Zane, Sue, Hu, & Kwon, 1991). In an intimate relationship in Japan, direct complaints signal the end of the relationship. Mind reading and avoiding self-assertion are ways in which partners assure one another of their closeness and commitment (Rothbaum, Pott, Azuma, Miyake, & Weisz, 2000). It thus becomes important to interpret emotional expression through the particular cultural lens with which people identify. The encouragement of direct expressions of love may signal conflict or distress to some people. Alternatively, it is important not to interpret an absence of strong expressions of love or affection as symbolic of a lack of love in a relationship. Finally, given that identity is such a strong motivator and forms the basis of relationships, the influence axis of interactions may be a stronger focus of the relationship.

In many instances in non-Western cultures, the marital relationship thus is typically a more pragmatic, institutional one rather than an emotionally charged, romantic one. This is reflected in emotional communication. Romantic passion and positive emotions such as love and joy, related to connection and empathy, appear to play a less central role in communication. Verbal and nonverbal communication in arranged marriages appears to be used more for matters of daily living than for emotional closeness or excitement. The Indian arranged marriage couples appear to settle their differences through verbal reasoning and problem solving (Yelsma & Athappilly, 1988). Less emphasis thus is placed on receiving positive emotional arousal from one's spouse. Israeli women value mutual support and understanding in marriage rather than emotional excitement. In Asian cultures, there appears to be less concern about arousal of the passions or attunement to emotions, especially related to intimacy in marriage; this may be in part because the role functions of husbands and wives related to intimate behavior are relatively stable (Yelsma & Athappilly, 1988).

There is some evidence, however, that the relative importance of emotional intimacy in relationships may be changing, especially as countries such as India and China continue to modernize and become influenced by Western culture. Couples increasingly approach marriage as a personal choice rather than a formal arrangement. A study by Friedman (2000) showed that in the mid-1990s in China, the growing popularity of an ideal of romantic love encouraged a widespread desire for conjugal intimacy among young men and women. With such changes, Eastern cultures will likely have to confront increased emotional arousal and expression related to intimacy in couples. Conflict may increase, and the probability of distress and divorce will as well (Epstein, Chen, & Beyder-Kamjou, 2005).

It seems, then, that culture influences the experience and expression of emotion in relationships such that the structure of values may alter the meaning of emotions across culture. As therapists, we must be sensitive to the particular meaning of certain emotions for partners and be careful and measured in when and how we encourage their expression. It also seems noteworthy that the direct expression of affection may signal different meanings across cultures. Again, we must be mindful in expecting or encouraging open displays of affection. Finally, given the importance of status and hierarchy in mate selection and the formation of relationships in non-Western cultures, we can speculate that the influence axis of interaction may be of primary importance in cross-cultural and intercultural relationships.

MARRIAGE AND IDENTITY IN DIFFERENT CULTURES

Cultural norms also have a strong impact on the nature of interactional cycles in the formation of martial unions in many non-Western cultures. Relationships seem to be somewhat predicated on issues that exist on the influence dimension of the relational axis. Marriage has occupied a privileged status as being one of the major validating relationships for adults in most societies. In many non-Western cultures, the basis of the formation of marital unions and the success of relationships often depends more on concerns related to status, identity, and power than to an attachment bond between partners based on caring and love. For example, when asked to consider what was the biggest hesitation in their decision to divorce, a number of women in a Singapore sample of women attending a counseling center reported that the potential loss of their roles and identities as mothers and wives was the most important factor in their hesitation (Tan Tzer, 1998). In this study, the women's identities, based on societal approval, acceptance, and even prestige accorded to the roles of wife and mother, were more important than many other aspects of their marriage. Most of the time, partners in functioning marital relationships more or less accept their position in the established hierarchy, and as long as their status is respected, there is no conflict.

Marital unions in India are largely built on concerns that fall on the influence axis. Decisions regarding mate choice, for example, are highly focused on status. In a comparison of Indian immigrants to the United States and their Indian counterparts in India, Siddizi and Reeves (1986) found that personal income, religion, and caste were significant in mate selection in India. According to a study by Yelsma and Athappilly (1988), attributes associated with marital satisfaction in India in arranged marriages were a sense of lifelong commitment and shared cultural tradition, whereas in companionate (love) marriages, the effectiveness of marital communication seemed to be the attribute most associated with marital satisfaction. Although romantic yearnings are indeed a muted narrative in marriages in India, and even though they find cultural expression in Bollywood cinema, popular music, and creative expression (Sonpar, 2005), marital unions are generally not primarily based on love. Security is provided, especially in more status-oriented marriages, but this is more a security provided by position and protection of position than by feelings of closeness and affection. Furthermore, when attachment and intimacy are at issue, these relate not just to one's partner but to the entire extended family and spread across intergenerational boundaries. A rupture of a bond in marriage therefore may not be simply between husband and wife but between wife and mother-in-law or other members of the extended family (Nath & Craig, 1999).

Similarly, according to a study by Shen (1996), Chinese people stress the importance of such factors as age, height, and status when choosing a mate. Both Chinese men and women agreed that men should be superior to women not only in schooling, occupation, and prestige but also in age and height. When asked about criteria for mate choice, Chinese men state that they hope that their future wives will be good at handling household matters, and women hope that their future husbands will be career minded. Men demanded that their future wives be "gentle and faithful," whereas women demanded that their future husbands be "resolute and steadfast."

When compared with U.S. couples, it was shown that Chinese couples held stronger standards supporting the exercise of power and/or control in the relationship. This included giving in to one's partner, trying to change the partner, and resisting control by the partner. Chinese couples also held stronger standards for sharing values. This was seen as reflective of a Chinese cultural emphasis on collectivist values, including harmony and devotion to the family (Epstein et al., 2005). Goodwin and Findlay (1997) examined cultural variations in love styles among British and Hong Kong Chinese student respondents. They found Chinese respondents to be more pragmatic (describing love in more logical and practical terms) and less erotic than British respondents. One of the authors and his wife, while traveling in China, met a 30-year-old female tour guide who espoused a strong commitment to "true love" but told them that she was being ostracized by family and friends for choosing to marry a calligrapher (who had the low status of a struggling artist) for true love and forsake another more established suitor who was a businessman and had money and status.

Studies have also shown that relationships in Japan emphasize loyalty and commitment and more pragmatic concerns over passion and intimacy (DeVos, 1985; Rothbaum et al., 2000). Research indicates that Asians, as compared with Americans, value companionable forms of love in which partners develop close, long-lasting friendships characterized by enduring commitment over romantic love (Dion & Dion, 1993). Although there is considerable emphasis on romance and love-based marriage initially, romance appears to be more of a premarital issue in Japan. A survey of 18- to 35-year-old Japanese women indicated that 63% of them want to marry on the basis of romantic love (Bando, 1992). After marriage and children, however, pragmatic concerns tend to override romantic ones, whereas U.S. partners continue to emphasize physical attraction and sexual intimacy (DeVos, 1985; Hendrick & Hendrick, 1986; Iwao, 1993). Pragmatic concerns for Japanese couples pertain to finances, work, and ingroup commitments and relate to community concerns; these all serve to link the couple to the wider social network. Romance is seen as fleeting and relying on it as glue for family cohesion is seen as undermining assurance (Iwao, 1993). Renewal is not a concern in Japanese marriages. In fact, Japanese obtain emotional intimacy in same-gender relationships more than do Americans. Because there is less reliance on marital partners to satisfy intimacy needs, it is relatively easier for them to meet each other's marital expectations and achieve harmony. It is the familiarity and ease of the relationship, not its novelty and passion, that sustain it (Iwao, 1993). Stability of marriage relates to complementarity in roles and the successful rearing of children (Iwao, 1993; Vogel, 1996).

There also is evidence that marriage in both urban and rural Africa is highly dependent on hierarchical structure, suggesting that marital unions are not based solely on love or an attachment bond. Amongst the Kel Ahaggar tribe in Saharan Africa, there is an elaborate set of rules designed to preserve the existing class structure dictating whom one can marry (Keenan, 1977). The ideology of male dominance is taken for granted as representative of the true state of affairs between men and women (Obbo, 1976). A study by Nwoye (2000) revealed that in contemporary Western and Eastern Africa, the themes in marital therapy, unlike most Western-based contemporary marital therapies, are grounded in a role-theory framework. The view guiding this is that obligations, expectations, and privileges are linked to the occupancy of social positions. Harmony and peace result when people occupying such positions perform their expected roles credibly, and disharmony and distress result when the opposite is the case. One form of African marriage therapy identifies the problem of marital discord as the inability of one or both partners in a distressed marriage to live up to the traditional marital role expectations of their position.

Mexican society is changing, and this is reflected in their views of modernity and the hierarchical structure within the marriage. Not so long ago in Mexican middle-class society, it was the accepted norm that women were subservient to their husbands, ready to satisfy their every whim and desire (McGinn, 1966). Hirsch (2003) revealed different findings in a study in which she interviewed both older and younger women regarding their attitudes toward marriage. For older women, marriage was not a union based on companionship, mutual affection, or gender equality. Older women defined clear gender roles, stating that they expected their husbands to define when they could leave the house, what they could wear, and when they would have sex. Their jobs were to cook, clean, run the household efficiently, raise the children, and provide sex for their husbands. Younger women stated very different expectations, however. They emphasized marriages based on mutual attraction, affection, and a more equitable division of labor and shared marital power, making statements such as, "From the beginning, I told him we were both in charge. . . . When the men give orders, they get really bossy with their wives" (Hirsch, 2003, p. 123).

In looking at the hierarchical structure of relationships in other cultures, one can clearly see that not all cultures explicitly value an egalitarian or love-based model as is more generally espoused in the West. And hierarchical structure appears to affect the manner in which couples resolve conflict. Many modern urban Indian couples have moved from the extended family setting to the nuclear one (Ramu, 1988). Research has shown, however, that traditional values and norms have been retained in perception and practice of marital role. In fact, husbands and wives reached a high degree of consensus about each other's roles: Husbands are viewed as the main bread-winners, and the wives are the homemakers. With regard to marital power, men retain the appearance of formal power to make critical decisions and to influence their wives. It seems, however, that men do closely consult their wives with respect to decisions and may be less authoritarian than before (Ramu, 1988). Young, unmarried women do learn through the socialization processes to avoid conflicts or to defer to men in conflict situations. Indian men are more control oriented and have more energy to engage in task inter-actions, instead of communicative interactions, than do women. Indian women also are more disposed to avoid or withdraw from conflict situations (Yelsma & Athappilly, 1988).

POWER, EQUALITY, AND MARITAL SATISFACTION

When the resource structure is asymmetrical, then, the control of the marital process lies in the hands of the powerful spouse. However, this does not lead to higher satisfaction for both members of the couple. In Western culture, equality and power sharing has been associated with marital satisfaction (Olsen & DeFrain, 1994; F. Rice, 1990), and women more often choose divorce over diminishment (Rampage, 2002). In India, as a consequence of women avoiding conflict and refraining from verbal and nonverbal aggression of self-interest, husbands in the arranged marriages develop higher marital satisfaction than do their wives (Yelsma & Athappilly, 1988). Rehman and Holtzworth-Munroe (2006) showed that Pakistani wives were significantly more likely to engage in unassertive demands than were American wives, whereas American wives were significantly more likely to use aggressive demands than were Pakistani wives. Pimentel (2000) showed, however, that in China, *egalitarian behaviors*—division of chores and decision making—and attitudes strongly affected marriage quality. Both urban Chinese men and women were happier in their marriages when they had an egalitarian outlook and shared household responsibilities and decision making. Hendrix (1997) examined predictors of marital satisfaction in preindustrial societies and showed that *role sharing*—the interchangeability of spouses in many tasks—was the most crucial factor in predicting marital quality. Similarly, a study of marriage in India showed that higher androgyny in sex role attitudes among couples was positively related to marital adjustment (Isaac & Shah, 2004).

Cultural factors are robust, and attitudes toward marriage seem to persist in part when people move and integrate into other cultures. In a study of couples in the United States in which the husband was Muslim of Middle Eastern descent and his wife was of European American or Asian American descent, the Arab men discussed their cultural expectation to be the provider and protector. Seeing their wives working and making significant contributions to their married lives was challenging for them. They also expected their wives to take more power in family decision making (Daneshpour, 2003). Goodwin and Cramer (2000) found that British South Asians integrated attitudes and values from their base culture (Hindu from Gujarat) with those of the majority populations. Thus, they maintained their collectivist values in the family but saw marriage as an expression of individual fulfillment. Individualist qualities of trust and friendship were valued. Singh and Kanjirathinkal (1999) found that Asian Indian immigrants to the United States placed a greater emphasis on the institutional aspect of their commitment than its more rational and emotional aspects. For the most part, the men in the study chose their spouse not through dating but through marriage bureaus; arrangements made by parents and relatives; and through "matrimonials" found in Indian newspapers that specify caste, ethnicity, and religion. They also found that women in the study tended to place a stronger emphasis on "marrying well," as they tend to view their marriage as an opportunity to move up in social status. They also pointed out that through marriage, Indians are accustomed to maintaining close ties with their extended families, which function as an important source of lifelong support. Satisfying relationships with extended family are seen as vital to the success of the marriage and nuclear family.

Conflict and Emotion

People in most social contexts resist being moved downward or diminished. The most characteristic reactive emotion to threats to status is anger; however, a person's culture often provides the outline of scripts for what is a threat to status and for how to handle conflict and competition. In male-dominant cultures, the privileges associated with male status and challenges to these are central in conflict. In India, although a movement is afoot to change it, dowry is an integral part of marriage. Dowry is a show of respect and entitlement claimed by the husband's family. Marriages can falter if rules of respect and entitlement are not followed. It is important to show subordination of the bride and her family to the husband and his family (Sonpar, 2005). We can thus assume, then, that in different cultural contexts, marital conflict involves conflict over rules and arrangements related to identity and self-esteem and not simply related to affectional attachment. Shame and fear of humiliation are key emotions; both partners will be attuned to preventing these, and much conflict will result from their activation. EFT-C therapists, then, need to notice, be attuned to, and work with these emotions.

In many couples, what also is important is how other people see themselves and their partners relating on the identity–influence dimension. Status in most societies is expressed by ideas of respect and even honor, and this involves not just maintaining one's own respect but also upholding a cultural view of what will maintain the respect of one's family or friends. This goal of being respected in society and being seen as being respected by one's partner is very important for some couples in some cultures. The perception of what earns respect is dependent on the particular cultural model of marriage. In Western culture, under the influence of the feminist era, how the woman is seen is very important to some couples, and feminism has been one of the most influential factors in the redefinition of marriage in the 20th century (Rampage, 2002). Often, one or both partners are very concerned that they be seen as being in an egalitarian relationship. Being seen that way can be as important as being that way.

Parental Approval and Marriage

In looking to determine what accounts for success in marriage in other cultures, particularly in the East, one needs to take account of the entire extended family as a unit, rather than focus on the couple in isolation. Satisfaction in marriage is clearly more dependent on parental and family approval than it is in the West. In India, one's partner is usually searched for and recommended by his or her parents (Yelsma & Athappilly, 1988). When a couple marries in India, authority and autonomy for the couple is not assured. Although the couple is expected to form a union and produce children, they also are expected to remain obedient to the older generation. Authority remains with their parents. A situation of reciprocity exists wherein obedience, respect, and deference are met with protection and guidance. Problems arise when reciprocity is not maintained or when those at subordinate levels seek greater autonomy (Sonpar, 2005). In Kinshasa, Zaire (now Congo), Africa, paternal authority is highly determinant of who one marries (Tambashe & Shapiro, 1996). Parents in China continue to powerfully affect their children's marriage (Pimentel, 2000). Completely arranged marriages now are increasingly rare in urban areas anywhere in the world, but many marriage decisions are still strongly influenced by parental input, either by parents providing potential partners to their children for their veto, or vice versa. Parental approval of the marriage is strongly associated with higher closeness and lower disharmony. One's own parents are particularly important, although in-law approval is also associated with higher marriage quality, except for women's marital closeness.

This review thus highlights that therapists need to explore cultural assumptions about marriage to better understand on which interactional dimension, affiliation or influence, and around which core concern, attachment or identity, conflict is most likely to arise. Although this may be shifting ground, it seems that marital unions in non-Western cultures are often formed on the basis of concerns about identity, and these values persist to some extent even when people begin to integrate into Western culture. When considering what expectations couples have and what goals they may strive toward, one must take into account existing hierarchical structure as well as the extended family system. It seems clear that identity and status are strong motivators in non-Western cultures, suggesting that interactional cycles on the influence axis often may be important for intercultural and multicultural couples. The EFT-C therapist must be aware of this and able to focus the therapy dialogue accordingly. In the sections that follow, we cover some of the factors that need to be considered in working cross-culturally.

Treatment of Multicultural, Interracial, and Bicultural Couples: The Relationships Among Role, Power, and Emotion

In the treatment of multiracial and bicultural couples in the West, one must take note of differences in issues that arise and modify or amend treatment accordingly. Issues of role, status, and power and extended family may be more prevalent for one member than another. It is becoming increasingly more common for interracial or bicultural couples (V. Thomas, Karis, & Wetchler, 2003) to seek therapy, and it is important that therapists be prepared with the necessary knowledge and skills to deal with such issues.

It is essential that therapists who work with multicultural or bicultural couples also explore and examine their own attitudes and beliefs about these relationships (Daneshpour, 2003; Tubbs & Rosenblatt, 2003) and not assume that problems are due to differences in cultural or religious values (Daneshpour, 2003). McRoy and Freeman (1986) suggested that biases are often evident when counselors or therapists either overemphasize a client's racial background or deny that race is an issue. The therapeutic cornerstones of objective and nonjudgmental attitudes must be present. It is also important for the therapist who works with multicultural interracial couples to be aware of cultural and experiential differences that clients bring to the therapy experience. These may include sociopolitical forces that have influenced the couple and language barriers that may affect the therapeutic relationship (Locke, 1992; Sue & Sue, 1990).

The general discussion and exploration of issues that arise in biracial or multicultural relationships is difficult because one must always consider the cultures involved as well as degrees of acculturation and whether one or both members are immigrants or born into the dominant culture. International marriages may be more fraught with difference than biracial marriages where both partners were raised in the same country. Ibrahim and Schroeder (1990) suggested that an assessment be conducted to help the therapist understand each partner's worldview and cultural identity. In treating multicultural and bicultural couples, it might be beneficial for therapists to assess couples' levels of acculturation and to investigate the motivations that drew them to one another. How much does each partner identify with his or her particular culture and its rituals, customs, and practices? It might also be helpful to explore perceptions of support from family and friends (Usita & Poulsen,

2003; Wieling, 2003), as they can have a strong effect on satisfaction and well-being. It would also be worthwhile to consider how much relationship distress is related to cultural racism of the larger, dominant society and their own cultural group.

When working with bicultural couples, one must consider differences in expression of emotion and communication, particularly language difficulties or metacommunication, expression of physical affection, beliefs of partners regarding roles, power distribution, cultural influences on the family structure, and the meaning of love (Okun, 1996). Differences between partners may arise with respect to these issues as well as differences in values, personality, family upbringing, family role expectations, and religion and related activities (Carr et al., 2006). Some of these issues and the EFT-C approach to them in biracial couples are addressed below.

Emotional Expression and Communication

As mentioned, cultural differences exist in patterns of emotional expression and communication, and this may represent a clash for the bicultural couple, particularly if one member previously lived in a different place. Some cultures value verbal communication; some value rational, dramatic, or expressive forms of communication. Conflict may be handled differently in different cultures, and this may depend again on power structure. In some cultures, conflict is handled physically, whereas in others, it is handled through withdrawal, teasing, direct confrontation, or indirect responses. Attitudes toward intimacy and dependence may vary and range from fearful and withholding to assertive and demanding. Cultural rules may dictate how partners express love and can be cause for conflict if expressions are misunderstood or misinterpreted. There also may be different attitudes and customs in dealing with grief and sadness. Some cultures value stoicism, others value expressive mourning, and still others are more celebratory of life in response to death. We see an example of cultural differences emerge when Grace, of Jamaican origin, and Billy visit his North American, Midwestern family.

Grace and Billy were going home to Billy's house for Thanksgiving. Grace always approached these events with a mixture of excitement, joy, sadness, and despair. She missed her parents, who had gone back to live in their home country of Jamaica. She liked Billy's family, his sisters, brothers, nieces, and nephews. He had told her many times how much his family liked her, but she never felt that way when she was there. She always felt somewhat put off by their Midwestern icy "friendliness." They said nice things when she and Billy arrived and asked all sorts of questions, but they never hugged them. Family members were very complimentary of Billy's parents' cooking and thanked them profusely. But in fact, no one in his family ever hugged. They all just shook hands or patted each other on the back. She always left feeling kind of cold and alienated after spending a day there. She needed to be reminded that Billy's family liked her and even that Billy loved her. Then she would get to wondering how she ended up with Billy. She would begin to withdraw. There would usually be a fight on the way home.

The EFT-C therapist would work to help the couple explore how each partner experiences and expresses love in the relationship. Such an exploration would include a discussion about how love was expressed and experienced in their respective families of origin and how they came to feel loved. Differences in expression and style would be explored. Grace would need Billy to reassure her of both his and his family's love for her and how he expressed it.

Attitudes Toward Extended Family

Bicultural and multiracial couples in general may have different approaches toward extended family. In general, Caucasian North American culture is relatively individualistic. Children will often move out of the house at college age and seek to live independently. Parents may no longer exhibit as great an influence on their choices. In other words, children are less dependent on parental approval for their identity formation. This may be different for non-Western people, however. They may remain close with their extended kin and seek both contact and approval. For the Western member of the couple, this may be unusual or uncomfortable and pose a challenge. He or she may feel it necessary to create stronger boundaries to prevent feelings of intrusion. This in turn might put his or her partner in a difficult position, feeling divided loyalty and not wanting to betray either their spouse or their family.

Raising Biracial Children

Racism can also be difficult, particularly when White partners in biracial couples see their children become victims of it. Brown (1987) reported that many people in interracial marriages experience conflicting feelings regarding themselves and their families, feelings that need to be addressed. These might include conflicting feelings toward family members and racial groups, guilt over conflicts faced by the biracial children, hostility and rejection of the biracial children, and guilt for the "transgression" of marrying outside one's own race. Although grief issues may not be specific to interracial couples (see chap. 11, "Sadness in Couples Therapy"), specific grief issues may arise that stem from racial issues. At any given point, one or both partners may deal with grief over the effects of racism on self, partner, child, or others. In addition, identity loss stemming from the interracial relationship as well as loss of family support may be issues in the relationship. From an EFT-C perspective, it is important for the therapist to acknowledge and validate grief, particularly in a culture that assumes that people can and should quickly recover from grief (Tubbs & Rosenblatt, 2003). It is important to acknowledge that for many people, grief will repeatedly return (Rosenblatt, 1996). It may be beneficial to help people symbolize their loss; this will in turn help their partners to witness it and validate its existence. Partners may need help to respect each other's need to grieve and accept differences in the need to grieve. Finally, in therapy, partners can be helped to soothe each other's grief.

Gender Role Expectations

An issue that is more common in bicultural and/or interracial couples than in other couples is differences in gender role expectations (Carr et al., 2006). Although feminist models have changed the thinking of both men and women in the West so that neither tends to have strong expectations that the other fulfill traditional gender roles, this may not be the case in non-Western cultures. Furthermore, these expectations may be implicit even for the spouse with the higher expectation, in part because he or she is attempting to fit into the prevailing culture. Thus, a South Asian or Latino man may expect his wife to cook dinner every night and be disappointed when this does not occur. Or he may expect her to play a hostess role in relation to his family or work colleagues. Of course, when feelings of disappointment or rejection arise, especially when unsymbolized, conflict is not far behind.

Cultural Customs

Other common differences in bicultural couples that potentially create problems are related to practices around food and dress. Thus, couples may have different eating habits and wish for their partners to partake or be interested in their culinary choices. Feeling they need to hide or not eat what they wish out of respect for their partner can create resentment. Another issue that may potentially create problems is choices related to dress. In particular, male partners from more restrictive cultures, for example, South Asian cultures in which Hindu and Muslim religious practices prevail, may find it difficult when their spouses dress in a manner that they consider provocative or overly revealing. If they choose to deal with their discomfort in a manner that is perceived as controlling, debasing, or humiliating to their partner, intense conflict might arise.

Below is an example of a fight that might occur between a bicultural White–South Asian couple dealing with the issue of customs. Melanie and Desh are getting ready to go out to a party. Desh waits anxiously downstairs, unsure whom he will meet at the party this evening. He wonders whether there will be anyone with whom he can talk. He finds these parties difficult. He knows he is pretty silent and feels uncomfortable about it. So far in the year that he has been in Canada, he has not found one party enjoyable. Melanie appears on the bottom of the stairs wearing a low-cut top. He cannot believe it. He is mortified. How can he be seen with her? And after she refused him for sex last night! He starts in.

Desh: You are going out wearing that?

Melanie: Yeah, what's wrong with it?

Desh:	Well, for one thing your top is very low cut. I can see everything.
Melanie:	What are you talking about? I love this top. I think I look nice.
Desh:	Yeah, well if you want to go out looking like that then you can go out by yourself.
Melanie:	Fine, I will. See you later.
Desh:	You look like a slut. You want to go out showing your tits to half the world, but you don't even want to have sex with your husband.
Melanie:	Yeah, go to hell. [*Leaves the house, slamming the door.*]

In EFT-C Melanie would be encouraged to tell Desh how she feels (e.g., criticized, put down, ashamed) when he comments on her body and dress in such a manner. She would also be encouraged to stand up to Desh in a firm but noncontemptuous manner so that he may know that it is alright to dress how she pleases. Desh, however, would be encouraged to move beyond his secondary anger and express feelings of disappointment and embarrassment that he may feel when he goes out with her when she is dressed in such a manner. He would be encouraged to share in a nonthreatening, nonimposing manner how her style would be seen in his culture and consequently how it makes him feel. He would also be encouraged to share feelings of sexual rejection. Finally, therapy would explore his feelings of homesickness. In keeping with the EFT-C model, he would be encouraged to explore intense pain and sadness that he may have and how this leads to him being detached and emotionally unavailable. Melanie would be encouraged to listen to his pain and to try to help soothe him through it.

Homesickness

When one partner is an immigrant, bicultural issues may be complicated by a complex overlay of strong needs to adapt and assimilate into the dominant culture. This is particularly true in the case of bicultural couples. For the immigrant partner, the need to adapt and be a part of the existing culture may be very intense. This can complicate emotional issues between the couple. For example, the immigrant's partner may value their partner's base culture and wish to celebrate holidays or take part in religious rituals, whereas the immigrant partner may want to assimilate and therefore not make this a focus. For immigrant partners, assimilation into, and acceptance by, the dominant culture is of primary importance. This is particularly true for new immigrants who feel a need to (at least temporarily) disavow the cultural values and practices from which they come and all emotional issues attached to it. This can, in turn, be confusing and disappointing for their partners, who are attracted to and interested in celebrating their partners' diversity.

At the core of such issues may be homesickness. Immigrant partners may miss home intensely and feel they have no way of soothing that pain. Those people who have difficulty regulating emotions may attempt to avoid or squelch the pain, and this will have negative repercussions in their relationships. Such emotions often get expressed in maladaptive ways, for example, through anger. The motivation to avoid the pain of homesickness is to avoid entering a bottomless abyss. This can be particularly difficult for men from cultures such as Latino, South Asian, or Asian cultures where it is even less permissible for men to feel or express vulnerable emotions. Their partners may be craving and wishing, however, that they reveal these more intimate emotions as they desire to be closer, and they nevertheless feel their effects, only in negative terms. Alternatively, the immigrant partner may be painfully aware of homesick feelings and not be able to focus on the present or their relationship. This can be difficult for partners who again wish for closeness or intimacy from their partner and feel only a distant wall. This can again be further complicated when partners attempt to deal with their partner's pain with denial in the hope that not focusing on it will make it disappear. The homesick partner may only feel further invalidated by such attempts.

Respect for Authority

A general respect for authority can be a more pervasive attitude in non-Western cultures, and differences can create conflict between partners (Carr et al., 2006). This might pose conflict within the couple, where the person with greater respect for authority becomes uncomfortable when they perceive their partner not being respectful. Emotional difficulties may arise if one partner is critical of the other partner in this regard. Criticism usually emerges out of anxiety that gets created out of what is seen as a bucking of authority. The nature of such conflicts are understood as specific to the bicultural context but still conceptualized in terms of the EFT-C model. If one member is critical and blaming, this is seen as either a struggle for dominance or secondary anger and blame that prevents the expression of more primary vulnerable emotions and needs. The goal will be to encourage the couple to express primary vulnerable emotions to one another, thus beginning a more healing cycle.

What does seem clear from the study and exploration of issues with multicultural and multiracial couples is that issues of respect and identity may be very important. Thus, respect for, sharing of, and even celebration of, differences in identity are necessary, and breakdowns and conflict may arise when this does not occur. In general, the exploration of underlying emotions related to issues such as shame, sadness, and pride seems to be helpful, although this may be mitigated once again by cultural norms regarding emotional expression. So, for example, display rules may be different regarding showing emotion to the other (Safdar, 2006), even the intimate other. In addition, it may be less sanctioned, particularly for men, to express vulnerability or turn to one's partner for help. The therapist then needs to understand, respect, and work with each individual's rules and norms related to emotional expression rather than expecting that he or she express emotion in the same manner. An explicit discussion of differences in emotional expression may be helpful in practicing EFT-C with such couples. At other times, the therapist may need to proceed more slowly (and respectfully) with those who have difficulty or strong internalized cultural mores surrounding emotional experiencing and expression.

GENDER

Gender is another contextual issue important in EFT-C. Certain emotions may be more difficult to process as a function of gender. Many men experience themselves as failing to live up to masculine gender stereotypes. Whether it be internalized demands for toughness, competitiveness, or sexual performance, the gap between the ideal masculine self and the real masculine self is a potent shame generator. Men are reluctant to seek help on their own and often only go into therapy when they are pressured by their partner, because they are afraid of their shortfalls and their sense of shame. Often, this is not in awareness. Men think that showing their weaknesses will lead to being put down, humiliated, or taken advantage of, which is why men are less likely to open up to their female partners.

Traditional masculine subculture disinclines men from normalizing and detoxifying shameful experiences through talking and connecting with others. Instead, it tends to reward and promote action, compulsive behavior, drinking, fighting, and the like. Denied shame often leads to problems such as substance abuse, rage, and sexual acting out. As opposed to normal feelings of shame that do not threaten identity, internalized shame from abuse or powerlessness can make some men prone to violence within marriage, especially when coupled with male socialization patterns related to power. Rage, however, is a defensive action caused by shame, and substance abuse in these men is a maladaptive way of coping with shame.

In this view, as a result of developmental and socialization pressures, many men remain extremely reactive to shame experiences. A father's rejection, lack of warmth, and physical and verbal abuse, as well as a mother's rejection, can lead to intense shame experiences for boys. According to Dutton (1995), "a cold, absent, intermittently abusive and shaming father produces a boy with a weak sense of identity. This is a climate that seems to destroy the soul, a climate wherein the central message is the unworthiness of the self" (p. 84).

Rather than being able to tolerate shame states, men are likely to react with avoidance, compensatory behaviors, primitive fight–flight responses, and rage (Bierman, 1997). Rage is a response to an attack on the self, a response to shaming. Shame or the possibility of shame challenges a man's sense of security of self. As a result, shame states remain unintegrated and threaten the integrity of the masculine self. Vulnerable and needful feelings are minimized and disallowed, hidden behind a cool pose. In a more extreme form, when shame is reactivated in conflict situations and cannot be tolerated, rage and sometimes accompanying secondary violent, abusive behaviors result. The use of contempt (projection of shame onto the other) as well as the shame–rage–guilt cycle represents externalization strategies favored by men.

Men have consistently been found to have a propensity toward externalization and objectification (Cicchetti & Toth, 1991). Both strategies serve to protect the vulnerable self by shifting the focus from the self to either its activities and accomplishments or its objectified or externalized appearance. Lewis (1971) first identified the bypassed shame affect. *Bypassed* means that affect is isolated and dissociated from experience in an effort to manage the shame experience. From an emotion-focused perspective, *bypassed* means that primary shame is bypassed in favor of secondary emotion such as rage. In this case, the affective component of shame is reduced to a twinge and the cognitive component is amplified. The self is objectified and seen from the perspective of the other; self-consciousness is extreme and takes the form of "How am I doing?" or "How do I look?" Bypassing shame in this manner protects the self from being overwhelmed by it. In Western culture, men are less likely than women to experience and report overt shame but are more likely to objectify themselves and project critical qualities onto the other (Krugman, 1995).

There are a number of factors seen as making it more difficult for men to integrate and tolerate shame. In Western culture, men are expected to dissociate the comfortable association and identification with the nurturant mother at perhaps a premature age and stake out autonomy and physical independence quickly. This suggests that in early experiences, men are shamed for having "soft" feelings, such as sadness, fear, vulnerability, and seeking soothing for such feelings. Thus, it is still the case that when boys are hurt, they are discouraged from "running to Mommy" and encouraged to "take it like a man." Masculine ideology in this culture thereby overemphasizes autonomy at expense of relatedness and connection (Krugman, 1995).

Extrapolating from population studies of child maltreatment and familial alcoholism, Real (1997) estimated that upwards of 20% of boys grow up in a family in which physical violence, sexual abuse, or alcoholism are present. In families in which caretakers are a source of shame through either physical or sexual abuse or through neglect or disdain, boys withdraw emotionally and learn to protect themselves by disallowing true feelings.

Conflict between parents profoundly affects boys' development of a shame-based identity. For example, when mothers are humiliated by fathers, boys frequently feel confused and unsure with whom to identify. Consciously, boys may identify with the humiliated mother and fantasize heroic protection of her while feeling ashamed of their helplessness to rescue her. Alternatively, he may identify with his aggressor father while feeling ashamed of abandoning mother. Additionally, high-conflict families who are unable to process primary emotions may use countershame or shaming of the other in lieu of conflict resolution, thus resorting to secondary anger and sometimes violence as a way of tolerating unpleasant painful feelings.

The loss of the father through death, divorce, or emotional unavailability also seems to leave boys with more vulnerable senses of self and thus prone to a shame-based identity. The absence of a positive male object of identification sensitizes his attachment to his mother and his own insufficient sense of masculinity. Identification with a failed or vulnerable father may leave the boy ashamed of both his father and himself. In the case of a divorce, when the ex-husband is maligned and the boy identifies with the discredited ex-husband, awareness of vulnerability gets translated into aggressiveness toward women.

In a normative environment, fathers sometimes shame sons in the course of teaching them "manliness." All too familiar is the situation in which a small boy who has hurt himself seeks comfort from his parents. His father minimizes the injury, and his mother nurtures. This dynamic may leave the boy feeling not only small and ashamed of his neediness but also infantile, particularly in front of his father, because of his mother's acceptance.

The typical expectation that men be prepared for the possibility of aggressive encounters means that fear and anxiety are often not symbolized, as they require vulnerability, and as such, these emotions are replaced with secondary shame. By contrast, for women, the need for connection and belonging requires a more flexible, tolerant stance in relation to the experience of shame in everyday life so that vulnerable states are more easily symbolized and thus integrated into the self.

Boys' fears of self-disclosure and one's secrets of shameful inferiorities, doubts, insecurities and fears breed social and emotional isolation. Normative doubts become painful secrets. Typically, men are doers and problem solvers, not talkers. Women's greater sociability, however, leads to a readiness to put feelings into words, thereby making shame integration more likely. Men, lacking experience in speaking of their vulnerabilities and shame, are much less likely to find ways of integrating shame-producing experiences, except in relation to women, who then become privy to their vulnerabilities. This in turn may be perceived as threatening to their well-being.

Men, therefore, are very likely concerned with their identities and will often be involved in influencing interactions to confirm their identities. They will show anger and be dominant rather than disclose more vulnerable feelings of shame and fear. They often may be more concerned with status and fear diminishment and loss of control and thus may be quite sensitive to identity threats. Thus, in the context of the interactional cycles, they are more likely to be dominant on the influence dimension. In addition, because they also fear dependence, they are more likely to be distancing on the affiliation dimension.

LESBIAN AND GAY RELATIONSHIPS

Common presenting problems for gay men and lesbians include, among others, separation versus connection, power equality versus complementarity, and permanent versus temporary relationships (Okun, 1996). These topics as well as emotion are touched on in the sections that follow, and it is suggested that readers consult a growing literature on what therapists need to know in working with lesbian and gay couples.

Attachment and Power

Lesbian and gay couples do not differ from heterosexual couples in that issues relating both to intimacy and to power arise; however, these need to be understood in the context of homophobia and heterosexism (Okun, 1996). It may be beneficial to clinicians treating same-sex couples to expose themselves to proposed stage models of homosexual couples development (Green & Clunis, 1989; Okun, 1996) to understand how the context of issues may differ from those of heterosexual couples. Because gay men, lesbians, and heterosexual people alike are all socialized in the same "heterosexual culture," all are prone to overlay stereotyped gender roles on same-sex couples. Heterosexist assumptions are inaccurate and potentially damaging when applied to same-sex couples. Some gay men may be more masculine identified in self-concept, whereas others may identify more with being feminine; others may be more androgynous. Similarly, some lesbians may be feminine identified; some, masculine identified. Some gay men and lesbians are flexible in their expression of gender-identified behaviors and scripts.

A frequently mentioned characteristic of lesbian relationships is that of strong closeness and connectedness, particularly early in the relationship. The female path of development is thought to be based more on a relational trajectory than is the male path, as girls are socialized to be more empathic and nurturing, with more permeable ego boundaries (Gilligan, 1982; J. B. Miller, 1976). The emotional intensity of female–female relationships is said to be stronger than gay male relationships (Okun, 1996) and sometimes than heterosexual relationships. Pearlman (1989) pointed out that "relationship merger" may be more prolonged in lesbian relationships. This is often attributed to attunement and emotional connectedness in relationships between women. Lesbian couples tend to be quicker at moving in together. This may also serve as an event to solidify their couples relationship. All of this may be helped by an intense type of high-energy romantic love that is all-absorbing.

At this point, of course, couples are not likely to present themselves for therapy. In general, however, fused or merged relationships are pathologized in psychological theory. In keeping with the EFT-C perspective that makes it a goal to create and maintain bonds as an antidote to conflict and problems, this sort of closeness should not be pathologized but rather should be understood. Merger exists at the beginning of any relationship: gay, lesbian, and heterosexual alike. It is typical to idealize partners, avoid disagreements, or feel bereft away from the relationship.

Fusion or merger can be problematic if gay and lesbian couples isolate themselves from family and friends in the early stages of the relationship. Later on, when ready to individuate, they miss a social support system, particularly if a larger family system or community support network is absent or thin. Overall, merger can pose difficulties when needs for independence and autonomy create conflict and the relationship cannot flex to allow them. It then becomes essential that the therapist explore how a merged choice developed for the couple and whether it is still preferred or whether it has become part of a rigid attachment or identity concern and then to discuss with the couple relationship models that include interdependence and individuation. This means healthy separateness and togetherness wherein both partners are comfortable and able to express basic needs without reprisal. This may mean reassuring one or both partners that separateness does not indicate that the relationship is flawed or a failure. This may also mean confronting fears of aloneness and isolation that arise when separated. It may also mean coaching one or both partners toward self-soothing when the other is absent and the partner feels abandoned and alone.

Identity-validation is also crucial in gay and lesbian relationships. Given that the partners often feel invalidated by society at large and often from family and even friends, partner validation is crucial. In addition, validation of identity as "butch" or "femme" or as the more masculine or feminine partner is crucial, as this is a very important aspect of each partner's identity and is not specified by sex. Having struggled often against family and social pressure to develop a gender identity, partners are very sensitive to its invalidation. Thus the type of birthday gift one partner gives the other, for example, can be a symbol not only of love but also of validation of identity.

There is a strong norm of equality in lesbian relationships, particularly around household tasks, finances, and decision making (Searight, 1997), and this may be in part why, when compared with gay men, lesbians tend to report higher levels of relationship satisfaction. Men are typically socialized to be aggressive, independent, and unemotional. This can make relationships difficult for gay men in that emotional intimacy is the essential glue that holds them together. Typically, women are the primary relationship caretakers. Men may have to work harder to relinquish stereotypical masculine roles and develop emotional communication skills. For example, they may find it particularly challenging to be vulnerable, accept weakness, or admit needs. The EFT-C therapist may have to work hard with the gay couple to establish emotional intimacy.

Gay male couples may experience power struggles within the sexual arena of their relationship. Men are typically more likely to take a more active and able role in sex. Men may expect high performance from themselves and their partners, and this can be a source of feelings of inadequacy if sexual desire or performance does not meet their own standards. This can further trigger feelings of insecurity with respect to masculinity. Intense and competitive power struggles can ensue (George & Behrendt, 1987). Such conflicts thus may belie identity struggles. EFT-C therapists will focus on underlying feelings of shame and inadequacy that may have originated in earlier relationships and may need to work with partners to heal underlying wounds.

Emotion in Lesbian and Gay Relationships

Jealousy and envy may be more likely to arise in lesbian and gay relationships and indicate distance regulation problems (Okun, 1996). One partner may feel threatened by the other's earlier or current relationships. Heterosexual relationships may also trigger feelings of jealousy that could indicate internalized homophobia and feelings of inadequacy and a sense of not belonging. Here, the EFT-C therapist will help couples understand and normalize jealousy as natural. Therapists can encourage partners to refrain from acting on jealous feelings with controlling behavior. If accurate, they may connect jealousy and envy with earlier experiences of abandonment and engulfment in significant relationships. They will help jealous partners with self-soothing in the face of threat, and they will help their partners to offer reassurance when necessary. Identity-validation may be a greater issue in lesbian and gay relationships, and shame may be more prevalent, particularly if people have developed shame around their identities. This can be the result of societal and familial disapproval, leading to internalized homophobia. Whatever the cause, it can emerge more readily in the relationship and become a focus of therapy.

Permanent Versus Temporary

An issue that is more common for gay and lesbian relationships pertains to commitment. In fact, Berzon (1988) referred to the gay and lesbian national anthem as "Why don't we just break up?" Too often, gay men and lesbians accept dissolution as a resolution to relationship problems. This is attributed to heterosexist socialization and internalized homophobia (Okun, 1996) and a lack of support from society in general. Therapists need to be aware of such issues and encourage couples to question heterosexist assumptions of relationships such as the implicit expectation of failure. Couples must learn that it is acceptable to disagree without breaking up as a solution. It is possible to experience anger and conflict and stay connected (Okun, 1996).

Given the isolation and aloneness that gay men and lesbians may have experienced in being marginalized, one could imagine that the threat of the dissolution of an attachment may be very distressing. However, given the identity-invalidation they likely experienced by certain factions of society, partners may be highly sensitive to identity threats.

CONCLUSION

The nature of pair bonding is different in different cultures. Rules related to emotional experience and expression vary across culture, and the EFT-C therapist must adjust for this in practice—expressions of anger, sadness, fear, and shame and direct expressions of affection are more or less dangerous in different cultures and different marriages. Within non-Western, nonurban relationships, status, power, and identity issues may be more central, and identity concerns may be more central in conflict than attachment. Identity concerns also can potentially be a source of conflict in intercultural relationships and will need to be specifically addressed in therapy. The influence dimension of the interaction may be of higher importance and in need of greater focus in non-Western relationships. Finally, the EFT-C therapist will likely have more success in therapy with multicultural and gay and lesbian couples if he or she is aware of the different significance of some attachment and identity issues that may arise. The EFT-C therapist needs to be sensitized to, and prepared to work with, the different concerns raised by different cultural groups. Because in dealing with emotion, therapists are touching the deepest, often tacit, and most culturally embedded aspect of people's inner world, great sensitivity needs to be shown to the different cultural rules and meanings given to different emotions and their expression. Couples also are helped by making their assumptions around attachment and identify concerns more explicit and understanding how these affect their relationships, especially as cultures begin to assimilate some, but not other, aspects of their differences.

II

COUPLES THERAPY: AN EMOTION-FOCUSED PERSPECTIVE

7

INTERVENTION FRAMEWORK

All emotions are pure which gather you and lift you up; that emotion is
impure which seizes only one side of your being and so distorts you.
——Rilke (1934/2004, p. 56)

Emotion-focused couples therapy (EFT-C) concentrates on problems
in the emotional bond between the partners in a couple. This bond is constituted by each partner's emotional experience, by the calm or sadness and
fears from attachment longings and needs, by the esteem or the shame and
fear from lack of validation and confirmation of identities, and by the joy
and liking of attraction. EFT-C strives to uncover how each partner reacts
emotionally to relational events causing negative interactional patterns. These
negative patterns are seen as being created by the partners' expressions of
secondary emotions, often anger, that obscure their primary, often more vulnerable, emotions and needs, such as their basic attachment fears and needs
and their shame at, or fear of, diminishment and invalidation. The fractured
emotional bond is healed by transforming the negative interactional cycles
that dominate the couple's interaction by expressing underlying primary at-
tachment- and identity-related emotions. The essential goal of EFT-C thus
is the creation of new, healthy patterns of interaction by using emotion to
restructure interactions. The following are the original nine steps of treatment of EFT-C laid out by Greenberg and Johnson (1986b, 1988) to promote this change process.

Original Steps of Treatment

1. Delineate the issues presented by the couple and assess how these issues express core conflicts in the areas of separateness–connectedness and dependence–independence.
2. Identify the negative interaction cycle.
3. Access unacknowledged feelings underlying interactional positions.
4. Redefine the problem or problems in terms of the underlying feelings.
5. Promote identification with disowned needs and aspects of self.
6. Promote acceptance by each partner of the other partner's experience.
7. Facilitate the expression of needs and wants to restructure the interaction.
8. Establish the emergence of new solutions.
9. Consolidate new positions.

These steps have been discussed extensively (Johnson, 1996; Johnson et al., 2005; Johnson & Greenberg, 1988) and were subsequently organized by Johnson (1996) into three stages of a negative cycle: de-escalation, restructuring the negative interaction, and consolidation and integration We present here an expanded 5-stage framework with 14 steps that explicitly spells out the process. This expansion includes more steps that focus on self-processes than in the original framework. These additional steps serve to integrate more work on each individual's emotional process, to promote self-change with the work on changing interactions that was more of the focus in the original framework. The five stages are validation and alliance formation, negative cycle de-escalation, accessing underlying feelings, restructuring the negative interaction, and consolidation and integration.

THE FIVE-STAGE FRAMEWORK

Although the stages that follow are described as though they occur in sequence, it is best to think of the stages as overlapping phases. In addition, therapy moves back and forth between stages, and many stages, such as the validation and alliance formation stage, are relevant throughout treatment.

Stage 1: Validation and Alliance Formation

The first stage emphasizes the creation of safety and the development of a collaborative alliance. It involves the following steps:

1. Empathize with and validate each partner's position and underlying pain.
2. Delineate conflict issues. Assess how these issues reflect core problems in the areas of connectedness and identity.

Stage 2: Negative Cycle De-Escalation

The second stage emphasizes reducing the emotional reactivity between the partners and involves the following steps:

3. Identify the negative interaction cycle and each partner's position in that cycle, and externalize the problem as the cycle.
4. Identify the unacknowledged attachment- and/or identity-related emotions underlying the interactional positions.
5. Identify each partner's sensitivities and vulnerabilities and their historical origins to help broaden the understanding of the negative interactional cycle.
6. Reframe the problem in terms of underlying more vulnerable feelings related to unmet attachment and identity needs.

Stage 3: Accessing Underlying Feelings

This stage emphasizes the actual experiencing and revealing of the underlying emotions. The following steps embody the core of the emotion-focused work:

7. Access unacknowledged feelings and needs underlying interactional positions and reveal them to the partner:
   - Blamer expresses fear, sadness, or loneliness.
   - Distancer expresses anxiety or anger.
   - Dominant expresses shame, fear, or anger.
   - Submitter expresses anger, boundaries, or fear.
8. Identify and overcome intrapsychic blocks to accessing and revealing emotions.
9. Promote identification with disowned needs or aspects of self, integrating these into relationship interactions.

Stage 4: Restructuring the Negative Interaction

This stage emphasizes the enactment of new ways of being with each other, with Steps 10 and 11 embodying the core of the interaction-focused work and Step 12 again emphasizing the self:

10. Promote acceptance of the other partner's experience and aspects of self.

11. Facilitate the expression of feelings, needs, and wants, to create genuine emotional engagement, and restructure the interaction by
    - softening the blamer,
    - distancer reengagement,
    - dominant going one down (de-escalating), and
    - submitter asserting.
12. Promote self-soothing and transformation of maladaptive emotion schemes in each partner, to facilitate self-change and more enduring couples change.

Stage 5: Consolidation and Integration

In this final stage, both interactional change and new narratives are supported; the following steps embody the behavioral and narrative focused work:

13. Facilitate the emergence of new interactions and solutions to problematic interactions and/or issues.
14. Consolidate new positions and new narratives.

THE NEW STEPS

This 14-step manual expands some of the original steps and adds some key self-focused processes to the original framework, in which only the original Step 5, owning disowned feelings and needs, was focused solely on the self. Step 5 in the new framework now focuses explicitly on identifying each partner's sensitivities and developing an understanding of some of the family of origin or psychogenetic determinants of each person's attachment or identity concerns that make the partner sensitive to particular interactional triggers. Steps 4 and 7, which focus, respectively, on identifying and on accessing unacknowledged feeling and needs now emphasize the difference between the verbal identification of the underlying feeling in Step 4, and actually viscerally accessing and facially expressing the emotion in therapy in an aroused manner in Step 7. Step 8 now focuses on the ways in which each partner may interrupt, avoid, or block his or her emotional experience and expression and on overcoming these. Step 12 also adds a focus on self-change in the form of emotion self-regulation and self-transformation. This step draws specifically on individual emotional change processes (Greenberg, 2002a, 2002b) and is an important development that introduces the new self-change process of transforming emotion with emotion, which has become a key concept in individually oriented emotion-focused therapy (Greenberg, 2002a). This highlights the importance of facilitating self-soothing when the partner is unable to provide responsive soothing.

The stages are summarized in the sections that follow, and examples of some of the added steps are provided.

Stage 1

The most important initial goal of the first stage is establishing safety and a collaborative alliance. This stage involves the therapist developing empathy, genuineness, and positive regard for each partner and forming a bond with each partner without alienating the other. This allows clients to feel safe enough later to reveal their vulnerabilities and their position or role in the cycle. This requires affective attunement to, and validation of, each partner's experience. Validation of feelings and needs by the therapist helps calm each partner's anxiety; the empathic understanding by the therapist of each partner's emotional pain, to some degree, soothes the hurt of not being heard by the partner. When therapists validate the wounds that the partners feel, they will begin to feel more trusting and will begin to reveal their wounds to each other. The therapist's ability to join, form an alliance with, and empathically resonate with the partner's pain thus will ultimately help the partner open up.

The therapist's task in the company of the partner is to empathically reflect and express how each one really feels, deep down; people want their partners to hear how they feel, even if their partners do not want them to know this. This helps in overcoming avoidances. Defenses will not hold if people feel understood. If there is difficulty establishing an alliance, the therapist might meet with each partner to facilitate this. Similarly, if at any stage of the process the therapy becomes stuck, individual sessions might be held to promote progress. While establishing the alliance and focusing on each person's pain, the therapist is also assessing the negative interactional cycle and the underlying emotions creating the negative cycle.

Stage 2

In the second stage, the therapist describes the negative cycle, helps the couple identify their unacknowledged attachment- and identity-related feelings, and reframes the couples' presenting problem in terms of the relational cycle. This helps externalize the problem as the negative interactional cycle, which then becomes the target of change. The therapist in this stage thus relationalizes the couples' presenting problems in terms of the cycle and begins to focus on helping partners label their underlying emotions. Often, it is helpful to ask couples for a specific instance of an argument to help get at the cycle. Another intervention that is helpful in identifying the cycle is the promotion of an enactment of the conflict in the room. Both of these interventions provide more concrete experiences from which to infer the cycle and identify the underlying feelings.

The step of identifying sensitivities and vulnerabilities, and seeing how these interact to produce the negative interactional cycle, has been added to this stage to help make this intervention more explicit. Once the cycle is identified, the most important thing to do is to identify and explore the underlying core sensitivities that are being activated in the cycle. Key questions for therapists to ask themselves are "What are each of the partners' sensitivities?" and "What is each of their core pain?" The therapist also explores to see whether there are some important psychogenetic origins of the wound. Getting a sense of partners' family-of-origin stories also helps to identify interacting sensitivities or vulnerabilities. If the sensitivity is not from family of origin, it may come from previous relationships or life experiences. These sensitivities are not viewed as pathological but as understandable vulnerabilities and are still seen as adult unmet needs. Once a picture of the cycle and underlying feelings has been formed, the therapist will frame the problem in terms of these underlying sensitivities. For example, with one couple, the frame offered was as follows:

> What I'm understanding so far is that you, [wife], feel anxious and untrusting when you think [husband] is being evasive, and that you worry about what he is not telling you. When that happens, you feel like you just have to find out what the truth is and make him see it too and you try very hard to get information from him? . . . I guess when she does that, [husband], you start feeling apprehensive about what's coming and without even thinking about it, you sort of step out of her way to protect yourself. So what's it like for you, [wife]? You know, somehow you are trying very hard to get the truth, and he seems to be evading your efforts to do that.

Having identified the cycle, the therapist then explores the partners' vulnerabilities. In this case, knowing some of the history of the wife's sexual abuse by the father, the therapist conjectures that the wife is understandably vulnerable to feeling anxious and invalidated because the mother had invalidated her revelations of the abuse. The wife's core feeling of needing always to know what is true and her fear of being invalidated is then linked to her husband's sensitivity by the therapist saying,

> No wonder the cycle gets going or that you feel the way you do because your [to the wife] sensitivity to invalidation which is so understandable from your past, interacts with your [to the husband] sensitivity of feeling cornered or swamped by your mother. When she tries to get you to tell her what's going on, [husband], you feel kind of apprehensive that somehow you're going to get criticized or be rejected for what you are thinking or doing? I guess when that happens, you try and make a sort of safety zone for yourself by softening things so you don't end up feeling the way you used to feel when your mother would try to control you or get you to do things the way she wanted them done.

Vulnerabilities or sensitivities are similar to a set of lenses through which people view the world. They are a construal system, or a basic mode of processing, set in motion by the activation of a core emotion scheme that scans for such things as "Is it unsafe?" "Are you going to leave me?" and "Will I be invalidated?" So therapists need to look for each person's core vulnerability, or core set of lenses, because ultimately threat is experienced in these terms. There are all kinds of complexities on top of the vulnerability, multilayers and multifaceted issues, for example, feminist, gender, cultural, and social issues or factors that influence the couple. But ultimately, partners construe the world through the eyes of their core emotion scheme, and it is this that we are aiming for. It is like the bull's eye at which we aim to access and reveal the core emotion scheme, reflect on it, and ultimately, if it is problematic and based on childhood unmet needs, to transform it.

There is so much content and complexity in working with couples that the best guiding principle is, Once the cycle is identified, then explore and focus on the interacting sensitivities. So the therapist does this by saying to one partner, "Tell me more about this feeling of being afraid and insecure." And to the other partner, the therapist says, "Tell me about feeling alone." Even better than inquiring into feelings is having the therapist voice these feelings for them, especially when partners are unable to, or not used to, doing this. Then the sensitivities are linked to their psychogenetic origins, if these are apparent. For instance, the therapist might say,

> Your father was an alcoholic and the world was an unsafe place; you never knew what was coming. So no wonder you feel very insecure and very sensitive to whether your husband is going to give you the safety, and you are very sensitive to whether you know what is going on.

And to the other partner, the therapist says,

> And for you, you were the sixth child of a family of eight children, and your mother was never really there. So no wonder you want so much to have someone to talk to, to tell about your inner world and have them listen. When your wife doesn't, given this need, it makes it seem that she is not interested in you, and then you pull back to your normal way of coping, saying "I just have to do it all on my own."

The therapist wants the partners to affectively explore their vulnerabilities, to name them, to place them into a context of the person's life story or narrative, and to provide a narrative about how they fit into the interaction.

The exploration of the historical origins of each partner's particular sensitivity to an underlying emotion is often done in the first few sessions and gives both the therapist and the partners a sense of the depth and origins of their particular sensitivities or vulnerabilities. Awareness of sensitivities helps contextualize and normalize the problem so that the partners can feel "no wonder I or my partner react this way, given our past histories." This can help people disengage from both other-blame and self-recrimination and therefore begin to own and explore their role in the perpetuation of the cycle. Note, however, that the therapist does not switch the focus at this point in the couples sessions from an interactional focus to an intrapsychic focus to work on dealing with unmet childhood needs, and the therapist refrains from working in-depth with the psychogenetic problem, beyond accessing the vulnerable feeling and identifying how it relates to the partner's roles in engaging in the negative cycle. Ultimately, the therapist wants to have the vulnerabilities shared and revealed in the room, without blame or judgment, such as statements along the lines of "I feel very lonely" and "I feel very insecure." If the psychogenetic information is not available, all the therapist does is say, "You are sensitive to security. Who knows why or what the origins are, but for some reason you are. Can you share that?" In brief couples therapy, the sensitivities are identified to serve as tools for deblaming. Identifying origins of sensitivities is not for insight; rather, it contextualizes the issue in a much deeper fashion. If the therapist can get to "You had this sensitivity before the couple started," that is what is most useful, because then partners no longer believe that "It is because of you I feel this." Identifying the source of the sensitivities also helps evoke more feeling and get to core emotion schemes. The partners, however, can also each be seen in an individual session early in the process to explore their position in the relationship and/or their family-of-origin issues. If it appears that there are major individual issues that need to be dealt with, such as past abuse, severe avoidance, inability to symbolize emotion, high emotional reactivity, inability to regulate emotion, extreme self-criticism, unfinished business, or symptoms of depression or anxiety unrelated to the relationship, then working with individuals alone for a number of sessions may be useful. These sessions may be interspersed with couples sessions. Here, the therapist may focus on individual issues and childhood unmet needs, with the focus on achieving the type of change that will help break impasses in the couples therapy. Thus, working with a very blocked man to help him access his feelings or with a very explosive woman on self-soothing may be particularly useful, and this may include two-chair and empty-chair work and other techniques to help evoke and regulate emotion (Elliott, Watson, Goldman, & Greenberg, 2004; Greenberg, Rice, & Elliott, 1993).

Also, we try not to end the session simply with an understanding of the cycle and sensitivities; this is still too conceptual. Rather, the sensitivities need to begin to be revealed, each to the other in the session. It would be like this: "I guess you are feeling vulnerable to being insecure. Can you tell him about your insecurity?" We want the partners to taste what it is like to open up in that way and not leave them in their heads. Then, the goal becomes one of doing more of that type of revealing to each other. The vulnerability always is linked back to the cycle. The therapist thus says,

When you are insecure, what ends up happening is that you blame. What we are going to work on is for you to share your insecurity and to experience it, and for you to hear it rather than to end up blaming and defending.

This process is engaged in with each partner.

The following is an example in which the therapist in Session 3 is inquiring into the history of each partner's sensitivity that he or she brings to the cycle.

> *Therapist:* You were the second youngest? But [wife] said something about you not getting from your mother necessarily or not being seen as much as you might've liked to have been. That's her interpretation. . . .
>
> *Husband:* Mm-hm.
>
> *Therapist:* . . . Um, and maybe you feel some sense of—you want to make sure you get what you need, and you didn't necessarily get it in the family. I mean, do you agree with that? We ended up last time sort of talking about you as a good boy in a way, or doing what your parents wanted, and being angry but also silently being sort of difficult, but do you agree that somehow there was some feeling you had, maybe of not getting enough attention in your family?
>
> *Husband:* You think these problems stem sort of around how my childhood was?
>
> *Therapist:* Well, I think in all of us, who we are now is connected with who we've been throughout our lives, and we're sensitive to whether our partner meets our needs or not. . . .
>
> *Husband:* Mm-hm.
>
> *Therapist:* . . . But our needs were formed outside of this relationship, and I think for both of you that may be true. Did you think about that at all?
>
> *Husband:* I have thought about it. . . .
>
> *Therapist:* Yeah. And what do you think about that? I mean, because somehow there's a lot; you're very angry with your wife now, but you don't say it out loud. And, I mean, you may or may not agree when I say that. . . .
>
> *Husband:* Yeah.
>
> *Therapist:* . . . But, I mean, you seem angry! And you do try to not be angry, but the thing is you're angry about her availability intimately and sexually and that feeds into your anger; you see, I think each of you brings something into the relationship, a vul-

nerability or a sensitivity, and that will eventually get activated. It doesn't matter who sat in that chair as your wife, eventually you would start to feel how you feel, . . .

Husband: Mm-hm.

Therapist: . . . and [*to wife*] similarly you would start to feel how you feel, . . .

Wife: Mm-hm.

Therapist: . . . and [*to husband*] feel angry about, that somehow she's disappointing you . . .

Husband: Mm-hm.

Therapist: . . . in not living up to certain expectations, in not giving you what you want, you would end up feeling used and exploited, . . .

Husband: Mm-hm.

Therapist: . . . and so on, right? Um . . . so, does that relate to your childhood at all, or what did you bring here? What's your main vulnerability?

Husband: [*clears throat*] Well, my mother ignored me, and I was, like, the second youngest and kind of, like, no one paid attention to me or, is that what you mean?

Therapist: Yeah, I mean, is that, is that true? Did you feel that?

Husband: Sure, at times, probably yeah. Other times, I didn't. . . .

Therapist: Right, sure.

Husband: . . . I mean, I'm looking at it now compared to the family we have, we have one child who gets a hell of a lot of attention. . . .

Therapist: Right.

Husband: . . . Okay, I was the fifth of sixth so I didn't get as much as he did.

Therapist: Yeah, and what was the most painful thing that you experienced growing up and what, what was, how were you formed by that? . . .

Husband: Okay.

Therapist: . . . To be sensitive to not being attended to, or?

Husband: Yeah, maybe that was it; I wouldn't call it painful, though, I mean, I never experienced anything traumatically painful. I always felt loved. . . .

Therapist: Yes, yes.

Husband:	. . . Right? I felt as a kid growing up a certain amount of pressure put on me to do well and to excel. . . .
Therapist:	I see, I see.
Husband:	. . . I know that, so to this day I still feel that.
Therapist:	And that came from who?
Husband:	My father, who would want me to be, excel and stuff even when I phone him, whenever I phone him it's like, "What are you doing now?" Fact of the matter is you're not really; there's not major accomplishments that occur at work, right . . . maybe, you know, when you're in university you're doing things, it's different.
Therapist:	I see. So you would report back to him?
Husband:	Right! I'd report back, exactly. . . .
Therapist:	Uh-huh.
Husband:	. . . What are you doing now?" . . .
Therapist:	Yes, yes.
Husband:	. . . "I'm doing this or that," right? As opposed to when there's a certain dialogue . . .
Therapist:	Mm-hm.
Husband:	. . . um, just conversation, right?
Therapist:	Okay, yeah.
Husband:	To this day, yeah, there's that, and ah, certainly as a child you're competing for attention, and I guess I didn't like always having to achieve.

Stage 3

In the third stage, the therapist works closely with partners to experience and express their underlying emotions associated with their vulnerabilities in an attempt to uncover and reveal the partners' attachment and identity feelings and needs. This allows partners to express vulnerabilities and self-doubts, and it prepares them to ask for what they need and receive comfort and validation. Disclosing changes partners' interactional stance and enables them to become more approachable, emotionally expressive, and communicative with their mates.

It is only once an initial therapeutic relationship has been established, and once the cycle has been described and understood, and the therapist feels that the partners are ready to move further in therapy, that the therapist would concentrate on accessing the unacknowledged feelings underlying their cycle and then reframing the problem in terms of these vividly experienced feelings. Because often it is through each other's faces and through each other's eyes that partners see themselves, the other's facial affective expression exerts a profound influence on how partners feel and see themselves. When partners interpret the other's facial expression or affective tone and expression as hostile or critical and directed toward the self, then their negative scripts about themselves (e.g., "I'm unlovable," "I'm unworthy") are easily triggered. When they see expressions of vulnerability that are not blaming, caring scripts are evoked. It is thus crucial to have the partners see the face of the underlying emotion.

Empathic exploration and empathic conjecture are key interventions that help access feelings (Elliott et al., 2004). These interventions rely on listening attentively to the words of each partner, as well as reading nonverbal signals, to capture what is most poignant. Once the feelings are accessed, it becomes clear that their fears and shame, not their anger or withdrawal, are what need to be dealt with. In Step 7, different underlying emotions associated with the different positions have been identified as a guide for what to listen for. These emotions are further elaborated in later chapters 10 through 14 on working with specific emotions. Access to these feelings helps in restructuring interactional cycles.

The therapist also always contextualizes the evoked emotion in terms of the negative interactional cycle. For example, the therapist first would describe how the husband's angry pursuit in a demanding and/or blaming fashion leads to the wife placating and stonewalling, which then only fuels the cycle even more. The cycle would then be reframed in terms of the underlying emotions—that the husband feels lonely and unloved and that the wife feels afraid and unworthy. The underlying emotions would now be accessed by the therapist. Then the anger of the husband would be replaced with his expression of the vulnerable feeling of loneliness and his fear of being abandoned, and the withdrawal of the wife would be replaced with expressions of feeling unworthy and unsure of herself. Once the cycle is reframed, the therapist would weave in the couples' respective attachment and identity needs that correspond to the primary emotions and then present that to the couple—in this case, his needs for closeness and her need to be validated.

An important skill an EFT-C therapist must learn, to help access underlying emotions, is how to identify blocks to, and interruptions of, underlying feelings and how to help overcome them. If the couple is ever to move beyond talking about their feelings to true revealing, they have to feel safe enough with both the partner and the therapist to overcome their usual avoidance of their core feelings and their fear of revealing them. One of the main methods for dealing with interruptions and avoidances is to treat them as needed protection and to understand their protective function.

Therapist operations that are helpful in overcoming blocks to revealing, especially when an injury or betrayal has occurred or when there is a lot of distrust and vulnerability in one partner, are reaching in and speaking for, focusing on the fear of opening, and finally, restructuring. When a partner has withdrawn because of a feeling of being wounded, the injured partner often puts up a protective wall. Reaching in by empathic conjecture and naming the anxiety underlying the partner's lack of trust and heightening the attachment and identity feelings and needs that the partner is not yet ready to express, for fear of being re-wounded, creates the possibility of a softening. Here the therapist needs to make explicit what is being protected and what is not being said and say it for the partner. The person may not state out loud their difficulty in opening or trusting, but it is apparent in the interaction. The therapist needs them to reach in and pull out the underlying vulnerability (this is reminiscent of Virginia Satir's, 1988, sculpting method of teaching where she would have someone act as the vulnerable child part of the person and she would pull it out through the person's legs). Here, however, it is the distrust and vulnerability or block that needs to labeled, validated, and expressed for the partner. This might sound something like,

> I understand how much a part of you needs to be comforted, you want to connect and feel together but you still need to protect yourself. Another part, maybe the stronger part right now, feels so afraid of opening and getting hurt. This part tells me "stay back and protect."

It is important to identify the nature of the fear that is organizing the protection. The therapist needs to focus on the fear of reaching out or of letting the other in. The self may fear what the other may say or do (e.g., reject, criticize), or the self may feel worthless, ashamed, or afraid of being unlovable. Whatever the fear is, the therapist may need to formulate the unformulated and say this for the client. If one partner is having particular difficulty opening up and revealing vulnerability, the therapist may even have that partner say this to the other partner. For example, the therapist might say, "Can you tell him this now: 'I feel vulnerable, and I need to protect myself. I just can't let you in right now. I am afraid.'" The final restructuring step, which is the goal of the next stage, involves a therapist directive to "say this to the partner." Having reached in and named and validated the wall and, when the client is ready, having pulled out the frightened child feeling and having obtained the client's confirmation that this is what was felt, the therapist then needs to say, "Can you tell him that in your own words?" and then support and validate when it is done.

Partners' avoidances or defenses thus are validated as protective, and the need for them is empathized with and explored until such time as the readiness for change emerges. Thus a block is validated, and the need to protect the self is owned until such time as the resulting feeling of isolation and desire to come out from behind the block begins to emerge. Once both partners have acknowledged their underlying feelings and needs, they are encouraged in Step 9 to work on repeatedly reclaiming the previously disclaimed feelings and needs. Partners at this time may be given awareness homework to notice times they feel afraid or ashamed during the week and what they do at these times. If partners have already expressed some empathy and acceptance of underlying vulnerabilities in the session, they may also be asked to express these core vulnerable feelings at least three times that week to their partner. Thus, one partner might say, "I'm feeling ugly and fat. I need reassurance you still love me," or "I feel afraid and worried you see me as useless."

In more general instances in working with characterological blocks to emotion in highly defended or avoidant partners, where for example, one person is superrational or another is highly deflecting, therapists need to help the individuals first become aware that they are avoiding emotion. Then the therapist helps them become aware how they are doing this, be it by changing the topic, making jokes, or squeezing their muscles. Only when people are aware of their blocks to emotion and begin to own this process can the therapist help them access and reveal what they are really feeling. How to work with the self-interruptive process in an emotion-focused way is described in more detail later in this chapter in the section Overcoming Self-Interruptions and has been elaborated more extensively in books on individual emotion-focused work (Greenberg, 2002a; Greenberg & Paivio, 1997a; Greenberg & Watson, 2006).

Stage 4

In restructuring the interaction, it is the partners' acceptance of the expressed vulnerable underlying feelings that is paramount, and it is this that sets up a new interaction. When one partner has nonblamingly revealed a primary feeling about an identity vulnerability or attachment insecurity and the listening partner is unable to respond with validation or caring, attention needs to be turned to what is blocking more bonding and validating responses from the listening partner. Generally, one finds either a wall of protection or mistrust, as noted in the previous step, or maladaptive emotional responses of anger or fear based on a negative learning history that prevents responsiveness. The partner's maladaptive, nonaccepting emotional response then needs to be focused on and transformed. One husband, for example, who did not respond to his wife's tears of loneliness and instead became rigid in response to her vulnerability, revealed after exploration that his mother's tears used to be followed by such rage that she once scratched him and drew blood. When he saw his wife's tears, he would freeze to avoid an anticipated rage attack. As his fear was focused in therapy and he was encouraged to breathe and to begin to discriminate between the past and present, he was able to see his wife's sincere vulnerability and need, and he was able to respond to these with newly experienced compassion. This identification of the nature of any blocks to acceptance and responsiveness is extremely important, as it helps contain the couple and hold the one partner while the therapist works with the other to explore what may be blocking him or her from responding more acceptingly and compassionately to a revealed vulnerability. Labeling the block to acceptance and responsiveness as a problem helps prevent the revealing partner from retreating and thus turning back any progress made in therapy. Understanding the block to acceptance also provides a cognitive framework for both partners of what problem is preventing a partner's responsiveness and helps sets goals for future therapeutic work.

Once acceptance has been achieved, the expression of, and response to, heartfelt needs is promoted. This is often expressed in an enactment in which the partners turn toward each other and express and respond to each other's feelings and needs. These expressions result in a change in interaction. Important processes in this stage involve the softening of the criticism and blame from the pursuing partner, while encouraging the distancing partner to reconnect and a softening of contempt and/or control by the dominant partner, while encouraging the submitting partner to reassert. Now, the blamer no longer attacks but softens into disclosure, and the withdrawer comes forward, reengages emotionally, and expresses his or her feelings and needs. Dominants go one-down rather than taking their customary one-up positions, and submitters stand up and express their feelings and needs rather than complying. Clearly, this step overlaps with and is an extension of the step of accessing underlying feelings and promoting the owning of needs. The goal of enactments here is self-directed interaction that results in successful resolution of problems; promotes secure attachment; promotes mutual identity-validation; and reduces defensiveness, stubbornness, withdrawal, anger, and conflict. When therapy goes well, couples engaging in enactments will usually be able to craft idiosyncratic solutions that are better adapted to their values, beliefs, and relationship styles than any ways of behaving the therapist might propose. Enactments, however, do need to be carefully monitored to keep them focused on central relationship concerns and to prevent explosive or destructive interaction.

We have added an additional self-soothing step toward the end of this stage. Once partners are more accessible and responsive and interactions have changed, to ensure enduring change, individuals also may need to develop the capacity to self-soothe and transform their maladaptive emotional responses, which often are responses to unmet childhood needs or past trauma rather than to the partners' lack of responsiveness. The capacity to self-soothe also is important for times when the partner is not emotionally available or responsive. Whereas with less distressed couples restructuring the interaction involves first developing more responsiveness to each other, with more dysregulated couples, the work of restructuring often first requires helping partners learn to self-soothe when the other is not responsive or available and to transform their responses based on unmet childhood needs. Work with dysregulated partners involves focusing on how they can soothe and transform their own affective responses so that they can change how they interact. Thus, self-regulation of affective storms often is a needed first step in couples in which partners are prone to rage. This is also the case with those who engage in extreme forms of behavior such as banging their heads against the wall, hiding in a cupboard, or punching holes in walls when frustrated or hurt, or those who self-harm. The focus on self-regulation of emotion, be it an early step for more extreme behaviors or a later step to facilitate more enduring change by focusing on transforming responses based on childhood unmet needs, involves helping people to tolerate their own painful emotions, soothe themselves, make sense of their emotions, and use them for constructive action and interaction.

In working to promote self-soothing, the therapist often is the first to provide the soothing of the underlying vulnerability by empathic responsiveness. This serves both a holding and a containing function for the individual and the couple overall, as well as modeling soothing and empathic responding for both the partners and for the individual him- or herself, who over time needs to internalize this empathy to self-soothe. At this point, the therapist also explores difficulties with self-soothing or objections to it. Some individuals object to providing soothing to themselves, feeling that this is a violation of their relational expectations. They believe that their partner should provide it. Exercises such as establishing a safe place to go to when distressed and other ways to self-nurture are discussed, and beliefs that self-soothing means the other does not care or will never be responsive again are explored and challenged.

When a partner's underlying emotional vulnerabilities are clearly understood to be maladaptive and based on unmet childhood needs or past trauma, such as the internalized shame of feeling worthless or the inability to tolerate even the smallest sign of abandonment, more individually focused work to transform these states by accessing more adaptive internal emotional resources is necessary. This can occur either in the couples sessions or in some individual sessions with each of the partners alone. It is here that the principle of changing emotion with emotion is most applicable. Core fear and shame schemes will be accessed and transformed by accessing client's internal resources, often based on accessing adaptive sadness at loss, and anger at violation (Greenberg, 2002a, 2002b). This helps strengthen the self as the person's automatic processing is no longer governed by fear and shame responses, and the person's adaptive responding is now more habitual.

By the end of this stage of restructuring interactions, once underlying emotions have been accessed and accepted and needs have been expressed, the couple is now more emotionally engaged, with a greater sense of attachment to each other and to the relationship, and each feels a greater sense of validation. Partners now are more expressive and responsive and also are more able to tolerate the anxiety of ruptures in the bond without needing immediate repair, as they are able to self-soothe. In addition to enhanced engagement with each other and greater closeness and connection, self-esteem is enhanced and the partners now may be engaged in continued self-work on how to transform their own maladaptive vulnerable feelings by accessing new adaptive feelings. They thus are less likely to respond with fear of abandonment and shame, because they have developed stronger senses of self-worth.

Stage 5

The final stage of couples work involves consolidating new interactional positions and strengthening positive, nurturing, and validating cycles of interaction. How these can be integrated into their everyday relationship is discussed. Partners are asked to reflect on what is different and also are asked to identify what they could each choose to do to precipitate the negative cycle if they wanted to return to a more dysfunctional way of relating. This gives them a sense of their own role and responsibility in, and control of, their interactions. In addition, the new ability to take a "self" focus rather than an "other" focus is emphasized and practiced. Although maladaptive states may not be fully transformed by the end of couples therapy, partners are now better able to understand their own and their partner's deep vulnerabilities and are working on how to both soothe and transform their own states, how not to trigger these states in their partner, and how to respond to them if they do. The consolidation and integration of change is helped by the therapist reviewing changes that each partner has made that have led to the transition from the negative to the positive cycle. The therapist also encourages the articulation of a new narrative of their relationship and of each partner's self by eliciting examples of their personal and relational growth.

EMOTION COACHING

EFT-C differs from most other approaches in its treatment of feelings because it confronts the feeling directly rather than, for example, promoting management of feelings such as anger management. The therapist is viewed as an emotion coach who guides partners toward feelings that are there but are implicit rather than explicitly stated. Emotion coaching involves both following where partners are in the moment by reflecting back to them one's understanding of their experience and leading the partners forward to deeper feelings by guiding the type of processing in which they engage. Thus, the emotion coach constantly encourages exploration of deeper underlying feelings. The concept of "coaching" is based on the premise that partners have sources of growth and possibility within them and that these can be developed by emotion coaching. An emotion coach focuses on strengths, possibilities, and resources and uses language that is prizing and appreciative to help partners move forward by accessing positive emotional resources within. Coaches facilitate emotional growth first by focusing people's attention on their positive emotional potential and helping them mobilize their inner resources. For example, in working with secondary anger, an EFT-C therapist reframes a partner's anger in terms of underlying vulnerability, guides the person's attention to the visceral feeling of vulnerability, and promotes expression of the primary hurt. The therapist then also guides the person to express the newly accessed, more vulnerable, and underlying emotions to the partner, thereby changing the interaction. The therapist is thus constantly sensing what the client is feeling and guiding a next step in the processing of experience and its expression. In addition, in change-focused enactments within sessions that focus on revealing vulnerabilities and needs, the therapist coaches couples to engage in new behaviors within the therapy session and carry them over outside the session. This behavioral, change-oriented focus allows couples to restructure the negative interactional cycles that previously had led to volatile and anger-charged communication cycles. In our experience, the best treatment to help resolve couples conflict is to guide people to develop their capacities both (a) to increase emotional awareness to express, regulate, reflect, and transform emotion and (b) to change their behavior to respond in empathic and comforting ways to each other.

Homework

Giving homework is an aspect of coaching. There are two major types of homework: awareness and expression homework. These are associated mainly with the steps of block identification and identification with disowned needs and aspects of self. Homework is marker guided, needs to be given at teachable moments, and is construed more as promoting learning through practicing some change that has already occurred in the session than itself being the main site of the change process. For example, at some point early on in treatment, the therapist gives both partners awareness homework. The husband is asked to pay attention to what he feels when he is criticized and to try and find the right words for it. The wife is asked to pay attention to what happens inside her when she feels invalidated. The following week, they report that the husband feels belittled and diminished and the wife feels both shame at feeling worthless and fear of not being believed. The wife's feelings relate to childhood wounds of abuse that were not validated by her parents, whereas the husband's feelings relate to a highly critical, over-controlling mother.

Marker-Guided Therapy

Although the five-stage framework is presented as a set of sequential steps, the therapist does not follow a step-by-step plan but rather takes advantage of the readiness of clients to engage in certain experiments or to explore the implications of certain suggestions whenever an opportunity arises. To take advantage of clients' readiness, emotion coaches need to recognize the signs of such readiness; this is referred to as *process diagnosis*, which involves the recognition of markers of therapeutically relevant states that present opportunities for interventions (Greenberg, Rice, & Elliott, 1993). The therapy is thus process sensitive and marker guided (see next section) rather than linearly structured. For example, if the therapist has evoked the wife's feelings of loneliness, she has expressed a need for closeness, and the husband does not appear to be responsive to her expression of feeling, then the therapist needs to intervene at this point because the wife has expressed underlying vulnerable primary emotions, and to do that involves some very real personal risk. If the husband does not respond in a way that validates her feelings, the chances of the wife again risking emotional expression of primary feelings are reduced. Thus, disclosure of vulnerability, which itself is a marker of asking for a partner's response, when followed by nonresponsiveness or lack of empathy from the partner, is a clear marker for intervention of a particular kind—one that will aim at promoting responsiveness or at exploring the block to responsiveness. Intervention can thus be seen as marker guided and focused on promoting the steps as outlined in the framework previously provided.

Each step in the framework, from alliance creation through accessing emotion, to consolidating new positions and new narratives, can profitably be seen as defining marker-guided therapeutic tasks. Thus, steps such as identifying negative interactional cycles, promoting the disclosure of underlying vulnerabilities, facilitating soothing of self, identifying blocks, and helping people own vulnerabilities and express needs are all discrete tasks, and the marker for their use is completion of the previous task facilitating compassion and expressing appreciation. Thus, for example, once partners feel validated, the task is to promote understanding and acceptance of the cycle as the problem. Once the cycle is accepted as a problem, this is a marker for identifying the underlying feelings driving the cycle. Once underlying feelings have been identified and their origins explored, this is a marker for accessing the underlying feeling. It is not helpful to jump ahead and access feelings before safety has been established or before the cycle has been identified and reframed in terms of underlying feelings. It also is not good to take a self-focus by asking partners how they can soothe themselves before having taken an other-focus and having promoted partner responsiveness and validation of underlying vulnerabilities. Other important processes discussed later in this chapter in a section on accepting difference also can be thought of as engaging the couple in a particular task appropriate at a particular juncture. Each of these steps and processes can thus be seen as tasks with particular markers that best fit interventions and specific types of resolutions.

In engaging in intervention within the general framework, it is important to recognize that affects are at the very core of partners' communication with one another and are the ultimate target of intervention. Affective tone through nonverbal expression is thus one of the most important markers of what is occurring between partners. Intervention then is not just about a set of therapeutic procedures that will promote the steps, on the basis of the content of interaction, but is about picking up on the subtlety of the affective tone of partner's communication to each other so as to get at the real meaning of the interaction and then to intervene appropriately on the basis of this. The affective tone of communication is conveyed by look, voice, and use of language. Partners are highly sensitized in intimate relationships to their partners' affective tone that always qualifies the content of the communication. They rapidly pick up on any single word or gesture that might convey something negative about them. Affective responses often are automatic, and so people often convey what they feel without intending to or knowing it. Angry partners, for example, try to hide the feelings by the words they use, such as saying they are disappointed rather than angry, but it is difficult to hide the affective tone of anger accompanying softer words. Thus, asking a partner to focus on underlying hurt while the tone of their communication remains harsh will not work in accessing the underlying hurt; sensing when the voice or face indicates hurt and then intervening will be more successful.

Communication in intimate relationships thus clearly is not restricted to the words that are spoken—it is the tone in which the words are said that is important. The affective tone of partner's communications conveys the meaning of an interaction and defines interactional positions. Because it is so determining of interaction, affective communication therefore must be the focus of therapists' attention and intervention. To guide intervention, therapists must pay more attention to how something is said than to what is said.

EMOTION ASSESSMENT: FOLLOWING THE PAIN

Within the five-stage framework, identifying secondary and primary emotions and accessing core feelings are central tasks. An often-asked question is "How does the therapist identify and access core underlying feelings?" Overall, and especially in the beginning, the therapist does this by following the primary pain in each person. The therapist also keeps asking him- or herself, "What is each partner's core feeling? Is this partner feeling lonely, sad, unlovable, unworthy, inadequate, or angry?" Then, on the basis of the internal answer to these questions, the therapist conjectures empathically about what partners may be feeling.

When the couple first enters therapy and the therapist inquires about what brought the couple to therapy, the therapist can feel overwhelmed with the amount of information being presented. The couple embarks on recounting recent fights and stating their positions, which are often entrenched and defensive. The therapist must wade through a great deal of material, often presented in terms of secondary instrumental emotions with little reference to underlying primary, more vulnerable emotions. As we have said, when couples present their problems in therapy, the therapist first validates, listens for, and tries to understand the negative emotionally based interactional cycle. Through the unpacking of the couples narratives and reconstruction of core conflicts, the therapist forms an understanding of both the attachment and identity cycles. The therapist, actively but empathically, conjectures into the pain underlying the initial presentation. The therapist does this by listening for changes in vocal patterns or increased emotional energy behind statements that provide a window into each partner's underlying pain that drives the core cycle. The therapist continuously makes empathic conjectures that are essentially informed guesses about each partner's painful primary emotions and meanings. Clients, in turn, will either confirm or disconfirm these conjectures; through this process, the therapist learns and comes to understand the nature of couples' core interactional cycles. When therapists are accurate in their conjectures, clients often feel the relief of being understood and begin to reveal more about what underlies the cycle. The therapist needs, constantly, to affirm each partner's underlying pain. Although clients may be initially reluctant to reveal their pain to each other for fear of attack or nonreceptivity from their partner, the therapist, by naming the pain, can provide an initial staging platform that allows individuals to reveal pain and receive support, understanding, and soothing from the therapist before revealing it to their partner. This can reduce distress for both individuals and couples and provide an overall containing function for the couple. Following the pain allows the therapist to get to the emotions underlying the negative interactional cycle more rapidly.

The therapist also needs to note whether the partners are more self- or other-focused. That is, are one or both members of the couple very focused on self-sufficiency and independence within the relationship but not accustomed to responding to the partner or asking for support, or alternatively, are one or both members very focused on getting the other to respond or trying desperately to get the other to change without any capacity to self-soothe when necessary? This will determine whether to focus more on activating other-soothing or self-soothing.

In working with emotions that are presented, as well as activating underlying painful and vulnerable emotions, the EFT-C model follows the principles of working with emotion from individual therapy (Elliot et al., 2004; Greenberg, 2002a)—in particular, tracking ongoing experience, empathic exploration, and empathic conjecture regarding primary emotions. These are key empathic tasks used in both individual and couples therapy. Although the initial stages that involve structuring the interaction and de-escalating the negative cycle requires particular interventions that are specific to EFT-C, subsequent stages require the therapist to adopt many of the empathic response forms used in individual therapy.

Fundamental ways in which working with emotion in EFT-C diverges from work with emotion in individual therapy arise largely as a function of needing to respond to both people in the room and facilitating a new form of interaction between them. First, in couples therapy, emotions are occurring in the present in the room and in response to the partner and are far more fluid. Emotions are communicated between partners in split seconds through facial and bodily expressions, tone of voice, and so on. Partners throw out statements that quickly evoke responses in their partners in part because they know each other well. The therapist must stay attuned to these interactions and track what both partners are feeling, being careful not to lose one person. This does not allow for the same type of elaboration and exploration that is a hallmark of the individual model. Emotions change quickly in response to changes in the partner, and the therapist is more concerned with following and tracking changes than with dwelling too long on emotions that have already passed.

There also is far greater use of empathic conjectures in the couples model. Although it is important to allow individuals to explore and symbolize their own experience, the importance of moving clients out of the painful negative interactional cycles that have brought them to therapy at the outset becomes of primary importance. Empathic conjectures aimed at primary emotions that underlie the negative interactional cycle are a primary means of doing so. It is important to note that empathic conjecture is more failsafe in the couples context. That is, people can check therapist's conjectures against their own present experience to see whether it matches what they actually feel. This reduces the risk of imposing meaning or feelings on clients and unduly influencing them. In couples therapy, people often have quicker access to felt experience because their partner is sitting across from them and the interactions between them provide ready stimulus for emotional responses. In addition, the focus of therapy is the relationship between partners, not the relationship with the therapist; therefore, therapist's conjectures and directives are less about defining each individual than about defining what is going on in the relationship at the moment and therefore are often less threatening to each individual.

One of the important skills of the EFT-C therapist is to be able to emotionally hold both partners at once. The therapist makes sure that the deeper exploration of one partner's experience does not create a sense of invalidation in the other. Thus, the therapist is constantly checking back with one partner even through a quick glance while exploring underlying emotion in the other. This serves a number of functions. It communicates that what both partners' experience is equally as important, that both are responsible and have a role to play, that one partner's emotions affects the other, and by corollary, that a change in one partner's emotional responses will change the other. It also allows the therapist to freely explore with one partner without violating or breeching the relationship with the other.

EFT-C uses more confrontation than is used in individual therapy. At times, this can be done by the therapist saying such things as "I think it's your fear that stops you from getting close" or "It would be good if you could respond to your wife's need right now"; however, it often is best done by having one partner confront the other or by unbalancing the system by, at any one moment, supporting one partner against the other. Thus, therapists will support a fearful or lonely partner to turn directly to the other and state what they need without fear of reprisal or shame. The therapist validates the importance of needs, thereby giving courage to partners to voice them. Or the therapist will encourage a submissive partner to set a necessary boundary and stand up to his or her partner, thereby bringing him- or herself to the table in the interaction. Ultimately, this facilitates a healthier interaction between partners.

What Do Therapists Need to Do for Couples to Change Interactions?

Therapists need to promote the processes of disclosing underlying vulnerabilities, owning vulnerabilities, taking a self-focus, and soothing self and other. They also need to identify self-interruptions and blocks to responsiveness, to facilitate the experience and expression of compassion, and the acceptance of difference, and finally, to encourage the appreciation and expression of positive feelings toward the other. Promotion of these processes is described in the sections that follow.

Disclosing

The first and best thing a therapist can do to change interactions is to help partners to present their primary adaptive feelings and needs as honestly and openly as possible in such a way that their partners are most likely to hear and see them. We have found that partners generally soften their stance toward each other by sharing both vulnerable attachment- and identity-related feelings and needs and also by witnessing these in their partners (Greenberg, Ford, Alden, & Johnson, 1993; Greenberg, James, & Conry, 1988; Johnson & Greenberg, 1985a, 1985b). When people focus on themselves and genuinely express their needs for closeness or identity-validation in a nonblaming manner, their partners relax and listen. Then, once partners are feeling heard and seen, they are much more likely to be able to participate in a more conciliatory engagement.

It is important to note that it is the display of emotion that is so important in organizing interaction. Seeing the face of the other evokes experience. People are impacted by the ways others face them, and they feel others feeling them by what they see on their faces. How people imagine the face of the other also is important in how they feel and what they do. It is important to note that the face, however, still is an ambiguous text, open to interpretation, and so how people react to others is also subject to their interpretation of the other. It thus is important to put facial and nonverbal responses into language to make them crystal clear. This is also why it is important to have partners face one another while talking and encourage them to read and report what they are actually seeing. This helps ensure that partners are responding to each other in the moment and not to an imaginary or prior response from the partner. In therapy, we thus want the person to express both facially and verbally in such a way that there is no doubt about what is being felt so that it is not misinterpreted.

Table 7.1 is a worksheet that can be used both in a session and more usually as homework to reinforce a process that has already occurred in the session to help partners access their primary feelings and needs. Partners write down on the worksheet the frustrating situation, followed by their own secondary emotion and behavioral reactions that follow. Partners then are encouraged to search for what else they feel at a deeper level, in addition to the secondary reaction, and to write this down. Once they have identified a more primary feeling, they are asked to identify what they need when they are in that feeling state, first globally and then much more specifically.

Focusing on Self

Therapists need to help partners take a self-focus and regulate their own emotions, so that rather than blame or control, they are able to disclose their subjective experience, one to the other. This provides material that will evoke caring for and empathy from the other.

When partners are able to take a self-focus and ask themselves "What do I need to change or understand to improve things?" they are moving toward successful therapeutic change. A stance of "I will change my reactions to my partner if my partner changes his or her reactions to me" is highly problematic. This type of quid pro quo mentality is not the route to intimacy. Marriage is not a bargain; it is an emotional bond. Partners need to be able to take both a self- and an other-focus, to regulate their own responses and to be both emotionally accessible and empathically responsive to the other. They thus need both to be more able to recognize the other's feelings and needs and to regulate their own affective responses to momentary ruptures in the connections or slights to their identity so they are more able to be responsive to the partner's feelings of loneliness, needs for connection, feelings of diminishment, and need for validation.

For example, a wife goes out one night without consulting her husband; he considers this to be really inconsiderate and criticizes her harshly for it. She then feels accused, reacts defensively, and runs out of the room in a huff.

TABLE 7.1
Emotions and Needs

Category	Situation	Emotional reaction	Behavioral reaction	Deeper feeling	Underlying need
	A. Frustrating patterns	B. Secondary feelings	C. Reactive patterns	D. Primary emotion (fear, shame, sadness, anger[a])	E. Needs: global specific
General	When you . . .	I feel. . . .	And react by	This hides my	What I really want is . . .
Specific	are late.	angry.	criticizing.	anxiety and feeling rejected.	to feel important to you. for you to call

Note. This worksheet guides the client in identifying primary emotions and needs. The client should start by describing the stimulus situation and his or her emotional reaction to it. The client should then describe his or her behavioral reaction, and, finally, identify the underlying primary emotion and need.
[a]Behind anger often is a hurt, and accompanying each hurt is an unmet longing or need.

At this point, if rather than feeling entitled to his contempt and taking the first opportunity to scold his wife further for her running out of the room so childishly, the husband takes a self-focus and becomes aware of his own primary feelings and concerns about closeness, and if he is able to regulate his anxiety and feelings of rejection, then things will go better. Rather than moving to anger and expecting her to change, if he can focus on himself, find ways of tolerating and regulating his own loneliness and thwarted desire for closeness, he will contribute to preventing the eruption of a negative cycle. He can do this by breathing, soothing his anxiety, and either contacting a sense of the enduring reliable nature of his bond with his wife or connecting with his own ability to entertain himself on his own. Only then will he be able to regulate his anxiety and loneliness. Rather than blaming her, if he reveals to her "I feel lonely and miss you but I understand that you do need to go out," he will simultaneously be changing his self-organization and the interaction both by revealing himself and by validating her. She, in turn, needs to be responsive to his disclosure, reassure him that he is loved, and show concern for his feelings. She, too, needs to feel able to regulate any anxiety or shame his disclosure may produce in her so that she can be responsive to him rather than feel put upon, blamed, or guilty.

A self-focus is thus necessary to promote healthy relating and change interaction. The best way of taking a self-focus is by revealing primary or more core vulnerable emotions rather than secondary or defensive emotions. This requires emotional intelligence. It requires the ability to attend to self; to label what one is feeling; to accurately identify the emotion triggers to regulate one's arousal; and to express the emotion to the right source, at the right time, and in a constructive manner. The best way of being responsive is to take an empathic other-focus and rather than self-protect and react defensively, to listen to other as a subject who just like one's self feels pain and seeks happiness.

Owning Vulnerability and Weakness

What is missing from much intimate relating is ownership of a sense of personal vulnerability, weakness, and powerlessness. When partners cannot acknowledge weakness, they often slip into patterns of dominance and submission. Given the actual powerlessness that goes along with being in a relationship based on relying on another to meet many of one's needs, all partners have grounds for feeling vulnerable and powerless. Yet dealing with feelings of vulnerability is complicated in the context of interpersonal struggles. Partners need help in attending to their more vulnerable feelings in such a way that they can assimilate these feelings into their identity rather than become dominant.

The therapeutic support necessary for owning vulnerability comes from focusing on being aware of inner experience and being encouraged to accept weakness in both one's self and others. The recognition of felt vulnerability needs to be cultivated, and coaches thus must help people slow down the pace of their experiencing and increase attention to their inner worlds so that they then can pay attention to their human frailty and need for others' support and so that they can feel comfortable communicating these to others.

Self-Soothing and Self-Compassion

In any difficult fight between intimate partners, at least one partner probably entered a core maladaptive state of anxious attachment or shameful inadequacy. That is probably why the interaction escalated into a fight. One of the partners reacted from a place of vulnerability, lost perspective, and suddenly felt that unless this was resolved and they got close right away, were validated right now, or were left alone, their relationship or they themselves would not survive. Partners who enter distressed states related to security or identity threats feel that unless they are responded to or heard right now, they forever will be abandoned, invalidated, or overwhelmed by their partners. Neither partner necessarily believes this realistically, but an anxious or shamed part of each of them begins acting their part in a cycle in a do-or-die effort to protect something. Unfortunately, the attempted solution—protecting by trying to point out, convince, blame, or attack the other or withdraw—usually becomes the problem. What is needed is to be able to calm one's self with images of past security and caring, or past experiences of being valued and validated, and feeling good. Partners need to work with their own anxiety and shame to soothe it by learning to breathe, by reassuring themselves that "this too will pass," and by remembering the experience from the past and understanding that it has changed. Therapists thus need to help their clients self-soothe at times when their partners are not able to be responsive and, ultimately, to help them to regulate and transform those maladaptive states that interfere with intimacy so they no longer respond in this way.

The ability to tolerate a partner's nonattuned responsiveness is greatly helped by having the client develop the capacity to remember that the partner was available or attuned in the past and will again be so in the future. This faith in their partners' overall responsiveness allows people temporarily to move away from their presently nonresponsive partners and even though they are not satisfied, to be able to turn to themselves graciously for internal support. If people are later able to turn back to their partner without resentment, but with humor, the ability to laugh at themselves, and the philosophical acceptance of the inevitability of conflict, this will help foster reconnection.

At certain times, especially when partners are unable to respond to each other's needs or soothe one another, each partner has to exercise the capacity for self-soothing. To help partners deal with their own maladaptive emotional vulnerabilities that are evoked in a fight, therapists, acting as emotion coaches, need to help partners learn to soothe their own feelings.

Individuals' vulnerabilities, as therapists know, often come from their developmental histories of traumas or relational injuries that produce deep-seated fears of abandonment, disintegration, annihilation, or shame-based feelings of worthlessness or diminishment. Thus, when pursuing partners who are vulnerable to feeling unloved and are unable to get a response to their needs for emotional or physical connection, they have to find ways of soothing and compassionately embracing themselves, so that they do not become enraged and attack their partners. Withdrawers who feel so overwhelmed and intruded on, or need more distance to maintain balance and be free of intrusion if they wish to be in a relationship, have to find ways of soothing themselves when they feel impinged on. They need to find the internal resources to come out and make contact. Likewise, dominant partners with underlying narcissistic vulnerabilities have to learn to tolerate and soothe their own shame and be able to step down or apologize, whereas submissive partners have to learn to overcome anxiety and step up. Ultimately, for more enduring change to occur, it is helpful for partners also to focus on personal transformation of vulnerabilities by learning to access other emotionally based resources that can help them transform core maladaptive states (see Greenberg, 2002a; Greenberg & Watson, 2006).

Some people are unable to self-soothe because they lack the internal emotional structures or processes to relax and/or to calm or nurture themselves. They may not have received enough of this as children and may not have built an internal nurturing caretaker representation of another on which to draw. When relationships are momentarily derailed, they feel desperate and have difficulty holding on to the sense of security generated by the lived history of their present relationship. Then it is difficult for them to buffer even minor disruptions, and they are unable to project a vision of a secure future to the relationship. They experience tremendous threat or a sense of violation, as though the current distance or slight rupture means the relationship is over and they will be abandoned and alone or unloved forever.

When people enter these deeply vulnerable feelings and are unable to self-soothe, they need to learn first to breathe, and then to breathe into that place in their body where they feel the awful feeling and begin to symbolize it in words. Naming the deep vulnerability, such as "I feel like I can't survive," "I feel like I'm falling apart or disappearing," or "I am despicable, disgusting, and don't deserve to exist," helps get a handle on what one is feeling. Once having named the dreaded state, a little bit of distance from it has been created. Now some perspective needs to be gained. At this point, deliberate efforts at regulating to change one's mood such as treating one's self to a favorite activity, listening to music, relaxing, taking a hot bath, going for a walk, or calling someone for contact and support are self-comforting behaviors that can be helpful to handle relational ruptures.

People then need to develop a sense of greater relational or identity constancy by being able to hold on to what exists even when it is not occurring in the moment. Those with a deep fear of abandonment when overwhelmed with a current relational rupture need to be able to develop relationship constancy by focusing on the fact that the relationship was good prior to the current rupture and will be good again in the future. They need also to be able to self-soothe by generating a comforting, nurturing image to evoke more secure feelings in the present, to help calm and soothe the deep anxiety that has been evoked by the rupture. Those who feel deeply defective or flawed when criticized or slighted need to be able to hold on to and remember that prior to the invalidation, they felt valid and had a sense of self-esteem and that in the future they will again restore it. They need to access images of being valued and validated and connect with their strengths. Vulnerable partners also need to be able to broaden their narrow vision of where they can get validation. They need to make contact both imaginally and in the real world with the support they can receive from varied other sources. This helps them not feel as desperate. Finally, and most important, they need to connect with their own internal resources and literally be able to soothe themselves by imagining themselves being compassionate and validating and taking care of the vulnerable part of themselves. It often is helpful at this point for the therapist to use self-soothing and imaginal restructuring interventions (Greenberg, 2002a). Here, the therapist can ask the person to imagine him- or herself as an adult compassionately soothing, validating, or meeting the unmet needs of the wounded self in the prior traumatic or painful situation, often when the person was a child. Sometimes even more powerful is imagining a previously nurturing other soothing one's vulnerable part. As the partner witnesses this, it helps him or her feel both less blamed and more compassionate.

A specific method to promote self-soothing that we have found most helpful is to ask a person to engage in a psychodramatic type of dialogue with an imagined other to evoke compassion and self-soothing. This is most usefully applied at appropriate markers of dysregulation such as when partners experience a lot of anxiety, shame, rage, or withdrawal in response to partners' rejecting or critical comments (Greenberg, 2002a). In this intervention, the therapist, acting as an emotion coach, asks the dysregulated partner to imagine a child who feels the kind of anxious or ashamed feelings he or she feels, sitting in a chair in front of them, a child who has suffered what that person has suffered in life. To evoke the child's plight, the therapist then describes the most poignant details of the person's history and asks, "What would you say to that child who felt these things? What do you feel toward the child, and what would you say to this child?" This typically evokes a compassionate response toward the child and its circumstances and a recognition of what the child needed.

For example, with one partner, the therapist says, "Imagine an 8-year-old girl sitting here," and holds his arm out to the side with an open hand to create a point of focus for the client to look at an imagined child. The therapist continues, "Her mother hardly looks at her, never mind talks to her. Her father emotionally draws on her for all the love he can't get from his wife and then rejects her when he doesn't need her. She feels so misused. What do you imagine it's like for her?" The therapist might also ask, "What would you say to her if she were your child?" The client answers, "I know she would feel so alone, so out of control, without anyone she can trust." The therapist might say, "What does she need? Can you give her some of what she needs?" Once the person recognizes the child's need and responds in a soothing manner to the child, then the therapist asks her to respond to the child in her, in the same manner. In this intervention, it is important to start with a universal child, not with the part of the self that needs soothing, nor with the person's own child within. If one starts with the self, this often evokes the person's unresolved self-contempt. Even though people understand the implication of what they are being asked to do when working with the universal child, they seem to be better able to soothe a child in general than to soothe themselves. Once the softening into compassion has occurred in relation to a child in need, it is easier to transfer this feeling to the self. Questions a person can be asked at this point relate to how they can feel this compassion for themselves or what would help them do this. To evoke compassion for the self, the therapist can ask clients what they would need to feel supported, what they would say to someone they care for, or what they would like someone who cared for them to say or do. Ultimately, the goal is to have them imagine a self-supporting part of themselves being compassionate to themselves and have them feel the warm, empathic understanding and acceptance of this. Doing this, in conjunction with the empathic soothing provided by the therapist's affective attunement, helps to develop the person's self-soothing capacity over time.

The development of the capacity to self-soothe explicitly, to find within the self resources to feel more secure, and asking partners to practice this, are very important in helping resolve couples conflict outside the therapy situation. Bringing the deep fear and shame out in the open and exposing these emotions to personal reflection, to help make sense of them, to new experience from within (Greenberg & Watson, 2006), and to new experience with the partner helps develop the capacity to later self-soothe at a more implicit level. The development of implicit regulation and self-soothing means that the person does not react with such intensity to conflict or momentary ruptures, as they automatically regulate the feeling of threat, and it is not nearly as intense.

Overcoming Self-Interruptions

When one partner is unable to access an underlying emotion, self-interruption work may be needed (Greenberg, Rice, & Elliott, 1993; Greenberg & Watson, 2006). Here, as in Step 9 (working on blocks), the therapist works in a three-stage process. The first stage is helping the person become aware that he or she is interrupting or suppressing an emotion. This is often done by asking, "What just happened then?" when a person interrupts their experience. The second stage, and this is the main work, is helping the person become aware of how he or she is doing this. Then the third stage is helping the person become aware of what is being blocked. Once people are aware that they are interrupting, the goal is to help them recognize their agency in the avoidance process. This involves them becoming aware of what they are doing to stop themselves from accessing their underlying emotion. The block might be cognitive in nature, like a belief such as "It's weak to cry"; a thought such as "If I cry, my wife will think I'm weak"; a deeper physiological block such as squeezing muscles in the jaw, holding the breath; a behavioral block such as looking away or changing the topic; or an affective block such as feeling anxious and worrying, or feeling angry, rather than feeling the underlying sadness. Once the interruption is identified, the therapist helps people become aware of their agency in the interruptive process by asking them to actively do what they do to interrupt. Once they are aware both that they are doing something and what it is they are doing to block the emotions, the emotion that is blocked can be attended to. Once the previously blocked emotion is accessed, it is expressed, usually first to the therapist and then to the partner.

Sometimes it is important to do preparatory work either to prevent or to overcome impasses caused by the inability to access underlying feelings. Here therapists can meet with each partner separately, coaching one to acknowledge some previously undisclosed underlying vulnerable feeling and possibly coaching the other to be able to receive the disclosure or respond to it if it occurs.

Being Compassionate

Partners can be encouraged to access compassion for a partner by focusing them on their partner's pain and highlighting that although it may not have been their intention to hurt their partner, it appears to have been the effect of whatever they did or are doing. Therapists need to promote the partner's ability to recognize both the self and the other as subject rather than object. This leads to seeing the other as being a person just like one's self, and evoking compassion for the other, who like one's self is in pain and seeks happiness. In addition, this capacity to see the other as a subject, a person like one's self, and an agent, with feeling needs and intentions, is required for empathy. Buddhists meditate and use other exercises to develop their ability to be compassionate, and prayer is used by some to send out loving care to the partner or pray for the partner's health and well-being, and they do this especially when they are angry with their partner. These are all ways of activating one emotion, in this case compassion, to change other emotions, such as sadness or disappointment or anger or resentment. Discussion of practices like these, if they fit the person's worldview, can be explored and supported.

Accepting Difference

Attempts to change one's partner are probably one of the biggest causes of conflict in couples. Partner renovation plans are always a problem and are rarely successful. Acceptance is the solution. Acceptance of the partner's feelings and desires is crucial if couples are to live in harmony, otherwise partners are always judging each other. Nonjudgmental acceptance of each other's feeling and desires is crucial to feeling safe. The statement "I just want to be accepted for who I am" is uttered very often by one partner in couples therapy. In addition, accepting that each partner's view of reality and view of the relationship has validity and that each partner's views are worth attention and respect is important. Given that one of the major problems in couples is their attempted solution to difference, acceptance of the difference solves the reactive problem. Differences in sexual interest, types of activities, or even beliefs about child rearing bring on attempts to change the partner. These evolve into reactive demand–withdraw, attack–defend, and dominate–submit patterns that become the problem. Emotional acceptance of difference and behavioral compromise are the solutions to the reactive problems. Acceptance leads to more emotional openness and generosity to the other's desires and to creative problem solving by the couple. In addition, forgiveness is particularly important at times of betrayal and is helpful in promoting reconciliation. In fact, success in marriage may be based on the ability to forgive the other for being different.

Encouraging Appreciation and Resentment

Another important piece of getting along is feeling and expressing appreciation of the other. People need to be able to express both positive and negative feelings to their partners. Although it makes sense that people need to express more positives than negatives, people in relationships soon forget this golden rule (Gottman, 1999). Some couples get into trouble because the positives are so taken for granted that they end up just expressing the negatives. However, some couples feel they are not allowed to express the negatives and avoid them altogether. Neither of these strategies is constructive. Therapists need to coach people to express appreciation for each other and engage in giving behaviors that make each other feel cared for. A little bit of positive goes a long way in helping people maintain good attachments.

Engendering and Expressing Positive Emotions

Along with appreciation, therapists need to promote experiences and expressions of caring, enjoyment, and excitement in the relationship, as well as respect for, and pride in, each other. Having couples engage in caring days, novel experiences, dating, and holidaying all help engender more positive emotions. Other structuring strategies that are useful involve suggesting couples protect time to talk, make sure they touch more, kiss on departures and returns, and give more compliments. The last often decrease too quickly in relationships because of familiarity and taking the other for granted. Increasing mystery and novelty also promotes excitement that spices up a sexual relationship, which after years together can become too familiar or predictable.

A NOTE ON THERAPIST EMOTIONAL PROCESSES

It is essential that the EFT-C therapist stay attuned to the ongoing, moment-by-moment emotional processes of the couple to maintain the therapeutic alliance with both partners, as well as to help partners to increase emotional awareness and regulate emotion. Therapists need to suspend their own value frameworks and be careful not to reach for closure too quickly. A high tolerance for ambiguity is demanded of the emotion-focused therapist. Therapists bring a number of cognitive–affective capacities to their ability to be empathically attuned, the most important of these being imagination (Greenberg & Rosenberg, 2002; Rogers, 1975). By actively imagining clients' experiences, therapists infer what clients feel, asking what they themselves might feel in response to what clients tell them. This provides the basis for empathic exploration of partners' inner experiences and allows therapists to make process distinctions between partners' expression of core emotions and other secondary and maladaptive emotions (J. Watson, Goldman, & Vanaerschot, 1998).

Such attunement requires therapists to be fully congruent and able at a given moment to recognize their own emotional experience so that they can take note of it and use it productively. EFT-C therapists, therefore, need to be sufficiently emotionally aware so that they do not miss important aspects of partners' emotional experience or become overwhelmed by their own emotional experience. It is thus necessary for therapists, at times, to pursue their own emotion-focused therapy or to seek supervision or consultation if they do not feel able to be fully present and empathically attuned in such a relationship.

CONCLUSION

Therapists help couples move through the 5 stages and 14 steps of EFT-C focusing on emotion and interaction. Both the states of the interaction and the partners themselves are used as markers of how to intervene differentially. They also attempt to promote certain states and processes that lead to greater connection and validation.

Marital therapy is most effective when both partners develop the ability to reveal their underlying feelings in a nonblaming and validating manner when they have felt wronged or misunderstood and to respond empathically and nonjudgmentally to each other's feelings and needs. This requires the ability to take both a self- and other-focus. Partners who become more focused over time on how to change and regulate the way they themselves respond to the upsetting things that their partners say or do, rather than trying to blame or change their partner, will achieve harmony far more than partners who focus on blaming and trying to get the partner to change the things they find upsetting. Two key concepts in helping couples resolve conflict thus are helping partners focus on themselves to regulate and reveal underlying feelings rather than blame their partners and helping partners to be responsive rather than defensive to the other's concerns.

8

THERAPEUTIC TASKS: FOCUSING ON INTERACTIONAL CYCLES

In all things there is a law of cycles.

—Publius Cornelius Tacitus

In this chapter, we describe and give examples of the different interactional cycles and how to work with them. We start by describing the different types of cycles that occur on the affiliation dimension, where both partners' main concern is attachment related, then we describe cycles on the influence dimension, where both concerns are identity related. We follow this by describing cycles where partners are on different dimensions so we have interactions crossing the affiliation–influence dimensions with mixed attachment and identity concerns operating.

THE BASIC NEGATIVE CYCLES AND INTERACTIONAL POSITIONS

Negative cycles on the affiliation dimension can be described alternately as pursue–distance, attack–defend, cling–push-away, or demand–withdraw, but all have to do with handling the dynamics of closeness. Negative cycles on the influence dimension are dominate–submit, lead–follow, define–defer, complain–placate, or overfunction–underfunction, but all have to do with the dynamics of influence. In these cycles, the more one partner engages in one action, such as pursuing for closeness, the more the other engages in a reciprocal reaction, such as distancing to protect. The more the one partner distances, the more the other partner pursues; the more one partner controls, the more the other resists or submits; so we get a circular escalating interaction—and the struggles for connectedness and validation begin. In one major type of cycle, the pursuer pursues for emotional closeness but does so by blaming and criticizing, and the distancer distances for emotional protection. In another major type of cycle, the dominant person controls, or overfunctions, makes all the decisions to feel secure, and then often ends up feeling burdened or disdainful of the other. The underfunctioning partner, who feels more insecure, unsure, or submissive, does not do much but then ends up feeling inadequate or invisible.

Negative interactional cycles are scripted by unmet attachment and identity needs driven by the desire to overcome loneliness and fears of abandonment or feelings of shame and/or powerlessness. In some couples, cycles occur mainly on one dimension, focused primarily either on maintaining closeness or on control. Although some cycles are described as affiliative, and others as influencing, many still have both a closeness and a control aspect. For example, in a struggle predominantly about closeness, pursuing spouses may feel controlled by their withdrawing partners, whereas withdrawn partners may feel controlled by their nagging spouses. In affiliative cycles related to closeness or sexual intimacy, the more active pursuer usually feels less powerful than the more distant partner, and it is generally held that it is the partner with lower sexual desire or intimacy needs who often controls sex and intimacy in the couple.

In couples whose interactional cycles involve a mix of attachment and identity concerns, each of the partners may pursue both closeness and validation at the same time. For example, one partner may offer friendly advice that is both somewhat affiliative and somewhat controlling. The other partner in turn may ask for such guidance in an affiliative and submissive way but may then ignore the advice as a way of asserting his or her identity.

In another important type of mixed cycle, the mixing occurs because partners are on different dimensions. For example, one partner may be concerned about attachment and pursue for closeness, whereas the other is primarily concerned about identity protection and controls or withdraws. For example, a wife may feel sad and lonely and pursues for closeness, but her husband may feel a fear of loss of control and/or a sense of inadequacy and stonewall or withdraw to protect his identity. This leads to her becoming angry, and she nags, criticizes, and demands. She is concerned about seeking closeness and feels primary anxiety about separation. Her husband, who feels criticized and controlled, hears confirmation that he is inadequate, and he feels ashamed, or he feels fear of loss of control and further resists her influence. His concern is not about closeness and security but about identity and control. In this cycle, stonewallers or withdrawers resist influence because their identity is threatened.

In one couple, in this type of mixed cycle, the wife, Abby, says she often feels lonely and unloved in her relationship, like she is living in a desert. This clearly involves an attachment need. Her husband, Paul, whose self-esteem is vulnerable, says he has doubts about whether he is capable of loving and has feelings of not being good enough because he cannot meet her needs, and he frequently becomes silent and withdraws. This does evoke a secondary attachment concern and fear that "She will abandon me if I'm not good enough," but it is important to see that the primary issue that he needs to resolve is the fear that "I'm not good enough." It is important to reveal this and be validated, but he also needs to be able to self-soothe when he feels defective and to find his own strengths. His is clearly primarily an identity concern, not an attachment concern. Abby's typical stance to loss of connection is to criticize and become angry, saying, "You never respond to me. I can't count on you being there; you don't care. You don't make me feel loved." Paul's characteristic internal response to his wife's demands for contact is to feel like a failure because he cannot give her what she needs. His typical outward response, however, is to defend and then to withdraw for fear of being seen as flawed. To his wife, it appears that he does not care, rather than that he is protecting himself, so she criticizes him. This confirms his feelings of inadequacy, and he withdraws further to protect himself.

In another cycle with partners on different dimensions, one partner, who is predominantly shame based and concerned about self-esteem, is controlling and the other is anxious, concerned about closeness, and submits. For example, the husband may feel inadequate about his manliness and may control his wife's activities and appearance, and his wife complies for fear of losing him if she does not defer to his will.

In these mixed struggles, attachment and security needs in one partner interact with identity and self-esteem needs in the other partner. These cycles often develop in the following manner. If Partner A's needs for closeness wane after the honeymoon period, and caring and even commitment start to diminish, Partner B will experience his or her security as being threatened. If this anxious partner then begins to devalue Partner A for not caring enough, Partner B will experience his or her identity as being threatened. If one partner feels threatened in the attachment domain, this partner often attacks the other in the identity domain. Now the conflict is in the realm of both security and self-esteem, with a resulting loss of safety for both. If conflict is not resolved, most people move to protect their identity ("I'm okay"), attack the other's identity ("You are not okay"), and they distance to do so, thereby threatening the attachment bond.

This understanding of the difference between the affiliation and influence dimensions of interaction in conflict is made more complex by the observation that at times dominance and coercion can be used, by at least one partner, in the service of meeting attachment needs. Dominance thus can manifest when connection has been ruptured, as an attempted solution to regain connection. Here, the source of conflict is who is right and has the right to set rules about closeness or who has the right to determine how things are and should be in relation to intimacy. Thus, we have an influencing interaction superimposed on a more fundamental pursuit for closeness. We now discuss and exemplify cycles on the different dimensions.

Pursue–Distance Cycles

The most common cycle on the affiliation dimension involves a blaming or demanding spouse interacting with a defending or distancing partner. In this pattern, the pursuer is pursuing for closeness by either requests, appeals, and actions that can become demanding to achieve this end or by criticizing; blaming; or condemning the partner for intimacy deficiencies, for being inattentive or absent, or for other failures. For both distancer and pursuer, the inability to regulate affect can play a significant role in the escalation of conflict. The distancer, to protect self and regulate affect, avoids closeness and absents him- or herself. The fear of intimacy of distancers is based on a sense that being close is a threat and will disrupt their ability to regulate their affect. Rather than finding closeness soothing or comforting, it is anxiety provoking because it is either currently disappointing or damaging or has been so in the past. For these partners, closeness is dangerous because it will lead to boundary intrusion, engulfment, annihilation, or abandonment, and so avoidance of closeness becomes the attempted solution to prevent or regulate anxiety. This involves shutting down, not listening, not looking at, and not responding to the partner. This response mode in the distancer cues anxiety or anger in the other partner, who, unable to regulate these feelings, responds desperately by attacking (e.g., "You're useless") or by threatening (e.g., "If you don't respond to me, I'll find someone who will").

Below we see how a therapist helps a couple, Fran and Mike, identify a pursue–distance cycle in their relationship.

Therapist:	Yeah. So, as I'm beginning to understand—it's like you [*to Fran*] have ended up in the pursuing position, and you, you know, you're the active one who sort of seeks closeness, touches, and sort of, . . .
Fran:	Right.
Therapist:	. . . and, . . .
Mike:	[*Clears throat.*]
Therapist:	. . . when there's a difference, you know, a disagreement or something, and when you might start getting angry, and we haven't understood yet exactly what the anger is all about, . . .

Mike:	Mm-hm.
Therapist:	. . . but, you withdraw as a way of trying not to get too upset, . . .
Mike:	Right.
Therapist:	. . . but then, is it the case that, you know once the wall is up, then, you keep needing the connection, so you keep sort of trying to, to get contact with him, but you've learned a little bit . . .
Fran:	Uh-huh.
Therapist:	. . . to, to give him some time, but in a way, the wall has the effect of making her, come after you more, . . .
Mike:	Mm-hm.
Therapist:	. . . and the more you go after him, though, the more difficult it is for him to let down the wall. . . .
Fran:	Uh-huh.
Therapist:	. . . So you kind of get caught . . .
Fran:	Full circle, yeah.
Therapist:	. . . in a circle, right? And you know one of the things that will be important bec—, and you know, I imagine this covers arguments about your daughters.
Fran:	Everything. Oh, sure.
Therapist:	That there's a kind of a pattern. You know, and so it's this pattern is one of the difficulties because, I think, you know, his withdrawal will be very, [*to Mike*] she says "he withdraws for a few days, sometimes," I mean, that's what she said. . . .
Mike:	Mm-hm.
Therapist:	. . . and [*to Fran*] that's very painful and difficult for you, and you must try all kinds of ways to pull him out, but then, when she tries to pull you out, . . .
Mike:	[*Clears throat.*] It, sort of doesn't give you the space you need, so you kind of keep the wall up, and so, somehow we've got to, we'd have to help find a way of dealing with differences so that you don't get into this cycle. [*Identifies the cycle as pursue–distance and links to presenting concern.*]
Fran:	Right.
Therapist:	Because the cycle becomes the problem.
Mike:	Mm-hm.

Therapist:	You know? Um, and the more he withdraws, the more you feel lonely and pursue, the more you feel lonely and pursue, you kind of maybe get angry . . .
Fran:	Uh-huh.
Therapist:	. . . at him, and you try banging the wall down, right? . . .
Fran:	Yeah?
Therapist:	Is that, is that true? Yeah? [*Identifies links between her underlying and secondary feelings.*]
Fran:	I would say that [*laughing*].

Most other interactional patterns in the affiliation domain can be seen as variants of the basic pursue–distance pattern and are concerned with the need for and anxiety about closeness. Cycles such as attack–defend and cling–push away are fundamentally about seeking closeness and regulating distance. It is important to note that although many marital researchers have pointed to the corrosive qualities and negative effect of conflict for marital well-being, Roberts (2000) demonstrated that it is partner withdrawal in response to confiding behavior (intimacy avoidance) that contributes to marital dissatisfaction over and above the couples' level of conflict. Distance and disengagement may be more damaging than open conflict.

When helping the couple identify their negative interactional cycle, it is important to also emphasize that the positions in this cycle are not personal failings but attempted solutions to problems that have now become the main problem. This helps externalize the interaction as the problem rather than either partner's perceived shortcomings.

The Influence Dimension

Because cycles on the influence dimension have not been as fully described as the cycles on the affiliation dimension, this chapter provides more detail below on the influence cycle (for more information on the affiliation cycle, see Greenberg & Johnson, 1988; Johnson et al., 2005). There are a variety of cycles on the influence dimension. Two major cycles of dominate–submit and overfunction–underfuction are described and exemplified in the following sections.

Dominate–Submit Cycles

The most common generic cycle related to identity, power, and control involves concerns about asserting or protecting identity, boundaries, or position. In the classic pattern of this type, one partner dominates, controls, or defines reality, and the other submits or defers. The dominant partner determines decisions, defines reality, and generally proposes that he or she knows what is best. The submitter defers, follows, and often even looks to the dominant partner for direction. The dominant partner's position is often somewhat structurally maintained, such as by being the major income earner, being the more achieved or educated one, or the one who knows more, and the positions become entrenched in the couple's everyday interactions. This pattern becomes overtly conflictual when the dominant partner's position is challenged.

Dominant partners, when challenged, often feel fear of loss of control or shame at diminishment and exert power to regulate their own negative affect by maintaining a one-up position to protect their position and identity. They often use rational argument, contempt, or anger to prove they are right. They never admit to being wrong, and for them, saying, "I'm sorry" or "I'm wrong," is tantamount to saying "I am worthless" and to losing a battle and feeling defeated. They require the other's compliance to feel okay. Submitters, however, lack confidence, doubt their own abilities, and feel fear of disapproval. They often look to the other for direction and for self-definition and are involved in both placating and bolstering the other's self-esteem. Not all submitters, however, are passive or placating. Some do not initially adopt a submissive position. They stand up and argue, but in the end, they defer. The dominant partner also can be a fixer, who in the name of helping the partner, tries to fix things. Fixers attempt to correct things and put it back on the track they see as right. This undermines the other partner's functioning and helps create dependence in the partner. The fixers may be motivated by their anxiety to make things right, but this still often becomes controlling behavior. Most cycles in the influence domain are variants of dominate–submit cycles, and they pivot on whose definitions of reality prevail.

"I Feel Invalidated"

In the example that follows, the wife, Helen, felt she could not rely on the husband, Rick, who felt controlled and micromanaged by her. In the following fifth session, we see the therapist identifying an influence cycle and encouraging the submitter to assert. The couple has been arguing about the husband being scolded and lectured by his wife about not bringing in the wash. At this point, the therapist steps back and offers an observation that defines both partners' feelings.

> Therapist: You're each, okay let me, let me; each of you are saying—and this is complicated because there's layers of stuff that even I am not appreciating at the moment, okay? But somehow, what I think I'm hearing you say [to Rick], you're feeling like you can't say how you feel, that'll get rejected, and you're saying that you feel like if you're angry, like you can't be angry because that it'll get rejected. . . .

Helen:	Right.
Therapist:	. . . and—and isn't that interesting because both of you in fact are feeling the same thing: "If I say how I'm feeling, I'm going to get rejected." . . .
Helen:	Yeah. Invalidated.
Therapist:	. . . Invalidated.
Helen:	You feel it, and I feel it. [*Note the dominant partner differentiates her feeling and clarifies that it is invalidated not rejected. This is what is of concern to the dominant partner.*]
Therapist:	So, so something . . .
Helen:	Is wrong [*laughs*].
Therapist:	. . . it's something about what happens when each of you tries to express negative feelings.
Helen:	Well, I do it [*laughs*], . . .
Therapist:	That . . .
Helen:	. . . it doesn't stop me.
Therapist:	. . . No, no, but when you, when either one of you expresses a negative feeling that's directed towards the other person, . . .
Helen:	Right.
Therapist:	. . . you [*to Rick*] get to feel rejected and you [*to Helen*] feel invalidated. And this, it threatens . . .
Helen:	The self.
Therapist:	. . . the love that you have, your selfhood, it, it invalidates the other person, makes you lesser.

About 15 minutes later with the same couple, the therapist defines the cycle.

Therapist:	So the question is, Is it something that you do or is it something that you're ready to react to? . . .
Rick:	Right.
Therapist:	. . . I don't think that what goes wrong is in you, or in you, because it's in neither one of you. It's the interaction between the two of you. It's a cycle, there's something when you feel . . . rebuked or, you know, and I can't even, we're not even going to figure that out today . . .
Rick:	Right.
Therapist:	. . . but, when you respond to Helen—out of feeling inadequate or whatever that word is that we didn't find—then you're un-

	comfortable with her anger. It's as if a cycle gets put in place, and it runs its course in ways that are puzzling to both of you, . . .
Helen:	Right.
Therapist:	. . . and what, what I'd like to come back to next week is kind of figuring out how that cycle gets kicked off, and you know, I'll bet it's sometimes you, it's sometimes you, it's, it's, but there's some kind of interacting sensitivity a, ah, somehow something primes you to go into the cycle, . . .
Helen:	Mm-hm.
Therapist:	. . . and we need to know what that is. The how of it. . . .
Helen:	Yeah, I do hear what you're saying.
Therapist:	. . . It's really, it's, there's something that is triggering this cycle, . . .
Helen:	Okay.
Therapist:	. . . and, and that's what we need to figure out, . . .
Helen:	Right.
Therapist:	. . . my assumption is that the triggers are inner experience, . . .
Helen:	Right.
Therapist:	. . . what goes on inside of each of you that's invisible to the other person. So it's like you have inside information, you have inside information, that's what you need to share with each other so that it's not a mystery anymore, . . .
Helen:	Right.
Therapist:	. . . and when it's not a mystery anymore, you can kind of say, "Oh look what we're doing" and then "let's not do that, let's not go there, let's, let's do it a different way." Okay?
Rick:	Yeah, but, yeah, because last time we talked about this issue that's exactly what I did. I sort of put her in a place where she said she felt that I wasn't loving her or . . . ? . . .
Therapist:	Mm-hm.
Rick:	. . . Because I wasn't, that I didn't listen, was that sort of the trigger that created her sort of scolding?
Therapist:	There's a button, there's a button you pushed, the "you're not listening to me, button," and "I don't feel."
Rick:	Right, because she said she felt—I don't know, was it unloved— not unloved but just . . .

Helen:	I felt invalidated. [*Again, note this is a feeling related to identity, not connection.*]
Rick:	. . . invalidated, right.
Helen:	Because you weren't, like, a part of . . .
Rick:	Right.
Helen:	. . . things going on . . .
Rick:	Right.
Helen:	. . . and, like, "I'm all wrong. I'm bad," or "My view doesn't count."
Therapist:	Uh-huh, so like, discounted: "My perceptions don't count, and that's reasonable."
Rick:	Well, well, yeah, it's definitely reasonable . . .
Therapist:	Mm-hm.
Rick:	. . . and, and that gives me somewhere to go with that because, I mean, I find that, yeah, that's the big thing with her.
Therapist:	But you see what's important then is what happens inside of you when you feel invalidated? That's the mystery for you, Helen. What is it that kicks off in you when he does something that leaves you feeling invalidated? The goal will be for you when you're feeling invalidated to turn to him and say, "Rick I'm feeling invalidated, I'm feeling not seen, because"—then you don't fight about hanging up the clothes at all because the clothes don't matter. What matters is "I'm feeling what I'm feeling right now, and I don't want to feel this way," . . .
Helen:	Mm.
Therapist:	. . . and then Rick can respond and say, "I don't want you to feel that way either, I you know I love you, I," you know, and then it's not about the clothes, . . .
Rick:	Sure.
Therapist:	. . . it's about the two of you connecting in important ways, to validate each other the way you need to feel validated.
Rick:	How do you do that? You know, like, how do you do that? . . .
Therapist:	Well, . . .
Rick:	. . . I know it's easy to say, . . .
Therapist:	Yeah.
Rick:	. . . but how do you do it. You know? I mean, it's a second, . . .

Therapist:	Yeah, it's, it's . . .
Rick:	. . . you're going to go from like, "Why did you do that?" to [*laughs*] "I feel invalidated," you know, it's more of ah, . . .
Therapist:	Uh-huh.
Rick:	. . . the power is in that.
Therapist:	Some of it is we need to, some of it is, and, and my own experience is I have to recognize the feeling of being invalidated. . . .
Rick:	Right.
Therapist:	. . . And I have to feel myself feeling invalidated so that I can name it, you know? . . .
Helen:	Mm-hm.
Therapist:	. . . We're, we're, you know, doing a kind of retrospective understanding, um, but there could be characteristic feeling that goes with being invalidated, a kind of sick-in-the-pit-of-my-stomach, . . .
Helen:	I don't know.
Therapist:	. . . you know, a physical sensation, . . .
Helen:	Absolutely.
Therapist:	. . and only when you know how it is you're feeling, then, then you can talk about that feeling instead of about the clothes. Does that make sense?
Helen:	Yup. It's that awful feeling like I'm being wiped out.
Therapist:	So we're getting more and more clarity the [*mouthing out the words*] and um, so it was interesting. Today was um, bringing it alive, it happened right here, . . .
Helen:	Okay.
Therapist:	. . . right? And I'm the, the monkey wrench in the system. I come along and stick my wrench in and everything sort of shutters and groans and we sort of go, "Ooh! How did that happen?" . . .
Helen:	Right.

Submitters also play an important role in unresolved dominance cycles, as they often are unable to assert themselves. While they may be able to express their vulnerability about being dominated, they do so in a way that is decidedly more despairing and hopeless than those who are successfully able to move out of a submissive role. Rather than simply disclosing vulnerability with a sense of openness toward their partner and themselves, they express pain related to feelings that they have little hope of transforming (Sharma, 2007). This hopelessness or powerlessness is related to their perceived lack of agency in their relationship. They experience themselves as passive victims of their partner's dominance with no control over the interaction. An example of this is as follows:

Therapist: Then how do you let his view dominate? I mean, you articulate intelligent points of view like now, but then his view dominates, and you become useless and wrong and of no value.

Beth: Well, I don't think I see myself that way all the time. I certainly don't operate with the rest of the world as if that were the case.

Therapist: But as you say, you're rather depressed, and I can see you in your primary relationship . . .

Beth: Well, I mean, after a while it's just like, you know, if you leave the stone under a place where it's dripping, eventually it's going to wear a hole [*laughs*].

Therapist: . . . exactly. And in your primary relationship, if you allow the other to define you, and they define you so negatively, it's like you either start standing up and saying "I won't take this," or you get depressed.

Beth: Yeah, well, there's nothing really to stand up against—because it's all, it's sort of insidious, it's all implied criticism, there's nothing really . . .

Therapist: . . . but you know exactly what it is.

Beth: Sure, but [*chuckles*] how can I say "Don't think that way about me, stop thinking like that"? I mean, if he's not actually doing or saying anything specific, there's nothing to object to [*feeling a sense of powerlessness*].

Therapist: So it's just the silent judgment behind his eyes that is your tormenter?

Beth: [*crying*] Yeah, basically.

Here the therapist has to work at the leading edge of the client's capacity to assert and support possibilities of doing this. In another excerpt from the same couple, we see the wife beginning to stand up.

Beth: Yeah, I don't know that he can do that, though, because he, like I say, he sees that as weakness. If you need to be encouraged and you need to be complimented in order to do a good job, then you're just . . . weak. You shouldn't do that, you should be [*laughs*], this is, this is the man who, when, yes, he knows what I'm going to say, when our children were infants, he would go out of his way to stop them from starting to suck on their thumbs,

saying that they should comfort themselves with their minds
. . .

Therapist: Yeah, yeah [*laughs*].

Beth: . . . we're talking about, less then 6 months old. I mean, are you a lunatic? Babies don't comfort themselves with their minds . . .

Therapist: Mm-hm.

Beth: . . . it's not real, but I mean, that's what he thinks everybody should, should do to be a real, strong, and fulfilled person, and I can't be like that. I'm *not* like that . . .

Therapist: Mm-hm. Tell him this.

Overfunctioning–Underfunctioning Cycle

The concept of "overfunctioning and underfunctioning" (Bowen, 1978) often captures an important aspect of the influence cycle and is a helpful concept in talking with couples about their roles, as it does not have the negative connotation of dominate or submit. The overfunctioners are anxious about loss of control and try to manage situations, whereas the underfunctioners are afraid of failing and prefer not to take responsibility, and if they do, they usually find themselves corrected by their partners or taken over, so they stop trying. One context in which an overfunctioning–underfunctioning cycle emerges is when one partner has a disability. Below, we look at a therapy session in which the husband has multiple sclerosis that has impaired his functioning. In the session, a recent fight is being discussed, and their conflict is reframed in terms of a negative interaction cycle, which emerged with the disability. In this, the wife, Dianne, is the leader, and Bob, the husband, is the follower.

Bob: But there are certain things, and the way she says things, everything has to be done her way, at her time, no matter what. And sometimes, like, I don't mind doing it most of the time, but it's every once in a while I get to a point where I go, "No! This is me as well," like I get to pick. Like, I probably would pick, like, if someone came up to me and said, "You know what, Bob, you should start reading these things or looking after these cause you gotta look for a job." I would go, "Yeah. You're right. Okay. Give them to me." But it's not that attitude sometimes with her. She has a different attitude. It's like, "Do this. Do it right now. Do it now."

Therapist: So, Bob, let me just clarify to make sure I understand. So it feels like it's one order after another and you usually say yes, but then something inside of you sometimes snaps and you say, "No more"?

Bob: There are certain ways that I perceive it, I guess, or it's given to me that I'm not going to accept it like that. Even though I know it's the right thing to do. It's stupid on my part, I realize that. There are certain things that I have to do, but I'm not going to accept them because it's not given to me how I feel it should be given to me.

Dianne: But he normally perceives anything I say as if I'm giving him an order.

Therapist: Okay. For Dianne, it is like, "I can't say anything without it being seen as an order," and for you, Bob, it feels like Dianne is giving it to you in that way. And then you kind of say, "Enough is enough"?

Bob: I do, I guess, a little, snap. It's one of those type of things. I do something stupid [laughs].

Therapist: Okay. And then it escalates.

Bob: Yeah. I guess our problem is that we don't know how to say, "Time out. Let's count to 10. Let's relax for a second. Let's talk."

Therapist: It's getting out of control.

Bob: We just keep going, and it's getting crazy.

Therapist: Okay, because there is this voice inside of you that says, "This is not the way you should be talking to me," so you react, and then you counterreact, and then it starts.

Bob and
Dianne: Uh-huh.

Therapist: Okay, because I was thinking, you know how in most interactions it's kind of like a dance, you know. There is always a leader or a follower. Someone has to take the position of the leader, and the other person has to take the position of the follower.

Bob: Oh, yeah.

Dianne: [laughs] I know where this is going. You should see when we actually really dance [laughs].

Bob: We're fighting when we're dancing. We're stepping on each other.

Therapist: So that's a good analogy [laughs].

Dianne: Oh, yeah [laughs].

Therapist: But it's just a position that has to be taken. Right? There has to be a leader that has to initiate the moves. And also, the leader is responsible for the pace of the dance. Right? So I just had the impression that in your relationship, Dianne, you were always a little bit of the leader and Bob, you were a little bit of the follower.

Bob: Uh-huh.

Therapist: And you really felt comfortable doing that. Like, this dance was always flexible enough. Like, you could be the leader sometimes and you could be the follower but generally the tendency for you Dianne was to be a little bit more of the leader, it kind of fits with your personality and what you bring to the relationship. And for Bob, you were talking about making everyone happy and going with the flow, so maybe it was more natural to be more of the follower.

Bob: Uh-huh.

Therapist: Okay. And I am kind of thinking how with Bob's illness, and long-term implications, and so on, it's kind of, it kind of got you confined in those positions of the leader and follower. Right now, the problem is that this dance has become inflexible.

Dianne: That's a good analogy.

Therapist: Okay. So now for you I guess it feels like you got to be the leader all the time. It's all on your shoulder. The dance is always your responsibility. You can never rest and let Bob take lead and you can just follow. And it also feels like the dance always felt like it has to be fast, fast, fast because there were lots of things to do.

Dianne: Yes. I almost feel the anxiety of being unprepared to be overwhelmed soon. Okay. That's, I think, that's why I'm sensing that. Because I am thinking about all the stuff that's gonna have to be done in case of this, in case of that. You know, I've already been making phone calls and trying to find out information.

Therapist: Okay. So as a leader you are responsible for planning the next step and right now in your head you think, "What is the next step?" And I guess for you, Bob, it felt like maybe you became stuck in the position of the follower?

Bob: Uh-huh.

Therapist: Because also with the implications of MS, you know, we were talking about implications such as physical and also those memory and concentration problems you've been talking about and so on, so it's a lot more difficult now to lead.

Bob: I think it is a lot more difficult now, and I find it very frustrating sometimes because there are times when I'm not able to look after myself.

Therapist: Uh-huh.

Bob: Which is frustrating.

Therapist: Right. So now you follow, not necessarily because you choose to in this dance, but you are kind of forced to.

Bob:	Yeah.
Therapist:	You have no choice. And that's a frustrating position.
Bob:	Uh-huh. Okay. I was kind of thinking about how this dance got out of control.
Dianne:	Yeah. I think you hit the nail on the head right there because it used to be much more flexible, where either of us could take the reigns. And there wouldn't be a problem, but now we are stuck in these roles.
Therapist:	And that's very challenging. I think that's, it's always a problem when you get stuck in a position and you are confined to a certain position and you don't have space to move in it. I can imagine how draining it must be for both of you to always have to, you know, you always have to be following, you always have to be the leader. It's like you're not really a true leader now. The dance is the leader. Right? [*Emphasizes that the cycle is the problem.*]

Although not always easily apparent, dominance often arises when one partner needs another partner to bolster his or her sense of identity and compensate for perceived deficits in the self or make up for past losses or fears. Escalating efforts at coercion thus often need to be understood as attempted solutions to the problems of satisfying underlying identity needs. The insecure, dominant partners need to feel superior to their spouses, build in an inherent sense of competition in the relationship, with the dominant spouses always needing to be one up or prove they are right. These relationships often start off with the dominant partner being helping or encouraging to the weaker partner. Helping can maintain the dominant's status as superior and soon involves pointing out faults, in subtle and not so subtle ways, in the submissive partner's behaviors. Criticism is offered as just helping. Growth in the underdog, or increasing assertion of an independent identity, as occurred often in women in the 1970s, during the feminist revolution, often leads to more open competition and exposes the dominant partner's insecurities. When the knight in shining armor no longer has a damsel in distress who needs rescuing, he may find he becomes a frog!

Processes in the dominant partner that appear essential to resolution are first allowing a previously disavowed core emotion of fear or shame. This facilitates the dominant individual both to change his or her interactional stance and to carry forward his or her experience of the self into new territory. Acknowledging reveals to the other and also opens the self to the possibility of self-soothing and transformation. Accessing deep-rooted fear or shame related to threats to identity makes possible the assertion of unmet identity needs, and finally communicating a genuinely felt vulnerability to one's partner promotes a "softening" of each partner's position.

Dominant individuals tend to deflect, avoid, or distance themselves from vulnerable emotions, never allowing themselves to fully experience *any* primary core emotions. Perhaps for this reason, they remain unable to move from the level of dominance. When partners cannot (or are unwilling to) find the words that accurately capture their felt experiencing of a situation, they remain stuck. However, when they allow themselves to focus on feeling and verbalize what is implicit in their bodily felt reactions, they can "carry forward" their experiencing into novel territory (Gendlin, 1996). Further change then becomes possible by self-soothing and by accessing other, more adaptive feelings of worth and value. Finally it seems that it is the affiliative emotions of liking and loving their partners that provide the motivation for dominants to change themselves. It is these that need to be evoked to help dominant partners be willing to confront their own dominance issues.

Reciprocal Cycles

In addition to the complementary cycles previously described, couples engage in symmetrical cycles. These often are the result of failures to resolve complementary cycles in which one partner changes position to match that of the other partner.

Attack–Attack Cycles

These cycles periodically occur in the affiliation domain, when the distancer eventually changes position, turns to attack, and fights back when attacked by the pursuer. These cycles can escalate into very hurtful name-calling interactions that partners later regret. One partner may say hurtful things such as, "You're a baby, so needy and demanding, grow up." The other partner may say, "You're so cold, ice wouldn't melt in your mouth, open up." In most cases beneath reciprocal cycles we will find that there was originally a complementary cycle—in this case, attack–defend, which turned into attack–attack when the defender changed positions and began to counterattack. Attack–attack interactions sometimes can occur as a result of dominance struggles where both partners are vying for control.

Withdraw–Withdraw Cycles

In the withdraw–withdraw pattern, both partners are reluctant to engage emotionally, and in the face of conflict, both will withdraw further. Although this may be the couple's basic pattern, it is more likely that a more basic pursue–distance or dominate–submit pattern underlies it. The withdraw–withdraw cycle frequently occurs when the pursuer has given up trying to reach the partner and withdraws or when the control struggle is so intense that a cold war has resulted. These cycles, in which there is a refusal to engage, are difficult for a couple to maintain over time. If they do, they are unlikely to bring themselves to therapy.

Control–Control Cycles

The control struggle often is the most difficult cycle to work with. Here, one partner may initially have been dominant and the other submissive, but now both need to be right and neither submits or defers. Being right, winning, or having one's definition of reality dominate becomes the key concern for each partner. Here, both partners are competitive, fighting to preserve their identities, fearing some sense of loss of control or annihilation. All couples engage in some mild control struggles, but in some, these struggles can become intense and highly destructive. The classic struggle between Richard Burton and Elizabeth Taylor in *Who's Afraid of Virginia Woolf* (Nichols, 1966) is an example of this type of destructive struggle, in which winning is more important than surviving. It is interesting to note that symmetrical submission is not usually found in couples therapy, although it can appear when both partners present as sicker or weaker or more depressed than the other and constantly react by going one-down.

Mixed-Dimension Cycles

As discussed above, in mixed-dimension cycles, the partner's main concerns differ, with one partner pursuing for closeness and the other withdrawing to protect identity. Interventions in these cycles can become complicated in that the threats and ensuing emotions in one domain for one partner often activate threats and emotions in the other domain for the other partner. EFT-C intervention, which involves accessing underlying emotions, thus is complicated by the fact that threats and emotions in one domain, in one partner, often activate threats and emotions in the other domain, in the other partner. In demand–withdraw cycles, the demanding spouse often is pursuing closeness while the withdrawer is protecting identity.

Below, we see a mixed cycle in which Linda's attachment needs are not met, and she feels abandoned and worthless, and this interacts with Brad's identity needs, and he feels like a failure. They are talking about an incident in which they were going to the theater, and he was running late because of chores he wanted to finish. The wife yearns for closeness, but this is not the core experience of the husband. He yearns for acceptance, for validation, and to feel adequate and valued rather than to feel close, but given the importance of attachment needs and their interaction with identity needs, he, of course, yearns for acceptance and validation from someone to whom he feels close.

> *Linda:* I feel that I don't ask you for a lot. I don't ask you for time every day, I don't ask you for much. It's like you are having an affair with your work, then you come home and, still I'm not important.

> *Therapist:* Uh-huh. It leaves you feeling lonely and not important.

Linda:	Yes, he's in love with his work, not me [*looking sad*].
Therapist:	Tell him how you feel. [*Empathizes.*]
Linda:	It makes me feel unloved, it makes me feel lonely and worthless, like I'm not important.
Therapist:	Like, "I am not worth much to you."
Linda:	Like I am not worth you wanting to put me as a priority. This is such an important day. We are finally able to do something together, to me, it is the pinnacle of the day and of the month. For you, going out is just another thing you need to get done.
Therapist:	Uh-uh, "I feel so disappointed because it is very special to me." [*Focuses on feeling.*]
Linda:	Yeah, I feel so disappointed that you don't feel it is equally special to me [*cries*]. I feel lonely, like you just don't care. Your paint cans are more important than me.
Therapist:	What happens when she says this now. Are you tensing up inside? [*Focuses on his reaction.*]
Brad:	I feel bad that I am letting her down again.
Therapist:	Somehow it is just like, "I'm letting her down." It sounds to me like it must feel awful that it is always like a failure, and the failure prevents you from responding to her loneliness. Can you tell her that you hear that she is lonely and feeling unloved? [*Symbolizes his shame-based feeling of failing her and coaches him to respond to her.*]
Brad:	I understand what you are saying, that you are feeling that I am not loving you and that you are lonely. I am sorry that I put you through that.
Therapist:	Are you able to say sorry without condemning yourself or feeling like a failure? [*Coaches him by focusing on apology rather than self-blame.*]
Brad:	Yeah, I can.
Therapist:	Because you can focus on, "Oh god, I'm no good," that's not really responding to her. She needs you right now to hear her. She really needs you, and it sounded like you are more focused on "I'm a failure," and, . . .
Linda:	It sounded like he failed me that he is guilty, it doesn't feel to me like you, you look at it like a character flaw, rather than it is a mistake of judgment.
Therapist:	What do you need from him? [*Focuses on her asking rather than blaming.*]

Linda: I need him to acknowledge it, and say, "Next time I will do it different, it is easier for me to."

Brad: I do feel sorry, I guess I didn't make a judgment appropriate, I should prioritize. I am sorry.

Linda: Yeah.

Brad: I realize the importance of being out together, or being together once we are doing it.

Linda: I feel validated.

A little later in the session:

Therapist: Clearly, Linda has a need for you to be there with her [*turning to Linda*]. You end up feeling that "I'm not as important as the paint cans." But for you, Brad, something important is going on for you that the paint cans are important to you—that the paint cans take on a significance in your life, but what is it? That's what I think we need to get at. Is it like, "I am uncomfortable, if I don't get to them"?

Brad: Well, I don't know, I do feel like I need to get them done. I feel a lot of pressure. They have to get done.

Therapist: I don't know, is it like you feel coerced and get angry? What is going on for you when the paint cans become important? It is something that drives you. Linda's need is clear, but you also need something, you are driven by certain anxiety that you need to get things done or something, but it is harder to talk about exactly what is driving you. If you don't get the paint cans done, what would happen? [*Empathic conjecture into his feelings and concerns.*]

Brad: The paint brushes will dry up, it will be more money, I could have done it another time, as long as my hands were in it, it is just one of those things, it is just the job that needs to be done.

Therapist: Chores will have to get done. When do you remember this beginning, having to keep up or get things done whatever? [*Identifies origins of the concern to finish things or be perfect.*]

Brad: I guess I can reflect back, my mother was very productive that way, my father was very driven but not successful in completion in his jobs, I vowed that I would never be like that. If I started something. I would finish it.

Therapist: Did your mum get at him about it? [*Explores family context.*]

Brad: She was a task master.

Therapist: She was a task master for him or for you so that she makes sure that you got it done. How did you react? Did you comply, or did you rebel? [*Explores his past pattern.*]

Brad: I would try to sleep in late and do it reluctantly, but in some cases I did an incomplete job.

Therapist: And then what would happen?

Brad: For the most part, she would get angry.

Therapist: What was it like for you?

Brad: I felt inadequate, I guess.

Therapist: It sounds like that must have been difficult. Somehow you had to learn how to protect yourself. [*Touches on his vulnerability to feel shame and feeling inadequate from the past.*]

Brad: I assume all families will go through this process, how do we get around that?

Therapist: It has left its mark on you. It sounds to me like it felt bad, you felt afraid of her anger . . . [*Identifies vulnerability.*]

Brad: More of my father's anger, he would give it to me.

Therapist: What was it like? Was it scary or . . .

Brad: My mother was not too scary, yes, she got very upset when I don't fulfill my duties, and my father would be verbally and physically abusive.

A few minutes later:

Therapist: The feeling that, I better push and push to get enough done, so that I will be able to relax, I guess, you need to get everything done so you can . . .

Brad: feel a sense of accomplishment

Therapist: So what drives you is a sense of accomplishment, is it crossing-off-my-list accomplishment or I-have-won-the-race accomplishment?

Brad: I think it is the list accomplishment that I have.

Therapist: So you kind of walk around carrying a bag of chores, if you can empty it . . .

Brad: Mm-hm.

Therapist: . . . right, then you can feel lighter [*laughs*]. [*Identifies his core concern.*]

Here we see he is concerned about adequacy and has a need to complete things. He is not afraid of closeness but organizes his world more instrumentally. She has higher relational needs and feels unloved and pursues. The more he is preoccupied, the lonelier she feels, and the more she demands, and then he feels inadequate and withdraws and also feels like a failure that he cannot give her the love she needs.

A further complication may arise because secondary emotions in the identity domain often obscure more primary emotions in the attachment domain in the same partner. For example, if a wife feels that her husband is not committed, she will experience attachment-related emotions of primary fear associated with insecurity. But her experience of threatened attachment also can lead her to feel he is not committed because she is inadequate or flawed, and she may feel she is in some way responsible for his reduced commitment—a primary feeling of shame in the identity domain. She may then defensively criticize him and stir up his feeling that he is inadequate as a person (a primary emotion of shame in the identity domain). He then can become afraid that she would not want to remain with him—a secondary feeling in the attachment domain. Thus, in many conflicts, emotions from both dimensions can be alive in both partners.

Sometimes, conflict within a person may also cause couples conflict. For example, a person may want to be close to someone and, at the same time, free to pursue his or her own interests, or he or she may want, but also fear, closeness. This type of intrapsychic conflict can produce relational difficulties and set up complex interactional patterns of moving close and pushing away and may ultimately need individual therapy in addition to couples therapy.

Positive Interactional Cycles

There are two forms of positive cycles, one related to closeness and the other related to identity, and they tend to merge, but it is useful to identify two different components in positive cycles: nurturing and validation. When partners nurture, they take care of each other, offer support, and attempt to meet each other's needs for closeness and security. Responsiveness to attachment needs ranges from caring and soothing the other emotionally, to doing helpful and nurturing things such as cooking or fixing things for the partner. When partners validate each other they are doing something different— they see and understand the other, treat their identity needs as important, and confirm their identities. They value and respect the other, are sensitive to the other's preferences, and see positive qualities in the other. We thus can think of positive cycles as either more nurturing or more validating. The former provide safety and security, the latter are more confirming and strengthening. In nurturing cycles, people feel caring and cared for, whereas in empathic cycles, they feel understanding and understood. These two positive feeling behaviors do interact because people generally feel cared for when they feel understood by their partners and feel understood when cared for. However, it is helpful to see that a person could feel nurtured or cared for by a mother or a nurse, for example, but not feel understood or validated, whereas one could feel understood and validated as a good person by a teacher or relative, say, but not nurtured or cared for. In fact, it is possible and often occurs that people feel nurtured by parents or spouses who meet needs for security, but they feel the caretaker is critical, makes fun of them, or is not proud of them, and therefore they do not feel validated. Couples do best when they both nurture and validate each other. For example, one partner may offer both by saying, "Losing that account must have been really disappointing. You worked so hard, and to have it snatched away like that would make me sad and furious. What can I do? Would you like a cup of tea, a hug?"

PROBLEMATIC EMOTIONS IN INTERACTIONAL CONFLICT

It is instructive to look at predictors of divorce to see how central emotion is in marital conflict and to discern which emotions are most problematic. Gottman, Coan, Carrère, and Swanson (1998) found that observer-rated facial expression of emotion was the best predictor of divorce. The wife's facial contempt and/or disgust, as well as the husband's fear and miserable smile and the wife's miserable smile, were the strongest predictors of divorce. Accompanying these facial expressions of contempt and fear, both partners were found to be more defensive (e.g., made excuses, denied responsibility). Wives complained and criticized more, whereas husbands stonewalled and disagreed more. The prototypic process leading to divorce appears to be one in which husbands become physiologically aroused in fear or shame. The wife tries to reengage, becomes physiologically aroused, and blames. The wife then expresses criticism, contempt, and disgust, and eventually withdraws. There is then a lack of emotional engagement, and they live parallel lives. Facial communications of affect seem to regulate this whole process.

The most troublesome overt emotions in couples conflict, in our clinical experience, are the expressed secondary emotions of anger and contempt. The most problematic unexpressed emotions are the unexpressed primary emotions of fear and shame. Couples conflict, as we have seen, results from negative interactional cycles supported by the expression of secondary emotional states. Thus, there are cycles of attack and defend, supported predominantly by secondary anger that obscures underlying fears of abandonment, and there are cycles of dominate and submit, supported predominantly by secondary emotions of anger and contempt that obscure underlying shame of diminishment or fear of loss of control. The troublesome emotions fall essentially into two broad classes. The first class involves the relationship-destructive approach emotions involved in attack or blaming, the second involve the relationship-eroding withdrawal emotions involved in walling off or avoiding. The attack emotions involve the hostile triad of anger, disgust, and contempt. Empowering anger, however, can be adaptive and relationship enhancing. It is an adaptive response to feeling unfairly treated and helps sets boundaries. It also is an adaptive territorially and hierarchically related emotion that is a response to challenge and that protects identity. It is only in maladaptive and secondary forms that it leads to attack, promotes attempts to destroy, and is focused on the other rather than on protection of the self. In these destructive states, people use "you" language to blame, for example, "You are bad, wrong, [and so on]." Related to anger is disgust. Disgust comes from distaste, in which one spits out what is rotten, whereas contempt comes from "dissmell," in which we lift our noses to move away from a bad smell (Tomkins, 1963). In their healthy form, these emotions help people get rid of and stay away from what is bad for them. In their unhealthy form, they become insult, indignation, and denigration.

The withdrawal emotions in conflict are fear and shame. Fear, in its healthy form, helps people escape, and shame, in its adaptive form, involves shrinking away from the gaze of others to avoid being ostracized and protects one's belonging to the group by ensuring he or she does not engage in nonnormative behavior. In their nonadaptive forms, fear leads to avoidance, shame leads to hiding, and both lead to withdrawal from connection. These two primary emotions generally are obscured in couples interactions by secondary avoidance responses. These secondary responses often are more behavioral, such as stonewalling (an emotional expression of anxiety) and dominating and controlling to regulate the shame and fear, or submitting, also to regulate the shame and fear. Sadness, the response to loss, can generate an approach or a withdrawal response. An initial response to loss is to cry out for the lost object, but if there is no response, to withdraw to conserve resources. So sadness may lead to pursuit or to withdrawal.

Another problem is that oftentimes positive, relationship-enhancing emotions either are not being felt, are not being expressed, or simply are absent. A couple may have developed a secure base and may respect each other, but because of familiarity, routine, child-rearing responsibilities, or stress, they may no longer be enjoying each other. These are marriages that are stable but not flourishing. The remedy here is not resolving a conflictual cycle but engendering more positive emotion through new kinds of interactions and experiences. This involves increasing the positive emotions. Feelings of cherishing and being cherished and enjoying and being enjoyed need to be stimulated.

Emotions Underlying Interactional Positions

In EFT-C, we facilitate access to unacknowledged emotion and promote the soothing and regulation of dysregulated emotion, as well as the

TABLE 8.1
Emotions Underlying Interactional Positions in Cycles

Position	Primary emotion	Secondary emotion
Affiliation (attachment) cycles		
Pursuer	Fear of abandonment	Anger
	Sadness at loss	Contempt
Distancer	Anxiety or inadequacy	Emotion avoidance
	Resentment	Disregard
		Depression
Influence (identity) cycles		
Dominant controller	Shame or fear	Contempt
	Anger	
Submitter	Fear or inadequacy	Caring
	Anger	Placating
Positive (virtuous) cycles		
Affiliation	Caring, endearing, cherishing	Neutral, task focused
(both partners)	Enjoyment, pleasure	No emotion
		Lack of pleasure
Influence	Pride, liking, respecting	Taking other for granted
(both partners)	Excitement, awe, curiosity	Boredom

Note. Primary and secondary emotions in each interactional position in affiliation, influence, and positive cycles are shown.

expression of previously unexpressed, vulnerable feelings to partners. This leads to change in self and in interactions. Table 8.1 shows the primary and secondary feelings in both affiliation and influence cycles, and these are described in greater detail below.

The Affiliation Cycle

Threats to attachment–security produce fear and sadness followed by anger and protest. This is a very important emotional dynamic in conflict. Caretaking, however, involves warmth, nurture, and compassion. This occurs naturally in response to expressed fear and sadness but is not a natural response to anger and protest, which rather begets defense, withdrawal, or counterattack. As shown in Table 8.1, the primary emotion in the pursuer in response to threats to security in the affiliation cycle is fear, but the expressed secondary emotion is anger. In the distancer, the primary emotions are fear of intimacy of being overwhelmed or intruded on, or there may be anger at intrusion, but the expressed secondary emotions are complex expressions related to avoidance and involve depression, a protective wall, indifference, or defensive rejection. The distancer longs to be connected but is anxious and afraid of disappointment or fears intrusion. Expression of the underlying fear or sadness at loss by the blamer helps the distancer let down the wall and brings the distancer closer. Expressions of underlying fear of being rejected or overwhelmed or anger at intrusion in the distancer is reengaging and provides much-needed contact for the pursuer.

The choice of which partner's underlying experience to focus on at any moment depends to a large extent on who is most receptive and accessible. Thus, the Mao Tse Tung saying "dig where the ground is soft" is the best guide. However, in our experience, we have found that with pursue–distance couples, it often is easier to first access the hurt beneath the blaming position of the pursuer. Attempting to get a strongly distant or withdrawn person to come out puts the therapist in the position of a pursuer, and pursuers have less power than withdrawers to change this type of interaction. However, empathy to a withdrawer, accepting and respecting the protective function of the wall, may help them come out. In heterosexual couples, when the man is a nonresponsive distancer, the woman may be reluctant to express her needs for closeness without any sign of his receptivity. He, however, is also unlikely to let down his wall if he feels he will again be battered. The sequence question of whether to first access a pursuer or a distancer therefore is best seen as a case of asking the wrong question. The couple, rather, is best seen as a mutually regulating, dynamic system in which both are changing little by little until one partner changes position, makes a state change, and reveals underlying feelings.

The Influence Cycle

When the conflict is in the identity domain, the threat is not to connection or security, as such, but to partners' identities. Here, the dominant person's identity, self-esteem, or status in the relationship is challenged. As shown in Table 8.1, when people's dominant roles or view of self are threatened, they respond with secondary or instrumental anger or contempt to protect their position in their own and in others' eyes. The primary emotions that are felt when there is a challenge to identity or dominance come from shame at diminishment or invalidation and fear of loss of standing or control, in the eyes of others and one's self. In the submissive partner, complex secondary responses to being controlled can be seen, as well as responses of placating, caretaking, or pleasing that obscure the more primary emotions of either fear of, or anger at, annihilation or inadequacy fears, or both. Expression of underlying shame and fears in the dominant partner would beget nonsubmissive, more empathic and compassionate responses from the previously submissive partner. Assertive expression of fear or anger from the submissive partner helps dominant partners to become more aware of and confront the problems inherent in their dominance.

Dominance, however, can also emerge in the pursuer in affiliation cycles, in service of getting needs for closeness met when attachment is threatened.

Thus, dominance also can arise to achieve closeness and results in a demand–withdraw pattern. When dominance emerges in an affiliation cycle, however, it is not shame based, but fear based. And the fear is fear of abandonment, not the fear of loss of control that occurs in threats to identity.

The Flourishing Cycle

Table 8.1 shows the type of deficits that arise in positive emotions. The deficits often can be recognized by the emotions that are present as a function of the deficit. When there is a paucity of the more primary experiences of attraction, enjoyment, cherishing, pride, respect, excitement, and pleasure, we are dealing with a more pragmatic task-focused relationship that lacks warmth. There is a lack of pleasure in each other, and the partners take each other for granted. This often is coupled with feelings of boredom, which can be described as the desire to have a desire. These are couples who do not necessarily have conflict but there is no life left in their connection. Therapy then needs to engender more positive emotions by having people both remember and reexperience the desire for each other and the positive feelings that brought them together. This can be done with questions such as, How did you fall in love? What do you most enjoy doing together? What is the most excitement you have felt with each other? or What do you respect, or are proud about, in each other? In addition, homework exercises to engender more positive experience in their daily living can be helpful. Here, positive actions, such as giving presents or flowers, going on dates, sharing activities, and creating couple time are all helpful. Positive emotions that help promote positive cycles thus are encouraged. The experience of expression of emotions such as joy, love, compassion, and excitement provide a reservoir of positive sentiment that acts as an inoculation against further conflict. When there is a storehouse of positive feelings, negative reactions are less likely to be evoked.

CONCLUSION

Destructive cycles, be they purely about closeness or identity, or mixed, all result from unexpressed primary emotions and needs. The cycles form around partner's most sensitive concerns. They are based on what each partner feels most vulnerable about and needs most.

Our goal, then, is to help people reveal the underlying and generally more vulnerable emotions of fear and shame, and in the case of withdrawers and submitters, the empowering emotion of anger. We also want to help people to begin to engage in validation and empathic responsiveness and appreciation of each other. In addition, we need to promote more positive emotions. People, however, find it difficult to acknowledge and share some of their more dreaded emotions, and therapists need to coach them to approach, tolerate, regulate, understand, and transform these states. Partners also have difficulty expressing positive emotions, often feeling shy or embarrassed, and they need encouragement and structure to expose softer positive feelings.

9

THERAPEUTIC TASKS: FOCUSING ON INDIVIDUAL EMOTIONAL STATES

The secret of getting ahead is getting started. The secret of getting started is breaking your complex overwhelming tasks into small manageable tasks, and then starting on the first one.

—Mark Twain

In the previous chapter, we described common negative interaction cycles in couples and examined how the therapist can best intervene with couples to transform these cycles. Although this involved some individual work in terms of helping each partner self-soothe, the focus primarily was on the interaction: helping couples identify and label negative cycles; disclose to each other underlying vulnerabilities; express to each other their needs; and respond to each other with empathy, compassion, and appreciation.

In this chapter, we explore individual work in the context of couples therapy. Previous work in individual emotion-focused therapy (Greenberg, Rice, & Elliott, 1993) underlies this approach, in particular, the use of markers of emotionally based problem states along with the corresponding therapist interventions that best fit these markers. This approach, as we described in previous chapters, is based on the idea that the therapist uses different interventions at different markers to promote different types of emotional processing and different types of problem resolutions. In these marker-guided, task-focused interventions in individual therapy, the therapist generally guides the client to pay attention to important aspects of his or her emotional experience or the evoking situation that he or she might not have registered in conscious awareness. One of the goals is to evoke new experience. The new experience and information makes a difference in the way the client feels, perceives his or her situation, and makes sense of his or her response. In couples, some of these same processes plus others specific to working with couples will apply. The markers and interventions from individual therapy that we have found most relevant to, and have adapted to, couples therapy are (a) systematic evocative unfolding of problematic reaction points, (b) focusing on an absent or unclear felt sense, (c) empathically affirming vulnerability, and (d) undoing self-interruptive splits. We have adapted these interventions to fit the couples context. The first three are discussed in the sections that follow. The fourth was discussed in the section Overcoming Self-Interruptions in chapter 7.

SYSTEMATIC EVOCATIVE UNFOLDING OF PROBLEMATIC REACTION POINTS

Evocative responding involves an attempt by the therapist to reevoke a problematic experience to bring it alive in the session to help people expand, differentiate, and reprocess reactions of theirs that they found puzzling (L. Rice & Greenberg, 1984). In the context of couples therapy, the problematic reactions generally are fights or arguments in which one or both partners see their own responses as problematic, such as when one or both say, "We had a pretty good week, except on Sunday we had this fight. It just came out of nowhere. We just got into it. I'm not sure why I or we responded that way." They view their responses as undesirable or too intense and as inevitably evoking negative responses in each other but are puzzled as to what triggered them or why they respond as they do. An example is one partner's sudden and instant frustration or attacking behavior to the other partner's silence as a response to a seemingly harmless request, such as a query as to what they might do today. Another example is the sudden explosion by a husband in response to his wife's request to turn down the radio. Such fights usually come from automatic emotion-schematic-based emotional responses that the partners had in the situation.

The three elements of problematic reaction points (PRPs; Greenberg, Rice, & Elliott, 1993) adapted to couples are (a) the partners recount a particular instance of a disagreement or fight they had during the week in a particular situation; (b) the partners' responses are felt to them to be problematic; and (c) there is some indication that the partners view their own reactions as problematic or puzzling, not simply as an unfortunate consequence of their partner's behavior. When such a problematic couples reaction presents itself, then the therapist uses evocative unfolding to revivify both the situation and each partner's reactions to help them better understand what occurred. It is the understanding of each partner's problematic reaction in terms of their perceptions and underlying feelings that is important. The first step before engaging in this type of exploration is to ensure that there is a good alliance with the therapist. The task then for the therapist is to ask the partners to vividly reconstruct the situation, encouraging each partner to be as detailed as possible about what occurred for them in the situation. There are two aspects of a PRP that need to be linked—the stimulus situation and the person's subjective response. The stimulus is generally some aspect of a partner's communication, such as his or her voice, although it could be a broader aspect of the situation, such as the cold, dark room, that evokes the feeling of loneliness. Therapists can use questions such as "What were you aware of then?" and "What did you feel when that happened?" to aid in the reconstruction of the situation. Reflections and conjectures as to how the client might have felt and what the experience appears to have meant to him may be used to help the partners bring their automatic perceptual processes and their responses into awareness. These questions, reflections, and suggestions are offered in a supportive manner to allow the partners to attend fully to their experience.

The earmark of the intervention is that it uses sensory connotative language to unfold inner subjective reactions to the stimulus situation. For example, the therapist attempting to vividly evoke the stimulus that triggers the partner's reaction might say, "Just the way she was up there at the top of the stairs looking down her nose at you." This will help him begin to get to his unacknowledged subjective response of humiliation that led to his reaction of "feeling depressed for the whole day." Attempting to evoke a wife's anxious dependent subjective response to her husband when he came home from work, the therapist might say, "Feeling like a little puppy dog just pattering after him," or to evoke the husband's nagging response of fear that he will never be good enough, the therapist might say, "This feeling of not quite good enough is always there just nibbling at the edges." The partners, with the help of this connotative evocation, can reenter the scene and begin to reexperience what occurred for them. They can then bring to awareness previously automatic responses and begin to form more idiosyncratically accurate, complete constructions of their own experience. Given that the problematic reaction of, say, getting inexplicably angry or suddenly withdrawing is an automatic response, each partner's reaction was triggered by some stimulus that activated the partner's tacit emotion scheme that constitutes the base of half of the negative cycle in which the couple is caught. The basic idea in working with PRPs is to help the partners recognize that the puzzling aspects of their reactions are explicable in terms of the unacknowledged ways that they tacitly construed the stimulus situation and the emotional response this evoked. Once this is achieved, it may be possible to make the link from this one situation to the way the partner construes things in the relationship more generally. Ultimately, the goal is to build on this new experience about how the partners construe each other and what responses this evokes in them, to restructure their constructions and, ultimately, their interactions.

Stages of Therapist Operations in Evocative Unfolding

Greenberg, Rice, and Elliot (1993) identified four stages of therapist operations in evocative unfolding, which are described and elaborated on here.

Stage 1: Positioning for Exploration

- Identify relevant marker: "So you are puzzled by your reaction to that conversation";
- verify problematic aspect: "It is the way you're depressed and the withdrawn feeling that is so puzzling"; and
- suggest exploring the problematic reaction: "Let's explore that a little more."

Stage 2: Experience Reevoked

- Stimulate reexperiencing the scene: "So there you were. Agnes was standing at the top of the stairs in her night gown; you, at the bottom, briefcase in hand, were ready to leave for work" and
- facilitate search for salience in the stimulus: "It was just the way she was looking down her nose at you."

Stage 3: Tracking Construed Personal Meaning of Stimulus Situation

- Maintain client's focus on emotional reactions to stimulate them: "Just a sinking feeling inside";
- maintain client's focus on construal of demand characteristics of stimulus situation: "They look like they are saying 'What do you know?' or 'What . . .?'"; and
- acknowledge and focus on client's spontaneous recognition of meaning bridge between stimulus and reaction: "I see, just I try so hard but, like, I never seem to be able to please her. I felt that quite strongly and begin to feel hopeless."

Stage 4: Facilitate Broader Self-Exploration

- Facilitate client's reexamination of emotion-based self-schemes: "Like, I never feel good enough";
- facilitate broader reexamination of emotion-based self-schemes in other relationships: "Like, I always felt this sense of wanting to hide from my father's disapproving looks"; and
- acknowledge and focus on client's new understanding of own emotion-scheme-guided vulnerabilities, dysfunctional styles,

and the new implications for self-change: "I know I am vulnerable to feeling inadequate, and I know she is not really saying this to me and that actually I do a pretty good job, and she often tells me so."

In applying these steps, the focus initially is on one partner, but at some point the focus shifts and the other partner's perceptions and reactions are explored. In addition, partners interact during this process, and this leads to new input, which helps deepen the explorations and also leads to restructuring, as partners often discover their partners were not feeling, thinking, or doing what they thought they were.

Often it is best for the interactional cycle to have been labeled before engaging in any systematic evocative unfolding. For example, if a cycle already has been labeled as pursue–distance, then if a husband talks about a recent troubling experience where he just felt that he had to get away from his partner, adding in a self-annoyed tone that this now feels like an overreaction on his part is a marker of a PRP and an opportunity for systematic evocative unfolding. It is useful to note that it is important to follow the person's primary response of "needing to get away," not his secondary reaction to it, his self-annoyance. What often occurs, however, at the point of stating a PRP is that the person and then the therapist will focus on his or her current response, in this situation, the husband's response of self-annoyance at his reaction, instead of focusing on exploring his initial reaction. So if he begins to talk in such a way that the therapist senses that he is discounting his initial reaction as bad or wrong, the therapist has to bring him back to a discussion of his troubling withdrawal reaction in the original situation. The following steps are then promoted.

Reevoke Experience

The therapist suggests that the partners try to get back to the situation and that they attempt to reevoke the experience of what happened. The therapist now promotes both partners' reentry to the situation by trying to get a vivid picture of the situation just before the interaction becomes negative and then focusing them on their initial reactions. The therapist does this by attempting to paint a picture of the situation (e.g., "So there you were in the kitchen"), describe what the physical environment was like (e.g., "it was sunny"), include what was going on in the situation and what the partners were saying to each other (e.g., "She was sitting at the table having coffee and saying what?"), and what their thoughts and feelings were at the time ("What were you feeling in your body? What was going through your head?"). The therapist thus focuses them on, and tries to get them to describe, what it was like for them just after their initial reactions. In addition, getting a contrast between what it was like just before and after the triggering incident helps give a better sense of what triggered the problematic reaction. When the experience comes alive in a vivid way in the session, the therapist takes another step.

This next step involves searching for what was salient in the situation for each partner that triggered their reactions. It is extremely important not to try to anticipate what might be salient for the partner. Thus a husband might say, "It was your silence in response to my saying I would like to spend the morning together that got to me," whereas the wife might say, "It was the demanding tone in your voice that upset me." The therapist then goes back and forth between helping the partners get a flavor of the quality of their feeling reaction and helping them to become more aware of how they construed the situation, especially each other's behavior. Thus, the husband is able to describe holding his breath and tensing up inside at his perception of her cold aloofness, while she contacts a memory of the knot in her stomach and feeling angry at his demandingness. Of course, the feeling and the construal (automatic appraisal) are linked, but it is important to separate them, especially at the beginning, because it will help each partner achieve more vivid experiential awareness. Concerning the feeling reaction side, when a client begins to use emotional terms to describe how he or she felt, therapists can help by reflecting the feeling to increase the focus on the feelings and can conjecture or provide tentative suggestions as to what each partner may have felt to deepen the feeling. Thus, the therapist might conjecture to the husband "feeling unloved, unwanted" and to the wife "feeling trapped."

The therapist helping the partners focus on their construal of the other needs to recognize anything new in the client's discussion of the situation. An example would be a client's identification of a "smug look" on a partner's face or, as we discussed earlier, "just the way she looked down her nose at me." When the partners describe self and other in connotative and sensory language, the therapist knows they have revoked the situation and the partners are reexperiencing their feelings and perceptions.

The last step for each partner is to make the link from this particular instance to how he or she generally experiences the other. The therapist helps the client explore these links in such a way as to avoid intellectual analysis and maintain a focus on the client's own inner awareness as the search proceeds. Therapists do not anticipate the areas toward which the search should move, or try to direct it toward particular conclusions. Rather, therapists empathically reflect the newly emerging edges of the client's experience. Often in the earlier stages of therapy, the exploration stops here, with the partners' understanding what drove their own response such as "I just felt so dismissed, that's why I withdrew, and it does happen in other situations too." As therapy progresses and partners are able to take more of a self-focus, the therapist will also explore some of the psychogenetic origins of the partners' perception and reactions that lead them to be particularly sensitive to these triggers and react in these ways.

What follows is a segment of a session with a married couple, Herb and Wilma, in which she pursued for closeness and he felt inadequate and withdrew. He was more introverted, and she sought out other people. In the past, at the beginning of the relationship, there had also been issues of her interest in another man and her trustworthiness. In the segment that follows, they are discussing a situation in which they had had a fight after being out at Herb's company Christmas party.

Herb: In the beginning, I felt up and then was enjoying myself and felt good.

Wilma: And he was talking with everybody . . .

Therapist: Yeah.

Wilma: . . . he was very animated.

Therapist: Mm-huh, so when, at what point does this change?

Herb: It changed when, I think—you know, we got up and went dancing for [a] few times and came back, and as you know, you know as time went on, there are less and less people staying at the table, and you may migrate off to different areas as well.

Therapist: So, like, you are sitting there at the table, and how do you feel about that? [*Focuses on the situation and his reaction.*]

Herb: Well, at times it is okay 'cause it was, there's no people there, but finally when it was just Wilma and I who came back to the table, and it was just an empty table, we sat down, and then she said, "I'm going to get a drink," so I am now by myself.

Therapist: So this is the first moment of sort of "I'm alone." [*Focuses on internal reaction.*]

Herb: So, I'm thinking, well, yeah, it's sort of the start of it, well, I'm thinking, "I'm by myself, she will be back, so I'll just enjoy the music. . . ."

Therapist: Yeah.

Herb: . . . It was alright for a while, and then I look around and than I start seeing the other people that used to be at the table, and then I think I start doing something, I don't know, I think, I start playing head games with myself . . .

Therapist: Yeah, yeah.

Herb: . . . and I start thinking things like, "Oh, I guess I'm not good enough to keep them here at my table." It's stupid things, like, that I start saying to myself . . .

Therapist: Uh-huh, uh-huh.

Herb:	. . . and it's the old—old tape recording that goes on that is very neurotic, um, and it's very stupid . . .
Therapist:	So it's somehow, sort of the "I'm not good enough" feeling there that emerges when you see all these people out there, somehow there is the sense of, "If I was good enough, they would want to come talk to me or they would . . .
Herb:	Yeah.
Therapist:	. . . stay at the table. . . ."
Herb:	Yeah.
Therapist:	. . . Okay, I see that you are sort of angry and frustrated with yourself for doing it, . . .
Herb:	Yeah.
Therapist:	. . . but it's something that happens, especially if you're faced with this "I'm all alone here, and they are all out there." It's a feeling of rejection, sort of like a maybe a feeling of wanting to shrink inside. [*Focuses on internal reaction, connotative use of language.*]
Herb:	Yeah . . . and the feeling, I can't seem to overcome it because I now don't don't feel confident enough in myself to get up and go and sit and just plop myself down in someone else's conversation.
Therapist:	And going and finding Wilma is hard.
Herb:	Um. Yeah.
Wilma:	Yeah, that's what I wondered about, like why didn't you just come and find me?
Herb:	I guess because I was sitting there at the time waiting for you to come back, you've just gone to get a couple of drinks so I kept thinking you won't take long, "She's only going to be a minute," then . . .
Therapist:	Right.
Herb:	. . . already 20 minutes go by . . .
Therapist:	And by that time, the tape in your head has started.
Herb:	It has already started, yeah.
Therapist:	So you sit down, you're alone, she's gone, a little bit of time expires, you start looking around, and what do you focus on? [*Focuses on stimulus side.*]
Herb:	Well, yeah, that's the thing, like, I'm still fine, I'm watching people dance, and I'm enjoying the music and all of the sudden I feel like people are watching me.

Therapist: So it's also that they are watching and thinking . . . [*Focuses on salience in stimulus.*]

Herb: They're thinking, well, you know, "He's sitting there all by himself . . .

Therapist: Yeah.

Herb: . . . you know he's no good."

Therapist: . . . "He's no good," so that's a painful kind of thing; so you look at her, she smiles, what happened? [*Focuses on present interaction.*]

Wilma: Well, because he knows he's not no good . . .

Therapist: Mm-hm.

Herb: I know, that's the thing, but that night towards the end of the night I got very . . .

Therapist: Yes.

Herb: . . . angry with myself . . .

Therapist: Mm-hm.

Herb: . . . because I was thinking of myself, "You are 35 years old, what's going on here? This is not high school, this is a very childish thing," I just thought of.

A few minutes later, after she has tried to reassure him that other people speak highly of him:

Therapist: Once you are planted, it's like you begin to withdraw, that's the difficult part, you begin to withdraw, and it is hard to signal to Wilma that this is happening. One way would be to try and say something. [*Suggests disclosing to change the interaction.*]

Herb: See, that's the thing, that it doesn't occur to me to do that, to tell her you know what it is I'm a little bit embarrassed by all of it.

Therapist: Yes, this is the struggle—this is the conflict, right. You are feeling this, and you feel like you shouldn't be feeling it, and that's the withdrawal effect you get so put out . . .

Herb: Exactly.

Wilma: The problem is that it gets progressively worse and worse and worse until we go home, and he didn't say a word to me the whole way in the car, which is almost a half an hour drive, and I'm sitting there going, . . .

Therapist: Yes, what happened?

Wilma: . . . "Here I go again. I don't know what I've done, I guess I must've done something wrong he's withdrawn again, all my dreams for the end of the evening go poof! . . ."

Therapist: Yeah.

Wilma: . . . We go to bed, actually the baby was up when we came home, we go to bed, and he doesn't start talking to me, he doesn't say a word to me, he doesn't say good night, he doesn't say a word, nothing, and here I go, I'm lying here in bed again feeling like I'm dead, he's next to me.

Therapist: And now you're feeling deserted. [*Focuses on her response.*]

Wilma: And I thought that I can't do this anymore, I can't stand it, and I got up and went to the next bed, next bedroom like, I'm not going to lie here, it's so awful for me, like, I just . . .

Therapist: You don't know what's happening.

Wilma: . . . it's like I'm lying almost, like, in a coffin, and you can't, and I'm totally alone but you're not, you have someone lying next to you . . .

Therapist: Mm-hm, mm-mm.

Wilma: . . . I'm lying on the bed in the next room and I think, "This is so stupid," and I got up and I said to him, "God damn it, what's going on? . . ."

Therapist: Mm-hm, mm-hm.

Wilma: . . . Like, the whole way in the car I was hoping he would say something, or like, I don't want to always be the one to solicit this information because, like, I sort of, like, it's not my place either, I'm not his mommy, I'm not his babysitter, I don't want to have to "What's wrong, honey," it was like I was waiting for him to tell me what was going on, and finally when I got to the bedroom, he said he told me what was going on, and he said, "I can't talk about it, I can't even recognize it when I'm in it. . . ."

Therapist: Mm-hm.

Herb: Well, the thing, like, obviously I know something is going on, but I, at the time, I felt embarrassed by it, and I didn't want to talk about it because I wasn't sure exactly what was going on and what it was that I was angry about, there was a lot of feeling nervous and clueless.

Therapist: Nervous, right, there was a lot of nervous . . .

Herb: Yeah, a great big knot.

Therapist: . . . at the time, it's kind of hard to unravel a little, that's the difficult part, you can't just speak about it at the time . . .

Herb:	Yeah.
Therapist:	. . . and that's what you both have to figure out, how to make sense of that and then [to Wilma] "What was going on?" . . .
Wilma:	Mm-hm.
Therapist:	. . . and then he said what? [Tracks the interaction.]
Wilma:	I can't really remember what he said, but he said, "I'm very depressed," and he said, "and I can't really talk about it while I'm depressed," or something, and it sort of came out in little bits and pieces, and I sort of understood what was going on. He said, "I felt abandoned, I felt, you know," and I don't think you said, "I felt no good," it was in little pieces, enough was said that I understood what was going, that I could recognize it . . .
Therapist:	Mm-hm, mm-hm.
Wilma:	. . . and he kept saying over and over how he felt so stupid . . .
Herb:	I feel very, in that situation or state of mind I feel very vulnerable . . .
Therapist:	So it's hard.
Herb:	. . . it's hard to talk about it because I feel even more vulnerable . . .
Wilma:	Yeah.
Therapist:	Yeah.
Herb:	. . . and, um . . .
Therapist:	You see this is an important, like, prototype for you, like of, How do you two handle this? See, I understand, on the one hand, for you [to Herb] it's like, "This is an internal struggle for me and it's really difficult," on the other hand, when you feel internally withdrawn, you've [to Wilma] got cause from your past, it's understandable you could personalize and somehow say, "I have done something wrong," and then you could start getting really isolated and feel deserted and closed out, and you have a high need for contact and if he is away, you feel really isolated. [Describes each partner's subjective responses.]
Wilma:	I have a high need for contact and for information.
Therapist:	Yes, so you're saying information would be enough contact, right, right?

The therapist now guides them back to the situation in the car to explore her reaction, and this further unpacks what happened for both of them.

Therapist:	So tell me, when did you first notice this total silence, so you were saying it was right after Herb, were you still at the table, or were you leaving or in the car? [*Focuses on the stimulus for her.*]
Wilma:	It was because of the silence in the ride going home in the car. It's like he's punishing me.
Therapist:	I understand, but you know, I understand, well, I think he's probably trying to handle whatever he's feeling, . . .
Wilma:	Mm-hm.
Therapist:	. . . his intent is not so explicitly if he was so in control that he was dealing out punishment to you, he would be in a much different place, I think this is part of the difficulty in that when he withdraws, it feels very punishing to you, and you sort of see him as punishing you but actually he is struggling . . .
Wilma:	Hm.
Therapist:	. . . now if we hear now what happened to him . . .
Wilma:	Yeah.
Therapist:	. . . he was a bit mad at you, but when he was sitting in the car also feeling "I shouldn't feel what I am feeling." [*Reframes and focuses on the experiences evoked.*]
Wilma:	You are probably right, and meanwhile I'm getting angrier, hmph! and angrier and yeah.
Therapist:	You're feeling, "This is really unfair, why do you do this, why are you doing this to me?"
Wilma:	Like here we go again, I'm kind of, you know, working myself up because I still have a lot of residual anger that I have.
Therapist:	Yeah, right, so you can hook you can hook, your inside feeling . . .
Wilma:	Yeah, yeah.
Therapist:	. . . 'cause I think you know you're saying [*to Herb*], "There's a lot of turmoil inside sort of feeling trapped, you know, a knot and it's complex and hard to grasp myself and tell you." And you know you [*to Wilma*] feel it's kind of intentional withholding from you, but it is more complicated. [*Reframes.*]
Wilma:	No, you're right, yes it is.
Therapist:	But so, there still is the issue of how do you signal when you're both feeling vulnerable, not mad, because you know the difficulty for all of us, it is, it's kinda hard but can you build sort of a better understanding of differences, like this is your vulnerability, this is your sensitivity, and you can end up feeling quite

	abandoned in a situation and no good—and then you'll withdraw.
Herb:	Yeah, I was, I mean, I was in that state and withdrew.
Therapist:	Right, so so that's now a real.
Herb:	A signal.
Therapist:	And for you it's easy for you to represent him as punishing and deserting you.
Wilma:	Oh, yeah.
Therapist:	You know, and also it is easy for you to sort of feel she's let you down and "she's the cause of my problem," and there's some anger that'll just feed your pain . . .
Wilma:	Mm-hm.
Therapist:	. . . and you feel this desertion and punishment . . .
Wilma:	Yeah.
Therapist:	. . . but what's really happening is you're really in a knot, and you're really feeling like, "I really need some information" . . .
Wilma:	Mm-hm.
Therapist:	. . . a minimal level, perhaps, and once you get the information and you know he's not actually punishing you, then things can be even more nurturing. [*Symbolizes underlying vulnerable feelings.*]
Wilma:	Oh, yeah, then I can, even if the information, even if he was to say to me, "I'm angry at you," at least it's still some information, it kills me not knowing.
Therapist:	Right, at least it would be information, it's the silence that's so maddening, right, it's crazy making for you, I guess, that activates all your . . . What's it like to be in the silence?
Wilma:	I just becomes very cold, and I feel very cold towards him, and I feel very angry, that's not me, that's not my natural state . . .
Therapist:	Yeah.
Wilma:	. . . that's not my natural state, and I start almost hating him.
Therapist:	Yes, but we talked about that before, the way the anger is your second reaction. . . .
Wilma:	Mm-hm.
Therapist:	. . . What happens first when he gets all distant and cold, what do you feel? [*Focuses on primary feeling.*]

Wilma:	Well, I feel abandoned myself . . .
Therapist:	Yes, yes.
Wilma:	. . . all of the sudden, I start feeling lost again and I feel like I have no purpose, and I don't think I have. I wonder if he even realizes, I wonder if you even realize how important you are to me in my life, how much of a focal point you and our child, it's like everything I do, I do for my family, that's what I love to do it, I want to take care of my family, and it's like a slap in the face . . .
Therapist:	Uh-huh.
Wilma:	. . . and you do everything you can for them.
Therapist:	His silence is like a massive slap in the face, kind of like suddenly it's, there's a massive hollow there . . .
Wilma:	Yeah.
Therapist:	. . . and also it's like a punishing vacuum, you want a lifeline to hold on to, and at certain times you feel terrible and lonely and lifeless. [*Uses connotative language.*]
Wilma:	He's, this may sound funny, he's more than a spouse, I mean, now that I'm home, he's also my job, it's my job to take care of him, nurture him, look after him, and make his life easy for him, particularly at this point, to do everything I can to make it easy for him because he has this project, and that's well, because he works full time and I don't, and every time I do all these things, all the time I keep him in mind, and I want him to do well, and when he does that to me, it's like . . .
Therapist:	Hmm. So alone, and almost you've failed in trying.
Wilma:	. . . well, yeah exactly that's part of it, so like a double negative, not only do you withdraw from me, just saying to me, "I'm no good I never tried . . ."
Therapist:	. . . uh-huh, uh-huh, and then you get mad at him, "I'm trying really hard, and I really do care, and you don't appreciate it . . ."
Wilma:	Yes, there's all those components to it.
Therapist:	Right, right.

From this point on, the process is much more reflective, positive, and solution oriented, with both husband and wife further examining their feelings of inadequacy and abandonment, respectively, and how to handle these in their relationship.

Focusing on an Absent or Unclear Felt Sense

Before partners can make themselves accessible and responsive to each other, they must be able to attend to, be aware of, and reprocess their own experience of what is occurring in the relationship. Another major task of emotion-focused couples therapy (EFT-C) involves guiding partners to focus on their unattended-to or unsymbolized emotions to help them articulate what they are feeling. Such emotions often will have the quality that Gendlin (1996) called an "unclear bodily felt sense." The focusing intervention is especially helpful early in therapy, as it involves teaching a skill that will be useful in accessing feelings later. The marker applied to couples generally is an unclear feeling about something in an interaction or when a partner is feeling vague, stuck, or blank about something that seems important. As the partners relate an event that provoked a reaction but are unable to identify the triggers or what they felt or are unclear about a current reaction to a partner, the therapist can use focusing to ask the partners to attend internally and to pay attention to what they feel in their bodies.

The steps of focusing and some directions outlined by Gendlin (1981) and adapted by Greenberg (2002a) are given here.

1. *Clearing a space.* Start by relaxing and helping the person clear his or her mind. Ask the person to get in a comfortable position and close his or her eyes; you can help your client relax by getting him or her to breathe deeply. This is especially useful for clients who have a hard time settling down or are having distracting thoughts. You might start by saying, "What are you feeling in your body? Let what comes in your body do the answering."

2. *Attending to the felt sense.* Ask the person to bring his or her attention inside his or her body where one feels things, and notice the physical sensation that is happening there right now. If the person reports that he or she does not feel anything, you could suggest to your client,

   > Think about this issue that is standing between you and feeling good about your relationship, or pick a particular issue that is troubling you right now. As you reflect on this issue, notice the physical sensation there in your body.

3. *Searching for, and checking, potential descriptions (get a label, a symbolic representation; check the accuracy of the label).* This step is referred to as getting a "handle" for the felt sense. Ask the person to describe the physical quality of the sensation that is happening and where it is happening in his or her body. You might ask, What is the quality of the felt sense? What

one word, phrase, or image comes out of this felt sense? What quality word would fit best? You can even ask clients to put a caring hand where it is happening in their body. Remember, you are looking for a description of a physical sensation, such as tightness, a knot, emptiness, heaviness, or pain. If the client describes something such as "I feel fear" or " I feel rage," ask him or her how that fear or rage feels in his or her body, "What is the quality of that physical sensation? What is the sensation in your body that you call 'fear'?" See whether the word that describes the felt sense fits; this usually brings some relief. If the person is having a hard time describing it, it is important to help him or her articulate the felt sense. Say,

> Go back and forth between the word [or image] and the felt sense. Is that word or image right? If they match, have the sensation of matching several times. If the felt sense changes, then follow it with your attention. When you get a perfect match, the words [or images] being just right for this feeling, let yourself feel that for a minute.

Note that it is important to ask your client whether it is okay to pay attention to that sensation, because it might be scary or overwhelming. Also, it is helpful to suggest the client be gentle and accepting toward the felt sense. You can help your clients accept and feel comfortable with their felt sense by suggesting that they be caring and interested in their sense, even though it is uncomfortable, and that they accept the sensations in their bodies as an important part of themselves.

4. *Feeling shift.* At this point, suggest that people focus their attention on receiving, from the felt sense, information about what the felt sense is about. Ask, "What is it about the whole problem that makes me so _____ ?" When stuck, ask questions such as "What is the worst of this feeling?" "What does the felt sense need?" "What does the felt sense want?" "What would make it feel better?" "How would 'okay' in your body feel?" "Let the body answer. What is in the way of that?"

5. *Consolidating.* Finally, guide the person to welcome what comes and to recognize that it is only one step in working on this problem, not the last. Suggest that he or she appreciate, accept, and consolidate the feeling shift without self-criticism.

The best times to use focusing are when a partner is having some difficulty in identifying just what it is that he or she is feeling, or when there is an absence of any underlying primary emotion. Externalized descriptions of relational problems offer a variant marker for focusing. Thus, if a partner is talking in circles about an issue and not getting to how he or she feels about it, you can use focusing techniques. Focusing helps people access their more primary feelings when the feelings being talked about openly are secondary and are masking more primary ones. If the nonverbal–experiential component of what is being talked about is missing, then the felt sense may be thought of as absent, because the client is not aware of it. However, if the client does have a sense that there is a feeling there but is unable to talk about or describe it, then it makes sense to think of the client as experiencing an unclear felt sense. Although the set of instructions provided suggests the client engage in focusing as a solely internal process, we suggest the use of interactional focusing, in which the therapist interacts with, as well as guides, the client at each step.

For example, in a couple in which the husband is in the role of the withdrawer, the therapist helps him focus on, and become aware of, his underlying feelings of anger, resentment, and fear. The husband, Mike, starts talking in an external manner about the content of a misunderstanding related to what his wife, Sue, meant when she said he was not to smoke. (This misunderstanding is the focus the couple has already taken when discussing this fight at home. This is a content focus, and it has resolved nothing.) The therapist now focuses him internally on his feeling rather than staying with the content.

> *Mike:* Well, I misunderstood. I thought she meant don't smoke when we are at the party.
>
> *Therapist:* Yes, but how did you feel when she said that?
>
> *Mike:* I said, "Fine." [*His response shows that he is not yet able to focus on his feelings, because he reports what he said.*]

The next set of turns by the therapist and the husband restates his current level of understanding.

> *Therapist:* And then you let up.
>
> *Mike:* Yeah, well, I misunderstood, and then she blew up.

The therapist now intervenes more strongly to have him focus on how he felt.

> *Therapist:* You have discussed how sensitive you are to what you call "put-downs." Somehow, I am just wondering how you felt when Sue commented on your smoking. If you pay attention to that place inside where you feel things, what did you feel there?

This facilitates the development of an internal felt sense, because the husband needs help in focusing on his feelings and the therapist's linking of his wife's reaction to the smoking incident and previous put-downs may help him along. His next turn confirms this.

Mike: Well, it's like, you are nauseating, you know, she's so logical and right, it's like, I'm nauseating.

Here, he has moved from talking about the misunderstanding to his construal of how his wife sees him. With this new focus and the issue of put-downs still in his mind, he is ready to talk about his feelings. And now the therapist just needs to ask him about how he feels.

Therapist: What are you feeling right now as you say that?

Mike: I feel hurt. I did feel put-down.

Now the therapist moves to helping him to find a label, or handle, for the feeling. Such handles can be key descriptive words, but here the handle is an image of a person, and we can suppose that the reference to the person represents many important descriptive words for him.

Therapist: Like your step father, Charlie. [*Brings up an image the client used earlier in the session.*]

He confirms that this handle is appropriate.

Mike: Yeah, like he was just a puppet, all those women, if they said jump, he said how high, and they commented on him all the time.

Once the therapist senses that this handle might fit his feeling, he or she can reflect the label and/or focus the client on his bodily felt sense.

Therapist: How do you feel when you talk about this now?

Mike: I feel angry. I'm sure as hell not gonna be another push-over like Charlie.

Now the therapist can resonate the label by checking to see whether the label really does fit.

Therapist: Yeah, was that what you were saying to your wife when you put the cigarette in your mouth?

Mike agrees, but his response is minimal.

Mike: Hmm.

So to make sure he or she is on the right track, the therapist checks again.

Therapist: So it sounds like you felt put down, and you also heard her telling you what to do. Is that right?

The last two sets of turns show the husband exploring the labeled feeling more deeply, and the therapist reflecting that feeling.

Mike:	Yeah, and I sure as hell felt you're [*to Sue*] not my goddamn mother.
Therapist:	"I'll show you. You can't hurt and dominate me."
Mike:	Yeah, I'm not going to be like Charlie.
Therapist:	So, "I'll do what I like."

At this point, Mike may be ready enough to explore how this reaction to Sue is a common way in which he handles his relationship with her.

We have just seen how the therapist used focusing to help the husband access his vulnerable feelings. Even though the example mainly concerned his feelings of anger and resentment, a withdrawer may also feel intimidated and incompetent with respect to his or her partner. And this was also the case with this husband. Here, the therapist elicited the anger and resentment, and, eventually, later in the session, the sense of threat that underlay this client's sullen and distancing behavior became accessible.

Key to accessing the experience of the body and the conceptual sense the person makes of it is the felt sense, the experience of being in a living body that understands the nuances of its environment by way of its responses to that environment. The felt sense is the experiential totality of that gestalt of brain and body, psyche and soma, all acting as one. The felt sense is the vehicle through which people experience themselves as an organism; it is the narrative of the whole. In the body's felt sense is to be found a seamless, integrative, coherent, and cohesive narrative of the person's experiences as mediated by the brain.

This type of somatic experiencing aims to change the focus from the head (cognitive, intellectual, and verbally dominated) to the body (somatic, sensory, visual) by fostering a process of moment-to-moment tracking of the body's shifting experiences. Initially, in focusing there often is a lack of clarity—that is why it is important to talk about physical sensation. Also, it is important to note, the felt sense is different from categorical emotions. The sense occurs bodily, as a physical, somatic sensation, not as a full-blown emotion, such as anger, with an action tendency. Often, it is sensed in the chest or throat, some specific place usually in the middle of the body. It is an internal sensation. It also is important to make the distinction between this and a more external physical sense, such as when tight muscles or a tickle on the nose is observed by the self from a more objective vantage point. Thus, for a person to have an emotional experience, the body must be involved and sensed from the inside. "The body" here means something very complex. It includes the collection of biological and/or emotional intelligence with which people are born. It also involves the complex feedback and integration between the body and all of the regions of the brain where body state and homeostasis are mediated (Damasio, 1994, 1999).

EMPATHICALLY AFFIRMING VULNERABILITY

The third marker that is highly relevant to couples is the vulnerability marker. *Vulnerability*, as it is used here, refers to a complex state in which the sense of self, the acceptable definition of "self," is at risk, resulting in considerable insecurity, anxiety, and painful affect such as sadness, shame, fear, and/or a sense of loss. Vulnerability can involve such feelings as a deep sense of having been hurt, despair about the future of the relationship or of ever finding the love one hoped for, intense shame of feeling defective, or a sense of total isolation from others. In couples work, before working on either partner's vulnerability in a more focused manner, the therapist first elaborates on how the partners' vulnerabilities interact to create a sense of deprivation and alienation, as described in previous chapters. As we know, the therapist constantly reframes cycles in terms of underlying vulnerabilities and suggests that certain emotional reactions can be seen to be motivated by these unacknowledged vulnerabilities.

When, however, partners are feeling intensely vulnerable in the moment (R. N. Goldman & Keating, 2003; Greenberg, Rice, & Elliot, 1993), therapists need to stop whatever operations they are engaged in and pay attention to this fact. When a partner is feeling this intense vulnerability, therapists should try neither to have them explore these feelings to get clarity nor to have them focus on the interaction; instead, they should empathically affirm these feelings. When the partner is in this state, the therapist uses empathic responses of prizing, affirmation, and validation, which provide support, rather than empathic exploration or conjecture, which are used to promote further exploratory processing. Empathic affirmation, rather than exploring, involves conveying a sense of understanding and validation of what this really means for the client. As one therapist affirming a client's vulnerability says, "There's just this very deep part of you that's really feeling very, very wounded and feels just so broken." Therapists responding in this way use a slow and gentle manner, encouraging clients to stay with their despairing or distressing images (e.g., "It's just like drowning" or "I've nothing left to give") and invite them to let the tears flow during this time of so much vulnerability. Therapists validate partners' experiences by understanding that this is what they are feeling and that what they are feeling makes sense. Therapists at this time also assist partners in emotion regulation, asking them to breathe and to slow down the physical symptoms of too painful emotional arousal.

Therapists assist the vulnerable partner in expressing what is so painful and bad about the situation. They reflect the intense feelings of hopelessness and powerlessness of that partner's experience, as well as the hollow feelings inside, and convey how understandable these feelings are. They find ways to reflect the immense pain of this state and convey a sense of being with the partner. Therapists validate the client's fears and feelings of responsibility and inadequacy, if these have emerged. In helping the client share this difficult experience, they provide a connection for the client that serves to break through the client's sense of isolation. Affirmation is expressed by the therapist verbally as well as nonverbally through signs of attentiveness, voice quality, posture, and facial expression. It is important to note that the focus until almost the end of this process is totally on the self. In addition, it is only once the emotion has been accepted, symbolized, and regulated and the person begins to reemerge from the vulnerability that the therapist, having modeled a soothing response, turns to the partners to encourage a response from them.

The six steps of working through vulnerability when it emerges in couples are as follows.

1. *Identify marker of the emergence of vulnerability.* The person expresses an intense, self-relevant negative emotion and is clearly feeling vulnerable at that moment. There is often a shame-based sense of feeling deeply flawed, such as "I'm a failure as a human being," or a despair about the possibility of connecting. This is usually accompanied by feeling exhausted, overwhelmed, passive, and weak. The feeling seems to be a more pervasive one that colors a variety of experiences. Clients also experience a sense that this feeling has always been with them. With this comes a sense of holding back, and a quality of the feeling being expressed for the first time. Vocal quality, posture, sighing, and facial expressions indicate the intensity of the vulnerability, even a feeling of being at the end of the road.

2. *Initial deepening.* As clients approach their vulnerable and shameful feelings on a deeper, more specific level, they are more able to describe the particular form of vulnerability, with images that are specific and concrete. One client described it as a "ship that hit the iceberg and crashed," and another said, "it's like living in black and white, when everyone else lives in color."

3. *Intense deepening: Touching bottom.* Here, clients are able to allow and to express the dreaded emotion in its full intensity. For one client, this meant expressing that he was just "a waste of space," and another simply said, "I'm so ugly." The client touches bottom and gets to the fragile core of this experience. Feelings that have previously emerged are deepened and become more visible in statements such as "I can't stand all the pain," or "I feel so fragile." Clients' level of distress increases as the pain comes to the fore. Sometimes, clients state directly that the pain is intense and feel that they cannot deal with it. Other clients describe being "shut down" physically or share feelings of being "suffocated and oppressed."

4. *Turning back to growth or hope.* This stage is characterized by a shift that involves turning back toward hope. Clients begin to express needs or tendencies associated with primary adaptive emotions. Some are related to adaptive empowering anger, as with, "I can beat this down." Another client shared, "It makes me mad, then sad." Sometimes, these are embedded in statements about the desire to change in some way, as with, "I want to change this." Clients also express the sense of being deserving of a better experience. There is also an increased sense of strength and self-efficacy.

5. *Appreciation and/or reconnection.* In this stage, the client expresses reduced distress and greater calm. The client may also convey that it was alright to have someone with him or her in this very fragile and vulnerable place, and this is shown by a willingness to share the newly emergent feelings. In most cases, the affirming other in the session first is the therapist; in those cases in which the partner may be able to respond in this way from the start, such responding is encouraged, but it is rare because partners usually want to make things better, thereby not affirming the vulnerability. This is a key and important stage in couples therapy in this event where the "vulnerable" partner comes out and reconnects with his or her partner from the more vulnerable place but from a position of strength, not weakness. Their vulnerability is now more integrated into their overall personality. His or her partner needs to be helped to acknowledge his or her witnessing of the vulnerable place and validate it. This means expressing acceptance of it to his or her partner and a desire to be with the partner in the vulnerable place.

6. *Full resolution.* In the stage of full resolution, the client expresses a new sense of self as whole and capable. Clients are able to allow sadness, loss, or other previously disowned states to emerge, to receive information from these feelings about what they need, and to have these feelings recognized.

The following example of vulnerability emerges when the therapeutic discussion is focused on how to break a negative cycle wherein the wife, Fern, criticizes and blames and her husband, Mario, distances. The therapist is encouraging the wife to express her more adaptive, primary feelings of fear, anxiety, and pain related to betrayal and abuse. The excerpt illustrates the therapist operations used to work through vulnerability.

    Fern: So, I should be working on not expressing my anxiety and fear and not do it in such an aggressive way too then, right?

Therapist: Right.

Fern:	Is that not something I need to work on?
Therapist:	Well, rather what I'm saying is your task is to say "I, I feel anxious, . . .
Fern:	Right.
Therapist:	. . . help me," to be approachable.
Fern:	Yeah, that's a good one. . . .
Therapist:	Mm-hm.
Fern:	. . . [*sniffles*] which is like going with the vulnerability, but you're already in a, you can't find yourself. Uh-oh that can be very bad! That would be very hard.
Therapist:	In some ways, it's being more like Mario. And . . .
Fern:	Right.
Therapist:	. . . living out of your heart, . . .
Fern:	Oh.
Therapist:	. . . but you very correctly said that you're able to put up whatever defenses you need . . .
Fern:	Right.
Therapist:	. . . to protect yourself. And you're good at that . . .
Fern:	You're making me cry again [*laughs*]. I said there was no way I was going to cry today, there's nothing to cry about anymore. [*Sighs heavily.*]
Therapist:	You're all cried out.
Fern:	Apparently not [*laughs*]. Apparently, that would be the bottomless well of tears. There will always be things. Oh gosh!
Therapist:	What is it that you're feeling? That it'd be—that's, that's scary to think of that, of that place?
Fern:	Well, that's the place where all the pain is, . . .
Therapist:	Mm-hm.
Fern:	. . . you know, and there is no protection against that. So that's like saying, "Oh well, here's a big stick. Feel free," or you know, "Here's the wound and you can just keep jabbing it," like that, it just feels like—it's a very scary place for me [*crying*].

As the client shares this state, the therapist now responds with empathy, affirmation, and validation. The therapist acts to bridge the client's sense of disconnection with an empathic presence. As vulnerability emerges, the therapist reflects the fragile feelings and assists the client in self-soothing. Using a slow, gentle manner, the therapist acts to slow the process.

Therapist: Can you speak from the pain and the tears and tell us what it is like. "I hurt . . . ." "I am . . . ."

Fern: It is just so hard for me to do that. I guess there is a good part of me that does not believe Mario would really understand . . . 'cause sometimes I try to tell Mario things, and he is just not there. I know he's busy and he gets easily distracted, and you know, I just know with myself that I know how to take care of me. I am good at it. I have always done it, and I know how, and with Mario, well, he's got his own stuff going on, and that's understandable, but I am not sure if he knows how to be there.

Therapist: So it's very painful. . . . You always had to take care of that little girl 'cause somehow if you didn't, nobody else would.

The therapist continues to use affirming empathic responses to deepen the process, conveying a sense of understanding of what this really means for the client. The therapist assists the client in expressing exactly what has been so difficult about being open and vulnerable in the past. This involves reflecting what is worst here for the client and dwelling on the vulnerable feelings.

Fern: [crying]

Therapist: Just so vulnerable?

Fern: [crying] I just feel that this is the painful part, and it doesn't stop. . . . I cannot stop crying . . .

In this stage of intense deepening, the therapist reflects how difficult this is but affirms the importance of allowing and staying with the dreaded feelings, despite the confusion and pain. The therapist also reflects the sense of confusion, exhaustion, and hopelessness that the client experiences. The therapist encourages the expression of tears.

Sensing the client has reached rock bottom, the therapist focuses on the need to promote adaptive reorganization.

Therapist: What do you need from Mario when you're feeling like this?

Fern: I don't really know . . . it's hard to answer that. I guess . . . he knows how to comfort me because he has before, and at times he does. I just need him to stay with me and understand.

Therapist: Mm-hm. Tell him what it is. Tell him what he can do.

Here, the therapist creates connection by encouraging the client to express needs to her partner from the vulnerable place.

Fern: [*crying*] He can be reassuring and just let me know he cares, that he is there if I need him.

Therapist: Can you let him do that now?

Fern: I am kind of scared to do that right now.

Therapist: Maybe you could start with that. . . . Can you tell him that now?

The therapist is attentive for signs of a shift, so the client begins to turn back toward growth and hope; the therapist validates her adaptive emotion of being afraid and encourages her to express it to her partner. Encouraging her to express the fear is helpful because it provides her with the self-protection she feels she needs. Remaining vulnerable with her partner by expressing her fear helps her partner not feel attached. Once she expresses her feeling and need, the therapist asks the partner to respond.

Fern: Okay. [*Breathes and sighs for 10 seconds. Turns to partner.*] It is hard for me to say this . . . it is hard for me to let you see this . . . I am afraid you won't respond to this part of me. I am afraid it is too much for you. Sometimes I just keep this to myself.

Therapist: What is your response, Mario, when you hear this?

Mario: Well, I can see it is very hard for you, and I know you hurt and this is hard, and I am sad that no one was there to take care of you when you really needed it, and I know that sometimes I am not there, at least not in the way you need me to be. But I want you to know that I want to be there with you. I love this part of you.

Fern: [*crying*] That feels good. I am glad to hear you say that.

Here the client is beginning to reconnect, but from the vulnerable place. Her partner's expression of acceptance is an important piece promoting a corrective emotional experience. The client is now able to reconnect from a more integrated place.

Therapist: It sounds like you really appreciate hearing that from Mario, that it really touches you inside. And Mario, you really want to be with Fern in this place.

The therapist reflects adaptive emotions and action tendencies. She affirms the partners' desire to reconnect from the vulnerable place. The therapist affirms the client's expression of growth needs.

Fern: Yes, well, at this moment it feels okay. In fact, it feels good, and I like having his comfort. I need it.

Therapist: Yes, it does feel supportive, and it is okay to let him in and let him comfort you. You are taking a big risk, but it feels good to let him in.

In the final stage, the therapist supports and assists clients in highlighting the changes. The therapist will continue to validate the client's sense of reconnection to herself and to her partner.

CONCLUSION

Accessing emotion and working with specific types of in-session emotion states and problems is the hallmark of an overall EFT approach to therapy. This chapter has focused on how to work with specific individual problems in EFT-C. More specifically, the markers and interventions—adapted from individual therapy—that were described in this chapter are problematic reaction points and systematic evocative unfolding, an absent or unclear felt sense and focusing and empathic affirmation of vulnerability. These interventions help couples therapists to work in different ways at different times with each of the partners to help explore their inner worlds.

III

WORKING WITH SPECIFIC EMOTIONS

10

ANGER IN COUPLES THERAPY

Anyone can become angry. That is easy. But to be angry with the right person, to the right degree, at the right time, for the right purpose and in the right way—that is not easy.

—Aristotle

Anger is one of the most powerful and urgent emotions in couples conflict. Scherer, Wallbott, and Summerfield (1986), in a research study of people across four continents, found that anger is most often directed at loved ones on the basis that the feeling that the loved one has wronged them. Anger has a profound impact on relations with a partner in marriage as well as on the expresser's self-organization. Anger can be stimulated by many sources. Many types of anger responses are possible—some positive, others negative, and only some aggressive. Anger is a natural, adaptive response to threats; it inspires powerful feelings and behaviors, which allow people to fight and defend themselves when they feel attacked. A certain amount of anger, therefore, is necessary to people's survival. An instinctive way to express anger is to respond somewhat aggressively, especially to communicate aggressive intent. The typical expression of anger, however, seldom involves actual aggression but is rather directed to correct the situation or prevent its recurrence. This is the empowering type of anger that some partners need to be helped to feel and express. Anger thus should not be conflated with aggression. Feeling angry does not necessarily mean behaving aggressively, and it is important to note that people can be aggressive without feeling any anger at all.

Like other emotions, anger is accompanied by physiological and biological changes, such as increased heart rate and blood pressure, as well as elevated levels of energy and hormones, including adrenaline and noradrenaline. The action tendency associated with anger involves breathing, vascular, vocal, muscular, and facial responses that ready a person to thrust forward and attack or defend against boundary violation. These responses organize one for action but do not actually produce behavior. The actual behavioral response results from a complex interaction of the action tendency with cognitive processes that follow the initial action disposition. The strength of the tendency to action varies, as does the subjective experience of anger, which can vary from irritation to annoyance, anger, and rage. Anger can be activated by conscious thoughts, but more often than not, anger is evoked without thought. The first cry of rage of the infant does not depend on conscious thought. Adaptive, primary anger is often activated automatically without one really knowing why. Partners sometimes know what made them angry, but often their reactions are often automatic. They do not necessarily have any conscious thoughts such as "You have wronged me." They just feel offended. Then they start to think angry thoughts and need to reflect to make sense of their anger.

Often, especially in Anglo Saxon cultures, people experience quite a lot of personal anxiety and fear disapproval from others about being angry. They have been taught, and taught well, to suppress their anger. For example, Joan is offended by constant jokes made by her husband at her expense. She smiles but grows increasingly resentful. She knows she is being criticized and feels angry, but having been taught not to express anger, she says nothing. Afterward, she feels depressed and cold toward her husband. It is far better to let her anger move her to assertively express herself than to feel deflated. With the energy and power that anger has provided, she can show that she has teeth and can protect herself from being taken advantage of. We are not advocating anger as a first line of defense and believe sincerely in the importance of conciliatory efforts, but ultimately, we do see anger as an indispensable part of human makeup, and partners need not be too afraid of receiving and sending its message.

In emotion-focused couples therapy (EFT-C), we emphasize the therapeutic effects of accessing and expressing previously unacknowledged primary adaptive anger that leads to distance and avoidance in relationships. Awareness and expression of anger needs to be followed by exploration of the meaning of anger, as well as awareness of the associated needs, and it needs to be followed by accessing the softer feelings alongside the harder expression of anger. In many instances, people would not be angry if they did not care or want to be cared about.

Although expression of primary anger at feeling unfairly treated can promote bonding by communicating a feeling of being wronged, expressing anger inappropriately also can be one of the most relationship-damaging emotions. Without doubt, one of the most important ways couples get into difficulties is related to their inability to deal with their own and their partner's anger. The problem with anger is that it is so difficult to express it without somehow shaming or belittling the other or becoming demanding and controlling. Yet if partners do not express it, a wall of resentment begins to build. Although, as we have said, anger in response to violation is a healthy feeling that needs to be expressed, anger very often is a secondary response to a more primary feeling of hurt, to the fear of feeling unloved or unsupported, or to the shame of invalidation. Many of the harder emotions partners express, such as anger, resentment, and contempt, may often be responses to primary fear or shame and are aggressive attempts to protect themselves from their partner or to protect themselves against their more painful softer emotions of sadness, fear, and shame. In addition, partners' responses to anger often are defensive or angry and lead to escalatory interactions.

Part of what makes the expression of anger so problematic is that angry interactions quickly escalate as partners respond defensively and recruit past grievances to bolster their position. As each person takes a more extreme position, they bring in past scenes from the current relationship in which they felt wronged, misunderstood, neglected, or used. Anger in the present can also activate memories of such scenes from other relationships, fueling the flames of anger in the current interaction and prompting partners to take more and more extreme positions.

However, many couples are frightened of any expression of anger, assuming that any argument is a sign of a troubled relationship. It is important for the therapist to help these partners see that angry feelings are part of being human and that the expression of anger can be wholesome and adaptive, especially when it is balanced with gentleness and compassion.

Compassion and gentleness, however, are hard to experience and express when adaptive anger has been suppressed. When partners have been wronged or their boundaries have been violated, therapists need to coach partners to express their anger openly, constructively, and directly. For example, a spouse may be coached to say, "I feel angry because you were so late for our dinner date." Such directness is not only informative but will clear the air, especially if the other partner is able to apologize.

Some partners who have bottled up their adaptive anger for a long time may suddenly blow up, expressing their anger in destructive ways. These partners also need to be coached to express their anger more appropriately. Although acknowledging that such outbursts may temporarily feel good, the therapist emphasizes the potential for damage to the relationship and to the partner's feelings of self-worth. Rather than yelling, "You are an inconsiderate slob," the partner may be coached to say, "I am feeling angry at you for ignoring my requests to tidy up." The therapist again stresses that the goal is to communicate anger for its information value, not for the relief of stress.

Of utmost importance in angry interactions is that power between the two partners remains equal throughout the ensuing emotional storm. Affect is contagious, so anger begets anger. In a quarrel, virtually anything, however innocent or well intentioned, if perceived as unsupportive can unexpectedly reignite anger that has already begun to subside. In couples in conflict, power must be equal for the affective storm to abate. A tendency during outbursts of anger is to take all the power by threats of various kinds, including ultimatums. The most dangerous threat is the threat to leave. In the midst of anger, one partner may be driven to express futility about the relationship and, feeling powerless, may threaten to leave or may walk away. The result of an ultimatum of this sort is that the other partner is immediately rendered powerless and will have to issue an equally volatile threat to offset his or her sense of powerlessness. Such threats in the midst of anger are highly counterproductive because they invariably up the ante, promoting further shaming and retaliation.

Therapists thus need to help couples understand that in situations in which anger is the problem, the purpose of conflict is to arrive at a win–win compromise resolution. There is not a one-up, one-down solution. Each partner must feel that they have something to gain and also that they relinquish something when coming to an agreed-on solution.

WAYS OF DEALING WITH ANGER IN RELATIONSHIPS

The three main approaches to dealing with anger used by partners are either expressing, suppressing, or calming the anger. Expressing legitimate angry feelings in an assertive manner is the healthiest way to deal with anger in a relationship. To do this, one must learn to make clear what one's needs are and how to get them met without hurting one's partner. Being assertive does not mean being pushy or demanding, it means being respectful to both one's self and one's partner using "I" language and communicating well. Anger, however, can also be suppressed and then converted or redirected. This occurs when one holds in anger, stops thinking about it, and then focuses on something positive. A danger in this type of response is that if the anger is not allowed outward expression, it can turn inward, and it certainly does not lead to problem solving. Anger turned inward may cause hypertension, high blood pressure, and even depression. In addition, it can lead to pathological expressions of anger, such as passive-aggressive behavior or a personality that seems perpetually cynical or hostile. The third approach to confronting anger is to be able to calm down inside and soothe one's self. This means not just controlling outward behavior but also regulating internal responses, taking steps to lower the heart rate, and letting the feelings subside. This too is a good coping response, but if it is being done repeatedly, without addressing the message one's anger is giving one, how one feels wrong will not be addressed. Humor also helps defuse low-intensity anger by providing a more balanced perspective on a situation.

There also are individual differences in proneness to anger, which need to be recognized in working with couples. Some partners are quick to anger, and some are slow. Some people stew and simmer, whereas others burst or explode. These individual differences need to be recognized. In different cultures, rules about anger expression also differ. In addition, women appear to experience and express anger in ways different than men. Some women tend to be inhibited in their expression of anger and often cry when angry, whereas some men tend to be freer with their anger. In general, men are perceived as more comfortable with the emotion of anger than women and use the externalization of anger to express it. Women often are socialized to express their emotions more openly, with the exception of anger, which is viewed by society as unfeminine. Women often are reluctant to express anger because they fear adversely affecting the relationship. When women express their anger, it is often in terms of feeling hurt or disillusioned, and their feelings of anger are interwoven with hurt, frustration, sadness, and disillusionment.

Although men and women may differ in their mode of expressing anger, this difference is not related to the degree of anger experienced (S. P. Thomas, 2003). The main gender difference is that men cry less than women when angry (Averill, 1983). Men are generally considered to be more aggressive than women. Anger may be displayed when a man has lost control of a situation or feels the behavior of his partner does not conform to proper human conduct. Anger can escalate in men if they perceive their feelings and opinions to be ignored. Situations are made worse when men feel that they have lost control and are unable to fix what has gone wrong. Although some men may manifest their anger by withdrawing from the situation, others may react by physically lashing out or by striking inanimate objects. Men have been socialized to express anger more freely, and this may explain why such outbursts are quite common. Often, vulnerable emotions such as disappointment, hurt, and shame (emotions considered too unmanly to express) may get funneled into anger.

How anger is, or is not, expressed thus varies depending on many factors including temperament, gender, and the culture or social environment to which an individual belongs. Identifying the different forms of anger described in the sections that follow and intervening differentially is particularly important in couples therapy.

VARIETIES OF ANGER AND DIFFERENTIAL INTERVENTION

As we have said, process diagnosis is at the heart of working with emotion in couples therapy. The type of anger expressed suggests the type of intervention most helpful at that point. The different categories of anger are described in the sections that follow.

Primary Adaptive Anger

Primary adaptive anger is empowering—it is a survival-oriented response to boundary intrusion and violation. The two major anger-related relational problems come from too much or too little anger. These are problems of over- and undercontrol and over- and underactivation. These are not mutually exclusive problems, as illustrated by the bottle-up–blow-up syndrome, in which the chronic overcontrol of anger leads to inappropriate and explosive anger. Repeatedly suppressing anger, to even small degrees, in response to situations that are perceived as attacks prevents assertive action. This, then, exacerbates a feeling of weakness and disempowerment, which engenders more anger. Spiraling sequences of this sort leave people feeling "full of anger" and result in an exaggerated, explosive, and ineffective expression of anger. Alternatively, anger suppression often leads to unexpressed resentment and withdrawal.

The automatic overcontrol of anger thus is as important a relational problem as is chronic undercontrolled anger. Partners often suppress their adaptive angry reactions at being violated or hurt, and for these people, control and management strategies are inappropriate. When anger is chronically overcontrolled, problems become infinitely more difficult to recognize and resolve. People are unable to assert their boundaries or defend themselves from attack or harm, and in these situations, primary adaptive anger needs to be acknowledged and expressed, rather than managed or controlled.

One of the potentially harmful consequences of holding in anger is that individuals avoid making clear statements about what they need, want, and think. Thus, couples problems commonly associated with anger avoidance are lack of assertion and boundary definition. As well, partners who suppress their anger begin to lose touch with what is important to them and begin to feel alienated from their own needs and wants. Partners who chronically interrupt experiences of primary anger often do this because of social injunctions against its expression. The experience of anger can be threatening because it signals potential disapproval, rejection, or loss of a needed relationship. Thus, many people (men as well as women) have learned to be submissive, unassertive, and to defer to their partners, thereby suppressing their own needs and swallowing their anger. Such chronic suppression can lead to depression and apathy. Having given up hope of ever getting needs met, partners lose touch with the assertive feelings, wants, and needs that define the self.

Therapists need to help couples see that chronically unexpressed adaptive anger creates distance and builds a wall that prevents intimacy. It also creates psychological and physical discomfort and lowers the person's threshold for getting angry about other things, especially things that remind the person of the original situation in which anger was suppressed. Appropriately expressed adaptive anger, however, enhances self-empowerment, facilitates assertive action, and creates the opportunity for unmet needs to be satisfied.

In coaching the couple to express anger constructively, the therapist stresses the need to do so without blame or insult and with a show of good will. Reluctant partners often find it easier to express anger by saying, "I don't want to feel angry, but I do feel angry at. . . ." This communicates a desire for harmony at the same time as it communicates that one feels wronged. Partners with pent-up anger should be coached to express their anger in a tone that conveys respect (i.e., not scowling or sneering).

Anger that asserts needs or informs a partner of a boundary or a boundary violation in a respectful way, although not easy to hear, is ultimately reassuring, particularly when couples are caught in a pursue–distance cycle. The expression of anger brings the withdrawer out of hiding. Much to the withdrawer's surprise, such expression brings relief rather than retaliation, as the pursuer finds the expressed anger easier to deal with than the distance. Such contact, although uncomfortable, enhances the couples bond.

Unexpressed anger at betrayal or injury is one of the major forms of adaptive anger that need to be identified and expressed in couples therapy. Partners in any of the interactional positions could feel this type of anger. This anger often is mixed with sadness and, sometimes, fear and devastation. Issues of betrayal and abandonment involve not only deep hurt and feelings of vulnerability from sudden loss of support but shattered trust and damage to self-esteem. The betrayed partner perceives him- or herself as having been abandoned, cast aside, unlovable, undesirable, and rejected or let down, wronged, and unfairly treated. The partner has not lived up to obligations, responsibilities, or expectations, and promises have been broken. Anger due to betrayal or diminishment also partly stems from frustration at lack of control over the situation, and anger helps reempower. In addition to helping the partner express anger in these situations, it is important that the therapist normalize and facilitate the expression of grief over losses experienced in the process of betrayal.

The first step in working with unexpressed primary anger often is identification and exploration of its avoidance. Markers of anger interruption are in-session verbal and nonverbal behaviors that readily can be observed and identified. These signs of interrupted anger include silence, helplessness, guilt and depression, numbing, intellectualization, rational control of adaptive anger, minimization, distancing of self from angry feelings with trivia or jokes, diffuse and inappropriate anger, and lingering bitter resentments. Even collapsing into tears can be avoidance of expressing appropriate anger.

In all cases in which unexpressed anger is involved, it is important for the therapist to help each partner differentiate feelings of anger from those of hurt, fear, and sadness. In the following transcript, the therapist helps a couple (Myriam and Ron) deal with anger as well as other feelings following the birth of their first child.

Anger and Hurt at Desertion

Myriam: I guess it was when I needed him most, he was not there. I remember that within a week after our son being born, Ron said something to me along the line that I had a really terrible labor, and he said, "I had never had more respect for you than when I saw you go through that labor," and he said, "but once you got the baby home all that went out the window, all that went down the drain." I felt like he just stabbed me, like "What you are doing, you are so anxious," and I was just trying to cope.

Therapist: It was this sort of scorn he had for you that felt so cutting. [*Empathically reflects the core of her injury.*] What happens when she says this, it must be hard for you. [*Probes for his response.*]

Ron: It is hard to hear, when she comes to that situation, she would say that I wasn't there for her, but I did so much . . .

Myriam: He did.

Ron: . . . in terms of taking responsibility. [*Defends his identity.*]

Myriam: Let me be clear: He did a lot in terms of taking care of the baby . . . it was so begrudging and he would turn to me . . . and say . . . "I am so angry, I am so angry at the baby," he was doing it [*crying*].

Therapist: Is she hurt or angry? [*Checks his perception to get it out in the open.*]

Ron: She is angry.

Therapist: [*to Myriam*] What are you feeling?

Myriam: I guess I am reliving it, it was like everything he did had a price, and I paid it. It was like he really didn't want to be there, he didn't want to help.

Therapist: There are two parts, sort of the anger and the hurt. You are saying, "I am angry at you." [*Begins to differentiate the complaint into hurt and anger.*]

Myriam: I realize I am very angry at you. It was the most difficult time of our life. I guess as a man he never really tried to understand the physical depletion part of it, the mental deficiency, the hormonal imbalance, I couldn't deal with it, with his desertion.

Therapist: I am angry that you deserted me, and I want to know you'll be there for me. [*Reflects the pure anger.*]

Myriam: It is more than that. He will be there when I am normal, but when I have a baby again and I am not physically up [*cries*], and I am hormonally, sleep deprived, and all the rest, postpartum, all the things I had at that time, he would desert me again.

<table>
<tr><td>Ron:</td><td>Your feeling is one of—but I didn't actually desert you, you were saying I was there. [Defends his identity.]</td></tr>
<tr><td>Therapist:</td><td>She does feel like somehow you turned on her and got angry at her; it was almost all the anger you had built from before towards her. [Validates both of their feelings.]</td></tr>
<tr><td>Ron:</td><td>I can understand how she feels that way, that I was angry. I know at the time I was very short tempered and impatient, I just felt that I was not in any kind of control of my life. [Acknowledges his anger.]</td></tr>
</table>

Here her expression of anger and his listening to it was an important part of the healing process. His seeing the hurt, alongside the anger, which the therapist was trying to separate from the anger and highlight, to draw out some compassion from him, helped him be able to respond to her anger in a more understanding and nonescalatory fashion.

Primary Maladaptive Anger

Anger as a person's first response to a situation is maladaptive when it does not function to express legitimate injury, such as a boundary violation or betrayal of trust in a current relationship. If a partner's anger comes not from the current situation but from an old wound or past maltreatment by others (such as a history of violence), this anger does not need to be expressed to the partner. It needs to be worked with and transformed, often in individual sessions. In individual sessions, the therapist focuses on helping the person soothe him- or herself, differentiate past from present experiences, and regulate the expression of emotion. This is the kind of work that was done with Donna, a woman who had been physically and emotionally abused by her father. Any time her husband approached her from behind and put his arms around her, she would explode in anger. After couples work in which she was helped to let him know how scared she was and her husband was helped to not put any pressure on, individual work helped her transform her hair-trigger rage by developing her ability to regulate and transform this primary maladaptive anger.

In couples sessions when primary maladaptive anger arises, it is important that the therapist acknowledge any primary adaptive anger that is contained in it (such as anger at not being heard by a partner that is experienced as abandonment) but then to redirect the person's attention toward the original source of the anger, such as the abandoning father. This helps the other person recognize that the partner has a vulnerability to feeling abandoned because of prior experiences. This in turn lays the groundwork for the couple learning how to modify interactions that trigger this feeling and how to handle the feeling appropriately when it is triggered.

Primary maladaptive anger is most often found in couples with dominance issues or violence, where the dominant partner explodes in hair-trigger anger at very slight provocation. Couples work with angry dominance involves labeling the anger as clearly maladaptive for the individual and the couple. Therapy then involves helping the couple recognize the triggers; help them not activate the anger, where possible; and learn how to soothe the anger and deescalate once it is activated. This includes behavioral methods of no-violence contracting, time-outs, and developing alternative coping strategies. Relaxation techniques, for example, can help a partner with maladaptive anger to feel calmer; experience less discomfort; and decrease heart rate, blood pressure, breathing rate, and muscle tension.

Individuals with borderline or narcissistic processes also may fly into rage when they feel rejected or slighted. Although originally a secondary response to hurt, this anger is now a primary maladaptive response in many situations and often manifests as rage because it becomes habitual and completely divorced from its origin. Maladaptive rage associated with narcissistic slights, feeling inferior, ashamed, or humiliated is recognizable because it is overly intense, chronic, or inappropriate. Intervention then needs to focus on accessing and changing the underlying maladaptive shame. Secondary rage over a minor insult, for example, can be acknowledged by the therapist, but attention needs to be focused on how the client felt deeply wounded and cannot bear even the slightest offence.

Adaptive anger also at times itself can become maladaptive if it is undercontrolled. Thus it is the intensity of the anger that is maladaptive. It is important to understand also that an initial adaptive anger reaction can escalate into maladaptive rage by a sequence of interactions, feelings, and thoughts that progressively intensifies the anger. In this sequence, every successive interaction acts as a provocation, which becomes a new trigger for further surges of anger, and each feeling of anger builds on the moment before. Anger builds on anger, and anger unhampered by attuned responses can erupt into highly destructive rage. Thus, in addition to accessing underlying helpless dependence or shame that leads to rage, it can also be helpful to unpack the interactions that contribute to rage.

Secondary Anger at Unmet Needs

Secondary anger is probably the most prevalent form of anger expression in couples. Most people tend to express anger when they are hurt. When anger is secondary and masks a primary emotion, it is not helpful expressing it. Rather, further exploration is needed to identity the partner's more primary emotion. Blaming anger is the most common negative form of anger expression in couples. This generally is a secondary emotion and needs to be bypassed to get at underlying softer, more vulnerable emotions. For instance, a husband who is angry at his wife for dressing too provocatively has to become aware that his anger is a secondary emotion and that it helps him defend against his primary emotion of fear and threat. Once the husband is open about his fear and expresses his concerns, he no longer is as controlling and blaming, and his wife is less likely to defend and more likely to respond to his concerns. An open disclosure is more likely to get an empathic response; will promote a bond between the couple; and will give partners a better understanding of their own emotions, as well as their spouses'.

Anger thus often is a reaction to underlying fear, shame, helplessness, or disappointment. In therapy, it is important for a therapist, after first acknowledging a partner's reactive anger, to focus on the person's underlying hurt, fear of abandonment, or sense of powerlessness. Having accessed the primary vulnerable feeling, the underlying need and implicit belief are then identified and worked with. Sometimes there is a desperate quality to expressions of secondary anger, which indicates clearly that it is not primary and suggests the underlying fear of dissolution or abandonment. This is the simplest form of anger, and examples of it are found in the next section on affiliative cycles, in pursuers' blaming.

A particularly important and difficult emotion sequence in couples involving anger is a shame–rage sequence when one partner feels primarily humiliated and then gets angry. This can vary in intensity, but when it is very intense, it can lead to violence in couples. Here, the partner's rage is generally a response to his or her inability to deal with the more core feelings of shame and powerlessness. Partners who feel rage or who rapidly escalate and become rageful in marital conflict need to learn how to calm the rage and to get to what is really at the bottom of it. Being aware and getting in touch with core feelings as they arise, then, is a key way to prevent the development of destructive rage. If one often gets very angry, one needs not only to control one's anger but to learn to experience and express the more vulnerable feelings beneath the anger. Expressing underlying sadness, fear, shame, or hurt will have a very different impact on one's partner than will expressing secondary anger. Partners thus need to develop the ability, when they are defensively angry, to feel and express the threat that comes before the anger. Emotion coaches need to help partners develop the ability to soothe themselves when angry and to also soothe their angry partners, rather than to escalate. This is one of the best antidotes to negative escalation—the ability to regulate affect in both self and other.

Instrumental Anger

Instrumental anger is a learned use of anger as a means of regulating others for secondary gains. This occurs more often in the dominant partner, who uses it to intimidate and control the submissive partner. It is also used by pursuers in attempts to get the withdrawer's attention. Anger expression is an effective way to control a partner but usually results in the partner becoming bitter, resentful, and distant. Instrumental anger is frequently observed by partners with more dramatic intense expressive styles and is expressed to get their partners' attention. It is a type of desperate attempt by a pursuer to get the distant partner's attention. The ineffectiveness of the use of this type of anger is brought to awareness, and an understanding of the client's underlying motivation and aims is articulated. The partner then is encouraged to learn alternative responses for achieving those aims. This form of anger is neither intensified, communicated, nor experientially explored; rather, its function and goals are brought to awareness.

Many partners may not be aware of the instrumental function of their anger, and it cannot be considered deliberate manipulation. For example, a partner in a gay couple was hurt and angry at his partner's lack of support and reacted by "punishing" him, "teaching him a lesson" by withholding his support. This is the use of instrumental anger mixed with primary anger at unmet needs. The therapist acknowledged and validated this partner's underlying anger at unmet needs for support but also empathically confronted his attempts to force his partner to give him what he wanted by responding,

> It seems that no matter what you do, however much you get angry or try to punish him, even if he gives in, he will not appreciate you, and all your efforts will simply push him further away. Your use of anger to get the closeness you desperately want doesn't help you get what you need.

This response brought to light the instrumental function of his anger and helped him let go of futile efforts to control his partner and, at the same time, supported his primary adaptive needs and motivation to get his needs met.

DEALING WITH HURT AND ANGER: TWO MAJOR ELEMENTS IN THE WALL OF ISOLATION

We now look at how anger manifests in the different positions in affiliation and dominance cycles.

Anger in Affiliation Cycles

Anger in the affiliation cycle is about not getting the closeness a person wants. Anger is often secondary but not always, and pursuer anger and distancer anger serve different purposes.

Pursuer's Anger

Secondary anger is probably the most prevalent emotion in couples therapy and generally manifests as blame and complaint. This is found in the partners pursuing for closeness who, after failed initial attempts to get their needs for closeness met, turn to anger as an attempted solution. The first stage of pursuit may contain appeals for closeness, but after repeated rejections or nonresponsiveness from the partner, the pursuers turn to blame or demand and begin to attack. The essential messages sent are "You are bad" and also "You don't love me." For example, Betty complained that her husband, Ray, spent most of his free time with his friends, watching football and drinking beer. She criticized him for drinking and complained that he always left the house when they started to argue rather than staying and talking things out. Ray kept repeating that he did not want her to raise her voice, and when she did, a wall went up and he left rather than getting mad because, as he said, "That is my way." He did not like to get angry. The work here with Betty involved getting past her secondary anger and accessing her underlying hurt and fear. Therapy involved simultaneously helping Ray coming out from behind his wall and expressing his underlying feelings.

In this, as in many marital situations, already-existing emotion, sensation, arousal, and stress precede and contribute to cuing anger-related action tendencies and anger-producing thoughts. Expression of secondary anger also helps people block the stress and pain that come from other feelings by removing them from awareness. Anger expression also helps release muscular tension and reduces high arousal levels associated with other feelings, such as fear or hurt. Thus in the interactions noted earlier, Betty first feels anxiety and fear of abandonment when Ray says he is going out to watch football with his friends. But already feeling deprived, stressed, and having had a poor night's sleep plus a frustrating day, she experiences and expresses anger at him as he leaves the house. This anger is secondary to her fear and loneliness but is due to a rapid sequence in which she, or rather her amygdala, appraises danger, feels afraid, then blames Ray for her fear, and gets angry, and the anger acts to help discharge the fear arousal. Similarly, a person who feels hurt when criticized or rejected is always approaching the situation in a preorganized state. When this is a feeling of being more vulnerable, the person is more likely to automatically appraise the situation as unfair, decide that the other should not have done what was done, and get angry. Similarly, anger momentarily erases guilt, depression, and feelings of unworthiness; thus, rather than feel guilty or worthless, one can blame or criticize one's partner. Rather than feel sad, one can get angry at one's spouse to obliterate the painful sensations and thoughts. The therapeutic goal, in all these situations, is to access the more primary feeling that leads to anger. The goal is to access the softer core attachment-related emotion of loneliness and fear at separation or the sense of shame at identity slights.

How does the therapist do this? For example, during one session, as the client spoke angrily about her partner's lack of attention, the therapist was aware of a desperate and panicky quality to her expressions of anger. This suggested an underlying anxiety at being alone. The therapist redirected attention to her experience of anxiety by tentatively reflecting back the panicky quality to her voice: "It feels so unfair, and it's almost as if you started feeling deeply abandoned, like, it feels so lonely, almost as if you'll be alone forever." Immediately, her eyes welled up in tears and she acknowledged her loneliness and deep fear of abandonment, which the therapist validated and accepted. The focus of therapy became communicating the unmet attachment needs, strengthening her sense of self, and looking for ways to get her needs met, rather than anger expression.

Pursuing partners sometimes distance themselves from angry feelings about past injuries by chronically blaming and complaining. The fusion of sadness and anger that underlies such blame and complaint needs to be differentiated so that feelings can be expressed in a way that leads to resolution, and it needs to be differentiated into the underlying primary emotions so that each can be expressed clearly and separately. Returning to Myriam and Ron in the following transcript, we see that when Myriam complains, Ron withdraws, leading to frustration for both of them. The segment begins with Myriam reacting nonverbally to Ron talking about his need for space. The therapist focuses on her hurt to soften the anger and prevent escalation.

Myriam: [*Face and gesture show anger and frustration.*]

Therapist: So, do you see her react? What do you do with this? [*Focuses on present.*]

Ron: I ignore it.

Myriam: This was a symptom of frustration. When we do talk about our needs, mine are always put second! I am always on the choke chain, whatever I want to do always comes second to what you want to do. [*Voice gets higher and higher and a cry of frustration begins to emerge.*] And if I communicate, and I do communicate it, what you want is always first, like you want to fix the shower this weekend. Things I want him to do or ask him to do wait for months, and I am so patient! I wait and wait and wait, and I don't say anything, and I put a sign on the kitchen fridge because I don't want to nag him. [*Voice is emotional, angry, and hurt; begins to cry.*]

Therapist: So you are saying to him . . .

Myriam: My needs are ignored. I always play second fiddle to him, to you, because somehow you just put yourself in a position or you appear to, the way you react, "My needs are more important, and I can't deal with them as well as you do, and I need this, and I need control, and that, I need time to myself and I need . . . ." He talks about his need to have time with himself and to play with his toys, and we have been doing that, but I said to him, before I went away. . . . I made real effort to give that to you and I still do, even this weekend, I will take [their child] and you will have a block of 4 hours to do whatever you want. I do that, and he forgets about these things.

Therapist: What are you saying to him? "I'm angry that my needs aren't being met"? [*Acknowledges anger but shifts focus to unmet need.*]

Myriam: It is so frustrating [*intense expression; clenching and banging her fist on her knee*]!

Therapist: What do you need from him? [*Continues focus on need behind the frustration guiding away from blame to access softer feelings associated with the need.*]

Myriam: I need him to hear me!

Therapist: Will you speak to him? Speak to him in a way that will get him to hear you: "I need you to hear." [*Continues to focus on a softer self-organization and coaches by asking her to say it in a way that he can hear.*]

Myriam: I need you to put a value to the things that I do as well, to give them value, because when you tell me all the time, "Oh, you are running around," it is like they have no value to them. Like, "What you do or need isn't important." And on the weekends, when I ask you to do something, it's "If I have time, I will get around it," and you know, how many things take him months and months to do, and I don't ask you to do much, there are so many things like that.

Therapist: "I need you to appreciate and to recognize what I do, do, and do for you." [*Continues to try to draw out softer part.*]

Myriam: To give me the same respect and courtesy back. It is not equal, it is not, and maybe I am partly to blame for that. He is the sole breadwinner even though, full time, even though I am a full-time mother and work part time. He's got more stress, and I do try to alleviate his load and try to cater to him a little more than . . .

Therapist: [*to Ron*] So what is happening now to you? You are not ignoring her? With all the emotions and tears, what do you do with it? How do you react?

Ron: I don't know.

Therapist: What happens inside you when she is angry? Do you tighten up, listen? Do you hear her hurt?

Ron: I listen, but I tend to back away a little bit.

Myriam: As soon as I say that I am angry with him, he feels unloved. I can see it in the look of his face, all of a sudden, there is this look of a little boy, "What, you don't love me anymore?" He told me that in his house when people get angry, they never make up, he has this idea when he was young, he has this idea, when people are angry with each other, it is over.

Therapist:	Do you feel unloved? Is it scary for you? You say you pull away.
Ron:	It is not because I feel like she doesn't love me, because I know she does, but it is more from this feeling that I am unable to cope with what she is doing, with her emotions.
Therapist:	So it's like, "I don't know how to handle this? It is a bit overwhelming," so you pull away, meaning what? "I don't know how to handle this," meaning what?
Ron:	How do I make it all better again? I feel I have a need to make it all better again.
Therapist:	But somehow that is how you deal with it? What I hear she is saying is "I need you to appreciate what I do and recognize its value," and she didn't say this, but "You need to learn to sacrifice some of your needs and not have to feel that I always have to meet your needs."
Ron:	As I am listening, I think it does strike a chord. [*The husband is able to overcome his self-protective response and move to a responsive rather than inadequate self-organization.*]

Distancer's Anger

In pursue–distance cycles, the person most likely to need help in accessing unacknowledged primary adaptive anger is the distancer. Rather than withdraw, this partner may need to show up in the relationship and express anger at being criticized, pressured, or blamed. The pursuer often finds the contact of anger preferable to the abandonment of distance. The distancer, however, often has to overcome years of fear of anger, of injunctions against anger, or of feelings of inadequacy to be able to access assertive anger and feel entitled to the need to be accepted. For example, Alan was a very quiet, introverted man who liked to spend hours playing his classical guitar. He was a school teacher who felt overwhelmed by his responsibilities and stressed by his responsibilities at work, always felt burdened, and repeatedly said he needed time to relax with his music. His wife, Alesha, began the therapy saying Alan was having an affair with his work and that she felt abandoned. In the early sessions, the therapist accessed Alesha's underlying feelings of lonely abandonment and desire for more closeness. She wept, and he began to see her more as sad than as angry and pressuring. Although things improved initially, this did not lead to him becoming consistently more available. She would make all kinds of appeals to him to be more present to her, to their children, and to his household responsibilities. He would apologetically agree that he was failing to do things and would promise that he would try harder. He would look down guiltily while his jaw would tense and his brow would furrow. He would promise to do better next time. Alesha, however, would make eloquent speeches about the importance of being connected and how much she tried to consider him and give him space, and she proclaimed that all she asked for was some concern for her in return. She would look imploringly at him, and he would sheepishly agree to her request. Occasionally, he said he was too stressed and needed space. The therapist, after a few sessions, helped him express his feelings of being overwhelmed and feeling pressured in relation to her needs. This highlighted how he withdrew in the face of Alesha's pursuit, which although apparently benign and well meaning, came from a lot of anger and was experienced by him as demand and guilt producing. Alesha then began to say how much she was trying not to demand and blame, but if only he would just do some of the things he agreed to, such as go with her to a play and fix the things in the house that he said he would. It was only when Alan, encouraged by the therapist, expressed his anger at her at being on his case all the time and said that he did not like her always pressuring him that the cycle really began to change. After overcoming his fear that his anger would push her away and that she would leave him, he became more empowered by his anger, and he began to say "no" to her more often and follow through more on the things to which he said "yes." The therapist helped Alesha recognize how her demands, although wrapped in cotton, still drove him away. She also preferred the clarity of his assertion to his previous failures to follow through. Both partners had to learn to deal with anger; he, by expressing his anger rather than withdrawing, and she, by acknowledging the anger beneath the sweetness but then the sadness beneath her anger.

Anger in Identity Cycles

Anger in identity cycles is more about dominance and submission than closeness. Anger in the dominant partner differs in function to submitter anger. The different types of anger in dominant partners and submissive partners are discussed in the sections that follow.

Dominant's Anger

Many people have difficulty acknowledging their own vulnerability, and rather than pay attention to internal experiences of feeling hurt or weak, or small or afraid, they turn this focus outward on the other, see the other as bad, and try to control the other. Dominance thus essentially is a misguided form of affect regulation. Rather than face and feel their vulnerability, people turn out and try to dominate the other, to manage or to prevent facing their feelings. The dominant partner sometimes expresses instrumental anger to intimidate, which is an effort to control, or maladaptive anger, which is automatic and can be abusive. Most often, however, anger is the dominant partner's secondary reaction to feeling a threat to his or her position or status and is shame based or fear based. Dominance in nonviolent couples often is maintained through the use of logic and reason, in which the dominant partners always prove their rightness through assertions of truth. Often, the dominant one asks lawyerlike questions for the prosecution, to which the other partner, feeling obliged to provide answers, defers or defends and generally succumbs to the dominant's superior arguments. Although this rational form of argument may not appear angry, it can be used as an aggressive form of control and can border on the contempt of a superior for an inferior. Dominant partners often only become angry if and when challenged, or when their superior logic or guidance is not followed by the more submissive partner. Dominant partners not only need to be right but also, and more important, are unable to say they are wrong. If submissive partners argue back, the dominant partners become more and more aggressive in manner and facial expression and only feel satisfied once the argument has been won and they have established that their definition of reality is again right.

A struggle for power and for balance of power often plays a pivotal role in the development of symmetrical escalations between marital partners. Anger is used in these to balance power. Usually, couples fight at the content level, often about practical things, such as where the pictures should hang on the wall, and are not aware that the real conflict is taking place at the relational level. This means that they are really arguing and fighting out of fear that their partner will dominate the relationship and their identity will be undermined. In some couples, this fight for recognition of rights and ultimately, identity, leads to frequent angry arguments that may escalate into verbal and even physical abuse.

Dominants generally often are unaware of the destructive effect of their anger, and on successfully dominating their partner, they feel that everything is again okay, that their identity or status is confirmed, and that their partners once again fit their image of who they should be. The conflict, however, is not resolved, it just goes underground because the submissive partners, in deferring, have suppressed a part of themselves. The therapeutic goal is to help the dominant partner to realize that this form of control by anger and dominance, by not recognizing the legitimacy of the other, will not lead to intimacy. The dominant partners need also to be encouraged to attend to their underlying feelings of threat and to use this awareness as a resource for reorganization. Once the underlying fear of diminishment, shame, or fear of loss of control are accessed, they present opportunities for restructuring the interaction. What is needed is first to acknowledge the vulnerable feeling, then to attend to it, and later to sooth it. Dominant partners need to learn to tolerate these feelings, to express them, to open them to soothing by their partners, and to be able to self-soothe and to access alternative internal resources such as compassion for their own pain, and pride in their own accomplishments. The latter helps them transform the core fear or shame that makes them feel so unworthy or powerless.

Dominant partners also need to work at recognizing the validity of their partners' feelings and needs. Fear of losing their partners' love can often help motivate the dominant partner in recognizing the partners' independent validity, but this occurs only if the submissive partners have also begun to recognize their own validity and assert themselves. Having the dominant partners reveal their underlying vulnerable feelings of fear and shame changes their positions in the interaction, and the submissive partners then have the opportunity to see their partners in a new way and to understand the underlying fears and shame that drive the dominant partners' control. The submissive partners then may be able to help soothe their partners' fears and shame, not by submitting but by genuine empathy for the newly expressed underlying vulnerability and by validating the partners' worth.

In therapy, it is important to encourage the submissive partner to assert. For example, Heather and Brian came into therapy because they were fighting a lot and also because Heather was feeling depressed and overwhelmed. Brian was soft-spoken, and Heather was more expressive. As the process unfolded, it became clear that Brian was pursuing Heather for more sex, and she felt pressure, found herself overwhelmed, and was not interested. They had two children, 8 and 11 years old. Over time, however, it became clear the major problem in the relationship was one of dominance and submission, in addition to his pursuit for sexual closeness, which of course was doomed to fail because of the unresolved feelings of anger from the dominance struggle. Brian defined Heather as too uptight and controlling, always wanting him and the children to march to her drummer, whereas he just wanted things to flow naturally. He just wanted everything to be fun, and consistently told her she was not enough fun. He never expressed anger, just witty and sarcastic comments and a lot of statements of how hurt he felt, which eventually, it became clear, had a "poor-me" quality. He could be defined as passive-aggressive in style. Although she would debate with him, Heather was submissive and would doubt herself and placate him. The transcript that follows presents a number of segments from an important session with the couple that addresses a complex dominance issue and gets to the shame beneath the control.

The Controlling Dynamic

Heather: The whole controlling dynamic that, you know, has still been an element for us, . . .

Brian: Like . . . ?

Heather: . . . the times when I am anxious, like, and I got my list and was checking it off, and you were feeling controlled, that kind of thing, because in a way, I guess what I am hoping, like, I am thinking, I see now with me that sometimes when I am afraid or I am feeling a certain thing, I am bringing so much of that to the picture, right, and the last time we had an episode where we verbally, openly talked about that, the issue of control coming in when we talked about it later, and I asked you, "How do you see it, how do you see your role and my role?" and you quite frankly said to me, "I frankly see it is all your fault. I don't see my role in it at all."

Brian: I am not clear what you are talking about.

Heather: That time we were sitting on the bed and talking about it, when we were heading for the high school, and I was presenting, and we were going skating after, and you want to put the hockey sticks in the trunk, and I want to get going, and I was anxious. I just wanted to see how you perceived the whole dynamic, and I guess I still do have a concern that you said, "I just see you as very controlling. I don't see me as coming with some issues maybe from my mum or whatever." I guess that worries me. I think that there is more than one side to it.

Therapist: Let me stop you now, Heather. Do you feel anxious now? [*Focuses on her fear, which is apparent in her nonverbals.*]

Heather: I do [*cries*].

Therapist: Can you tell him, "I am anxious"? So it is hard for you to . . .

Heather: [*cries*]

Therapist: . . . what happens is when I said, "Are you anxious?" it just crystallizes how difficult all this is. You are scared that you are going to get a negative reaction from him if you assert yourself. I am not saying this is what he will do. I think he is scared too. I just wonder if it is scary for you to say to him that "I want you to take some responsibility for this." [*Draws out her fear of standing up to him.*]

Heather: It is. I guess it hooks in to this whole thing that I can't do that, that I have to make it all better, not disagree with him, so I take all the responsibility myself.

Therapist: You are also responding to something in him, or the history of your relationship, which is what? [*Focuses on the present relationship as a way of encouraging her to confront him.*]

Heather: Yeah, I guess I have a fear in me that it will be hard [*to Brian*] for you to hear what I am saying and that you will feel defensive and you know, maybe, not look at it.

Therapist: That is the anxiety now?

Heather: Yeah.

Therapist: Can you tell him what you want, what it is important for him to look into? [*Promotes an assertive enactment.*]

Heather: I don't know that I can [*laughs*]. In terms of this issue? I guess I feel that it is important for you to look at why you feel so controlled and to look at in an instance when it happens, to look at what your part, your feelings are, as opposed to just me as the force inflicting this on you. I need you to give up some control and not always need to be right.

Therapist: How scared are you now?

Heather: Not quite so scared.

Therapist: But it is still difficult.

Heather: It feels like I am going like that [*hitting fist; being confrontive*], and I am not like that [usually submissive].

A few minutes later in the session, the therapist focuses on Brian's sensitivity to being controlled, which leads him to be very controlling by defining what is acceptable.

Therapist: . . . We have talked about it before, about your vulnerability to feeling controlled that sort of connects to your mother, to your family. But there is something that comes up there. And then, as in any couple, the issue becomes, Whose issue is it? Somehow [*to Heather*] your anxiety and unsureness leads you to often take on that you are not allowed to assert yourself in relation to Brian. And also, you always have to say, "I am not being controlling." [*to Brian*] She has always got to reassure you that she is not controlling, for herself almost. It is like being controlling is a fate worse than death. Somehow you, on the other hand, are very activated when you feel controlled. [*Begins to reframe who is controlling.*]

Brian: I feel activated when I feel controlled without the necessity of being controlled. [*Attempts to reframe that his response is reasonable.*] Like when we are doing an evening routine, if we are getting the kids lunch together and you are dictating what to do.

Therapist: The sensitive issue here is, unless you actually start asking yourself sometimes "How come I am so sensitive to being controlled, and how I can deal with it rather than . . . ?"

Brian: Yeah, I know I am so sensitive.

Therapist: . . . Yeah, it's great that you see that, but now it's important to look at "How can I deal with it?" rather than "It is only when you should not be controlling that I get upset about being controlled." So it is really, can you own and deal with your own issue of control? I am aware and she is aware, and this is where the difficult area is for you, and I imagine you must feel really anxious about somehow being, I dunno, not having your needs seen.

Brian: Yeah, it is in an area when I am perceiving that it is not necessary. [*Disagrees.*]

Brian continues to disagree, becomes very rational, and then minimizes the issue. A few minutes later, the therapist refocuses on the control issue.

Therapist: I think there has been a rule where you are not allowed to say to Brian, "Don't feel so controlled, or there is something about your feeling controlled rather than me being controlling."

Heather: [*whispering loudly*] That is why I brought it up here.

Brian: Say that again.

Therapist: There is a rule that has been generated in which she is not allowed to say to you, "Brian, your control is a vulnerability or sensitivity of yours. Deal with it as yours rather than laying it on me. Don't say I am controlling, own your own sensitivity to being controlled." The two of you have constructed your relationship where she tries not to be controlling, and she has bought into that she is controlling or that she is not allowed to be controlling, and she is not very happy with that, and she gets quite depressed about it. [*Confronts.*]

Brian: Sorry, you are unhappy because you are not controlling? [*Attempts to redefine her as controlling.*]

Therapist: Unhappy, she is unhappy that she is not allowed to name your control as an issue. [*Accepts as a way of minimizing and deflecting.*]

Brian: Okay. It is an issue. We have talked about it as an issue.

Therapist: There is not enough security. Twice today she tried to bring it up. She did bring it up with the safety here, both times she was very anxious. She is extremely frightened, so that the fear does not come from her past, but because she knows you will get protective of yourself and even out-maneuver her in the conflict, and it will end up with her being bad, and so she progressively silenced herself.

Brian: That sounds strange. Do you want to be controlling?

Heather: That isn't the question.

Brian: I am confused.

Therapist: She wants you to be less sensitive to feeling being controlled and to seeing her as controlling and to just accept what she does without labeling her as controlling or without seeing yourself as being controlled.

Brian: [*laughs*] Okay. I am going to be facetious: Do I just say "yes" to her and . . . [*Bows his head in a subservient gesture.*]

Therapist: What you need to do is to deal with your own sensitivity to seeing everything as controlling. Something, some feeling underneath, leads you to need to protect yourself.

Brian: Sure, there's also the daily interactions, you know, these interactions that we have in daily life [*nervous laughter*].

Therapist: You are very, Brian, as I see it, you are very sensitive to control. [*Confronts.*]

Brian: It doesn't come up a whole lot.

Therapist: I think it comes up a lot.

Brian: Ay, that is not true . . . [*laughs*]. Don't control me! [*Uses a humorous strategy to avoid confrontation.*]

Therapist: Exactly [*laughter*]. In your way of moving through the world, you have antennae like that to issues of control. You have needed them to protect.

Heather: [*to Brian*] You notice that I am not disagreeing.

Therapist: You have to develop these antennae to protect yourself, I understand that. [*Validates.*]

Brian: But I don't feel controlling. I only feel controlled. [*Disagrees.*]

Heather: When I am being controlling [*sarcastically*]!

Brian: It is once in a blue moon when, in my perception, when there is no need for this. [*Minimizes.*]

Therapist: Partly I think it is so much of your being, maybe, that you are not aware of how you are always reacting to control. Maybe you are so good at it that maybe you succeeded not feeling very controlled, but the person outside of you, especially your intimate partner, is exquisitely aware of how sensitive you are to control, as I am, and she feels very controlled by it.

Brian: [*laughs*] Okay. [*Minimizes.*]

Therapist: And so it is something, part of who you are and what you needed to do to survive in your family. That is not necessarily good or bad, but it can produce something. Somehow it is, like, it is sometimes hard for you to understand the effect you are having, and the other person feels you are very sensitive to control and sees what you do as often being very concerned about not being controlled. You have said it quite often, saying in these sessions, "Don't be controlling. I don't want you to be controlling," and controlling has got a . . . it is a bad brush to be painted with. She feels that, and also to some extent, she agreed or bought that rule that she can't say to you, "There is something about your being so sensitive to control that is a problem for me," but then the more she can't say it, the more she gets distressed.

Brian: Okay, I am trying to understand. [*to Heather*] Do you want to be controlling? [*Hard for him to change his view and focus on self.*]

Heather: I think that question misses the mark. Because to me, the concept of "controlling" is a perception, like it's that word doesn't even have to be there. Like, if I say to you, "I don't want you to put the hockey stick in it," it is based on some need in me. To see that as controlling or wanting to be controlling is a perception that, I don't know how to say this. It does not need to be seen as controlling. I don't see it as controlling; *controlling* is a very emotionally laden word.

Therapist: It's hard to be appreciative of her point of view. For all of us, this is hard. You could not even be aware of it, but there may be a hundred possibilities of what is right, but for you there will always be, "My way is right, and yours is control." If you didn't have a mother who was intrusive and controlling, you wouldn't have developed antennae with super sensitivity to control and won't apply them. But you do. You walk through the world, and you taste each situation in terms of "Am I being controlled?" or you perceive them that way, and Heather says this ends up being quite difficult for her because she always has to give way to you.

In this next segment, Heather expresses anger at Brian, and he acknowledges his anger and then his shame.

Therapist: Or you become resigned that she won't be fun, right, and then you feel sad, then I don't know if you withdraw or . . .

Brian: Right now it is sort of an acceptance thing, you know; I sort of will get my fun at home with my boys, and I can count on that. [*Said with a "poor me" tone and face.*]

Therapist: That sounds . . .

Heather: God, that hurts. It felt like a knife [*making a stabbing-in-the-heart gesture*].

Brian: It is not a knife.

Heather: I know, I am telling you how it felt.

Therapist: I am not sure if it is not a knife.

Brian: It is not a knife.

Therapist: "If I can't get my fun here . . ."

Heather: Just pardon me [*throws a stuffed toy that was on the table angrily on the floor*]. I am sorry, I am really mad. I apologize. I am really pissed off. I am not mad at you, [therapist].

Therapist:	Will you deal with him? What are you saying to him?
Heather:	I am saying that it really pisses me off. Part of me not being fun is what I just told you, you let us share our responsibility so that I was fun through university, I was fun through my youth, my trips, I don't want to not to be fun.
Therapist:	I think you are mad at her when you say that it is not a knife. You are angry with her . . .
Brian:	No.
Therapist:	. . . and I guess you feel very hurt . . .
Brian:	No.
Therapist:	. . . what do you feel?
Brian:	I feel sadness. I shouldn't have said anything all along, I am supposed to communicate your feeling. So I communicate my feelings. [*Complains.*]

A few minutes later in the session, the therapist invites Brian to take a self-focus.

Therapist:	I guess your anger is expressed in withdrawal . . .
Brian:	Okay.
Therapist:	. . . when you see a kid say, "I'll take my marbles and go home," he is hurt and angry, and I guess that is what you feel.
Brian:	I don't know, maybe if you are using anger in that way. There is certainly sadness, disappointment.
Therapist:	You don't feel actively angry. Actually you withdraw when you are angry, and to express anger is very scary, or you blow up on a few occasions in your life. I, too, never used to express anger in my life, but sometimes anger is important. [*Disclosure.*]
Heather:	I guess it sounded to me angry, like "I am taking my marbles and going home"; if you are taking your marbles and going home, for me there is our marriage. Saying, "I will get my fun from the boys; I will withdraw from you," that was a different way of saying that. "I won't look to you for that," is one way of saying it, another way is withdrawal.
Therapist:	One other issue is, then, it hits your anxiety button, which is feeling abandoned or left alone . . .
Brian:	[*silence*]
Therapist:	. . . so what is happening now? It is complicated, it is not easy for you.
Brian:	[*long pause*] I don't know.

Therapist: How are you dealing with what I am saying, with what she is saying?

Brian: I am pretty withdrawn. [*Genuine.*]

Heather: [*softly*] Can you see how this connects to when I brought up on the couch and I say to . . . however we choose to say it, to say what is true out there, "I am feeling incredibly annoyed," or whatever, and when that gets suppressed other things happen, . . . even when putting it down there. "I am really annoyed that those dishes are still there," you know, this is exactly how I see what [therapist] is saying. I just, I honestly love you, I do love you, and I do think that you have really a hard time with anger, even the concept of "anger," what is "anger"? I dearly wish you could kind of go to the shower about that, there are times when I am ticked off, and just get it out.

Therapist: [*softly*] Anger is loss of control for you or a bad thing—it is not a good thing. Like when you were in India and you almost hit the bus driver, but there is this thing you feel, and it is very difficult to handle anger, and you want to make it not there, that is dangerous.

Brian begins to reveal the threat to his identity ("I am bad") and his fear of losing her love when Heather gets angry.

Brian: I didn't see anger growing up, and when I see it occasionally, it is frightening.

Therapist: Were you frightened when you saw her throw . . .

Brian: I guess, yeah.

Therapist: . . . it is scary, I was shocked. Then what happened inside? You feel a need to run away to hide or what?

Brian: I just don't know how to deal with it. I'll become parental and protective of myself and parental of Heather. When she gets angry, I just feel like [*sigh*], like the way I do now, like "Way to go, Brian, you make her angry," the way I feel guilty, "I blew that one and now it is time," and go to her when she is lying on the couch or on the bed, like a puppy.

Therapist: I see, you become scared of her anger at you, that she will abandon you, or what, that you are no good? [*Therapist mistakenly focuses on attachment rather than identity.*]

Brian: I don't know that *abandoned* is the word, it's just, I hurt her, and I'm bad.

Therapist: Like the comment with the knife.

Heather: Does that happen to you, feeling like "I am feeling bad"?

Brian: No, like I *am* bad. [*Reveals vulnerability and core maladaptive emotion scheme of shame.*]

Heather: Yes, that is what I mean, it's "I stabbed her, she is angry. I am bad," like I have seen the little-boy feeling in you that says, "I am bad, I am not worthy," you know.

Therapist: Yes, so it's feeling "I am unacceptable, I'm not okay," is it like, if I understand it, it's what happened when you weren't picked for the hockey team as a kid? [*This is information from an individual session with Brian in which he worked on feeling humiliated in front of kids at school.*] [*Validates.*]

Brian: Yes. Like as a kid, the other kids would look at me and laugh, and I felt so humiliated. I was so much smaller and less developed, and I felt so ashamed, like I would never be good enough [*looking down, tear in eyes*].

Therapist: Uh-huh, like you just wanted to run away and hide, get away. But you really just needed to be accepted and valued as having something. That's what you need most, to be accepted as okay. [*Focuses on need.*]

Brian: But also with my mother I also wasn't okay. She was so controlling and critical, so I had to always be on guard. So I needed to always be on guard or on top of things.

Heather: It is so much easier to feel concerned when I hear how hard it was and how bad you felt about yourself—then it's not me, and I do care about you. [*Compassion.*]

Therapist: Can you let that in, Brian? You're okay in her eyes when you feel small or feel not okay—in my eyes, too—and Heather, I guess he really needs to hear that from you. Can you let him know that you do value him and what he says and do see his strengths? [*Promotes corrective emotional experience.*]

Heather: I do, and you know that I always value what you say. I always want your opinion and care about what you feel. But can I say one thing: For the record, I threw that doll because I don't want to be depressed in my life, and I will throw things in my life before I get depressed again. I threw that because that is breaking the pattern I have been living in my life, and I have to do that, but it is important for you to say what you were feeling. I was angry and I expressed my anger to stand up for myself.

Therapist: You need to throw things in order to express and to really get through to him.

Heather: I had to throw that, it is important. I felt angry, and I throw when I am not feeling heard.

Therapist: Ideally, let me say this as a teaching thing: You will find ways of being heard without having to throw things.

Heather: For sure, that is my goal.

Brian: Well, I guess you know that is where my boys are important to me. I can play with them and know I'm okay. As we talked about before in that individual session, the adult me can also tell the small me that I am okay, and I can take care of that painful part of me and of my boys, too, because now I am the grown-up. [*Articulates ways of self-soothing.*]

Submitter's Anger

It is the lack of anger, rather than its presence, that is most noticeable as a problem in the person who adopts the submissive role. Assertive anger needs to be accessed to help this person assert appropriate boundaries and rebalance the power in the relationship. The submitter's identity has been submerged to please or placate the dominant partner, but it leads to a build-up of unexpressed resentment. Often, fear blocks the expression of assertive anger by the submissive partner, who needs the therapist's support to stand up to the dominant partner. Rightful anger is one of the best motivators of assertive behavior. It empowers, giving the feeling of having been wronged and of having rights. Assertive anger challenges the dominant partner's assumed superiority and can produce change in the relational patterns.

Mae was a 32-year-old and was 10 years the junior of her husband Victor, a symphony orchestra conductor. They had met 8 years ago when she became a member of the orchestra. She was now a private music teacher, no longer a member of the orchestra, but she still deferred to his guidance, was very attentive to him, and tried to please him. He had had an affair, and his complaint to Mae was that it seemed to him like she wasn't really a person who could make him feel loved. On exploring this, it became clear that to him it didn't seem like she was really there as a separate confirming other because she was so compliant. In one session, the therapist asked Mae to tell Victor what she felt when he intruded on what was her domain, that of gardening, by standing over her while she was planting and telling her where to place the flowers. She was hesitant to say anything, smiling sweetly, but when the therapist conjectured that she resented him doing this, she readily agreed. Victor, the dominant husband, turned to the therapist and said, "How do I know you're not just putting words in her mouth?" The therapist turned to Mae and said, "Tell him in your our words what you feel," and she said, "I do resent you telling me what to do. I plant flowers every year without your advice." This was the beginning of a restructuring of their interaction on the basis of accessing her unexpressed resentment.

A NOTE ON CONTEMPT

One of the most destructive emotions expressed within a couple's relationship is contempt. The worst-case scenarios are when there is a very rapid escalation, with contempt and defiance. For example, if a wife says, "Wash the dishes," to the husband, and he says, "Yeah, make me, you bitch," these are signs of future divorce (Gottman, Gortner, Berns, & Jacobson, 1997). To regard one's partner with contempt is to demoralize and demean him or her; to feel disgust and disapproval toward him or her; or to insult, mock, and judge him or her. Behaviors associated with contempt include eye rolling, name calling, sneering, and an excessive use of sarcasm or cynicism (Gottman, 1994; Gottman & Silver, 1999). Contempt is heavily steeped in negativity and involves nonverbal or verbal behaviors that are fueled by long-simmering negative views of a partner. Contemptuous partners criticize, sneer, and exhibit sarcasm. Contemptuous partners are treating their spouses as objects and have lost sight of the other as a person just like themselves. As partners become more disgusted with the lack of response to their complaints, they begin to feel broadly fed up and lose positive affect toward the target partner. This lack of positive affect results in contemptuous behaviors, including criticism, belligerence, and disgust, which may have no situational significance (Gottman, 1999). This overall negativity toward the other is the main drive behind contemptuous words and actions.

Although contempt is closely linked to anger and disgust, it differs from these. Whereas anger is generally a nonmoral reaction to goal blockage or violation, contempt harbors a critical judgment against the target individual's worth. Additionally, contempt conveys a sense of superiority and elicits feelings of inferiority in the target. As a result of this negative evaluation, contemptuous words and behaviors elicit feelings of shame in the target partner. Shame involves being seen as defective in the eyes of the other or a vicarious experience of this.

Many argue that when partners express deep-seated contempt, little may be done to repair the relationship. How do therapists approach working with a couple in which one or both partners experience a strong sense of contempt? Is there hope for the contemptuous couple, or are they destined to fail? Gottman (1999) held that once one or both partners has become so negative that mutual fondness and admiration has been extinguished, the marriage is in dire trouble. It follows, then, that positive feelings of fondness and admiration are antidotes to contempt. If a partner feels concern, caring, or respect for a spouse, they are less likely to act disgusted with him or her when he or she disagrees. Bringing positive feelings to light during therapy is necessary to establish a healthy foundation for improving distressed marital relationships in general and as an antidote to contempt. How to get there, however, is not as simple as having partners write lists of positive qualities of their partners, or asking what attracted the partners to each other in the beginning. We do aim to evoke alternative feelings in the session toward the spouse and mutual validation rather than derision or contempt, but this has to be done in small steps. First, the therapist validates the contemptuous partner's dissatisfaction but suggests that the partner has a different view and that it is going to be important to hear both sides if change is to be achieved.

Contempt possesses similar characteristics to anger and may be worked with in similar ways. Like anger, contempt may be expressed as an attempt to protect one's self from experiencing more vulnerable feelings of fear, shame, or hurt. Contempt also serves to place an individual in a more powerful position, and like anger, is expressed by belittling and shaming a partner. Contempt is thus most likely to occur in the dominant position, but a pursuer for closeness may also eventually become scornful and begin to express contempt.

In essence, contempt needs to be treated more as an experience within the individual expressing the emotion than as organized by the immediate interaction, and treatment then is geared toward helping that individual recognize the origin of the feeling and learning how to regulate it, independent of the partner. Dealing with contempt thus often requires more of an individual focus. Often, this involves getting to a deeper hurt or shame in the contemptuous personality. Some couples in which there is too much contempt may be too entrenched in blame and may experience too high a level of emotion to work as a couple. At this point, the partners should be seen individually to reduce contempt, anger, and blaming. Initially, individuals with the contempt problem must step back and become aware of their own underlying feeling. Mindful awareness helps slow down reactions and helps people adopt an observer stance and thereby better regulate their reactions. The contemptuous person needs to learn to identify and explore the underlying feeling by asking, What am I truly feeling? Anger? Shame? Hurt? Helping contemptuous partners learn to develop the ability to explore their basic attachment or identity feelings or needs prior to entering an exchange with their spouse facilitates them in expressing their needs rather than the contempt they normally expressed. This helps them ultimately get their needs met far better than does expression of contempt. Contemptuous partners thus must learn to pinpoint the source of their frustrations before engaging a spouse. They need to develop the ability to regulate and reflect on their feelings of contempt and ask, Is this reaction going to help them get their needs met? If not, then perhaps an argument can be avoided. However, if partners truly feel wronged and cannot soothe themselves, then the discussion needs to take place, but without contempt.

For example, in a case where a husband is contemptuous of his wife for not having dinner ready when he returns, the therapist would want to work initially with the husband's contempt. The therapist validates that his expectations have not been met and then helps the husband attend to his internal emotional experience in the original situation when he arrives home to find his wife has not made dinner. Does he just feel contempt, or are there other feelings as well? Perhaps he feels neglected, unvalued, diminished, unloved, or pushed aside. The therapist also helps the husband try to be more specific regarding the particular event that triggered his reaction. Was it the fact that his wife had not prepared a meal, was it something from the previous night or week, or did it begin with other frustrations? The therapist would need to explore these and any other relevant considerations with the couple to get at the trigger.

In another couple, the husband, for example, expressed contempt by insulting his wife in various ways including saying she had grown fat and ugly. His contempt appeared to grow out of his withdrawal and normally mild-mannered personality as an act of desperation at feeling finally pushed to his limit by his dominating wife, who reminded him of his mother. His contempt was dealt with as resulting from the vulnerable, painful emotional experience that he was unable to acknowledge, of feeling dominated by his wife. These feelings of powerlessness and anger that he never had expressed before led him ultimately to treat his wife as a nonperson, with contempt. Once his core emotions of both anger and hurt were accessed, his expressions of contempt were understood and transformed through accessing his primary emotions and through asserting rather than submitting. His wife, after first protesting that she was not so dominant, began to listen to his complaints, and his contempt turned to assertion.

CONCLUSION

In EFT-C, when a couple comes in with one or both partners expressing anger, often anger that the other is not the way they "should be," this anger is almost always viewed as a secondary emotion, especially when the presenting problem is angry conflict. In these situations, anger takes the form of a defensive coping strategy that is counterproductive in creating change within couples. Then, the underlying more vulnerable feelings need to be accessed and expressed. Unacknowledged anger, however, can be primary and productive, and then its expression is encouraged, and it brings contact in place of withdrawal.

EFT-C differs from other approaches in its treatment of anger because rather than promoting anger management, it confronts anger and its underlying determinants directly. Rather than attempting to modify erroneous cognitions as would a cognitive approach, EFT-C reframes anger in terms of underlying vulnerability, guides the person's attention to the visceral feeling of vulnerability, and promotes expression of the primary hurt. From more psychoanalytic perspectives, anger might be viewed as regression to an immature state or, for Bowenians, a sign of low differentiation. In EFT-C, however, anger is not viewed as an immature emotion but as one that often prevents a person from attending to the true underlying feelings, which need to be accepted.

11

SADNESS IN COUPLES THERAPY

We are never so helplessly unhappy as when we lose love.

—Sigmund Freud

Sadness in relationships is a response to loss, to parting or separation from loved ones, and to the loss of connection. The behavioral forms of separation include being rejected or neglected by one's partner; being unable to communicate or express true feelings to one's partner; and of course, death or loss of one's partner. Sadness is an expression of loneliness, and the loss of closeness and connection is a source of sorrow. Sadness also somehow has something to do with love and people's capacity for empathy. Sadness deepens people's ability to understand the pain of others. The experience of sadness makes the soul tender and gives people wisdom. For many people, it is their personal pain that has been an important teacher. When partners feels lost, sad, alone, and unable to stop the hurt, their loved ones often can help them because they too have felt that way and understand how to respond.

Sadness is an important part of growing up. Life offers plenty of tragedy. People all suffer, and people all die. They need comfort from each other as they all face the pains of life: the surprises of fate and the inevitability of aging and death. Sadness prepares people to be kind, loving friends, parents, and mates. Sadness announces that people care. Many people, however, are afraid of sadness and refuse to feel it when fate gives them the opportunity.

The two action tendencies associated with primary sadness are reaching out to one's partner for comfort and succorance to reduce distress or withdrawing into self to recover from loss. Overall, tears of primary sadness com-

259

municate vulnerability to one's partner and can bring concern, compassion, and comfort. They also can be healing in and of themselves and bring with them a sense of relief, and release of tension and exhaustion. Sadness and grieving allow for acceptance of the loss, healing, integrating what was lost, and moving on to renewed interest in life.

In couples, partners feel sad when they feel they have lost the love, respect, or special connection with their partner. They feel sad when they experience being alone or neglected or when their expectations are disappointed. The losses that produce sadness in intimate relationships often are not separations or actual loss of the loved one but are disappointments and feelings of loneliness. This is an emotional process that leads to assimilating the loss and letting go of the goal and moving on.

Often, sadness that is suppressed is about significant losses—the death of a parent, sibling, friend, or worst of all, a child. When one member of the couple experiences a loss, the other partner grieves the loss as well. Most often, couples are highly connected and intertwined, identified with, and empathic to one another. The partner who suffered the primary loss will need to feel that his or her pain is sufficiently validated and understood by the partner. The partner will also need support and recognition that he or she is grieving. When they both suffer the same loss, as in the loss of a child or the loss of functioning of a child, this involves a major grieving process that can cause great mental stress to the parents. How people handle and wish to handle their grief can bring them together or tear them apart. A couple with, for example, an autistic child or a child who has a debilitating illness can handle their grief in many different ways. These differences often produce conflict. One partner may need the other to listen and support him or her as he or she expresses his or her feelings of grief, whereas the other partner may want to grieve silently, at least at first, and wants the other to respect his or her need to not talk about it. Expressions of sadness may evoke feelings of powerlessness, especially in men, who then try to propose practical solutions that feel unsupportive to the spouse. Some partners, especially women, may respond to their spouse's need for solitude with demands for sharing that leave the spouse feeling that their needs are being disregarded.

In addition to differences in processing grief, conflict in couples is often fuelled by adaptive sadness over loneliness. Feeling married but alone is a major source of sadness. Some partners have experiences of "being so alone" in the relationship or feel "Once again, it is me by myself. I am so alone. I cannot rely on you." Other core sadness experiences might include feelings such as "It's hard for me to admit it, but I need your support"; "I feel neglected; I want to know that I am important to you"; "I need you to take care of me"; "I want you to make me a priority"; "I feel like I work alone; I want to feel we are a team"; "My partner does not stick up for me"; and "He is always with his work buddies; I am so alone in the relationship." When this type of primary sadness produces couples conflict, it often relates to earlier experiences of loss in life in which clients felt abandoned and alone. Clients may access memories from early life experiences of "never being able to rely on anybody" or being "that lonely kid in the schoolyard," or even memories of abandonment and loss of one parent or another due to death, separation, or divorce. One partner may recount a sense of abandonment when as a child he or she began a new developmental stage such as puberty: "My father couldn't relate to me as I became a woman and was no longer his little girl." This maladaptive aspect of sadness relates to unfinished business with parents and leaves the person vulnerable to feeling abandoned by partners. Sadness also is often mixed with fear, and it is the fear of abandonment and loneliness that people so often want to avoid. These often are the underlying feelings that lie beneath one partner adopting a blaming, critical stance.

DISTINGUISHING SADNESS AND DISTRESS

Although tears often signify primary adaptive sadness, they can also signify other types of psychological distress. Clients in interactional conflict, especially women, frequently cry easily when distressed about the things that are bothering them. In this situation, crying signals one partner's distress to the other about the circumstance. It does not, however, necessarily indicate primary sadness at loss. In working with couples, it is important that the therapist determine whether crying is due to primary sadness or to other emotions involved in distress. Tears can accompany loneliness, fear, anger, shame, or helplessness. Sadness or loneliness can produce tears, but tears of loneliness differ from the distress cry that is more related to fear and danger and that is a signal that something is wrong. Sadness also can be evoked by disappointments or having one's hopes shattered. In situations in which distress does not signify pure primary sadness, it is counterproductive to focus on it. Rather, the task is to help the person identify other specific emotions associated with the distress until such time as the primary emotion emerges. One way of distinguishing between sadness and different types of distress is to observe people's responses and what is helpful to them. Distress is reduced by comfort in the form of soothing sounds, verbal reassurance, pacifiers, and physical contact from the other. Sadness also is reduced by comfort, but this form of connection involves breaking the isolation and loneliness rather than protecting from danger. Therapists need to distinguish primary adaptive sadness from secondary and instrumental expressions of sadness, which are discussed in the next section.

PRIMARY ADAPTIVE, MALADAPTIVE, SECONDARY, AND INSTRUMENTAL SADNESS IN COUPLES

Primary adaptive sadness is characterized by a kind of momentary surrender or giving up, and it is free of blame (Greenberg, 2002a, 2002b). Distinguishing primary adaptive sadness from secondary depression or a sad but more victimized helplessness is based on knowledge of the situation or couples' interactional styles and patterns, as well as on verbal and nonverbal cues, including vocal quality, facial expression, and manner of experiencing. The expression of previously unacknowledged primary sadness has a new, fresh quality that evokes a different feeling from chronic hopelessness and complaint that masquerades as relentless sorrow.

Primary sadness that is suppressed often manifests as hopelessness or anger and blame. Markers of suppressing sadness and emotional pain include intellectualization or minimizing damage and pain, tensing muscles, holding back tears, blaming the other, and avoiding contact with the other, along with an explicitly stated unwillingness to cry or go into the pain such as "What's the sense of crying?" or "It's best to just get on with it." Fears or concerns about being overwhelmed by sadness also are major blocks to sadness.

In distinguishing primary, adaptive sadness from secondary or instrumental sadness, the therapist needs to consider whether the expression of sadness promotes attachment in the couple or whether it preserves a negative interactional cycle. This assessment is aided by observing responses to interventions after the sadness is evoked in the session. When the sadness is acknowledged, does the partner seem to more fully experience the sadness and to respond to his or her partner's support with expressions of closeness and connectedness? Or does the person repeat the same feeling again without any noticeable change in the quality or intensity of feeling? Does the partner become more desperate as sadness is expressed, feeling abandoned and falling into a state of helpless dependence? The latter suggests problems with affect regulation and a core sense of weakness based more on fear than on sadness. In these cases, the continued expression of sadness is not productive and the therapy needs to focus on self-soothing.

Secondary sadness can also be distinguished from primary sadness by the temporal expression of emotion. For example, first, anger may be expressed but is quickly followed by tears. Or fear may be elicited but is covered over by tears. A good example of this is when in the midst of conflict, one partner threatens to leave the relationship and the other begins to cry. When the crying is explored, it becomes apparent that fear is often at the core of the secondary sadness. Secondary sadness often is an aspect of complaining about the other. This is pejoratively referred to as "whining" and is the case when tears are a form of protest, expressing how poorly treated the person feels. Here, anger and sadness are often fused, and the underlying anger needs to be separated from the sadness. If there is any primary sadness, it needs to be experienced and expressed free of the anger.

A common secondary reaction associated with sadness is depression. It involves a kind of generalized hopelessness or sense of powerlessness rather than genuine acceptance of loss. Depression may be triggered by childhood and family experiences of abuse and neglect, by more recent interpersonal experiences such as loss of attachments, by the loss of personal agency or potency in the face of abuses of power, by harsh criticism or contempt that gets internalized, or by some combination of these (Greenberg & Watson, 2006). When lingering depression in one partner results from stifled primary sadness at losses or any other suppressed primary experience, treatment involves unpacking the secondary depressive reaction into its underlying feelings and acknowledging and experiencing the underlying painful, primary adaptive emotion of sadness at loss.

In working with depressive states in one partner, within the couples context, the therapist may work both individually and interactionally, depending on the needs of the couple or the given constraints. It is often important to recognize the depression as a problem in its own right and help the depressed partner seek individual treatment while couples therapy continues. Some of the couples work may focus on the difficulties of one person and the way in which the partner might be able to assist him or her. In other cases, the work may focus on difficulties within the relationship and between the couple related to one member's depression.

Instrumental expressions of sadness in couples are observed when people cry because they are feeling helpless, dependent, and are crying to get help. People may not be aware of their neediness or the instrumental function of their tears. People learn to express instrumental sadness in earlier relationships in which it once served an adaptive function. However, this sadness does not primarily result from an experience of loss and often does not elicit the desired support. In current relationships, instrumental sadness serves as an interactional appeal, with the hope that it will evoke sympathy, support, or understanding, and they prevent the development of self-support. Instrumental tears function to get attention from partners or the therapist and are experienced as manipulative. Therapists will empathically challenge or interpret the function of instrumental tears in the relationship, access underlying motivations and needs, and encourage people to express primary needs to their partners.

For example, Joann and Dirk came to therapy after having been together for 6 years. They said they really loved each other but they were trying to decide whether they wanted a more committed relationship. Joann's major complaint about Dirk was that she was not sure whether he was strong enough for her. She felt he lacked drive and determination. Dirk's major complaint about Joann was that he was not sure she was honest and true to her word. He was not sure he could trust her. She had been involved in several other romantic relationships while they were together that Dirk had only found out about after the fact. When the therapist began to ask Joann about those relationships, Joann began to cry, saying it was very hard to talk about it as this brought up a great deal of sad, bad feelings. She felt that Dirk was mean to talk about these things and embarrass her. Joann was crying in part to divert the focus away from other feelings, especially her fear of intimacy, although this was not in her awareness. At first the therapist simply reflected her feelings of embarrassment and sadness, noticing internally that he did not feel compassion for her. A few sessions later, when the alliance had been firmly established, the therapist told Joann that he had felt shut out by her tears and wondered aloud whether Dirk felt the same. Dirk acknowledged that he felt pushed away by Joann's tears every time he tried to have an honest conversation about the meaning of those other relationships. The therapist supported the couple in recognizing that even though the feelings this topic evoked were difficult for Joann to discuss, they needed to continue to talk about them even through Joann's tears.

Attachment injuries are a source of sadness and loneliness (Johnson, Makinen, & Millikin, 2001). These injuries relate to earlier events in a couple's relationship in which one or both partners felt abandoned or neglected. Although couples may not first present their problems as an injury, it becomes clear over the course of therapy that one partner has suffered an injury by the other. This may take the form of a shattering of trust or lack of responsiveness at a significant time of need. In these cases, neither the injurer nor the injured may have recognized the significance of the act. Nevertheless, if not addressed, they can linger in the relationship and become corrosive. An example might be a woman who felt abandoned or neglected when her partner was emotionally unavailable when she had an abortion. In another couple, Susan felt injured when after extensive medical tests to determine why she had pain during intercourse, it was determined that she had endometriosis and that if she wanted to have children, she should do so immediately or consider surgery or medication. Susan did not feel in a position to have children at that point in time but knew she did in the future. She was afraid of surgery and did not like that option. She had relayed all of this devastating information to her partner, Ralph, and told him that she wanted to discuss her various options. Ralph, even though he had agreed at some point that they wanted to have children, had had little response and changed the subject. Susan had felt hurt and lonely at the time but decided not to bring it up again until Ralph was ready to talk. One week later Ralph approached Susan, saying he wanted to have sex. When she replied that she did as well but that he would have to wait 1 hour until her pain medication set in, he replied, "Well, we have to talk about whether you are going to have the surgery." In this case, Ralph's timing caused Susan to experience an attachment injury. By waiting to discuss the issue until he wanted to have intercourse, Susan felt he was not concerned about her or about having a child but only about his sexual needs.

In another example of an attachment injury, a man, Alan, was rushed to the hospital with a broken leg that he sustained while playing tennis. It turned out to be complicated and that he would need surgery. When his wife Catalina was called and informed, she had trouble deciding whether to go. She decided to send her teenage daughter instead because she was "too busy."

Alan felt this indicated how unimportant he was and began from this point on to distance and throw himself into his work. Attachment injuries can differ in severity, depending on the nature of the injury.

Although it is sadness that we are focusing on here, the core emotions that underlie attachment injuries are more often a complex combination of sadness, fear, and even anger, depending on the nature of the injury. We focus on sadness here because often the person feels alone and sad about the loss of connection but does not recognize or express these feelings at the time the injury occurred. The man with a broken leg felt alone and sad that his wife was not by his side at the hospital, but he had suppressed these feelings and only anger was experienced or expressed. He may also have missed a sense of family. He felt abandoned, and this may have provoked a fear of being alone in the future. Sickness or injury often evokes a sense of aloneness and abandonment. Those people who were ill as children may have felt abandoned when left alone in the hospital. Adult abandonment experiences can trigger childhood memories of abandonment and leave people feeling vulnerable and alone.

As we have indicated, it is important to differentiate between attachment and identity injuries, both of which may trigger sadness, although the sadness in identity injuries is secondary to the more primary shame of the injury. Sadness over an identity issue is about loss of status rather than loss of connection. For example, when a partner shows up drunk at a public event important to the other, the partner loses face and feels shame that is the result of identity injury. Or when a partner is promoted to a new position and the partner does not recognize the achievement, it is identity that is at issue. The partner feels diminished. She may feel, but does not say, "You don't recognize or celebrate my successes. This promotion is important for me, and I feel you ignore my achievements. You don't understand or appreciate who I am." This is the type of experience that partners can be very sore over for a long time and have a hard time forgiving or letting go of the bad feelings. There is a sense of a "one-time opportunity, a moment to shine," and it is lost. The unresolved feelings and the beliefs formed at this time often underlie the negative interactional cycles that couples present.

AFFILIATION CYCLES

Sadness in affiliation cycles is about loss. In the section that follows, we provide examples of pursuer's sadness and distancer's sadness.

Pursuer's Sadness

In affiliation cycles in which the concern is attachment, the partner pursuing for closeness is the one most likely to feel underlying sadness and loneliness. Within these cycles, primary adaptive sadness is a response to feeling a loss of the other's responsiveness or concern or presence. If one partner were to die or go away on a long trip, the other partner would miss him or her and feel sad. If a partner is often unavailable or nonattentive, the ignored partner would feel sad and lonely. The key to resolving with these couples is that the sadness needs to be expressed in a nonblaming and nonpressuring way. When and if this occurs, it has the potential effect of evoking compassion rather than withdrawal from the distancer. The following excerpt from a first session is a classic example of a pursue–distance cycle in which the pursuer, Eva, wants closeness and becomes persistent when her partner, Max, is not responsive. As is shown, her pursuit serves to push him away further.

Sadness and Loneliness and the Wall

Eva:	Sometimes he'll just sit in the background and be quiet . . .
Max:	Right.
Eva:	. . . and then he's mad; he's sullen and that's not good, then the kids see that, you know. Now there's no communication.
Therapist:	Yeah, so let me understand. So one of the patterns might be, you . . . [*to Max*] uh . . . sort of disagree, or don't agree with what's going on, . . .
Max:	Mm-hm.
Therapist:	. . . but to not get into things too much, you kind of bite your tongue, . . .
Max:	Yeah.
Therapist:	. . . right, and you sort of hold it in, but then you get down, you get sullen, . . .
Max:	Mm-hm.
Therapist:	. . . maybe withdrawn, right? . . .
Max:	Yes.
Therapist:	. . . and then you're not communicating. [*to Eva*] You notice that he's withdrawn, right?
Eva:	Mm-hm.
Therapist:	. . . and, then what do you do? [*Explores the wife's behaviors in response to the husband's reported withdrawal in attempt to get at the cycle.*]
Eva:	Um, initially in our marriage, I would just keep saying, "Honey," and talk "Na na na. . . ."

Therapist:	[*laughs*]
Eva:	". . . I mean, let's talk about this," and he's always like, "Just leave me alone for a while," and I'm like, "No, let's talk now, now, now."
Therapist:	Yeah, yeah, yeah. So, you really are kind of in the pursuing position. . . .
Eva:	Right.
Therapist:	. . . right, you're really after him, yeah? [*Identifies her position.*]
Eva:	But I think, "Now I'll give him 5 or 10 minutes?" It's still not much, but I'm learning. You know, and then, by, certainly by the end of the night I'm like, "Well," you know, "I'll try to talk to him about it," and sometimes he'll talk if I'm quiet long enough, and sometimes I'll just have to be quiet for quite a long time, for me . . .
Therapist:	Yes.
Eva:	. . . and then he'll talk to me, and we'll maybe reach a middle ground, or we'll just start arguing again if we just can't.
Therapist:	Yeah, so what's happening for you when you're going after him? [*Explores her feeling in that position.*]
Eva:	I'm super frustrated. . . .
Therapist:	Yes?
Eva:	. . . because I think I'm very Type A? You know, I'm ready to talk right now, "Let's address this now." I can't rest. You know, "Let's talk about this now."
Therapist:	Yes, right; so on the one hand, you're very active in trying to get the communication, but it must be uncomfortable to have to hold yourself back, right? . . .
Eva:	Right.
Therapist:	. . . and you've done that some, right? And it has some positive effect if you give enough space. [*Identifies the underlying feeling and highlights how backing off helps.*]
Eva:	If I, right, if I relax, I think so.
Therapist:	But actually, I'm imagining that inside it feels, I mean, I don't know you well yet, but maybe even a little lonely? Or kind of, it's like, "I want the contact, the touching." It's kind of hard for you if a wall goes up, . . .
Eva:	Right.

Therapist:	. . . it's kind of you being closed out? . . .
Eva:	Yep, that's true.
Therapist:	. . . and it's kind of a loneliness inside. [*Reaches in for underlying feeling.*]
Eva:	That's true.
Therapist:	Um, but what he gets is a kind of agitation, right? [*Identifies secondary emotion.*]
Eva:	Uh, yeah. [*Begins to tear.*]
Therapist:	Yeah. But so a tear comes, for you. . . .
Eva:	[*laughs, cries*]
Therapist:	. . . right? because it touches the loneliness. . . .
Eva:	[*crying*] Yep.
Therapist:	. . . mm-hm, so can you say a bit more about that? I mean, it's painful? [*Validates underlying emotion.*]
Eva:	Um, I don't know, just more.
Therapist:	Yeah, it's just sort of like, "I, I need connection, I need you to talk to me, . . .
Eva:	Yeah.
Therapist:	. . . when the wall goes up, it just leaves me, like, so alone. . . ."
Eva::	Right.
Therapist:	. . . yeah. "I just need you to reach out to me so that we can be in contact," right? [*Amplifies underlying feeling.*]
Eva:	Yeah.
Therapist:	Yeah, yeah. [*to Max*] Did you know about your wife's loneliness, in a sense? [*Gets husband's response to wife's expressed emotion.*]
Max:	[*inhales*] Yeah, I can definitely see it, and, and you know it's because . . .
Therapist:	But if I can just, interrupt—[*Blocks his attempt to rationalize.*]
Max:	. . . mm-hm, sure, okay.
Therapist:	What actually happens for you right now inside as she cries? You know, how is it? Do you tense up a little, or . . . ? [*Focuses on current internal response.*]
Max:	A little. I, I know that she deeply cares about me.

Therapist:	Yeah, and about the connection. . . .
Max:	Absolutely.
Therapist:	. . . so what do you feel right now in your body?
Max:	I dunno. I guess sort of sad.

In this example, the client does not initially reveal her sadness, and she may not be fully aware of it in the moment. This is, after all, a first session. When asked how she feels about being shut out by her husband, she responds by saying "super frustrated" and even tries to justify her experience by explaining that she is "Type A." Frustration is, however, an emotion secondary to her sadness. The therapist conjectures that underneath the frustration is loneliness, and Eva confirms it and even sheds a tear. Primary sadness, if expressed in its pure form without blame, can communicate needs for closeness and comfort from the other and potentially draw couples closer together.

In a posttherapy interview, Eva said of this session, "I was honestly enlightened to discover the words to what I was feeling, 'lonely.'" She also said of the whole therapy, which focused initially on the pursue–distance cycle and later on her dominance and his withdrawal, that the therapist

> unlocked closed doors that had been painted shut. Well, we can actually talk now and hear what the other is saying . . . he can cue me and say, for example, "You're rolling your eyes again!" and I smile and try harder to stop because now I know how it makes him feel—undervalued.

The Pressure of Passionate Love

In the following example, Alma, the female member of the couple, who pursues for closeness under the coaching guidance of the therapist, expresses her primary sadness at loss of passionate love in the couple's relationship rather than her more usual criticism of him being incapable of intimacy or emotion. This leads to her partner, Jose, expressing his sense of feeling like a failure, that he is a disappointment to her and his reaction of feeling pressured and tense.

> Alma: The realization that really hit me, that it actually hit when I couldn't ignore this feeling any more, we were sitting there watching a movie, our daughter had gone to bed, it was a very nice, cozy, relaxing evening, I felt very relaxed with him and there was kissing going on in the movie. All of a sudden I realize, he never kisses me, he does kiss hello, he does kiss goodbye, but beside that there is no kissing, not for years. I reached over, I said, "I really miss your kissing. I would really like you to kiss me." And he said, "I'll try not to feel pressure from that." He doesn't have the feeling where you want to kiss somebody. It is just not there [cries].

Therapist:	Yes, I understand it is very hard for you, it makes you feel like you're so unloved. [*turning to Jose*] What is your response when you hear her say this?
Alma:	I don't feel unloved though.
Therapist:	This kind of passionate love.
Alma:	I feel like he is my friend.
Jose:	When I hear this, I immediately feel that I am a disappointment to you, and when I feel that I have disappointed someone, I feel really that I am a failure.
Therapist:	This is the sort of thing that activates in you somehow, like "I am no good." Somehow, left alone, this can get quite escalating. You can get to feel quite unloved, passionately, and you could feel very inadequate. I am really pleased you are able to say this. I don't think you want to make him feel inadequate. [*Validates husband's expression and reframes wife's intention.*]
Alma:	This is not a criticism.
Therapist:	Yes, I understand that he can feel quite criticized. You are saying, "I feel very lonely for the passion." [*to Jose*] Something is happening for you, about not kissing, you are also saying something is missing for you. Let's try to understand it. Are you aware of what is going on for you? This thing about not kissing?
Jose:	I am aware of it, but it is definitely tied in with my state of mind, which I have been starting to see certain patterns. A lot of it has got to do with how Alma is feeling, when I feel that she is not comfortable with how things are, like she is feeling in the last few days, I know that she is feeling a certain way, I will start to get a bit depressed . . . and withdrawn.
Therapist:	So you are pretty sensitive, and if you feel she is unhappy, there is an implicit criticism that "I am not meeting her needs." You tend to tense up and withdraw rather than come out and feel like connecting or kissing, which is the opposite of what she wants, and this leaves her more and more feeling unwanted, undesired. [*Labels his behavior and the cycle.*]
Jose:	It's not that I don't want to be close and kiss, it's more, when I'm tense, I can't.

This excerpt illustrates a mixed affiliation–influence cycle, with the wife experiencing the attachment loss and the husband experiencing a threat to his identity. She feels sad and lonely as her pursuit for closeness fails. He feels shame and inadequacy. It is important for the therapist to validate her sense of sadness while still holding his sense of failure that is evoked by her statement that her needs for closeness are not being met. This allows the couple to begin to hear one another rather than repeat their pattern of criticize and withdraw.

"Anger Means I Feel Unloved"

Primary sadness often drives the pursuer's blaming, critical stance vis-à-vis the partner. Once the pursuer's secondary harder emotions are explored and the therapist has an opportunity to move underneath the blaming, critical anger, for example, the primary sadness will emerge in the form of missing, grief, and loneliness. For example, Holly and Sean came to therapy saying they felt very disengaged from each other and were not sure if they wanted to remain married. Besides the extremely explosive and hostile blow-ups that left both partners feeling very distressed, they described their relationship as a very functional one that involved comanaging the household and taking care of their two kids. They had a boy, 6, and a girl, 9. Sean was an independent filmmaker and artist and Holly was a lawyer. They had been married for 10 years. When they fought, Holly became very critical and hostile toward Sean, claiming he was just an irresponsible, inadequate provider who wanted to sponge off others, much like his good-for-nothing father had. Again, we see a mixed attachment–identity cycle, where she is the hostile and critical pursuer who actually feels abandoned and alone and he withdraws from her rebuke in shame and inadequacy. She also accuses him of being controlling, a "petty tyrant" with their children, saying he is overly hostile and critical with his children and not properly attuned to their needs. Sean called Holly the "sniper," saying that her anger could suddenly explode and grow out of control. Once she was in that state, she became "crazy," he claimed, saying contemptuous, mean, and hurtful things. At that point, he felt, he could only run for cover.

As the therapy progressed, Holly revealed that behind her resentment, criticisms, and complaints about Sean being a poor provider was a distinct sense of feeling sad, alone, neglected, and unloved. If he loved her, he would provide for her. In the third session, she talked about how alone and abandoned she felt just after their oldest daughter was born. All she wanted at that point was to be with her baby. She had trouble nursing her baby and felt that she really needed Sean's support and love at the time. Instead, Sean was out "exploring" his next film and even had to travel to do so. This film had never been produced, Holly claimed, and she had simply been left "high and dry. Deserted." When the baby was only 4 weeks old, she had to go out and work to support her family. This was, she felt, a great loss. Holly cried deep, heartfelt sobs as she relayed this story, talking about how alone and abandoned she felt, and what a loss she felt to have not been able to spend this time with her daughter.

Sean primarily experienced her angry wrath, was actually afraid of Holly, and felt he was doing the best he could. For Holly, this was an attachment injury. Sean, who experienced Holly as only competent, able, and fiercely independent, was actually surprised to hear Holly's vulnerable feelings and what she really needed, and he expressed regret at not having been more emotionally available to her. Holly seemed relieved to hear he cared and was more able to get in touch with her emotional needs. Once the time period of their daughter's birth had been revisited and the various underlying primary emotions revealed and responded to, the couple began to reconstruct what happened, voice to each other their underlying needs, and heal from the events.

Maladaptive Sadness and Unresolved Past Loss

Primary sadness may also be evoked in relation to loss in earlier relationships, such as loss of a primary caregiver or a prior divorce. In this case, sadness is potentially unresolved and maladaptive. It represents unresolved past loss that colors present interactions. Maladaptive sadness in the context of couples struggles related to attachment needs is usually more common on the part of the pursuer. In the case of Holly and Sean, the sadness she felt over not being able to spend time with her baby daughter after her birth was in fact adaptive and a response to a current loss. However, sadness episodes such as these may trigger earlier experiences of abandonment and be maladaptive in that their source is not in the current relationship. For example, Melissa, a mother in a similar position to Holly, felt lonely after the birth of her first child while her husband worked. She started to feel depressed remembering how abandoned she had felt by a depressed mother who had been unable to be responsive to her needs. It is helpful to both partners in these cases to identify the source of the sadness, to help individuals identify the historically related maladaptive components of the emotions, and to access more adaptive emotions. Melissa recounted how it was the silence in the house that she could remember—just an empty, lonely silence—and this is what she began to feel when her husband had gone away and she was left alone in the house and the baby was sleeping. She needed to know they were not alone, that her husband cared about them and would be there if she needed them. The therapist helped facilitate Melissa's husband to soothe and reassure her in the session and encouraged her to ask for it and him to provide it when she needed it. Once such work of contacting the emotion schematic memories of past abandonment and feelings of loneliness and sadness are evoked and shared, the partner can be brought in to help soothe the other and provide more corrective emotional experiences. The maladaptive sad responses of feeling abandoned can be identified as an ongoing source of sensitivity for the one partner, and the therapy can focus on strategies for the couple to work with this sadness when it emerges.

In Holly's case, a few sessions later, she also got in touch with sadness over the loss of her father's presence in her life once she hit puberty. After having a very close relationship with her father from an early age that she described as an almost romantic, affectionate relationship in which she felt she was the "apple of his eye," she then felt rejected and alone when she hit puberty. It was at this time that he seemed no longer interested in spending time with her. She felt awkward and alone and longed for his acceptance. When she began to talk about this, she cried uncontrollably, gasping for air, and began to feel like she was fragmenting. She began to describe feeling like she was floating and said she did not know why she was crying so intensely. This is an example of maladaptive sadness, elicited in the couples relationship, that belonged to an attachment injury from the past. It also illustrates a problem with affect regulation that needs to be dealt with as well. The therapist remained focused on and empathically attuned to Holly. Even though Holly was having difficulty symbolizing what she was feeling, the therapist provided empathic affirmations and reflections that helped capture her experience. The therapist also encouraged Holly to breathe and focus on the therapist and her partner, Sean. The therapist then turned to Sean and asked him what was happening inside for him as Holly went through this. Sean replied that he was feeling sad, and with help from the therapist saying, "So, you feel sad and concerned," he expressed compassion. The therapist then encouraged Sean to express his caring and concern directly to Holly.

Distancer's Sadness

Primary sadness is not often at the core of the distancer's position. However, an exception to this is when distancers react to an attachment injury earlier in the relationship, which is only unearthed when the therapist helps this partner explore the source of his or her withdrawal. Then it is discovered that the distancer reacted to the attachment injury by emotionally resigning or "giving up" while still physically remaining in the marriage. More often, the primary emotions of the distancer in the affiliation cycle are shame of inadequacy and/or unexpressed resentment. Thus, where one partner may have started off as a pursuer in the negative interactional cycle, he or she could shift, partially as a protective device or out of secondary anger, in response to an attachment injury and become the distancer. Furthermore, distancers can unwittingly create attachment injuries in their partners when their reaction to current feelings of abandonment is amplified by earlier attachment injuries in their own lives.

For example, by the time Parker and Lili entered couples therapy, they had been married 25 years and were stuck in a withdraw–withdraw cycle. However, this had not originally been the case. In the beginning of the relationship, Lili pursued for emotional closeness and Parker had a tendency to withdraw. When their first child was born, Lili felt unsupported and emotionally abandoned by Parker and suffered an attachment injury. Instead of pursuing, as in the past, she responded by withdrawing. Parker, however, had pulled away from Lili at that point because of an attachment injury of his own. He felt Lili had shifted her affection from him to the child, which stirred up significant abandonment experience from his childhood. Feelings of depressive sadness from the past caused him to feel unloved in the present, and he further withdrew from the relationship. In response to this and to her own injury, Lili resolved not to rely on Parker for closeness so that she would not be so disappointed again. She focused on motherhood and on pursuing her career instead. Thus, both partners were reacting to attachment injuries by pulling away from one another, and the withdraw–withdraw cycle became entrenched.

Over the years, the couple grew increasingly more distant from each other, reshuffling their efforts toward raising their children and pursuing their respective careers. They came to therapy after their children had left home, reporting strong disaffection and disenchantment. Parker had initially communicated to the therapist on the telephone that Lili had requested therapy for many years, and he had refused. He was now initiating therapy because he said that if they continued the way they were, he feared they would not stay together. They had not been sexually intimate in over 5 years, and the topic of divorce had been raised.

In therapy, Parker described Lili as cold, withdrawn, and unavailable. Lili described Parker in fairly derisive and critical terms, saying Parker was disengaged, somewhat antisocial, unsupportive of her, and generally not very competent. Parker did not protest Lili's characterization of him. He also disclosed that he had struggled with depression at different points in his life. He tended to have a slow, almost plodding style of talking and answering questions. It would take him a long time to answer questions, and when encouraged to reflect on his emotions, he would take a few minutes to try to get a sense of what he felt and then say that he just did not know or sometimes that he felt sad and hopeless. Although it was difficult for the couple to generate many current examples of conflict, Lili did identify that her withdrawn, busy stance vis-à-vis the relationship had not always been present. In fact, she was able to identify that her resentment toward Parker had roots in their earlier marriage, after their first child was born. Lili described tearfully her sense of stress, being overwhelmed, and abandonment. She said this time was a turning point for her, when she came to know she could not rely on Parker.

In the following interaction, Parker is describing a recent event in which he had wanted more attentiveness from Lili and found her unavailable.

> *Parker:* Well, as I was telling you, I am quite involved in this running club, and this past weekend was the half marathon. I have spent quite a bit of time training for it, and Lili of course knows that.

> *Therapist:* So you were there to cheer him on then, Lili?

> *Lili:* No, I had some work to finish up this weekend, so I ended up going up to the cottage for peace and quiet to do that.

Parker: Right, that's just the thing. So I came home on Sunday night, you know, pretty spent but proud of myself, and I find this note: "Lasagne in the freezer. Reheat if you like."

Therapist: So somehow I guess you were pretty disappointed then, it sounds like, Parker.

Parker: Well, no, maybe, I guess [*sighs*]. I am just used to it. Lili doesn't really care about what I do. I mean, she is busy. I just went to bed.

Therapist: Well, it sounds a little bit like you know how to protect yourself and take care of yourself, but it also sounds like there is some sadness there. Like, "I don't dare want this 'cause I have kind of given up on getting it, but it sure would be nice if Lili would celebrate my achievements just a little with me." [*Focuses on underlying feeling.*]

Parker: Well, yeah, I mean, I lived by myself for 5 years [*referring to an earlier time in their marriage where he had an appointment at a university in a town 4 hours away and would live there by himself during the week*].

Lili: [*snorting*] Yeah, sure. Parker's idea of taking care of himself is reheating frozen dinners. When he lived in [town] I had to cook for him all the time—either go there or send it with him. I don't even know that he owned a frying pan.

Parker: [*looking down, defiant and angry*] That's not true. You like to exaggerate.

Therapist: But somehow for you, Parker, it was kind of disheartening when Lili was not there. I mean, I don't know, maybe you would have liked her to be there when you ran the marathon, at the finish line cheering you on. And when you came home and you were expecting her to be there, you were disappointed. You did want to share your experience with her. [*Refocuses on his softer feelings of disappointment and his need.*]

Parker: Well, yes, I would like that. But we live very separate lives, you know. Lili does her thing, and I don't even expect that she is going to be there, and God forbid I should ask her to come to something I do [*resentfully*].

Lili: Well, yes, that is true. It is just the way it is. It's been this way for years. And Parker does not come to my events—he has never even seen the laboratory where I work. I know this is a sore spot for him, though, that I don't play the role of the doctor's wife. I wonder sometimes whether it is payback for that.

Therapist: So, this is how the two of you end up, very distant and kind of disengaged from each other. But somehow my sense is that

Parker, you would like more closeness, more intimacy. [*Identifies the problem and need for closeness.*]

Parker: Yes [*voice trailing off*].

Lili: But like I have told you, I don't even know if I believe him, and I certainly don't know where he gets off in wanting that [*face changing to anger and hurt, mixed*]. I mean, when Kyle was born, he wasn't even there at all. I mean, this guy just checked out.

Parker: [*Looks blankly at Lili as if frozen.*]

Therapist: So that was a really hard time for you, huh, Lili? [*Focuses on underlying feeling.*]

Lili: [*beginning to cry; covering her face for 15 seconds*] I was so alone. I didn't know what to do. Kyle just needed so much from me and Parker was no help at all. He just kind of checked out. I felt so alone, so unsupported.

Therapist: Lili, can you turn to Parker and tell him what you missed, what you needed? [*Promotes enactment of primary sadness and longing.*]

Lili: I really needed your help, your support.

Therapist: What happens when you hear this Parker?

When Lili began to cry, Parker simply looked bewildered and tightened up, saying he did not know what Lili was talking about. In this couple, Parker's hopeless, depressed, and withdrawn stance that prevented him from responding obscured his much deeper primary sadness. In such cases, it is useful to both identify the block and acknowledge the feelings it evokes in the partner. In this case, the therapist turned to Lili and said,

> I know it is difficult that he can't respond right now with the caring you need, but we now have to understand his block. If he could respond, you two wouldn't have this problem, so although it is painful, this is an opportunity to work on this impasse.

The therapist then turned to Parker and focused on his block to responsiveness by essentially labeling it as coming from some wound (a maladaptive emotional response). The therapist said, "What happens as she expresses her sadness? Something blocks you from responding. What happens? What comes up in you? What makes it difficult?" The focus became one of exploring his block. It was only later in therapy that Parker was able to describe how sad and alone he had felt when their first child was born. He had withdrawn because he felt rejected. He had felt abandoned by Lili as he felt her affections had been dispersed and he no longer felt important to her. Identifying this attachment injury helped him identify and explain an even more basic attachment injury from his childhood. It is interesting that this acknowledgment of his past injury and its current influence came only after a number of individual sessions in which Parker had worked through grief from his childhood. He had spent his young childhood in a country involved in political turmoil and strife. His parents had been forced to leave the country when Parker was 7 years old and he had been unsure of his fate at this point. He had been bounced around to different relatives. He experienced the situation as traumatic. He had only been reunited with his parents 3 years later. The therapist suggested taking some extra individual sessions to work with Parker's depression.

On a final note, Lili and Parker initially were quite disengaged, and Lili's not attending Parker's marathon could be conceptualized as an identity injury for Parker. Parker and Lili had both suffered a number of attachment and identity injuries by each other that they were not aware of. Career identities were important to both of them, and they were both fairly ambitious, driven, and accomplished. Yet, the relationship was structured such that neither recognized this as important, and they were both somewhat inured to hurt caused by the other. As therapy progressed, however, they both came to acknowledge needs for closeness, security, recognition, and validation from each other. As well as coming closer, they realized that recognition, support, and validation of achievements from each other mattered just as much as it did from the outside world.

INFLUENCE CYCLES

Sadness is not that central in influence cycles, although it can underlie dominance positions. Some examples are discussed in the sections that follow.

Dominant's Sadness

Primary sadness may be at the core of the dominant person's hostile pursuit of the other. Here, the dominant person is lonely but rather than criticize or blame, he or she tries to control the partner overtly with such phrases as "You should do this" or "This is what is right, you are wrong" or covertly by organizing things to get his or her way by controlling time and activities. Dominant partners become overtly demanding when they feel saddest, to regulate their sadness. Often, the dominance that results from unacknowledged sadness involves a demand for closeness and thus is related to pursuit for closeness in the attachment cycle. As we have said, however, this cycle is characterized by control, rather than by blame and criticism.

Being Powerfully Weak

In the following example, the therapist is encouraging a woman, Kaya, who is typically both dominant and blaming in the pursuit of closeness, to express her underlying sad loneliness to her partner, Omar. This occurs in the 12th session, and only after work has been done to increase awareness of the cycle and each partner's role in it. The partners are aware of their pursue–distance cycle and can identify and talk openly about it, but dominance issues have not yet been understood. Notice how, in the segment that follows, the therapist subtly communicates to the woman that she is powerful in her expressions of sadness and need. She is painfully aware of her own needy sense of deprivation but not aware of how controlling and demanding she can be and how this pushes her partner away. In the following example, the therapist brings this to her attention, mollifies and validates her feelings and needs, and teaches her how to communicate in a manner that will draw her partner closer rather than push him away.

> *Therapist:* So, when you were actually weepy and you just said, "I need . . . ," he was much more able to come close to you, when you can be vulnerable and ask without a demand or a criticism. See, often when you are vulnerable in your strength, you know, I sense in you, you are very powerfully weak, you end up telling him what he should be doing, and it pushes him away. . . .
>
> *Kaya:* Yeah.
>
> *Therapist:* . . . but when you are actually just weak and needy and can just speak from there, he seems to come through for you.
>
> *Kaya:* Yeah, I am aware of that. I have been . . . all of the sudden of the difference between being powerfully weak and weak. Because you know, he's always said "I'm intimidated" because he's intimated because I'm so strong. But I'm not strong, I'm vulnerable, but . . .
>
> *Omar:* You come across so powerfully . . .
>
> *Therapist:* You often say what you want him to do, but you focus on him rather than just saying, you know, "I really feel sad, I really feel . . ." there's always that hand that he feels [*referring to her hand, which often goes out in a controlling manner*]. I mean, it's very complex. So there's the history and the hurt is built up. But somehow when you just laid in bed and said, "I need a hug" or "I feel . . ."
>
> *Kaya:* I felt alone, I told him, "I feel really lonely."
>
> *Therapist:* Yeah, okay, so now, what happened when she just said that? She didn't tell you what to do. Or do you get your back up? You don't bristle or pull away . . .
>
> *Omar:* No, because of the way she is saying it. It's not a command or anything. There's no real expectation to it, it's done very softly and . . .

Therapist: . . . and you [to Kaya] are really just speaking about how you feel, and then he is much more able to respond to that. Now this is difficult, right, for both of you? Also, you understand sometimes that even when she's commanding, she's actually hurting. How do you not be so reactive [to Omar]? . . .

Omar: Right.

Therapist: . . . but also, how are you [to Kaya] going to speak from the hurt, not from the demand? [Labels the softer underlying feeling of the dominant and encourages perception of it by submitter.]

Kaya: It's hard for me to speak from the hurt, cause that's . . .

Therapist: . . . the most vulnerable place to be?

It is also possible for expression of sadness and weakness on the part of the dominant person, about matters unrelated to the couple's interaction, to create a softening in his or her partner. For example, Wilma and Enrique's cycle was one in which he was very rational and told Wilma what to do all the time. Wilma tended to feel humiliated and angry and simply withdraw in response to Enrique's criticism. Enrique was often angry with Wilma, as he felt she did not support his point of view or make him a priority. In fact, she would often make her daughters' (from a previous marriage) point of view a priority over him. Wilma had suffered a great deal of abuse and neglect in her family of origin and had difficulty expressing needs. She often felt invalidated by Enrique. Enrique had been married once before, years prior, and when they fought he tended to worry that Wilma was simply unhappy and not capable of happiness like his previous wife. At one point in therapy, he went through a great deal of difficulty because both of his parents were ailing and could potentially die at any time, and he had just lost a good friend. He cried as he recounted all of this in one session. His tears drew Wilma closer to him. The couple stated that even though they had a great deal of conflict, they were closer in times of crisis because it was at those times that Wilma was very supportive and soothing to Enrique. His tears made her feel closer to him as she was able to witness his vulnerability. This provided an opening to discuss the sadness and fear of loss that lay beneath his controlling behavior.

A Sad Little Boy

Maladaptive sadness can also underlie dominant pursuit of the other. Jim and Nancy come to therapy saying they did not know whether they could stay together but they wanted to see whether it was possible. Jim was 36 and Nancy was 28. They had been married 9 years. Jim felt that Nancy no longer loved him, and she said she was unsure whether she did but she did know she felt trapped. Jim worked for himself at home as part of a family business with his father and elder brother who lived in a city far away. He was carefully articulate in describing how Nancy seemed to have lost her affection for him. He said he was not sure she was ever happy being married and that probably she found marriage too constraining at the beginning and that it was a shock for her to move away from her home. He also talked about how she had been raped shortly before he met her and how the court case in which she testified during their early years probably stressed her and affected their marriage. Nancy said that Jim constantly wanted sex and was always "bothering her for it," even when they are fighting. In the seventh session, Nancy tells the story of how they were at a party recently, and she had not supported him in a discussion with his friends. He had expressed anger at her in front of his friends for contradicting him. Even though she had felt ashamed, humiliated, and withdrawn, he had suggested they have sex that evening after the party. When the therapist began to talk to Jim about this incident, Jim was able to acknowledge that at times he could be "condescending" and also "relentlessly pursuing" and that even though he wanted closeness, he in fact pushed his partner in the other direction by becoming like a school principal and requiring compliance. Underneath his critical, dominant anger was revealed a sad and needy little boy.

Nancy described how she felt controlled by Jim's neediness. She felt it difficult to spend time by herself, and Jim was often making her feel bad when she wanted to spend time alone with family or friends. With the therapist's prompting, Jim began to remember being a sad little boy whose mother had died when he was 9 years old. He recalled how after his older sisters and brothers left home, he had spent much time alone by himself, staring out the window and feeling an eerie sense of aloneness. He remembered dreading these moments alone and craving companionship. He began to sob and grieve for himself and his loss. The therapist helped him to work through his sadness and grief. Only after he had fully expressed the primary sadness and Nancy had responded to it empathically and compassionately did the therapist discuss with the couple how to help him self-soothe in moments of sadness, rather than control. He discussed with the therapist how Nancy could help reassure him that when she went out by herself or went away, she was not abandoning him in a permanent way and would return. Initially, Jim was not open to the idea of self-soothing, saying that Nancy's soothing was something he was entitled to in his relationship, or why have a relationship at all? With the help of the therapist, Nancy validated Jim's needs, but more significantly, asserted that her needs were important as well. Slowly, Jim began to open to the idea that sometimes it was acceptable and possible to soothe himself. He began to talk to the therapist about how he might take care of himself at times when Nancy disagreed or asserted a difference.

Submitter's Sadness

Primary sadness is not that prevalent in submitters and is not a central aspect of their submissiveness. Submitters who are generally dependent may feel secondary sadness about their lack of competence and feel helpless and sad when they do not have someone to guide them. Submission in a relationship is based more on fear and shame, and so sadness does not play a major role. Secondary sadness, however, often is expressed by the distancing partner in the context of identity struggles. For example, in the case of Jim and Nancy, when the therapist would explore with Nancy what she felt when Jim got upset with her for spending time alone, or with friends and family, Nancy would simply throw her hands up in the air and begin to cry. She said she simply felt despondent and hopeless and that she was going to have to leave the relationship. Crying in this case was not deep sobbing. She produced few tears and tended to talk in a high-pitched voice when she was crying. Her vocal quality was somewhat limited. Her crying usually petered out at these points. This is indicative of secondary or instrumental sadness. She was quite angry with Jim and had a great deal of difficulty expressing it. In this case, anger was her more primary emotion. Depression, hopelessness, and sadness in the withdrawn partner are a secondary symptomatic response to either underlying unresolved primary sadness or anger.

CONCLUSION

Sadness is one of the most important emotions to access in couples. This emotion is often an indicator of what is missing in a relationship and what type of injuries it has. It is important to distinguish between primary adaptive sadness and maladaptive sadness (left over from previous relationships) or instrumental sadness. Primary sadness should be expressed, and the therapist needs to support the partner feeling sad and encourage the other partner to be supportive. Sadness predominantly will be found underneath a blamer's criticism and misguided efforts at getting closeness. Expressions of sadness can bring the couple together in a caring and empathic way. If a partner becomes overwhelmed by feelings of sadness, the therapist helps him or her to self-soothe. However, if sadness is actually a cry of distress that is associated with other emotions, encouraging its expression is counterproductive and the therapist needs to validate the client's experience but focus on the primary emotion and associated needs.

12

FEAR IN COUPLES THERAPY

The only thing we have to fear is fear itself.

—Franklin D. Roosevelt

Fear is an attachment emotion that binds people to others in a way that no other emotion does. In that sense, it is double-edged. It motivates people to seek closeness and connection, but it can prevent them from choosing healthy separation or seeking shelter when they need it. Trauma, an extreme fear reaction, and other negative learning experiences stemming from past relationships can lead to overgeneralized or misattributed fear that prevents people from proactively meeting their needs or protecting themselves when necessary.

People seek to be close to others in part because it makes them feel calm and secure, and fear motivates them to seek this connection. When bonds are ruptured, people feel bad, and their fear of aloneness motivates them to repair damaged bonds or seek new ones. All adults, when bonded, feel some anxiety on separating or breaking a bond. Thus, in relationships, fear and anxiety related to separation protect individuals from danger. This is healthy fear that was originally associated with survival. Fear, however, is also at the center of attachment disorders. Separation anxiety, which is for the most part a healthy human experience, can become a key source of conflict as partners in relationships struggle to have their needs for security met. If there have been abandonments or traumas in the past, either in the person's childhood or in previous relationships, this anxiety can be maladaptive and the struggle for security can be destructive. It also is important to acknowledge individual differences in anxiety and tolerance of separation. Depending on both genetic and environmental factors, partners will differ in their degree of anxiety and need for connection. What triggers their anxiety is probably learned, but the intensity of their response and ability to soothe also are somewhat genetically influenced. Certain learning histories, characterized by loss, neglect, unpredictability, and problematic interpersonal control, however, can produce many interpersonal anxieties that influence how partners bond. Regardless of genetic predisposition or learning history, though, the intensity of anxiety felt at separation is mitigated by the degree of security partners feel in the context of the couples relationship. That is, within relationships, individuals may feel more or less secure, depending on how much comfort and reassurance is provided for in their primary relationship. This, in turn, will be partially a function of their partner's needs for closeness or ability to tolerate it or provide reassurance and soothing.

In this chapter, we discuss adaptive and maladaptive fear in the context of the affiliative and influence dimensions of relationships. We discuss how fear of intimacy, fear of abandonment, and past trauma in relationships cause major problems in creating and sustaining healthy connection. Case examples illustrate how to work with fear in therapy and provide solutions for how to shift maladaptive fear in the process of creating healthy connections.

ATTACHMENT ANXIETY

Bowlby (1973) said that when a person is confident that a loved one will be there when needed, "a person will be much less prone to either intense or chronic fear than will an individual who has no such confidence" (p. 406). Although angry protest, depression, or anxious hypervigilance are often displayed more outwardly, primary fear is the core driving emotion behind a partner's perceived threat of loss, rejection, or abandonment by their partner. Attachment responses to separation or loss seem to be organized along two dimensions: anxiety and avoidance (Bartholomew & Horowitz, 1991; Fraley & Waller, 1998). A primary anxious self-organization can be indicated by either an anxious or an avoidant attachment pattern. In both cases, the sense of self has developed from an aversive attachment history and at the core is a vulnerable self-organization.

Early experiences of emotionally unavailable, inconsistent, or nonempathically attuned caretakers; noncontingent or incompetent holding; prolonged separation; or traumatic abandonment can be precursors for insecure attachment experiences and self-organizations later in adulthood. It is important to note that although we see the early work on attachment behavior as very important in helping to identify the factors and conditions that contribute to insecure attachment and difficulty in relationships, we have not observed characteristic styles of attachment in adults that persist across all relationships and always determine the way people respond in intimate relationships. As we have said, people are dynamic, self-organizing systems, and their reactions depend more on their current state of fear and avoidance than on enduring structures. A dynamic-systems view of functioning allows for the possibility of change in brief therapy far more than a trait view of personality, such as attachment styles. Thus we do not see one partner's position in the pursue–distance cycle as necessarily related to a specific attachment style that defines his or her basic character. We have observed that people use more than one strategy, even in the same relationship, and that different people and situations will bring out different attachment behaviors.

We do recognize, however, that people adopt anxious styles of handling attachment conflicts in relationships and that they may be driven by anxious and/or weak or avoidant organizations of self in relationship. The more traumatic or damaging the developmental history, the more rigid is this organization. The person who organizes in an anxious and/or weak manner is fearful of separation and adopts more dependent, clingy behavior to try to avoid dreaded separations. The person who organizes avoidantly gives up seeking attachment and turns to self-sufficiency. Self-sufficiency, however, often is accompanied by feeling alienated and somewhat depressed when alone. When organized avoidantly, a person typically has a limited ability to explore or differentiate internal experience.

FEAR OF INTIMACY IN RELATIONSHIPS

Core states of fear-based vulnerability are often at the center of couples conflicts. People are fundamentally relational, need others, are afraid of aloneness and abandonment, and at times find it difficult to survive on their own. Given the vulnerability of needing others and the pain associated with past and possible future disappointment, people often organize to avoid facing these feelings and needs. Closeness also can leave them feeling out of control. This state of, and fear of, dependence on others complicates intimate relationships. They move into a self-protective stance that is driven by a fear of intimacy. If they dare open up themselves in current intimate relationships and become aware of needs, fears of getting hurt, disappointed, and belittled may reemerge and they will close off again. It becomes increasingly more difficult for them to open up again. In a sense, they become intimacy phobic. Hopelessness often accompanies this avoidance because as people get stuck in avoidant patterns, they cannot imagine ever facing such difficult fears and they are less able to get their needs met. Ultimately, fear in relationships is fear of either rejection, annihilation, or abandonment. This last fear is biologically built into infants to protect them from dangerous separations, and adults still carry the same programming. Fear of rejection and abandonment can cause people to put their needs aside for fear of upsetting or pushing away the other. This often produces resentment, however, and can create conflict in the couple. Alternatively, some people will organize to avoid intimacy because of the ultimate fear of dependence. Avoidance of intimacy by one partner can be frustrating for a more intimacy-seeking partner who craves, and eventually demands, the closeness required to sustain a healthy bond. The need to know the other is as powerful as the need to be known if engagement in the relationship is to occur (Fosha, 2001; Surrey, 1991). Fear of intimacy therefore can make for distant partners and conflictual couples.

Assessment and recognition of the fear of getting close in therapy is helped by knowledge of the person's attachment history, combined with in-session indicators of uncertainty, timidity, hypersensitivity, hypervigilance, detachment from partner, and extreme self-consciousness. Markers associated with a fear-based self-organization occur most vividly in therapy when clients show fear of exposing aspects of self to their partner. They are guarded or cautious about self-disclosure to their partner and to the therapist. They generally do not enjoy being the focus of attention.

FEAR OF INTIMACY IN WOMEN AND MEN

Intimacy-related fear may express itself differently in different genders. Although it is impossible to generalize about what is at the source of fears of intimacy for all people and it is best to understand this fear on a case-by-case basis, fear of intimacy may in fact work somewhat differently in men and women. On the basis of earlier experiences and social learning, people bring to relationships certain assumptions and beliefs about the same and the opposite gender. Fear-based negative voices influence many people's view of the opposite gender. In fact, men and women may be able to identify specific statements they learned from their parents, culture, and experience (Firestone & Catlett, 2002). For example women may have internalized voices that say, "You can't trust men; they don't have feelings; they are too dominant; you have to build a man's ego," and at the same time voices that say, "If you don't have one, you are a failure." Often running through men's heads are voices that say, "Women are too emotional, too demanding, too controlling," and at the same time voices that say, "If you don't make your woman happy, you are a failure." In same-sex couples, partners may also hold these internalized generalized voices about their same-sex partner. All of this creates great conflict in people wanting but fearing intimacy. Closeness can occur only when people overcome their fear and change the beliefs that appear to protect them but in effect prevent them from achieving intimacy.

In terms of their source, fears of intimacy and connection may arise from chronic disconnections among family members in the form of such things as secrecy in the family that involves the denial of an unacceptable reality; the inaccessibility of parents so that children do not have the opportunity to learn about or know them; and "parentification" of children, which occurs when children are placed prematurely in responsible, adult roles for which they are not ready and are not reciprocated (J. B. Miller & Stiver, 1997).

A major source of fear of connection for both women and men comes from parents' inaccessibility. When parents are too preoccupied or depleted to be responsive and are unable to share their own experiences, children will feel cut off from their own emotions and other family members. This can lead to children feeling helpless in terms of figuring out how to have an impact on parents and feeling connected with them. This is often seen in families with a depressed or alcoholic parent for whom inconsistency is the norm. If a child cannot rely on a parent being consistent and genuine, it can be terrifying to risk expression of true feelings. In adult relationships, people may fear self-disclosure, believing that partners might be disconnected and not acknowledge it. As adults, people then fear that their partners might be unresponsive as well.

Men's fears of intimacy are often connected to wounds sustained in relation to early paternal and maternal loss. Much has been said about the ill effects of absent or rejecting fathers (Bly, 1990; Dutton, 1995; Silverstein & Roshbaum, 1994; Snarey, 1993). The typical American father spends on average only 11 minutes a day with his children (Real, 1997). This seems to create an undeniable wound, such that a male child feels abandoned, and perhaps more important, a chasm with respect to his identity develops and he does not know how to conduct himself and feels lost, without sentinels to guide him. Without a clear sense of identity, it becomes difficult for men to know what they need and want. This creates ambivalence and trouble sustaining closeness. At times, he may need to assert identity at the expense of intimacy to ensure he is right, that he indeed exists. At times, he may need to assert his masculinity and be very sensitive to perceived threats to it.

Another important source of loss for men may indeed be what has been termed the "mother wound" (Betcher & Pollack, 1993; Real, 1997; Silverstein & Roshbaum, 1994), which can also contribute to fears about intimacy. In addition to the effects of the stereotypical mother who will not let go, there is the wound of the mother who, under social and cultural pressure, lets go too early. This is the mother who inhibits nurturing her boy before she feels ready to do so or senses this is what he needs for fear of "softening" him. This often occurs under overt or covert threats from fathers or men.

There are few good models in our culture of young men developing dependent closeness into adulthood to anyone, male or female. Maturity and connection are set up as choices to exclude one another. The instruction to turn away from the mother is not simply singular to that relationship itself but to intimacy in general. The diminished attachment to mother is a disavowal of all emotionally rich parts of the self. According to Real (1997), men's disavowal of emotion falls into two spheres, rejection of expressivity and rejection of vulnerability. Both are connected with intimacy. Boys and men are discouraged even from talking in an animated way, let alone expressing vulnerabilities and fears. The relationship between emotional numbing, or alexithymia, and depression has been well documented, and a case can be made for the relationship between alexithymia and addictive disorders (Khantzian, Halliday, & McAuliffe, 1990), which is a male disorder of choice.

TRAUMA IN RELATIONSHIPS

Past trauma that prevents intimacy in relationships may stem from childhood or prior relationships but may also come from injuries in the adult relationships (Johnson, 2002). Drawing on Herman (1992), Johnson (2002) defined *traumatic experiences* as violations of human connection that make closeness with others feel dangerous. In addition, trauma may be of two types: trauma from violation or trauma from neglect. Trauma as a result of physical or sexual boundary violation can be seen as active trauma, whereas trauma due to emotional neglect can be thought of as passive trauma (Real, 1997). Here, *emotional neglect* is defined as the absence of nurturance and failure to meet responsibilities normally expected of a caregiver or partner and is experienced as absence of connection. Both of these may create problems in relationships later on in different ways. However, these two types of traumatic reactions will express themselves somewhat differently in the couples context. Therapists should be prepared to recognize differences and work differentially with them in couples therapy.

Passive Trauma in Adult Relationships

The loss of a primary attachment figure in childhood can create passive trauma related to deprivation, loss, rejection, and abandonment (Johnson, 2002; Johnson & Whiffen, 2003). This may severely affect the capacity for intimacy in an adult relationship. The traumatic effects of losing a primary attachment figure early in life are well-documented (Bowlby, 1980). There is strong evidence that inadequate mourning early in life can lead to persistent pathological problems in relationships in adulthood. The trauma may manifest in the form of anger, sadness, or a general reticence and difficulty trusting partners. When this emerges in couples therapy, it is necessary to frame the partner's difficulty trusting as an understandable response to present circumstances but also as at least a partial response to past experiences.

Two other forms of passive trauma that may interfere with a current relationship are (a) when one member has a trauma from a past relationship such as, for example, having gone through a difficult divorce and carries fear from the previous relationship into the current one, or (b) when one member has had an emotional injury or betrayal in the current relationship, such as because of a partner's affair. We find it accurate to define these experiences with couples as *passive traumas* and clients often feel it helpful to have the word *trauma* to characterize their experience. These experiences represent injuries that consume one person's attention and prevent intimate relating from occurring with the present partner. Until the injury is addressed, the current relationship is in many ways stuck. Work must include revisiting the original source of the trauma and reprocessing it emotionally.

In working with couples in which one member has experienced an emotional injury in a previous intimate relationship of an attachment nature, such as a divorce or some form of rejection or abandonment, the therapist must be aware that that person may indeed be shell-shocked and find it difficult to trust again (Johnson, 2002). It can be helpful to reframe the anxious, shell-shocked partner's fear to the current partner as in part a response to a past trauma and not solely a response to the current partner. This will help the current partner to feel less blamed and more able to assist the traumatized partner heal from the previous relationship. It may also be helpful for the therapist to help the injured partner distinguish between the past partner and the current partner and to understand that his or her reluctance to trust may be related to the past injury. This fear needs to be validated as very real and understandable given the person's past experience but nevertheless a response influenced more by the past than by the current experience. It may be necessary for the injured partner to do some individual work to help resolve past injuries that did not originate in the current relationship.

In couples in which one member emotionally injured the other, such as by having an affair, the injured party often experiences symptoms that mimic those of posttraumatic stress disorder (Glass, 2003; Johnson, 2002; Pittman, 1989) immediately after the affair and for some time to come. The betrayal has long-lasting effects that make recovery challenging and difficult. Common symptoms include obsessive thoughts, flashbacks or intrusive thoughts, numbness and detachment, hyperarousal, and hypervigilance. Obsessive thoughts about what happened will only dissipate when shattered assumptions about the relationship are addressed and an alternative narrative has been constructed about the affair.

There are stages associated with repair after traumatic attachment ruptures such as an affair. Deeper emotional repair work may not be possible until some time after the affair has occurred. In working with couples in which one member has emotionally injured a partner in the relationship and the injury was more than 2 years prior, Malcolm, Warwar, and Greenberg (2005) found that it was very important for the injured partner to identify the idiosyncratic impact of the injury so that the unique meaning of the injury is addressed. In addition, this partner's need for a protective wall needed to be validated. Both partner and therapist needed to respect the others' need for a protective wall, and the therapist needed to help the injured person to give voice to the unvoiced wall and raise awareness of it and its protective function. The injured partners also needed to see themselves as having a real choice to let go, forgive, or withhold forgiveness. The injurer had to accept the partner's right to choose and had to refrain from setting the expectation that the injured person must trust, let go, or forgive. The therapist could help the betrayer to ask for, but not demand, forgiveness. It also appears, from a preliminary task analysis, that it was the expression of shame and/or empathic distress by the injurer that led to forgiveness by the partner. Finally, to resolve the injury, partners needed to take responsibility for their own part in the injury. The injured person then needed to express specifics of what was needed to trust again, and the partner needed to receive these requests without blame. An example of this is given in the next section.

Fear of Trusting Again After an Affair

Jules and Monica came to therapy 3 years after Jules had an affair. They stated clearly that they wanted to stay together but had doubts about whether they could recover and move past the trauma of Jules's affair. In the following excerpt from Session 7 of couples therapy, the therapist and Monica discuss the possibility of her trusting Jules again and her very legitimate fears of doing so. The therapist validates her need to protect herself against further harm. The therapist also conducts a very authentic and direct dialogue with Monica about what it means to trust again and what form that might take. The therapist encourages Monica to be honest and hold out for what she needs to trust again.

Monica:	I mean, I, I believe that he, he means every word that he says. I believe that he, you [*turning to Jules*], in the place that he's at right now, he really wants this to work and that he loves me, and I believe all of it . . .
Therapist:	Right, right.
Monica:	. . . but I don't know if that's enough for him, right, like I just, I just don't know that . . .
Therapist:	I don't know if what's enough for him?
Monica:	Well, even though he loves me and he wants all this, it doesn't mean that he's still not gonna cheat!
Therapist:	I see, yeah, so what do you need, I mean, it's a dilemma . . .
Monica:	It is.
Therapist:	. . . and then it becomes, What do you want or need to do, given this? It's difficult . . .

Monica:	Mm-hm.
Therapist:	. . . I understand. Do you want to trust him? I mean, on one hand, a part of you just can't trust him, there's a protective wall . . .
Monica:	Mm-hm.
Therapist:	. . . right, of hurt.
Monica:	Well, I don't think it's whether I can or I can't. It's degrees, I think.
Therapist:	Yeah, and I think that's a good point, right, . . .
Monica:	Yeah.
Therapist:	. . . to what degree?
Monica:	It's what degree, and I think that, ultimately, I just know that as time goes on, I'm more able to trust . . .
Therapist:	Right.
Monica:	. . . like every day that goes by, . . .
Therapist:	Right.
Monica:	. . . so I don't know how I'm gonna feel in 10 years, I don't know . . .
Therapist:	Mm-hm, mm-hm.
Monica:	. . . how I'm gonna feel in 5 years, you know, uh, maybe at some point if we continue to really work, I really will get past it . . .
Therapist:	So what is it that you think you need now, or what do you want to do with this time? You see . . .
Monica:	I don't know!
Therapist:	. . . you talked about being able to talk about your doubts, being able to talk about that you feel untrusting, you've been able to talk about—that you feel you don't know that you will ever trust . . .
Monica:	Right.
Therapist:	. . . him, and I think these are important things to be able to talk about, right?
Monica:	Mm-hm.
Therapist:	. . . And then he has to deal with them . . .
Monica:	Right.
Therapist:	. . . the best way that he can. I think that that's more important than bottling it up.

Monica:	But I think that that's something that has been one of the significant, I think, of our time here, is that he's accepted it or has an understanding of that it's important. Because it's important for me, it's important for us, for me to be able to talk about my feelings about it because up until this point I have just been, not able to I feel like, you know, he doesn't want to . . .
Therapist:	His reaction.
Monica:	. . . it's painful to him . . .
Therapist:	Yes, yes.
Monica:	. . . for me bring it up, . . .
Therapist:	Right, right.
Monica:	. . . so, um.
Therapist:	But he's going to have to suffer.
Monica:	Well . . . [sighs]
Therapist:	I mean, I don't mean that vindictively, I mean, that's part of the consequence.
Monica:	Yeah, that's, I mean, it's part of me getting through it, I think, so we can get through it, um, as hard as it's going to be for him, and I think he has a better understanding of how necessary it is.

The Effects of Active Trauma on Adult Relationships

Active trauma is the response to earlier physical or sexual violation by past partners or primary attachment figures. It can be highly distressing and seriously interrupt intimacy with current partners. This type of trauma leads to the development of an embedded core fear that was adaptive in response to the original threat but may no longer be adaptive in the current relationship. Traumatic events that originally involved actual threat or violation through sexual or physical abuse result in fears of connection. The presence of this type of traumatic fear can be identified when one partner reports feeling fear or panic related to closeness when the other partner is not being currently threatening or introducing danger. Another marker of this type of traumatic fear is extreme avoidance of intimacy or sexual contact. More intense indicators include intrusive memories of traumatic events that interrupt contact between partners or fantasies, memories, or dreams that get evoked when intimacy is approached. Accompanying this may be explicit statements of fear, as well as stuttering, shallow breathing, and sighing whenever traumatic material is evoked. Alternatively, partners may attempt to completely avoid traumatic material and anything that may evoke it (avoidance may be highly generalized), leaving their partners feeling frustrated, shut out, and powerless. The maladaptive fear response typically represents fears of reexperiencing the pain and powerlessness of the original traumatic event(s). Secondary anger reactions can protect against and be a sign of underlying fear. Trauma survivors tend to create emotional distance in relationships. A couple's relationship itself can help heal trauma (Johnson, 2002). Treatment involves accessing the maladaptive fear, identifying its source, reexperiencing the fear in response to the original situation, and mobilizing self-resources and partners' responsiveness to help provide a corrective emotional experience. The traumatized partners need to be able to face the fear and increase their capacity to self-soothe and ultimately transform the fear by accessing other emotions in response to the reimagined trauma situation. The nontraumatized partners need to be able to provide interpersonal soothing and validation in the form of compassion, empathy, and acceptance rather than any pressure or demand to change.

A Very Scary Place

In the following example, Ella, with the help of the therapist, is working on expressing the more vulnerable feelings of anxiety and fear that she previously has been too scared to expose because of past abuse in her life. The couple (Ella and Tim) is in therapy because Tim has had an affair, and until this ninth session, the therapy has been focused on repairing that attachment injury. It becomes clear, however, that the affair and Ella's past abuse by her father are intertwined and that the affair served to confirm her deepest fears that nobody, not even her closest partner, is trustworthy. In this next excerpt, they are discussing how to break the negative cycle wherein she criticizes and blames and he withdraws. The therapist is encouraging her to express her more adaptive, primary feelings of fear and anxiety and pain related to betrayal.

Therapist: Tell us about the pain and . . . what it would mean to say, "I'm hurting right now, and I'm frightened of it. It scares me."

Ella: I think for me—it's kind of, ah, my whole life has proven to me so far that, that nobody looks after that part of me. I have been very alone in terms of protecting that part of me, . . .

Therapist: Mm-hm.

Ella: . . . so the idea of having that part rethreatened with something that's going on, and not put up any kind of protection, it's almost—in a way me betraying me—you know, if, if Tim for some reason can't do what I would need him to do, which is his right being a separate person not always being able to know what I need, that would be devastating [*inhales*], that would scare me.

Therapist: Because you've always needed to protect that little girl who got abused because nobody else would listen, nobody else would be there for her.

Ella:	[crying]
Therapist:	Tell us what that's like—can you do that?
Ella:	[crying] I just feel that's the part that it just, can cry forever . . .
Therapist:	Mm-hm.
Ella:	. . . there's no end to that . . . [crying]
Therapist:	What do you need from Tim when you're feeling like that?
Ella:	I mean, it's everything that he always does, I mean.
Therapist:	Mm-hm, tell him what it is. Tell him what he does.
Ella:	[crying] He comforts me and makes me feel like he cares about me . . .
Therapist:	Tell him, "I'm frightened, I need to be taken care of." Can you tell him that? "And it scares me to even trust you with that part of me."
Ella:	[crying] It's scary because part of what was so painful about the affair [crying] was that, in a way, does that mean that I can't trust Tim either? Do you know what I mean? . . .
Therapist:	Mm-hm.
Ella:	. . . every single person who's ever been important in my life has betrayed that . . .
Therapist:	Little girl.
Ella:	Yeah, so, it's really scary. It's scary, it's just so scary to put myself out there, like, I feel that could destroy me, like I don't know what there would be left.
Therapist:	It's almost like, it'd be like putting a baby out in the snow, that a piece of you would be at risk.
Ella:	Yeah, I need to protect myself, but it feels better putting it into words.
Therapist:	It makes a difference because you're trusting, and he's right there holding your hand—and seeing his, that he cares about all of you—can you tell her some of that, Tim?
Tim:	You can trust me; I'm going to be here. Don't be scared.
Therapist:	May I make a suggestion, Tim? Tell her that it's okay to be scared and that you'll be there . . . to help protect the scared part of her.
Tim:	It's okay to be scared.

Therapist: And your response to that he will protect that part of you, there's some doubt, some hesitation?

Ella: [*sniffles*] I just feel like that never happened, you know?

Therapist: "I want to but it would be totally unchartered territory, it would be so, so different." And I guess you're saying that gives him a lot of power.

Ella: I mean, now he has this wall, . . .

Therapist: Right.

Ella: . . . and I know that if that wall goes up, he, like, sees it, and then I can kind of stop if he's going too far or if he's going too far away I can [*makes hand motion of pushing him away with explosive sound*], and he says, "Oh well, fine," and stomps the other way. That way I can kind of stop the onslaught. I mean, it just doesn't feel right to leave yourself so exposed. Like, ultimately, I need to take care of myself [*sighs*].

Therapist: You, ah, tried to get people to share that with you, and they betrayed you. Of course you'd be foolish not to have some protection, some wall that you could put in place and, and I think it's really important that you know that it's okay to keep that wall when you need it but also to entertain the possibility that Tim could come behind the wall with you and reinforce your sense of safety. It's like, don't get rid of the wall but go behind it together. It's a big risk, and I think it's really important, Tim, for you to hear how much control that would give you and how much you hold in your hands then.

Tim: It's so foreign, you know, I mean, it's understandable when she gets like that, it's the little girl trying to, you know. But when you don't see it, you know, you don't know it. But I see it now, and it's very awkward for me to have, for our arguments to be based on what happened to her so many years ago. It's hard for me to accept it, but I feel I just need to understand it, what it does in our relationship, because I couldn't, I can't picture her and that happening, they're two different people. So, it is almost easier to deal with the anger that she has against me than believe that that went on with her when she was younger, you know, so I don't put the two together.

Therapist: I think that what you're saying is that "I want to come behind the wall with you, but it is hard for me to see you like this, but if that is what you need, I can come behind that wall with you, so help me."

Tim: And I know it is the biggest thing you could ever do.

Ella: I don't even know if I can to be quite honest. I don't even know because I don't know how [*crying*].

Therapist: You're doing it right now. You are doing it right now by talking about it and showing how you feel, that's how you do it. You're being vulnerable right now.

Violence in an intimate relationship creates trauma. A couple that presents in therapy and reports that violence occurs regularly in the relationship, by one or both members, is not suitable for emotion-focused work. The couple should be referred to a specific treatment for violence, and the individual member of the couple who commits the violent behavior needs individual treatment focused on emotion regulation. Only when violence is under control is a more emotionally evocative couples therapy indicated. Emotion-focused couples therapy (EFT-C) is suitable when one partner has previously been a victim of violence in an intimate relationship. The effects of the violent behavior need to be understood and treated as active trauma. Partners need to describe the effects of the past trauma to their partner in the current relationship. They may be more sensitive to particular cues, leftover from the previous violent relationship, that indicate that violence might follow. Thus, they may be more attentive and start to feel afraid when voices get raised, when criticism begins, or when their partners get into negative moods. The previously victimized partner must describe in detail any idiosyncratic indicators that violence might start. Current partners need to be able to hear how the past trauma experience affects their current relationship without feeling hurt or defensive. They then may be able to be more sensitive to their partners and avoid fear-inducing behavior. They may also be able to play a more soothing and reassuring role with respect to the prior trauma.

WORKING WITH FEAR AND ANXIETY IN THE THERAPEUTIC SETTING

In working with fear and anxiety, the EFT-C therapist does different things at different times, depending on the nature of the fear and what the therapist deems necessary in the moment. Where one partner is avoiding the fear because of fears of disintegration, loss of control, or abandonment, the therapist will help the person face the fear so that he or she can realize that his or her worst fear is not founded. When the fear is of abandonment by the partner, the therapist encourages the partner to reassure the other that he or she will not be abandoned or rejected but also works with the fearful partner to develop self-soothing capacities. In other words, the therapist helps strengthen the partner's ability to be alone, to take care of one's self, and to regulate their own emotions. When the fear is related to shame anxiety[1] in

---

[1]*Shame anxiety* differs from *shame* in that *shame anxiety* is the anxiety that one will be shamed.

which the client anticipates potentially feeling embarrassed, humiliated, or mortified if he or she reveals core aspects of self-experience, the therapist engages his or her partner to help reduce the sense of shame by encouraging the partner to reassure, soothe, or even celebrate the person in their more vulnerable states. When partners fear being judged or misunderstood by their partners or are not able to disclose unless they feel safe, the therapist again encourages the partners to reassure them that they are not negatively evaluating them. When there is an intense fear of negative evaluation, the therapist judges whether additional work needs to be done for the individual to work with his or her own negative or critical self-introjects.

The EFT-C therapist helps partners identify and reveal both unexpressed feelings of adaptive attachment anxiety or fear and maladaptive anxiety or fear involved in the negative emotional interactional cycle. The former are used as a guide to inform communication and action; the latter need to be accessed to expose them to soothing and transformation. The EFT-C therapist (a) helps people acknowledge and express their primary adaptive fears and anxieties and vulnerabilities to their partners particularly when they are either putting on a facade of strength, thereby ignoring their relationship, enhancing fear or insecurity, or withdrawing to avoid dealing with the fear; (b) helps people access primary adaptive fears so that partners can learn to face them, rather than to avoid them; (c) helps people access their maladaptive fears; (d) focuses people away from future-oriented fear and brings attention to the present moment to control anxiety; and (e) accesses both failed ways of calming fears and other feelings, such as anger at violation that produced the fear and sadness at loss. This is the process of regulating fear and transforming it by changing people's self-organization.

The therapist thus helps people understand whether their fear is in fact adaptive or perhaps once was and now no longer is. The therapist helps partners understand how their fear or anxiety functions in the current relationship. Is it a reaction to an accurately perceived threat? Is there a climate within the relationship that breeds the fear? Is the fear signaling an important message to the person that needs to be addressed or acted on? Or was the fear perhaps functional in an earlier relationship or situation but preventing intimacy in the current relationship? The therapist helps partners identify what aspects of the fear are in fact maladaptive in the current relationship, parses out and access the adaptive components of fear, explore other associated adaptive emotions, and encourages partners to express and act out of newly constructed adaptive emotions. For example, fear may have been adaptive for a woman in response to her father's sexual advances but may not be in relation to her husband. There may be an adaptive component to the fear in that it is a signal that protects her; however, there are perhaps other more tender emotions that need to be accessed as well and brought forward as valid responses to a currently nurturing and safe relationship.

AFFILIATIVE CYCLES

Fear of being alone and separation anxiety are the dominant emotions pervading the affiliation negative cycle. Other difficult emotions, such as sadness and anger, also occur, but the fear or anxiety related to loss of connection is a core motivator of much couples conflict. When couples fight intensely and often, difficult and painful emotions can be evoked, including shame, anger, and hurt. Experiencing difficult emotions over time can be exhausting, and eventually people begin to withdraw. When partners sense each other's withdrawal, they feel disconnected and alone. Fears of abandonment are triggered and begin to pervade the relationship. Fear then potentially can be experienced by either the pursuer or the distancer. An important aspect of working with fear in attachment-related cycles is to get beneath the anger to access and reveal the partners' fear to each other and to help them understand whether it is adaptive or maladaptive.

Pursuer's Fear

In all cases of negative attachment-related cycles, the separation anxiety and fear of loss driving the cycle varies on a continuum of adaptive to maladaptive. All people need closeness, get anxious at separation, and fear rejection and abandonment. All partners have difficulty in expressing and negotiating these feelings and needs, and this can lead to conflict. Many people also have particular vulnerabilities and sensitivities. These are often based on their maladaptive emotional response.

"He Just Wants to Get Away From Me"

Lynn and Aaron described their relationship as "fairly compatible." Day-to-day activities were mostly enjoyable, and they felt they had a great many compatible interests and hobbies. They could have fun doing nothing together. They felt their intimacy was strong. They came to therapy because every 2 to 3 weeks or so, they would have a highly distressing explosive fight that would turn ugly very quickly. Tempers would flare, and the volume would be turned up from 0 to 100 very fast. Many corrosive and damaging insults would fly, and they would both feel remorseful later on. They came to therapy to try to figure out how to resolve fights better. In identifying the cycle with the therapist, they report that fights often occurred just as Aaron was planning to go out by himself with friends or family or even to attend a work function. As the couple talks more, Aaron describes how difficult it was for him to tell Lynn that he was going out because of his fear of her disappointment and wrath. He usually avoided telling her until the last minute, even though he acknowledged that avoiding tended to make things worse. He also talks about how he loved Lynn but felt stifled in the relationship. Lynn and Aaron describe how after Aaron would come from a party with his friends at 4 a.m., Lynn would be distant and say many derogatory comments to Aaron. Eventually, Lynn begins to talk about her primary fear that drove her contemptuous, hostile criticism when Aaron would leave: Her fear of being alone. She felt that perhaps Aaron's loyalty was not fully with her. She recognized that at times the belief that he would leave her was unfounded, and she understood that he needed to have "his space." The therapist and client then begin to talk about how the fear of abandonment was related to her earlier childhood experiences. Her parents had divorced when she was 7 years old. She had never felt particularly wanted by either parent and was "carted around" from house to house. She described how her mother was "inconsistently" emotionally available. At times, she was "lots of fun" and very empathic and understanding. At those times, she felt close to her mother. However, at other times, her mother was completely distracted. After her divorce from Lynn's father, her mother was preoccupied with her dating life. Many men would come through the house. Sometimes her mother had time for her, and sometimes she did not. Sometimes she would leave her alone in the house with "strange" boyfriends. At those times, Lynn felt terribly alone. She talked about how this related to her fear of being alone. She said that as a teenager and young adult, she had jumped from one relationship to the other, no matter how she felt about the partner, dreading the idea of ever being alone. The therapist and client begin to explore how she could learn to self-soothe in the face of abandonment.

In one session, the couple was discussing an upcoming business trip that Aaron needed to take. Lynn was feeling quite apprehensive about this and was saying things such as,

> I don't know why he has to go for such a long time. He is going for 5 days when I think he only really needs 4. But I think it is kind of a relief for him, even though he won't say it. He just wants to get away from me.

They began exploring Lynn's fears about Aaron leaving.

Therapist: I guess it really hurts that he is leaving you.

Lynn: [*Begins to cry.*]

Therapist: There is a lot of pain there.

Lynn: [*crying more intensely*] I don't know why I am crying, to be honest. I am fine.

Therapist: Somehow it is so scary when he leaves, as if he might never come back.

Lynn: Well, yeah, but I know he will come back really. [*Cries more uncontrollably, deeply sobbing and gasping for breath.*]

Therapist:	Somehow, you know, but it is so scary. We are here with you. Can you just stay with the feelings? Can you describe what is happening for you right now?
Lynn:	I can't really say. I just can't stop crying, and it feels like a big dark hole that has a bottomless pit. I am just afraid this is never going to end, this pain. And I will keep crying like this. It is like I am going to fall and keep falling [*continuing to gasp for breath*].
Therapist:	[*after 15 seconds*] So, somehow there's this fear, and it's so scary [*gentle, empathic voice*]. Lynn, can you take a deep breath and look at Aaron? He is sitting here, looking at you with a very concerned look. Can you turn to him now?
Lynn:	[*After sobbing and gasping a few more seconds, tentatively sneaks a fearful look at Aaron.*]
Therapist:	What do you see?
Lynn:	I see a concerned face.
Therapist:	Aaron, can you tell Lynn what is happening inside for you?
Aaron:	[*turning to Lynn*] I know it is scary for you. I am here. I love you.
Lynn:	[*Begins to take slower breaths.*]
Therapist:	So, Aaron, you really feel concerned and love her. Lynn, can you look at me now? What do you see?
Lynn:	I also see a very concerned face.

The therapist stays with Lynn while she explores her core fear of abandonment. Rather than attempt to "change something" such as modify the fear or, alternatively, allow the client to avoid it, the therapist stays with the client, encouraging her to explore it. By allowing and symbolizing it, the client faces the fear and realizes that her fear of abandonment is not founded. The client is encouraged to come back to the present moment and make contact with her partner, who is in fact sitting by and looking at her in a concerned, loving way. By encouraging her to make contact with her husband as well as the therapist, the therapist is encouraging Lynn to stay out of her head and make contact in the present. This helps Lynn see that nothing bad is going to happen.

After a few more minutes, the therapist and couple begin to work on ways to help Lynn self-soothe in Aaron's absence.

Therapist:	So, Lynn, it is hard for you when Aaron goes out of town or says he's going out with friends. You somehow feel left out, left out in the cold. At some level, I guess you know he'll come back and it will be alright, but it's hard to hold on to that in the moment. How can we help you with that, to sort of take care of

	yourself at those times? So when Aaron says he is going away or going out, what happens for you, in your body? What do you actually feel?
Lynn:	Well, I guess a bit panicky, 'cause I go a little weak in the knees and sometimes my stomach starts to hurt. I know it is irrational, but . . .
Therapist:	Yeah, but somehow that's what really happens. I wonder, when you start feeling like this or when he actually goes out, I mean, leaves, and you are all alone and you start to feel shaky, what can you do?
Lynn:	Well, I can breathe [*sighs*].
Therapist:	Yeah, that is a good start. And I notice you do that now. Can you do that again? . . .
Lynn:	[*Breathes again.*]
Therapist:	. . . good, and I wonder if you can somehow reassure yourself that it will be okay.
Lynn:	Like how?
Therapist:	Well, what can you tell yourself?
Lynn:	Well, I guess I can tell myself it will be okay. That nothing is going to change. We are still doing alright. Sometimes I can do that. Sometimes I even start to like being alone!

Trying to Thaw

At times, people can maladaptively fear rejection or abandonment and express a secondary emotion such as anger to prevent the exposure of their more vulnerable emotions. In the following example, Merril is afraid of being vulnerable and exposed. After a number of sessions, this couple became aware of their negative interactional cycle. Steve had explored his underlying shame and sense of inadequacy evoked by Merril's criticisms. Merril was more aware of her needs and how she blamed Steve instead of talking from a more vulnerable position. She had also learned how to take care of her own needs and self-soothe to a large extent. In some ways, this had been a positive shift, as it had given Steve a chance to move out of his withdrawn retreat. In the following excerpt, the therapist talks to Merril about her past hurts and disappointments within the relationship and her fear of making herself vulnerable once again and opening sexually. Notice how the therapist distinguishes between expressing blame and demand as opposed to vulnerability. The therapist also works with the fear, carefully validating its legitimacy, and encourages Merril to take full control of when to reveal her vulnerability.

Therapist:	Right, and somehow there's the subtle difference of needing and not demanding . . .
Merril:	Mm-hm.
Therapist:	. . . and I think it's the demand that he finds hard and most people find hard, . . .
Merril:	Yeah.
Therapist:	. . . but maybe the need isn't as, he's not as unable to respond to your need if, because that's what he's saying, he's sort of beginning to understand you are there and you have a need. . . .
Merril:	Yeah.
Therapist:	. . . You like doing things in particular ways, and that's you, . . .
Merril:	Yep.
Therapist:	. . . that's what makes you happy, and that's okay. So, somehow it's, can you let him see your needs and respond to them without there being the demand component and the rejection that follows?
Merril:	I don't know.
Therapist:	Mm-hm, it's like you need to put your foot in the water toe by toe.
Merril:	Yeah, yeah. Right now I don't want to go into the water though. . . .
Therapist:	Mm-hm.
Merril:	. . . I could float on it in a boat, but I don't want to put my toe in. . . .
Therapist:	Mm-hm, mm-hm.
Steve:	Well, that's a start; I could rock the boat [*laughs*]. No I'm just kidding, I could knock you out of there [*laughs*].
Merril:	I might swim away.
Steve:	Yeah.
Therapist:	The dance is different, though, because now it's you who is, it's unusual for you to be afraid.
Merril:	I know . . . it's not . . . I've never been this way with him before. . . .
Therapist:	Mm-hm.
Merril:	. . . I've never experienced . . .
Steve:	It's true.

Merril: this kind of, lack of, like he said to me he has needs, he's a man, . . .

Therapist: Mm-hm.

Merril: . . . I'm not meeting them. . . .

Therapist: Mm-hm.

Merril: . . . I don't . . . I used to have needs way beyond his . . .

Therapist: Mm-hm.

Merril: . . . and they were always intense . . .

Therapist: Mm-hm.

Merril: . . . and I was always bothering him about them, and now I just have nothing. There's nothing, it's, like, dead, and it's so strange.

Therapist: Do you know, when you say "dead," you are still alive, the way you say "dead"? So there's something with it still . . .

Merril: There's the hormonal part, but it's . . .

Therapist: I guess what I'm saying is, it's still painful to know you are dead. . . .

Merril: Yeah.

Therapist: So it's very, you know, you are dead to protect yourself.

Merril: I know . . . I can't . . . I keep trying to thaw, and I can't. . . .

Therapist: Mm-hm, mm-hm.

Merril: . . . So, it's like I have this war going on inside of me.

Therapist: Mm-hm. So you are saying you are actually aware of the struggles. . . .

Merril: Mm-hm.

Therapist: . . . of the war?

Merril: It's just easier to go along the way things are now. This is the best it's been in a long time, and I just . . .

Therapist: Yeah.

Merril: . . . I'm thankful that at least living together now is not as . . . before we were both incredibly . . . it's not as hard to be in the same room. We don't have to work hard to disguise or protect our daughter from our anger, because it's not there.

Therapist: So this is an important truce period? After a war, you don't jump into bed right after a war. I mean, it's smart in some way, sort of protective. But you are saying you are aware of a voice that says,

On one hand, "I want to thaw, or I want to somehow be in a place where I have thawed," versus another that says, you know, "No way."

Merril: There's a voice that says, "I should try and thaw."

Therapist: Right . . . I understand . . . it's not you "want," but you "should." I somehow sense that the other voice is saying, "I'm not ready, I'm not there. I'm scared, and I'm terrified."

Merril: Yeah, I'm terrified, and I can't go there. So . . .

Therapist: So I think everybody needs to help soothe the terrified part. You know, help reassure her.

Merril: Well, um, we're going away on vacation and that might. At least a change of scenery or pace . . .

Therapist: But yet, I think you need to not feel too pressured that you should thaw. I think you should only thaw when you feel safe, . . .

Merril: Okay.

Therapist: . . . you know.

Notice here that the client describes herself as once the pursuer. She has since retreated in self-protection and now accesses a tangible fear of rejection that she has never encountered before. The therapist clearly brings this to her attention as he conceptualizes the problem that faces the two of them.

Distancer's Fear

Fear in the distancer may be related to a fear of intrusion, that closeness will damage or destroy the self or to a feeling that showing needs for closeness or vulnerability is weak. In other words, the distancer may have established in him- or herself a firm commitment to not allow anyone to witness his or her weakness or vulnerability or to protect the self from intrusion. In these cases, people often have had negative experiences associated with exposing themselves or showing vulnerability and have learned that the most adaptive way to prevent further disappointment or rejection is to refrain from further exposing any vulnerable aspects of self or needs. They may even have adopted a position earlier in life that not having their needs met was so painful that they will never need anyone again. Men often adopt this position and wall off their vulnerability. The fear of showing vulnerability or of needing others may simply be a learned response through socialization or an automated protective response learned in the distant past from disappointment or loss. Injunctions against showing vulnerability, although often forgotten for many years, are recalled when prompted in therapy. People often can identify the time period when it began.

In the context of the attachment-related affiliation cycle, the distancer might also be afraid of expressing what he or she actually feels and needs for fear of pushing the partner away. Distancing prevents expression of primary emotion. It is ironic that distancers in this process achieve the opposite of their aim and that their attempts to not push the other away pushes the other away.

For example, Bree finds that at work she has a great deal of difficulty saying "no" to other people when they want her to take on extra jobs. She finds herself compensating for many of her coworkers', including her boss's, shortcomings and generally "holding down the fort." She is fed up working in a place where so many people are satisfied with mediocrity and incompetence, but she cannot help herself from taking on extra to make up for other's shortcomings. She comes home at the end of the day angry and exhausted and is short with her partner, Gilles. She starts opening drawers and cupboards and complaining how she hates the kitchen, how the refrigerator is too small, and so on. Gilles desperately wants Bree's attention when he comes home from a busy day of managing 25 people. He also works in an administrative setting. He, too, is overwhelmed and overwrought. He is hoping to connect with Bree and put all of their troubles at a distance. All he gets from Bree, however, is a cold shoulder. He starts to feel rejected and alone. He starts to wonder whether she really is happy and whether she can be happy with him. He thinks of how she left her home and her kids in another city so that they could move for his job. He wonders whether she wishes she could return. He starts to think about his first wife and how she left him, and then he starts to get scared. Finally, he blows his top and gets angry at Bree: "Why can't you just be happy? Why can't you look at the bright side of things? You are always so negative." Bree gets angry and yells back and then retreats further into her corner. When the fight is discussed in therapy, it becomes clear that Gilles simply wants to connect. Bree understands Gilles's need to connect but is so accustomed to handling things on her own that she does not consider opening herself to Gilles and talking to him about her problems as a source of comfort. Bree has a history of physical and sexual abuse and neglect. When she was young, her mother and father quickly divorced, and she was carted around from home to home as her mother "shacked up" with various men. She never felt protected by her mother and many times felt "sold down the river." At times, she was sexually abused by one of her mother's boyfriends and his son. She says she wants to open up to Gilles but is afraid she will be invalidated. She explains,

> Occasionally, he [Gilles] makes me laugh about it all, and that takes me out of my bad place, but I don't like to ask for what I need. It is very hard for me to do that. And if I do take the risk and don't get what I need and

feel invalidated, well, that is terrible. Where I come from, asking for what you need or for support is a sure way to get your hands burned.

Gilles cannot understand or reassure her that she will not get invalidated. He feels he is a victim of her past. He feels insulted and defensive that she feels that way and says, "I don't know where that all comes from. I don't invalidate her." He goes back into the place of feeling, "She is simply unhappy, and I can't make her happy, and she will leave me in 6 months like my first wife did." Bree, the pursuer, is afraid of rejection and humiliation; Gilles, the distancer, is afraid of abandonment.

Anticipating Rejection, Reject First

Carla and Luis came to therapy saying they were fighting a great deal and were considering whether to get married or end the relationship. Luis had been married for 17 years prior to meeting Carla 3 years ago, and Carla had never been married. They were both in their early 40s. Luis had 3 children, one with a severe disability. Luis maintained a very troubling and enmeshed relationship with his ex-wife. After a bitter and expensive custody dispute, a settlement had been reached whereby Luis took care of the kids one half of the time, rotating each week. When Luis was with his children, Carla spent a great deal of time with the family, and it was clear to the therapist that she wanted nothing more than to be a part of the family. She longed for the children's love and went to great lengths to be a positive maternal figure, spending much of her free time nurturing and caring for them, throwing lavish birthday parties for them, and generally indulging them as much as possible. She craved love from both Luis and his children. As each partner recounted his or her own story, the chief complaint that Luis made was that he felt criticized and "never good enough"; Carla, however, talked of feeling unappreciated, and this was attachment related. Note that Luis was reacting not to frustration of an attachment need but to a threat to his identity and that he reacted not with loneliness but with shame. This is thus a mixed attachment and identity cycle. Carla felt that although Luis at times did special things for her and bought her expensive gifts, he was not sensitive to her desires and needs and did not care about her. For example, he would forget her birthday and fail to buy her a present. This was very important to Carla, and she felt deeply wounded. Luis, however, felt that even though he did not always respond to her "whims," he was generally very considerate of her and had her well-being at the forefront of his mind. He always indulged her with special gifts, although for Carla, they were not the ones she wanted.

A typical fight would occur as Luis and Carla were preparing to separate after spending a weekend together. At the end of the weekend, there often was an extra-stressful event because Luis would also be preparing to part with his kids for a week and turn them over to his ex-wife, with whom he did not feel his children were completely safe. The children would begin to exhibit separation anxiety. Luis would begin to feel anxious and morose and express despondency about the next few hours. When this happened, Carla would feel he was withdrawing from her and anticipating a rejection, and so, she would reject him first. Thus, when Luis responded sharply to a question, Carla would adopt a withdrawing strategy based on her fears of rejection and say, "Fine, I am just going to leave then," and prepare her things to go home. Feeling hopeless, Luis would respond defensively, saying, "Fine. Leave." Carla would then pack her things and go. She would describe how going home was much safer and how relieved she felt upon being there. In many ways, she felt being alone was more comfortable than being attached. When the therapist would reflect how this was her natural response to growing up in a chaotic and unstable home environment and how she had learned it was unsafe to be vulnerable, she agreed. She did not want to explore the vulnerability further, however.

Carla told the therapist on previous occasions that when she was growing up, her mother had a bipolar disorder. Her father had left the home when Carla was very young. In general, her mother's caregiving was highly inconsistent, and for the most part, Carla took care of her mother more than she was taken care of by her mother. She recounted scenes when her mother would, in a psychotic state, wake the children in the middle of the night to clean the house. In response, and as a matter of survival, Carla had learned to take care of herself at a premature age and had become fiercely independent. She had learned that it simply was not safe to be dependent on her mother. She had carried this approach and adopted a caretaking role throughout most of her life, staying out of intimate relationships until recently (age 42) when she dared enter a serious relationship. Being in a relationship was thus an unfamiliar experience and one that she found at once to be compelling, meaningful, incredibly scary, and uncomfortable.

Carla thus was responding from a maladaptive fear of being neglected, and this required work in therapy to help her first to overcome her avoidance of approaching, experiencing, and exploring this fear in relation to her mother. Once she began to explore these feelings and access the legitimacy of her needs for caring and concern from her mother, the therapist worked with her on how to self-soothe and with the couple on how it would be safe to bring this vulnerability into the current relationship. They then explored how Luis could help soothe with his empathic understanding and compassion.

"He Probably Finds Me Disgusting, That's Why I Distance From Him"

As discussed earlier, distancers in the attachment-related affiliation cycle can also be experiencing core fear arising from trauma in the past. They are often afraid of any sexual or physical intimacy. Pursuing partners tend to be sensitive to rejection and unaware of how their behavior triggers a fear response. Thus, increasing awareness of how they trigger their partner may be an important piece of the work; however, the major work involves identifying the trauma and understanding how it functions to prevent intimacy in the current relationship. Then, it is helpful for the partner to be involved in promoting the healing of the traumatized partner. Let's go back to our couple Jim and Nancy from chapter 11. Recall that they have been married 9 years and are unsure of whether to stay together. Jim feels unloved, saying Nancy has "lost" her affection for him. Nancy says she is unsure whether she does love him, but she does know she feels trapped. Nancy was raped shortly before they met. Nancy feels that Jim has no problem publicly humiliating and shaming her, and then she feels indignant when he pursues her for sexual intimacy soon after.

In the 10th session, Jim and Nancy come in, saying things are much better. Nancy is not feeling that Jim is purposely humiliating her and Jim has stopped being so pushy. Jim mentions, however, that he has backed off from pursuing Nancy for sex, as he realizes that it only pushes her away further and backfires for him. He is tired of being rejected. He does admit, however, to feeling alone, "as if on a deserted island." He feels that if he does not pursue Nancy for sex, they will never have it. She agrees that she likely will not initiate sex and says she is just not all that interested in it. As they explore the issue further, the therapist begins to explore with Nancy what happens when Jim does initiate sex. She says that sometimes she feels angry and other times she feels a combination of anger and disgust. At other times she feels simply numb. Much of the time, she sees Jim as a needy predator who is simply interested in his own pleasure. As they talk further, Nancy admits that sex is mostly a negative experience for her and has been ever since she was raped. Although there were times earlier in her relationship with Jim when sex was pleasurable, it now reminds her of the rape. She then begins to recount the rape scene and reveal how violated and afraid she felt. The therapist listens, empathically following her experience and encouraging her to allow all the accompanying emotions to emerge. Considerable time is spent with her retelling her story and working through the many emotions associated with this experience, including anger. All the while, Jim is listening intently, looking empathic, concerned, and protective. The therapist is monitoring his facial expressions periodically. Eventually, the therapist asks Nancy whether she is aware of Jim's presence and encourages her to make contact with him. She says that he probably finds her disgusting and that is why she needs to keep distance from him. With the therapist's prompting and help, Jim talks about feeling compassionate and concerned. He also talks about feeling protective over her and not wanting her to hurt again. He expresses strong loving feelings toward her. The therapist then checks with Nancy to make sure she is making contact with Jim as he expresses his feelings. She says she is, and she looks at him somewhat incredulously, saying it is hard for her to believe he feels that way. She says she appreciates hearing that, and although it is difficult for her, she wants to allow the feelings to sink in and comfort her. She allows Jim to hug her in the session.

Angry but Afraid He Won't Stick Around

Fear also can appear in the pursue–distance cycle as a secondary emotion that prevents or defends against a more primary emotion such as anger. The distancer may, for example, feel resentful of perceived maltreatment by one's partner and so refrain from stating needs and wants, so as to placate the partner. One partner may feel afraid of being left or abandoned but, in fact, may actually feel quite resentful. For example, Jill always felt cold and distant after she and Ron returned from parties and social functions with friends. She was not sure why she felt that way toward Ron but knew she just felt kind of scared and alone. When they presented in therapy, Ron complained that Jill was a "cold fish." Jill did not appreciate the characterization of her but stated that she was aware she was driving Ron away with her distance. She thought Ron would eventually leave her but stated that this was kind of "to be expected, as everyone always did eventually." When the couple came to one session describing a recent fight after a party, the therapist began to deconstruct with the couple what had actually happened at the party before the fight. They described a scene where Jill had felt quite humiliated and put down by Ron in a conversation with friends. They had been discussing their earlier days in college, and Ron had told his friends that Jill was never a serious student who was passionate or committed to anything. "She mostly just slept around in college," Ron had told their friends, "a regular slut." Jill had in fact strongly resented this characterization of her but found that she was frozen and unable to defend herself. She described feeling sick to her stomach at the time and sort of wincing inside. She had quietly excused herself from the conversation and went to talk to some other friends as a way of distracting herself. What became clear as the couple discussed the incident further was that Jill was actually angry and seething inside. She had felt embarrassed by Ron but was afraid that if she described how angry she really was, he would "not stick around." She later revealed a dream where Ron was dead and she had to figure out how to dispose of his body. This was very difficult for her to disclose, and the dream had frightened her. She was encouraged to tell Ron how angry she was in a constructive manner in the therapy session, with the help of the therapist.

INFLUENCING CYCLE

Threats to identity are important in partners' efforts to control and influence each other. The different types of fear underlying partners' positions in the influence cycles are described in the sections that follow.

Dominant's Fear

In the context of the dominance cycle, the dominant person often fears that a major or catastrophic disaster will occur sometime in the future and experiences him- or herself as having to plan for and avert disaster before it happens. Partners, however, experience them as too controlling. The anxious dominant's rationale is that if he or she is not managing things and planning for the future, a disaster may indeed occur. This sends them into a hypervigilant state, and secondary emotions such as anger, blaming, and criticism may ensue when they feel others are not to be depended on. These types of partners often have an innate sense of responsibility and caring for others and likely have been saddled with a primary caretaking role in their family early on. Alternatively, they may have come from a chaotic home in which they felt responsible for their siblings or were in the role of preventing their parents from flying out of control.

Unseen and Taken for Granted

Elaine came to therapy before Jennifer did, saying she wasn't sure whether she wanted to continue in their partnership. She claimed that Jill did not take proper care of her and was too introverted for her liking. After a few sessions, Elaine agreed to bring Jennifer into therapy. Their description of their relationship was "communication breakdown." What became clear was that Elaine felt terribly criticized by Jennifer. She talked about having an alcoholic father who was verbally abusive and how hurtful it was that Jennifer was critical and "always on her case." She was tired of her always finding fault in her and of feeling like she could not do anything right.

Elaine described feeling inadequate and getting into a dark hole when Jennifer would say she does not plan and leaves it up to her. In response to this, Jennifer exploded,

> You have no idea. I am sorry she is so sensitive to criticism, but that just makes me feel like I cannot say anything in the relationship. I need to fight to make this relationship work. I feel so unimportant and exploited. I mean, I need some predictability. She prefers to live in this bohemian fashion, just assuming that things will take care of themselves. Meanwhile, I take care of all the finances, plan ahead, think about our family's future, while she sits idly by. I cannot stand her irresponsible approach. It makes me feel highly uncomfortable. She will not talk about anything. She ignores all my concerns. I have been trying to get her to sit down and make a budget with me for the last 5 years, and she simply will not. She always evades me and I feel unseen and taken for granted.

As they explore Jennifer's concerns, it becomes clear that she came from a family that lost all their money when she was 11 and their lives became chaotic, and she is extremely anxious that unless she knows what is happening, something bad will happen. In a response to threat that is somewhat more typical of men than women, she adopted a hyperresponsible role at an early age to deal with feeling afraid that things would fly out of control, and so she constantly feels she must avert disaster before it explodes. She is more rational and planful than her partner, and works as a computer analyst. Elaine, however, is a new professor in a creative field and does not find order to be her most pressing concern.

Submissive's Fear

"Stonewallers," as Gottman (1999) called them, are notoriously known as the "withdrawers" in relationships. More typically than women, men tend to shut down when their partners begin to attack, claiming emotional negligence. Rather than fearing closeness, these men fear criticism and feeling controlled. In therapy, they may sit and listen but have very little emotional response to their partners' tirades and rants. No matter how hard she goes or what insults she uses, he has little visible response. Gottman demonstrated, by rigging heart rate monitors up to couples and actually asking them to stage a fight in the laboratory, that these stonewallers do actually have an increase in heart rate despite outward physical signs. In fact, these people are feeling afraid, whether or not they are consciously processing it. This is often the passive response to an attack from the more dominant or active partner.

It is not uncommon to have a couple where one partner feels primarily afraid of the other and submits out of fear. Of course, the submitter tends to be the withdrawer. More typically than men, the woman in the relationship is more likely to be afraid of her husband's wrath, although it is entirely possible for the roles to be reversed.

Shutting Down

Upon entering therapy, Eli and Jane described how, for the most part, they got along very well. They would occasionally have bitter fights, however, and not speak for days. Jane was a photographer, and Eli was in journalism. Jane was struggling to get her own business off the ground and at times did not feel motivated. She relied a great deal on Eli for financial and emotional support. Eli did not have a problem with this arrangement, although at times he felt financially burdened and became critical of Jane. Jane, however, felt that Eli was often busy and consumed at work and did not make enough time for "the relationship." When she began to feel unhappy, she would tell Eli she was feeling lonely and that they needed to talk. The more she pursued Eli to talk and be more attentive, the more he withdrew. Eventually, Eli would get angry with Jane and tell her to stop nagging him. According to Jane, he would just shoot her mean looks and then blow up, becoming furious and ranting. Sometimes, he would put her down, tell her how useless she was, and ask her why she couldn't just be a more independent person and get her business off the ground. When Eli would rage like this, Jane would become afraid. She tended to shut down and withdraw. Then, she would not want to talk or be close to Eli for days. They discuss the issue in the following excerpt. Notice how the therapist rebuilds the scene of the actual fight, tracking what happened for both people behaviorally and emotionally. The therapist tracks both the secondary and the primary emotion. In this example, when exploring what happened for Jane, the therapist focuses on the exploratory reflection of her primary emotion, which in this case is fear.

Therapist: So, what happened for you last night, Jane?

Jane: Well, he came home from work late as usual, and I was actually looking forward to seeing him. I had lunch with a friend yesterday, and we had a little bit of conflict, and I wanted to tell Eli about it. I was feeling kind of weird.

Therapist: Uh-huh. So, he comes home, and you are looking forward to talking to him, and then what happened?

Jane: Well, he comes home, he barely pecks me on the cheek, and he just walks into the den and plops down in front of the TV. Clearly, the message was, "I don't feel like talking."

Therapist: Uh-huh, so what happened after that? Were you aware, Eli, that Jane wanted to talk? Or what was happening for you?

Eli: You know, I had a very stressful day at work. Very stressful. I had had this big fight with an editor, and I really just wasn't in the mood for talking.

Therapist: Uh-huh, so then what happened?

Jane: Well, I guess I was pretty mad, and I said, "You know, I am so sick of this relationship. I really just want to talk to you, and it is like pulling teeth."

Eli: You know this is it. She comes out with all these whacko statements. Like, as if I am not there for her. So, I don't know what happened, but I think I got pretty angry.

Therapist: So, you got pretty angry, and then what happened? What happened for you, Jane?

Jane: Well, he just lost it, and he started on his tirade, and he just blew up at me.

Therapist: And then what happens? What were you actually feeling, Jane, when Eli was raging like that?

Jane: When I start seeing that angry look on his face and, well, my muscles just tense and I start to feel sort of light-headed. I feel so small, and I guess I kind of just shut down.

Therapist: It sounds like, Jane, when you see that look on Eli's face, you get afraid and then immediately put your guard up.

Jane: It reminds me of when my mother, over the smallest thing, used to just fly off the handle and get really angry and mean and start banging the pots and pans around.

Therapist: So when Eli gets that mean look on his face, it reminds you of when your mother used to lose her temper and become abusive with you. You just kind of get scared and shut down, is that it?

Jane: Yeah, I feel so alone and kind of scared, to be honest. I start feeling all woozy and dizzy, like I am not going to make it. [*Stops for a second.*] Actually, I am sort of feeling that right now. It is hard to talk about.

Therapist: That sounds really hard. Can you stay with that feeling of woozy and dizzy and tell Eli what that is like for you? Instead of going away, can you tell him what that is like for you? Would that be scary? I imagine it might be hard? Can you tell him?

Jane: Well, okay, I think I could tell him. When you start getting really mad like you did last night, I feel afraid, and I start feeling like the bottom is dropping out [*beginning to shake and cry*]. And I guess it reminds me of my mother when she used to lose it. I know you are not going to hurt me like she did, but sometimes I guess I am not sure. I just get this sinking feeling in my stomach.

CONCLUSION

Fear is an important emotion to attend to in couples therapy. When adaptive, it brings people closer and helps create and maintain connection. It also serves the important function of protecting people against threat. People all need each other and need to feel in control. However, fear and separation anxiety can function maladaptively in couples relationships and become the source of heated and intense conflicts. In this chapter, we have discussed the positive, healthy aspects of fear in attachment but mainly focused on the different ways in which fear, trauma, and separation anxiety can play a corrosive role in tearing couples apart. We have outlined the different ways in which fear may underlie either affiliation or influence cycles. In working with fear, the EFT-C therapist must help partners determine whether their fear is an undisclosed, adaptive fear that underlies criticism or control and whether it needs to be acknowledged and should be expressed. Pure expressions of fear will be received and responded to far more empathically than will criticism. Maladaptive fear, when present, also needs to be validated but ultimately must be faced and transformed. Important methods for soothing fear within the self and the couple have been recommended.

13

SHAME IN COUPLES THERAPY

Shame is pride's cloak.

—William Blake

Shame has been recognized as a critical source of low self-esteem, play-ing a powerful role in directing, distorting, and even crippling identity. How-ever, shame is also a critical barrier to the realization of intimacy in couples. If therapists are to help couples succeed in achieving intimacy, they must help them face their shame and understand its disruptive impact on their relationship. Shame needs to be distinguished from anxiety. Although anxi-ety signals that one's survival is in danger, shame signals that one's accept-ability to others may be in danger. Rather than the danger being one of abandonment, it is the danger of being devalued and scorned. This may be followed by fear of abandonment, but the primary concern is about being defective.

THE EXPERIENCE OF SHAME

Shame is about feeling overexposed and found lacking in dignity or worth in the eyes of others. It involves feeling looked down on or seen as inferior, and this is most painful when it is one's most intimate partner who a person feels looks down on him or her. Shame is closely related to fear of others' devaluation. Shame anxiety makes people cautious about revealing themselves. It is at the core of a family of shame feelings, which include shyness, embarrassment, stigmatization, and disgrace.

Basic shame develops most fundamentally from the lack of caretaker attunement to a child's excitement or expressiveness, which forms the bases of their agency and sense of self. Beyond this, shame develops from being the recipient of others' scorn, contempt, and disgust and from failure in one's own or others' eyes. Shame thus begins with the experience of one's spontaneous expression of core self-experience being ignored. Children feel shame when no one pays attention to their efforts at exhibiting their prowess or when parents ignore or belittle children's emotional excitement at their success. When children excitedly yell, "Mommy! Daddy! Look at me!" as they stand on a diving board ready to jump into a swimming pool, and their parents ignore them, they will shrink away in shame (Kohut, 1977). As children grow into adolescence and adulthood, shame arises when they reveal their emotions to another person and do not receive validation or attention. When, for example, one is telling a story to a group, there is a shrinking away inside when one suddenly realizes that no one is listening.

Partners' capacity for intimacy is damaged severely by shame. Revealing a core aspect of self to one's intimate partner, even if it is a salutary aspect of self, leaves one vulnerable to being ignored or judged. If it is a vulnerable or damaged part of self that is being revealed, it is doubly dangerous. To experience intimacy, partners must be able to approach each other and must also be willing to be approached. They must allow themselves to communicate their excitement in connecting. In that process, they open themselves to each other and become vulnerable. Vulnerability is an opening of the self in union with another. For vulnerability to occur in safety, without shame, the partner being empathic must follow it. If the other also becomes vulnerable, the experience for both is completed and leads to deepened intimacy. When individuals are able to mutually unburden themselves of their shame and be vulnerable with each other, this shared experience can produce a tie that binds forever. However, when shame remains impermeable, unexpressed, and unshared, then intimacy is prevented.

Shame differs from guilt; when people feel guilty, they want to repair whatever wrong they did and seek a solution to the problem. However, when they are filled with shame, they just feel like crawling into a hole and dying. The hiding response characteristic of shame is captured in the expression "losing face." Thus, the shame response reduces facial communication as people drop their eyes and their upper body shrinks away and collapses. People in shame also experience blushing, pounding of the heart, and awareness of themselves; blushing increases the sense of looking publicly foolish or inferior.

Repeated lack of attunement from caregivers in childhood leaves adults vulnerable to feeling unworthy, inadequate, inferior, and defective whenever they are exposed to the slightest criticism or lack of recognition. They may also project their internalized inner critic onto the other and experience their partner as condemning them. To avoid these painful feelings, they often resort to dominance or to withdrawal, leading to feelings of isolation in both partners in the relationship.

The aversive nature of shame also leads some people to disavow parts of themselves, leaving them prone to projecting these parts onto their partner and then devaluing their partner as they were once devalued. For example, narcissistically vulnerable partners often induce shame in their partners to avoid their own painful feelings of shame. They need to feel superior to avoid feeling inadequate. Attacking or criticizing a partner can also be defenses to protect against awareness of normal longings for validation that were unmet and then experienced as inherently bad.

A variety of interactional scripts also develop to protect against shame (Kaufman, 1989). The dominance–power cycle described in chapter 8 is often used as a defense against shame. People often dominate others to maintain feelings of superiority and to bolster self-esteem. This protection against shame often manifests in sexual relations (Kaufman, 1989). For example, one woman had to control all aspects of sexual intimacy with her partner to avoid feeling exposed and vulnerable. Her partner at first enjoyed her dominance but later felt that the rigidity of the script was preventing real closeness from developing. Similarly, a gay man who needed to defend against intense feelings of shame found that the only type of intimacy he could tolerate was through sex with anonymous partners. Another man saddled with shame over needing intimacy had a number of affairs during his marriage to avoid feeling dependent on any one person.

Shame-bound individuals may be particularly vulnerable to being drawn into and staying in abusive relationships, feeling they deserve whatever punishment they are receiving. However, their shame often becomes coupled with rage over time. The experience of helplessness and victimization is disowned to escape the agony of being shamed. As they fiercely defend against the feeling of shame with anger, they are unaware that it is their underlying sense of worthlessness that both keeps them in the abusive relationship and results in their feelings of rage. It should be noted, however, that not all shame is maladaptive. In the sections that follow, we discuss the differences between adaptive and maladaptive shame, as well as further distinguish shame from guilt.

VARIETIES OF SHAME

Work with shame is central to working with identity issues. Identifying which type of shame is occurring aids different kinds of interventions. Different types of shame are described in the sections that follow.

Adaptive Shame

Adaptive shame helps people maintain acceptance in a group to which they belong by ensuring that they not alienate themselves by acting outside the group's norms. Shame can be an adaptive emotion if it is in response to violations of implicit or explicit personal standards and values, such as shame at engaging in deviant behavior; public loss of control; or having betrayed, injured, or abused a spouse. In these situations, feelings of shame need to be acknowledged, because they provide the individual with valuable information about socially acceptable behavior that one might choose to use as a guide to one's conduct. Adaptive shame informs people that they either are too exposed and other people are not supporting their actions, have broken a very basic social norm, or have violated standards or values that they recognize as deeply important. Shame thus can be adaptive because it simultaneously protects one's privacy while keeping one connected to one's community.

Shame also serves the important function of appeasing observers of social transgressions, evoking responses in observers that lead to forgiveness and reconciliation, and helping to reestablish social harmony that is inevitably disrupted following moral or rule violations (Keltner & Harter, 1998). Submissiveness is at the core of shame, which involves the sense of being both small and inferior as well as appeasement displays of gaze aversion and dropping of the head. Appeasement analyses indicate that shame evokes affiliative responses in others and brings about reconciliation (Keltner & Harter, 1998). In couples, when one partner has injured the other, such as by having an affair, expression of shame by the injurer or betrayer was found to be helpful in healing betrayals and injuries (Greenberg, Warwar, & Malcom, in press). If the betrayed partner sees that the betrayer is truly ashamed of what he or she did and is truly remorseful, he or she is more likely to forgive. The expression of shame here is adaptive, helps rebuild trust, and promotes forgiveness.

Shame, as we have said, needs to be distinguished from guilt. Although they are similar, shame is a core or fundamental emotion that concerns one's worth, status, or value as a person, whereas guilt is a more complex state that involves learned judgments about particular actions or behaviors. The action tendency in guilt is seeking atonement for wrongdoing, whereas in shame, it is to withdraw or hide. Hiding ensures that one's flaws and personal failures are not exposed. Findings in a study that examined the relationship of shame and guilt to constructive versus destructive anger also indicated that shame and guilt are distinct affective processes with strikingly different implications for anger-related intentions and behaviors (Tangney, Miller, Flicker, & Barlow, 1996). Shame often leads to destructive anger, whereas guilt does not.

Primary Maladaptive Shame

There is an important difference between shame as an adaptive emotional response to violating a reasonable social norm and shame that is experienced as a core sense of one's self as worthless or unacceptably flawed. When the contempt and disgust of significant others is internalized and directed at the self, feelings of maladaptive shame are generated intrapsychically. People who were emotionally, physically, or sexually abused or treated with contempt as children have internalized a sense of themselves as dirty, unlovable, or worthless. They learn to treat themselves the way they were treated by significant others, that is, with hostile self-blame and contempt, and this produces intense feelings of worthlessness and shame. The problem state or dysfunction also comes from the sense that the person him- or herself was responsible for a shameful act over which he or she had no control (in the case of sexual abuse) or somehow deserved the abuse and brought it on the self. Other forms of maltreatment that emanate from social rejection because of, for instance, race/ethnicity, poverty, disability, or gender, also can damage a person's identity and result in a core sense of one's self as flawed or inferior.

Internalized shame also occurs through child-rearing practices that teach children that certain feelings, desires, and behaviors are unacceptable. Shaming is a common child-rearing practice in the West, and to a certain extent, all people in the West are damaged by it. For example, boys typically are shamed for showing weakness and girls are shamed for not being relational or for being too assertive or sexual. Children's adaptive shame pulls them back from exposing those parts of themselves that are judged as unacceptable. Through repetition or even an intense single experience of being belittled or viewed with contempt, shame becomes internalized such that those feelings and behaviors that were scorned automatically evoke feelings of shame, whether or not the other is present. Furthermore, these internalized shaming messages can generalize from specific feelings and behaviors to condemnation of the entire self or core aspects of the self. Views of one's self as flawed, stupid, lazy, incompetent, or selfish often are based on early shaming experiences. If these are activated in a relationship, they lead to strong withdrawal, not for fear of closeness but for fear of diminishment. Partners who feel worthless are also unable to ask for support or assert their needs, because they feel so undeserving and unentitled.

Body shame is a major source of maladaptive shame and can affect intimacy. Evidence associates a positive body self-concept with protection from anxiety in sexual interactions (Goldenberg, McCoy, Pyszczynski, Greenberg, & Solomon, 2000). Because sexual interactions simultaneously expose many private aspects of the self, negative regard for one's body will most likely interfere with deeply intimate sexual interactions. The human body has been a source of shame for some time, especially in Western culture. The degree to which the body becomes directly associated with shame varies from culture to culture and has also changed over centuries. Shame has multiple sources; the image by which we are shamed is often cultural, but the transmission of shame occurs through the family and the peer group. Body shame stems most strongly from the period of adolescence, a time of universal vulnerability to shame, especially because of the uncontrollable ways that bodies are changing at this time.

Because of society's influence, girls appear more open to shame than boys, even at an early stage of development (Lewis, 1971). Girls, however, are allowed to show their shame in their interactions, yet boys are forced to conceal it. Many men experience themselves as failing to live up to masculine gender stereotypes. Whether it be internalized demands for toughness, competitiveness, or sexual performance, the gap between the ideal masculine self and the real masculine self is a potent shame generator. Men are reluctant to seek help on their own and often go into therapy only when they are pressured by their partner, because they are afraid of their shortfalls and their sense of shame. Often this is not in awareness. Men think that showing their weaknesses will lead to being put down, humiliated, or taken advantage of, which is why they are less likely to open up to their female partners. Traditional male subculture disinclines men from normalizing and facing shameful experiences through talking and connecting with others. Instead, it tends to reward and promote action, compulsive behavior, drinking, fighting, and the like.

When shame is not faced and dealt with, it often erupts as rage, dominance, and control. Internalized shame and being shame bound, as opposed to normal feelings of shame that do not threaten identity, can make some men prone to violence within marriage and intimate relationships, especially when coupled with male socialization patterns of needing to be in control. Rage and withdrawal are defensive actions caused by shame, and substance abuse is a maladaptive coping mechanism for dealing with shame.

The emotions of contempt and disgust play a central role in generating feelings of maladaptive shame. Contempt and disgust are directed at an object that is viewed as offensive or unworthy. Disgust is a function of being too close to an indigestible object and involves a desire to expel the offensive substance. It can be thought of as an aspect of distaste, which occurs when one tastes something disagreeable (Tomkins, 1963), as discussed in chapter 8 of this volume, but it is not limited to rejecting offensive tastes and smells. Disgust is felt in relation to anything viewed as offensive or dirty, including thoughts, values, and people. Thus people show disgust with, for example, laziness, stupidity, sexual activities, and ideas.

Contempt, however, as also discussed in chapter 8 of this volume, comes from "dissmell," which occurs in response to a foul odor (Tomkins, 1963). It entails rejection that is haughty and superior. The person raises their upper lip, pulls away his or her head and nose, and looks down on the other. This gives the face a look of arrogance, the perpetual critic in the presence of an offensive odor. Contempt and disgust, when directed at another for violation, serve the same adaptive function as anger, that is, they promote separation and boundary definition. However, when internalized and directed at the self, they produce maladaptive feelings of shame and self-loathing.

SECONDARY SHAME

Shame often coexists with anxiety in a complex sequence of feelings and cognitions. Secondary shame about internal experience is one example of this relationship. Specifically, one can be ashamed of particular emotional experiences, such as feeling hurt, weak, or needy, sexual, and angry, and feeling fearful that these experiences will emerge. This leads to an inability to express one's feelings or needs. This type of shame is often similar to avoidance of weakness and vulnerability because of fear. Intervention involves exploring partners' beliefs about what experience is acceptable and empathic affirmation from partners and the therapist to help tolerate the shame and face the disavowed experience. Shame that blocks acknowledgement of what one feels often blocks the partners from becoming intimate. Instrumental forms of shame, such as feigning embarrassment so as to appear socially appropriate, are not forms of shame that are prevalent in couples therapy.

TREATING SHAME IN COUPLES

Empathic attunement to emotion is the most general and fundamental principle of all emotion-focused intervention and is particularly important with shame. The first part of addressing shame in the process of couples therapy generally is to name the feelings of inadequacy, humiliation, or shame and empathize with it. Then, the therapist needs to identify the workings of shame in the system, including how each partner exhibits and experiences it; the origins of shame in their families of origin; and their individual and couples shame cycles. Next is recognition of the partner's protective defenses against shame. It is at this time that tracking the moments of shame in each partner that rapidly go underground becomes important, for instance, when one partner laughs embarrassedly when being corrected by the other partner. Finally, the time comes for active interruption of shame cycles, both within and outside of therapy. Each partner has to learn how to identify shame-related behavior in self and other and how to modify his or her conduct. When a person acknowledges shame, his or her feelings of worthlessness and inferiority are all too painful and obvious in therapy. However, when shame is unacknowledged because it is too threatening to a fragile ego or to self-esteem, a lot of work is required to acknowledge the shame underlying the more overt signs, such as contempt or dominance. Unacknowledged shame or narcissistic vulnerability is commonly observed in dominant partners and partners with problems of substance abuse, obsessiveness, and perfectionism, or in those with the grandiosity and bravado of narcissistic personality. Although these behavioral styles may protect against experiencing feelings of self-loathing and inferiority, they become maladaptive and interfere with couples functioning.

The literature on the treatment of shame in couples is sparse. Feelings of shame, or the attempts to avoid such feelings, are at the root of much relationship discord. In one study, shame was found to be one of the variables that significantly predicted distress at marital therapy onset (Horak, 2003). Another study discovered a negative correlation between shame and attachment (Bray, 2002).

Escalating shame most frequently occurs when partners get into mixed attachment–identity negative cycles. When a shame-based partner feels inadequate and withdraws, the pursuer wants more contact and reassurance and the escalation of pursuit and withdraw begins. An important element of this cycle is the fact that both partners often feel shame for their respective feelings or needs. The pursuer may feel rejected and shamed for "wanting too much," whereas the withdrawer may feel shame for either being inadequate or wanting more space. What is clear, however, is that each person feels criticized and invalidated (shamed) by the other, each not realizing that both are having the same experience of shame.

Overall, the first goal of emotion-focused couples therapy (EFT-C) interventions to counteract shame is the development of a supportive, empathically attuned relationship with each partner and with the relationship. The focus then shifts to helping the partner or partners recognize and overcome avoidance to their shame to acknowledge the painful feelings. Empathic responses such as "just wanting to hide," "feeling so wretched and small," and "humiliated and wanting to just disappear" are interventions that help clients bring alive, and stay in touch with, their experiences of shame, embarrassment, and humiliation. Helping partners symbolize these previously inchoate feelings in the immediacy of the session, as they occur, helps to make them more manageable. Rather than being controlled by the shame, people can begin to control the shame. The partner's compassion and understanding, then, is key in this transformation process by providing new interpersonal experiences of validation. Once the shame is regulated and the person feels validated by empathic mirroring of the therapist and compassion from the partner, the therapist may also work to promote self-soothing.

Evoking Shame

To get the partners in a couple to understand what they are truly feeling, the therapist often evokes childhood memories that bring out the vulnerable feelings of shame. The therapist thus focuses on the past if it helps activate core shame that allows the client to get a better grip on the here and now. Evoking memories that access maladaptive shame allows the client to have the important feelings right in the therapy. Paying attention to the client's nonverbal expressions, such as dropping of the eyes, is helpful to get at primary feelings. The therapist works toward the clients understanding and expressing their needs, goals, or intentions associated with shame, usually a need for acceptance and validation. With shame, it is often important to have the partner give validation before the shame-based partner can ask for it. Shame-based partners need a lived new emotional experience of validation to help transform their shame.

Feelings such as "feeling inadequate in response to mother always being dissatisfied with me" or "feeling unrecognized in response to my father never once praising me" will be activated by current interactions with a partner. Evocation of emotion schematic memories of past shame by a current situation is one of the most frequent sources of experiencing unregulated, maladaptive shame in adulthood. This often occurs in intimate relationships. Current interactions then reactivate memories of original scenes, long forgotten, and prompt the return to awareness of these old feelings. For example, even well-intentioned and affectionate teasing by present-day friends or partners may activate a core scheme of childhood humiliation and cause a person to reexperience deeply embedded shame. In a relationship in which a partner usually feels secure and trusting, this sudden and unexpected exposure can be very disorganizing.

For example, Jacob found himself feeling tremendously humiliated and angry at his wife and friends, who all started laughing at him lightheartedly one day for being such a "baby" about being afraid of getting an immunization for an upcoming trip to India. This had reactivated shame from an experience of school kids all laughing at him for being such a "baby" when he was 5 years old because he cried when there were no more cookies left for him at a class party. Activating each other's core shame-based vulnerabilities is inevitable in long-term couples relationships. As people spend more time together and grow more intimately connected, however secure or trusting the relationship may be, they eventually will evoke the other's shame. When core shame schemes are activated, they invade the present interaction, and if people become trapped in these maladaptive states and reexperience the feeling with all the original affect fully reawakened, they reenact the scene, but now with the person who currently activated the scheme. This leads to yelling or withdrawing and to puzzling conflict.

To alleviate these shame-based interactions, partners must become fully aware of their core shame and learn how to distinguish past from present. They also need to learn what triggers their shame and how to soothe their shame and regulate their anger at their partners in response to their shame. It is also important for partners to be aware of their partners' triggers, to avoid activating them, and to learn how to help soothe their partners' shame once it is activated. These are the best ways to sidestep automatically activating past shame schemes and being caught up in the ensuing emotional storm. Past small shaming traumatic scenes cannot be eliminated, but they can be transformed, first, by making them conscious; then by learning to recognize them with increasing skill; and finally, by changing one's emotional response to them by evoking new adaptive emotions, often empowered anger or pride.

For example, a wife says to her husband on his return from supermarket shopping, as he is bringing in the groceries, "Did you remember to get the tissue?" This casual question activates an unexpected affective reaction. The husband, already tired from shopping, snaps and becomes suddenly enraged, feeling his competence is being called into question. He experiences shame, which rapidly turns into rage. The wife was not criticizing or questioning his judgment, she was simply asking whether the husband had bought something she needed. After a few of these repeated scenes, the couple in therapy explored what was going on and the husband realized that his reaction came from his childhood, in which he recalled his parent never trusting him, accusing him of never remembering anything, and punishing him when he forgot things. This had felt so humiliating and unfair to him. He realized that this was why he invariably shouted at his wife when she asked him whether he had remembered to buy things. The shame-based scheme of his childhood had been reactivated and had invaded their interaction.

This shame was worked on by directing the husband's rage at his imagined parents. In the session, with his wife observing, he expressed his shame and hurt to them and then his longing for a more understanding response. She responded compassionately with empathic affirmation of how awful that must have been and affirmed that she saw him as reliable and competent. He then affirmed himself and was able, in imagination, to take his parents' perspective, and as them in imagination, say they were proud of him for his accomplishments, something the client had always wished for but never actually heard them say. The husband was then able to receive his parents' pride in him, as though they were really there, and his eyes filled with tears. This changed his emotional response in this situation to his parents. He felt pride where before he felt shame, and he felt sad where before he felt angry. His wife, witnessing all this, was moved to tears and felt compassion and understanding toward her husband.

Resolving his unfinished business (Greenberg, Rice, & Elliott, 1993) in this way allowed the husband to then deal emotionally with his current interaction with his wife in a new way. He was more able to soothe himself and not respond automatically with anger. The couple also developed new ways of handling the returning-from-the-supermarket interaction. The husband was less reactive, but they also changed their interaction so as not to trigger him. Either he told her or she asked him, more generally, what he had bought, rather than question specifically whether he, for example, bought tissue.

Shame in the Interaction

Shame is best handled by being approached and acknowledged and having the self validated. Partners need to be helped to recognize, rather than deny, their partners' feeling of shame, and never try to fix it. Rather, they need to let their partners know that they recognize their shame and see how badly they feel. They need to be compassionate and understanding. When a partner's body shame erupts, his or her spouse must first allow the shame to be given full expression for it to be ultimately faced and soothed. This is not an easy task. Tolerating someone else's shame demands patience and a willingness to be uncomfortable. This is true for therapists as well as spouses. The best approach is to try to enter the partner's experience by imagining one's self inside the other's shoes. For a moment, one partner needs to be encouraged to try to feel what it's like to actually be the other partner. They also need to listen to their partners' feelings of shame and to allow those feelings to be expressed fully. Shame is best healed through internalizing new empathic experiences.

Sometimes, partners unwittingly activate their partners' shame when they attempt to fix it by saying "no big deal" or by telling their partners that they are too sensitive. When one's partner's shame has been triggered by something a partner (or therapist) has said or done, it is important not to deny one's part in what happened. Instead, it is important for the shamers to admit whatever mistakes they might have made—which, in turn, requires them to be able to tolerate their own shame, which often is what makes apologizing so difficult. When people can tolerate their shame, they can more freely admit mistakes. The most important thing is for one partner to be able to own his or her own part in triggering shame in his or her partner. Although it's very challenging, he or she needs to be prepared to accept and absorb his or her partner's anger in response to having been shamed by him or her. When partners can say something such as "I know you're angry now, and you're right, but I hope you will end up forgiving me," the others' feelings are acknowledged without rushing them to "get over it" and they show the desire to stay connected.

Because a sense of one's self as inadequate, worthless, or defective can make people vulnerable to momentary feelings of shame, it is important in therapy for the therapist to track interactions closely for when a partner might be feeling shamed. Momentary shame about diminishment or loss of self-esteem is not necessarily the same as a core identity shame and can occur in any partner at any time in response to either the partner or the therapist. Laughter often is an indicator of the brushing off of shame but hides a source of potential difficulty in a couple. When one spouse refers to another as incompetent, unable to be intimate or talk about feelings, irrational, or too emotional, these criticisms often cut to the core. They produce shame in the partner. The couples therapist must constantly monitor communication to the therapist, as well as the couple's communication to each other, for signs of shame.

Therapists constantly need to be attuned and respond to nonverbal indicators of the emergence of shame-related experience. These indicators include downcast eyes, squirming or writhing in the seat, and laughter or shrugging off that serves to cover embarrassment. Empathic affirmations, such as, "It's hard, maybe, feeling somehow foolish talking about this," open the door for further exploration. Interventions aimed at acknowledging shame that is on the periphery of awareness require particular sensitivity on the part of the therapist. They involve, first, recognition of surface reactions that cover shame, such as cockiness, bravado at bad feelings, narcissistic anger, perfectionism, or other types of obsessiveness, and then, empathic conjecture about the underlying experience. These are phrased tentatively, on the basis of knowledge of the client, and are used only after a firm bond is established. An example of an empathic response to the shame underlying a client's social anxiety is, "Almost like, if they saw you for who you really are, they'd reject you." A response to bravado about rejection might be, "I hear the determination in your voice, like there's this part of you that puts on a brave front to fight against this other part that feels kind of insignificant."

For many clients, seeking psychotherapy is itself a shame-inducing experience; they feel humiliated to ask for help and to admit that their life is out of control. Clients may begin a session by saying how they had to talk themselves into coming, by joking about "hating" being there, by talking about how they feel "reduced to paying for help," or by giving any number of subtle indications that it is somehow degrading to be in therapy. Immediacy in attending to this reluctance is essential to establishing the therapeutic bond. Interventions—such as "It's embarrassing to talk about such private things" or "It's hard to ask for help, feel a bit like a child"—validate and open up the struggle for exploration.

Shame anxiety is another important problem that often is not easily distinguishable from feelings of vulnerability based on fear. This is anxiety about revealing internal experience for fear of being judged. At these moments of shame anxiety, interventions that attempt to change or interpret the person's protective processes act to invalidate what the person is feeling and intensify the innate action tendency to withdraw. The best intervention at these times is empathic attunement, support, and affirmation of the need to protect one's self. Thus, a therapist might say, "You are so afraid to show how bad you feel for fear your partner will see you as flawed, but look how concerned she is as you talk about this." Provision of safety and empathic affirmation of vulnerability reduces interpersonal anxiety and allows people to risk revealing themselves. This reduces isolation and allows the hidden aspects of self to be accessed, explored, and exposed to new disconfirming experience in the therapy session. However, once the intense vulnerability has passed and the person feels confident that their experience is accepted, exploration and transformation of shame experience also need to occur at a later stage.

Obvious and frequently occurring markers of interactional shame-related processes are explicit critical statements, such as spouses calling their partners "stupid," "lazy," or "bad." Therapist responses need to highlight the affective quality of contempt and disgust in the invalidating partners' tones of voice, the arrogant tilt of their heads, or the snarls or curls of their lips, and then, most important, how it must feel to be the recipient of such contempt. For example, when one partner constantly berates the other partner for not living up to expectations, the therapist can respond, "Sometimes your partner must feel that you really don't like him or her very much . . . it must be very painful for both of you to be feeling all this pain."

Work with shame in couples therapy differs from work in individual therapy. Compassion and acceptance from a partner are the relational antidotes to shame. In couples therapy, the first step is for a partner's shame to be heard—if not initially by the other partner, then by the therapist. The goal, ultimately, is to have the partner provide the affirming voice. Couples thus are encouraged both in and out of therapy to use shame as a signal to have a conversation about the state of the relationship. Such a conversation may be initiated by one asking questions such as "Is everything okay between us?" or "Did I say or do something wrong?" Statements such as "My feelings just got hurt" or "I'm feeling invalidated right now" can also start a conversation. Unfortunately, the painful experience of shame is so unbearable that instead of using it as an impetus to communicate, shame is often bypassed or avoided.

Intrapsychic work to promote self-soothing and self-support comes only later in couples therapy if shame persists after partner affirmation. Then, interventions such as "How can you soothe that part that feels so bad?" or "Breathe and see whether you can comfort that part of yourself, and what does that part need?" help promote self-soothing and expose the shame to new experience, thereby restructuring the maladaptive shame scheme. Awareness of the need to be validated within the shame often mobilizes a person's healthy strengths and resources, such as self-compassion, self-respect, and pride, which help the individual counteract shame experiences and construct new meaning of shameful experiences (see Greenberg, 2002a).

In individual EFT, work with individuals' internalized shame involves the therapist both providing empathic affirmation of the person's vulnerability and helping the person turn the contempt for the self into acceptance and self-soothing (Greenberg, 2002a; Greenberg & Paivio, 1997a). This work requires considerable trust, for clients have to reveal what they consider to be their deepest flaws, what is "wrong" with them, and those parts of the self of which they are most ashamed. Therapists need to reduce client's shame anxiety by empathically affirming vulnerability and by promoting self-acceptance. This helps to create new meaning and compassion for the self. The process of transformation also involves accessing the contempt and disgust directed at self, along with the painful reaction of the self to this harshly negative self-evaluation (see Greenberg & Paivio, 1997a, 1997b; Greenberg & Watson, 2006). In this way, the person's awareness of agency in producing shame feelings is heightened, and the adaptive tendency to protect the self spontaneously emerges as a reaction to the contempt and negative evaluations and acts to challenge the shaming messages. These more self-affirming voices are strongly supported. Clients then begin to reevaluate and become less harsh in their judgments of themselves. They become more self-accepting and self-soothing and develop the strength to reject the negative evaluations and counteract the contempt with pride. Both anger at being violated and compassion for the self are the self-soothing antidotes to shame.

Overcoming projected and/or internalized shame often becomes one of the central foci of work in individual therapy, but work on shame also may become a central focus in couples once the negative cycle has de-escalated. Through corrective emotional experiences with one's partner in couples therapy, a person's good self and other representations will ultimately come to outweigh the bad, allowing for the integration within the self of all good and all bad. This helps to gain realistic self-acceptance of a less than perfect, but good enough, self and relationship. In addition, intimacy and connection, the revealing of one's self to another and being accepted, is an antidote to shame. Couples therapy thus works to transform shame and replace it with acceptance and connection.

INFLUENCE CYCLES

Shame is the major underlying emotion pervading the influence cycle. In a pure influence cycle, either the dominant partner or the submitter can experience shame. In a mixed affiliation–influence cycle, the withdrawer generally feels shame once the pursuer begins criticizing, but usually the pursuer is not shame based. The main goal in working with shame in couples therapy is helping partners face, soothe, and transform the maladaptive shame, in self and other, that drives the negative cycles.

Dominant's Shame

Shame anxiety is often the emotion that is organizing the dominant partner's position as he or she fears diminishment or loss of esteem or status. Dominant partners assert their dominance to regulate their own negative affect—especially to regulate shame. Maintaining the one-up position is essential to regulating their self-esteem and protecting their identity. They often use rationality to prove they are right. Often, it is as though the lives of the dominant partners depend on their being right. If their definition of reality is proved wrong, their identity is threatened and they feel tremendously at risk. This form of dominance often arises when one partner needs another partner to bolster his or her self-esteem, compensate for perceived deficits in the self, or make up for past diminishment or humiliation. The dominant partners' whole sense of self depends on defining reality or winning if there is any dispute. This is the only way they know how to feel good. Perfectionists usually fall in this category. This often leads to competitiveness between partners, with the less dominant always trying to prove their worth but losing in the end and feeling inferior. Shame thus arises most often in dominant partners when their identity is threatened, and dominance is an attempt to regulate shame.

In identity-based dominance cycles, the dominant partners carry on in what is normal discourse for the couple, always proving their point, and their partners defer but end up feeling silently defeated and resentful or inadequate. When challenged, the dominant partners, to stave off feeling shame at diminishment, exert their dominance more actively by becoming more highly rational and insistent and then angry or contemptuous. Dominant partners often may have entered in the relationships in a helping or teaching role. They initially might tend to the other's anxiety or teach them about life, feelings, sex, or anything in which they are able to be in the superior role. As long as their view of reality prevails, all is apparently smooth, but if the other challenges, then sparks fly. It is important to dominant partners' self-esteem that they feel superior to their spouses, but as we have said, this builds in an inherent sense of competition in the relationship, with the dominant spouses always needing to prove they are one-up or right.

"I'm Right," or "I Am Only Valuable if I'm Right"

In an example of how complex dominance–shame can become central in couples conflict we will continue to look at the therapy with Heather and Brian, which was discussed in chapter 10, on anger. This excerpt comes from a session earlier than the one discussed in chapter 10 and demonstrates that issues are dealt with repeatedly over the course of therapy at differing degrees of intensity. This episode is a precursor to the more confrontive episode in chapter 10. Heather had come to therapy, initially, for her depression. She had described herself as feeling overwhelmed and unable to juggle all the balls of being homemaker, worker, mother, and wife. She also felt that her husband was critical of her, saying that she was not much fun and not that interested in sex, certainly not as much as he was, and she reported that there was a lot of marital conflict. Brian came in willingly, and it was clear early on that they were locked into a cycle of him pursuing her for sex and for her to be more fun, and her feeling pressured and distancing and becoming depressed. After some work on this cycle, it became apparent, however, that in his quiet way, Brian was very dominant. He defined reality, and she deferred but felt very trapped and inadequate. He defined her as being like a sergeant major and as not able to have fun, and he kept saying, "All I want is for things to be simple and peaceful." In dominance cycles, both partners often define the other as the controlling one. The issue for the therapist is to identify the core identity struggle and see who appears to be defining reality and who is responding to that definition. The dominance issue often is in the domain of struggles over definitions of identity rather than simply over who will do what. Here, Brian defines Heather's requests or demands as controlling, and it is around this definition that the real dominance struggles die.

In the next transcript, the therapist works with Brian's dominance. Brian, who doesn't like to make the children do their homework, defines his more laissez-faire way as "dancing" and defines his wife as "sergeant major," who wants them to march to her drummer. In this segment, the therapist reframes his view of being controlled as coming from a threat to his identity.

"Just Joking"

> Therapist: Something is making it difficult for you to hear what she wants you to hear, and it raises a lot of anxiety or threats, or something, for you?
>
> Brian: I don't know, it is not clear, but it might be, it might mean or, maybe, a lack of acceptance of who I am, you know, because I am saying that this getting-the-kids-to-do-the-homework thing again, that there are times when I will forget, and I am reading into your position, you're saying, um, either "You have got to change or you can't be like that, or you shouldn't be like that, or it is bad to be like that."
>
> Heather: I am not saying that.
>
> Brian: Well, I am reading into it, that is what I am feeling maybe. And no, maybe, maybe, um, I shouldn't be dancing so much, or maybe I should be marching maybe, you know . . .
>
> Therapist: Mm-hm.
>
> Heather: I don't want to march.
>
> Brian: I feel like you've got the drum, you know. . . .
>
> Therapist: Mm-hm.
>
> Brian: . . . and you are setting the rhythm, and you know, I mean, I will write a song about the capitals [*referring to teaching their children about capitals*], I want to dance and to get things done the same way, you know, and, mm, not march.
>
> Therapist: I think you do feel that she has got the drum . . .

Brian: Mm-hm.

Therapist: . . . and somehow when that comes up, then you do all kinds of interesting things, which end up in telling her she is just so complicated, and then, and then you say just "just be simple," don't sweat the small stuff. But really it seems something more threatening is happening for you . . .

Brian: Mm-hm.

Therapist: . . . that somehow you will be shaped or organized or forced to be someway that is not really "me," . . .

Brian: Mm-hm.

Therapist: . . . so you are ending up feeling quite controlled and, or potentially organized, you are trying to protect your sense of just who you are, so you sort of define her in a way that is leaving her feel very powerless. That is not your intention. Your intention is to survive as "you." But the more you kind of don't hear her, and tell her essentially that she's too stressed and complicated, the more she actually feels powerless and unheard, but she gets very angry that the homework doesn't get done unless she steps in. And then because she is active, she tends not to withdraw, she comes back with further and further effort to get your cooperation, and this is her attempted solution, you feel more and more controlled, and counter with defining her as not simple and too stressed. You try harder to show her she's wrong, but for you, somehow, it is, like, a sense of maybe, I don't know, feeling threatened or, like, your way isn't valued, that your way and you is being invalidated. [*Reframes the negative cycle in terms of him feeling threatened.*]

Brian: Mm-hm, that is our parental song and dance. My song and dance was feeling invalidated, and hers was not being heard, you know, being shouted at, being controlled that way.

Heather: Being criticized.

Therapist: Yeah, yeah, and I mean, you know, as we are able to sort of put the words to it between you, I mean, it fits your experience and it fits what I see, I mean, I see this stuff. I see you being active, and I see you [*to Brian*] trying to move around there to maintain something, for fear of losing your position, and [*to Heather*] the more he does that, the more criticized you feel, and you don't tend to withdraw, you know. I imagine, like you said, that sometimes you withdraw . . .

Heather: Mm-hm.

Therapist: . . . and you give up . . .

Heather: Mm-hm.

Therapist: . . . and you feel hopeless but you also come back. You try so hard, and you [*to Brian*] tend to move to ideals, "This is how we should do it, this is how it should be, 'be simple.'" [*to Heather*] That just makes you feel less and less heard, and so we go around, right. But there is something about him feeling so invalidated, that his view is going to mean nothing here, right, . . .

Heather: Mm-hm.

Therapist: . . . and there is something [*to Brian*] about her feeling criticized and invalidated. And you know that is not what each of you is thinking when you are doing your thing.

Brian: Yeah.

Therapist: . . . You are just thinking, "I want to be able to be me. . . . "

Brian: Mm-hm.

Therapist: . . . you are just feeling, like, "I just want to be able to be me," or you know, "I want to be heard." You are not thinking he feels diminished . . .

Brian: Mm-hm.

Therapist: . . . and you are not thinking she feels invalidated. . . .

Brian: Mm-hm, yeah.

Therapist: . . . Somehow until we start helping you each appreciate each other, you know what I mean, when you see her tears, I think, it must impact you at some level that she does feel invalidated. . . .

Brian: Mm-hm.

Therapist: . . . right, that is good, I think you do see that. It is harder sometimes for you [*to Heather*] to understand the feelings he has around feeling not in control, the anxiety, and I guess feeling not important or his self is threatened. [*Defines the cycle and some underlying identity protection motivations.*]

Heather: I can feel it, . . .

Therapist: Yeah.

Heather: . . . I definitely feel it. On Saturday night when we were talking, I could feel physically this bolt receding in the distance. We were talking, I felt, whether it was on the energy level or not, I just felt you leaving, you know.

Therapist: [*to Brian*] You had a pretty scary learning with your mother about losing yourself or needing to pull away in order to maintain yourself and not be controlled. . . .

Brian: Mm-hm.

Therapist: . . . I mean it really gets quite scary for you I imagine . . .

Brian: Mm-hm.

A few minutes later, the therapist works to unbalance the system by labeling Brian's hostility and helping him to be aware of his unacknowledged anger and to name it. This challenge helps Heather to begin to be more assertive.

Therapist: When she comes on strong, the more you, Brian, put your hands up with such intensity, the more she feels invalidated.

Heather: Yeah. It's like I feel just shut down.

Therapist: [*to Brian*] You are passionate when you make your statements.

Brian: That is not the kind of passion I want though [*sarcastically*].

Therapist: That is a little dig there. [*Labels his veiled hostility.*]

Brian: I was making a little joke.

Therapist: I think your joke comes from a source in you of hurt and anger, and she feels that she feels that, and it stings.

Heather: That hurts. I am thinking, "See, I have passion in me, I can be different." That's a dig.

Therapist: Brian, you never give up, you peck here and then there, and that is affecting; every time you do that, you push her away and she doesn't feel open to you.

Brian: Just joking.

Therapist: Your joking comes from a deep place that is expressing you, and you are experienced as that person.

Heather: I won't let you get off the hook this time.

Therapist: What is the most important is that it has an impact, the impact is not achieving what you want. You try to touch it lightly, but it comes from your hurt and anger, that light joking thing, naming that again and again and really recognizing it is important because these comments are affecting your relationship deeply.

Later the therapist turns to Heather to support her, label her underlying feelings, and encourage her to express herself.

Therapist: Something happens in you, and you feel deeply unsupported; I don't know exactly what, why. You have all those pressures, you juggle all these balls, there is something in you that feels unsupported. There is a piece of you that often you feel unappreciated and invalidated. [*Empathizes with feeling.*]

Brian: Is that your mom? Your dad not validating, not appreciating?

Heather: My dad was always a super responsible person, overresponsible, you are very different in that way . . . I am wondering whether I am matching up to mom.

Therapist: But there is something for you in this relationship that's important.

Heather: It is not from mummy and daddy alone. I think in a way it does, I feel invalidated because the things I have identified as important, like the kids' piano, it is important, and that's okay, I have aimed to please my whole life, please the teachers, please the parents, it is an anxiousness.

Therapist: You get anxious, that is why you need things done, but then you feel unsupported. He has to understand and hear more about the anxiety that drives you. He sees you as the sergeant major, nobody loves the sergeant major; he does not see the frightened girl inside who is trying to get approval. [*Identifies underlying feeling.*]

Heather: I feel like, yeah, that is not speaking to the sergeant major, that is speaking to the deeper me.

In the transcripts of another couple (see the next section), Richard, an engineer, had been feeling suicidal, trapped in work, and trapped in his marriage with Sharon. After seeing the husband for one session, the therapist clearly saw that the marital problem seemed to be producing his feeling of being trapped much more than the work situation, which seemed to have a solution. It appeared as though he felt he could not assert himself at all in his marriage. The couple had been in therapy 4 years before and had had a good alliance with their therapist. In this segment, we see first the husband come out of his submissive position, and toward the end, we see the wife access the shame that drives her dominance.

World Wrestling Federation Wrestling Babe

This excerpt starts with the therapist framing the husband's withdrawal as relational.

Therapist: Okay, let's just stop—we have one clear thing, is that you withdraw.

Richard: Yes.

Therapist: And . . . you end up feeling so mad that you want out. So the puzzle now is, do you withdraw because you've got a withdrawal mechanism in you, or do you withdraw because she turned the key on, in that mechanism, because you do have a mechanism in you?

Richard:	Yeah.
Therapist:	And so that's in both your hands, right? So that, on the one hand, it's, I mean, yeah, it would be great if you wouldn't withdraw and would stand up.

The therapist and clients later identify and discuss aspects of the dominance–submissive cycle.

Therapist:	So you are more active, you—but that's how you learned to sort of, cope with that, between you two . . .
Sharon:	Yeah.
Therapist:	. . . it involves both of you—it's, you know, this is not that other couples don't have to deal with this, there's usually one who's more . . . dominant, more controlling, quicker, faster, and there's one who's more . . . withdrawn or quieter. So I mean, it's like you've got to negotiate, but you've both got to be very clear . . .
Sharon:	Uh-hmm.
Richard:	Uh-mm.
Therapist:	. . . this parallels what we talked about last time, when you said you talk, talk, talk, and you actually do that to try to get him engaged.
Sharon:	I do . . .
Therapist:	Right.
Sharon:	. . . it's my way of trying to draw him out, there's a number of reasons why I do it, and I don't always want to do it, I don't always like doing it. Sometimes I wish I could be quieter [*laughs*]—and I have been, since we've had that . . .
Richard:	But you, you . . . gave, you know that, I tend to, speak slower . . .
Sharon:	[*Sighs deeply.*]
Richard:	. . . take longer time to think about things, pause between my thoughts, um—because that's just the way, my mind works.
Sharon:	I'm much more aware now of his pauses and how he needs time to think, and I have to—though the voice in my head goes to jump in, and I go "errarr," and it's like, I have to . . .
Therapist:	Uh-hmm.
Sharon:	. . . consciously, shut my mouth and let him finish. Because . . . just the house that I grew up in, everybody talked, at the top of their lungs and a mile-a-minute, "blah blah blah." To be heard, you always had to [*Snaps fingers four times.*] jump in and say what you needed to say . . .

Therapist: Uh-hmm.

Sharon: . . . because otherwise you just were, you were, no, you didn't get heard . . .

Therapist: Uh-hmm.

Sharon: . . . it's just the environment I grew up in—it's hard, it's a, it's a habit, it's . . .

The therapist brings the discussion back to a recent interaction in the room, again identifies their pattern, and now accesses her underlying feelings of shame.

Therapist: Right, but you know, it also comes, ultimately, I mean if we just go back, I can't remember the actual word that you said, but then you said, "Do I always have to agree with you? . . ."

Sharon: Umm, uh-hmmm.

Therapist: . . . what, what were you saying to her? Do you remember it was, y–, a while ago?

Sharon: About the household.

Therapist: If I make a decision around the children or something like that . . .

Richard: Yeah.

Therapist: . . . immediately you came back with, "Do I always have to agree with you?" Right?

Sharon: Well isn't, is . . . that is a valid, uh, question, because I . . .

Therapist: But then let's look at what's really happening.

Sharon: . . . okay.

Therapist: Right, he's saying, he's criticizing or . . . making a . . . complaint, right, he's saying, "You don't listen to me when I make a suggestion," right? That's the essence of what he's saying, now, if you were just a listener, you would say, "Oh, tell me more, about when that happens," right? Because this is embedded, in a history . . .

Sharon: Uh-mm.

Therapist: . . . and, my belief is, you know, and we're a bit away from it, but is you actually feel wrongly or unfairly criticized—then, you come back, with a defense, which is an attack, actually, you say, "Do I always have to agree with you?" very quickly. . . .

Sharon: Uh-mm.

Therapist:	. . . but actually you must be feeling wronged, or kind of, you know, you, you must feel hurt, I think, when he says that.
Sharon:	When he says . . .
Therapist:	When he says, "You don't always listen, you don't, you don't ever listen to me when I make a suggestion," you know, there was the essence of what he said . . .
Sharon:	. . . uh-hmm, uh-hmm.
Therapist:	. . . and you must actually feel . . .
Sharon:	[Sighs deeply.]
Therapist:	. . . sort of hurt.
Sharon:	Umm, um, I really, remember he says that I really do try and . . . examine . . . do I really do that?
Therapist:	But do you see that your comeback was, "Do I always have to agree with you?" I mean, that's like a debating comeback . . .
Sharon:	[laughs]
Therapist:	. . . right, to win the argument . . .
Sharon:	Uh-mm.
Therapist:	. . . but what I'm trying to say is, you see, you're very quick [Snaps fingers four times.] . . .
Sharon:	Uh-mm.
Therapist:	. . . but I'm saying, there's something else going on in you that you're not yet, really, paying attention to, right . . .
Sharon:	Uh-mm.
Therapist:	. . . and that is, you know, you're doing so much responding to criticism from him, it must hurt! . . .
Sharon:	Yeah.
Therapist:	. . . when he criticizes or when he says, "You're not doing this."
Sharon:	It does, it, it's, it's a, it's a whole 16 years of criticism.
Therapist:	Right. Built on top of a mother of criticism, right?
Sharon:	Yes, that's why I have a lonely child . . .
Therapist:	Yeah.
Sharon:	. . . [laughs] [in reference to her underlying feeling from the previous couples therapy] . . .
Therapist:	But a, a street kid, who comes back a legal street kid . . .

Sharon:	. . . uh-hmm.
Therapist:	. . . with very good defenses—right . . .
Sharon:	Uh-mm.
Therapist:	. . . automatic.
Sharon:	It's definitely a reflex—yes . . .
Therapist:	Yeah.
Sharon:	Yes.
Therapist:	But so somehow [*snaps fingers four times*] a lot of this is leading him to . . . feel, submissive to your dominance . . .
Sharon:	Uh-hmm, uh-hmm.
Therapist:	. . . somehow, underneath your very active dominant person is something else, which is actually feeling hurt, a fear of being mistreated, or a feeling of being not okay, not seen, misunderstood, but that's not what comes out, what comes out . . .
Sharon:	Uh-mm.
Therapist:	. . . is a kind of, uh, attacking, defense . . .
Sharon:	Uh-hmm.
Therapist:	. . . you know. I mean, those are strong words but, you know, what . . .
Sharon:	Yeah, yeah.
Therapist:	. . . comes out is a more active coping style . . .
Sharon:	Yeah.
Therapist:	. . . where you're sort of putting him on the defense then, and then he withdraws, right? [*Identifies the primary feelings of invalidation obscured by the more attacking style.*]
Sharon:	This is all a, a, a repeat with my relationship with my mother, really . . .
Therapist:	Yeah.
Sharon:	. . . very much so, 'cause she always criticized me, terribly, and I would . . . have to go on the defensive, to protect myself. So I guess that reflex is there [*snaps fingers*] whenever I feel he's criticizing me, the little voice inside me goes, "No, you're okay, defend yourself," and it, and I just "errrhm" because that's just, I had to with my mother . . .
Therapist:	Right. She was just a force to be reckoned with.

Sharon:	You, you couldn't be mealymouthed around her, right? Couldn't say, "I'm sorry," couldn't, you, you know, say, "You are hurting my feelings," you had to just, stand up and yell.
Therapist:	Yeah I understand. [*Empathic understanding.*]
Sharon:	So it's, that's how I had to be.
Therapist:	So, but the voice that says, "No, you're okay . . ."
Sharon:	Uh-mm.
Therapist:	. . . is a response to another kind of part that feels . . . "I'm being unfairly criticized," or, you know, I mean, it's complicated, I don't quite know what. But if you really slow down, felt very safe . . .
Sharon:	Uh-hmm.
Therapist:	. . . and I'm going to say this, with apologies to Richard, right. He's been putting you through hell—and it hurts . . .
Sharon:	Uh-hmm.
Therapist:	. . . and I mean he's telling you he's very unhappy, he wants to leave, he can't take you. That hurts like hell. [*Heightens to access feeling.*]
Sharon:	Yes right, and—I'm not going to cry today . . . [*laughs*]
Therapist:	[*laughs*] Because?
Sharon:	[*Breathes deeply.*] . . . It, it's just been a lifetime of hurt . . . people . . . [*sad voice*] basically telling me I'm no good, that's what I figure [*crying*] . . .
Therapist:	Right.
Sharon:	. . . my mother—for years and years and years, basically, you know, telling me, "One day you'll have a daughter as different from you as you are from me and then you'll understand" [*Breathes deeply.*] . . .
Therapist:	Yeah.
Sharon:	. . . well, I was different, but what was wrong with being different?
Therapist:	"I want to be lov–, accepted just for me." [*Empathic exploration.*]
Sharon:	For me, but there, it was always conditions, with my mother, same thing, had to jump through hoops, had to meet her guidelines in order to be accepted, love was withheld, unless I was, what she saw as her perfect daughter.
Therapist:	And you have replicated that here.

Sharon:	But that's, it's kind of replicated itself in a way.
Therapist:	Yeah, yeah, yeah, yeah, I understand.
Sharon:	You know, it's the same.
Therapist:	And unless both of you, . . .
Sharon:	[*Breathes deeply.*]
Therapist:	. . . are ready for that path . . .
Sharon:	Yeah.
Therapist:	. . . you'll just continue.
Sharon:	I know.
Therapist:	Right, so actually, you need to be able to show him how much it hurts—how much you hurt, how bad you feel inside, like "I'm not okay as I am, kind of, like, not good enough." [*Encourages revealing underlying feeling of shame.*]
Sharon:	[*Sighs deeply.*] . . . I don't know if he can accept me [*laughs*].
Therapist:	Uh-hmm. Can you . . . look at him? . . .
Sharon:	[*Sighs deeply.*]
Therapist:	. . . I mean it's a very tough place, right, to feel, "I don't think you can accept me . . ."
Sharon:	[*Breathes deeply.*]
Therapist:	. . . it's, there's s– s– [*deep breath*], but really, inside, it's like, "I really need you to, I want you, to, accept me as I am." [*Attempts to promote enactment to create contact.*]
Sharon:	Yes! And . . . doesn't, everyone want that?
Therapist:	Yeah, yeah, and "I want you to still be able to hold my vulnerable part and not criticize me, . . ."
Sharon:	Uh-hmm, right.
Therapist:	. . . that's the paradox . . .
Sharon:	[*laughs*]
Therapist:	. . . he's sort of saying, "When you are vulnerable, I can hold you."
Sharon:	Yeah, so when he . . .
Richard:	But I also feel . . .
Therapist:	Yeah.

Richard:	. . . when she's in that state, that vulnerable state, I can also feel that I can talk to her about, what's bothering me without her attacking me . . .
Therapist:	Uh-hmm.
Richard:	. . . like, she seems, to me, I, she feels, I, I feel that she's, she's vulnerable.
Therapist:	Lets you in.
Sharon:	Accessible.
Richard:	And accessible and, and . . .
Therapist:	So what will come back will be not so much of a defensive, kind of, uh, statement from her that puts you in the defense, right?
Richard:	. . . yeah, it's more of a, a, an open dialogue where we can get to the root of the problem. Maybe it's got nothing to do with her at all . . .
Therapist:	Uh-hmm.
Richard:	. . . it's something to do with me, but I'm not seeing it clearly— I don't know—but if it's, if I'm given a chance to, to talk.
Sharon:	[*Breathes deeply.*] I know what the pattern is. [*Sighs deeply.*]
Therapist:	Uh-hmm.
Sharon:	. . . I know what the pattern is, I think . . .
Therapist:	Okay.
Sharon:	. . . Um, when he wants to talk to me, my first reaction is [*sucking breath*], "He's going to criticize me again, he's going to . . .
Therapist:	Right.
Sharon:	. . . attack me again. He's going to talk about something I did wrong or something he doesn't like, or he's going to want to change another part of me, he's going want me to . . ." [*Breathes deeply.*] and I immediately [*snaps fingers*], almost . . .
Therapist:	Right.
Sharon:	. . . always, just that, "Whoop!" that wall goes up . . .
Therapist:	Right.
Sharon:	. . . "Okay, he's going to criticize me, hurt me, again." It's, hard to, it's no, it, it's, I immediately go into that, reflex mode . . .
Therapist:	Right.
Sharon:	. . . it's so easy, to bamboozle him . . .

Therapist:	Right, right.
Sharon:	. . . I can throw him [*snaps fingers*] off track so fast, and I don't mean to do it, I just . . .
Therapist:	Uh-mm.
Sharon:	. . . I've learned it. [*Newly symbolizes internal experience in aware-ness.*]
Therapist:	Yeah, I understand. That's what we've been talking about.
Sharon:	I've learned it, it's survival for me . . .
Therapist:	Yeah.
Sharon:	. . . I've learned it with my mother . . .
Therapist:	Yeah.
Sharon:	. . . I had to do it . . .
Therapist:	Yeah, yes.
Sharon:	. . . in my family I grew up in a family that said, "Sharon, you'd be a great lawyer." It's funny you used that analogy . . .
Therapist:	Uh-hmm.
Sharon:	. . . [*snaps fingers*] because I'm just so quick, and I know—it—I get his head spinning, and I know it . . .
Therapist:	Yeah.
Sharon:	. . . And it, it's just [*weak voice*] because I'm so afraid he's going to tell me I'm not okay—not good enough.
Richard:	I hate that . . .
Sharon:	I know.
Richard:	. . . words.
Sharon:	I know, I know [*laughs*] . . .
Therapist:	Right, right.
Sharon:	. . . and that's the pattern, it's like we [*laughs*]—that's what I do, that's my part in it.
Therapist:	Right, right, right, and I think to the degree that you can begin to do something different at that point. Let him see the feeling, criticized or hurt, rather than this . . . protective barrier that bamboozles him. He doesn't really see the real you, who feels so invalidated, and he hates the defensive, protective you, but it's not really you, it's like you're not really giving him a chance—now I understand that you feel scared as hell of being invali-dated . . .

Sharon: [*Breathes deeply.*]

Therapist: . . . like, "if I show him the real me, I don't think he'll actually accept me, love me, and accept me." [*Suggests disclosing underlying feeling.*]

Submissive Shame

At core, submitters often feel inadequate, worthless, or not good enough. They may have internalized shame from their past that makes them feel undeserving or they learned that they need to placate or please to be valued. When dominated, the submitter does not feel respected, and this eventually turns to anger. Submissive men often talk about feeling incompetent or inadequate or feeling like a failure. In women, shame in the submitter is often more tinged with a helpless sense of dependent inadequacy. The core feeling, however, is the shame of being unable, not good enough, or inferior to one's partner.

For example, Shelly came to therapy on her own, tearful and depressed, saying she had headaches, felt unhappy, was not interested in sex, and that her husband was angry at her and did not seem to support her. It appeared from what she said that if she ever tried to express her point of view, he put her down. Seeing the husband alone, to balance the alliance by getting his point of view, served to consolidate a view of a strongly dominant man and a dependent, submissive woman. The husband took the position of telling the therapist what was wrong with his wife, that she just was not able to cope, that she was often thoughtless, and that her work in the media did not require her to think things through, whereas he, working in industry, had to be on top of things. It was as though he was talking about a child. He was an orphan who had built himself up into a no-nonsense executive, whereas she had been a middle daughter seeking approval. Right from the start, it became clear that she would look to him for direction, which he freely gave, but if she disagreed, he swiftly corrected her. She would deflate and give in, but end up withdrawing.

Because intimate partners have provided each other with private information about themselves, they are very vulnerable to being hurt by each other. Intimate relationship partners risk being hurt in two ways. In the short term, they risk that the partner may show indifference or lack of responsiveness creating an attachment injury. In the longer term, however, partners may create identity injuries by misusing personal, private information they have learned about one another as weapons of criticism, attack, invalidation, or coercion during conflict. What is destructive about these conflict behaviors is that they attack the partner's identity. For example, knowing that one's partner may feel unattractive or has had past humiliations and then attacking these results in lasting identity injuries. The injured partner then feels doubly wounded and withdraws. For example, when Lorne, knowing his wife's difficulties in feeling competent, felt lonely, he would criticize his wife for not earning enough money and relying on him, and he would accuse her of being lazy. She would doubt herself, and this left her powerless and ashamed.

In one couple, Jan had recently had a very unsatisfying affair, which her husband, Timothy, had discovered. They came into therapy with the goal of understanding why she had the affair. He said he needed to know why, as did she, so it could be fixed and so that he could trust that it would not happen again. What was dealt with first was having him directly express his anger at her and helping her to hear it. Then the therapist helped her to express an authentic apology and express shame for what she had done to him by having the affair. After this, the affair was understood in terms of the marital couple's prior negative interactional cycle. She had always felt he was better than her. A feeling of inferiority and guilt began in her childhood but was perpetuated in her marriage by him always controlling and criticizing her. She said she lived in guilt with him constantly on her shoulder watching over her, a feeling she also had with her mother. She felt not good enough and unlovable and essentially sought validation outside the marriage. This backfired, and the relationship affair left her again feeling criticized and maltreated. The husband's anxious insecurity, a feeling of not being "man enough," had produced in him a jealous insecurity and a deep feeling of being undesired. This had led him to be controlling and critical.

AFFILIATION CYCLES

Shame is not the underlying emotion in pure attachment cycles, but to the degree that the cycle contains elements of control or attacks on identity and threats to self-esteem, shame will be activated. Shame, however, is prevalent in the mixed cycle in which the pursuer pressures for closeness or criticize and the partner withdraws out of a shame-based sense of inadequacy. Here, the withdrawer is involved in an identity-protection strategy, not an attachment fear.

Pursuer's Shame

Shame is not highly prevalent in pursuers who are motivated more by a need for closeness and by fear of abandonment, but some primary shame can be activated if they begin to feel the distancer does not care about them because they are flawed. This could activate any sense they may have of not being good enough. Some secondary shame also can arise in pursuers if they are shamed by their partners for being too needy, especially if they had been shamed as children for being too dependent. This may lead them to hide their needs for closeness and prevent their loneliness from becoming the focus.

Distancer's Shame

When distancers, who have less need for closeness or are less emotionally available, are criticized by their partners for being like a stone, incapable of love, afraid of intimacy, or frigid, it is their identity that is threatened. They feel inadequate, and their shame response is activated. In work with withdrawer shame, the therapist needs to encourage the partners pursuing for closeness to stop the criticism and rather to reveal their loneliness. The pursuer needs to be encouraged to respond to the withdrawer in a more validating manner and reassure that they will not diminish, invalidate, or look down on them. The therapist, however, must also work with the shameful partners to help them face the shame and transform it. When shame anxiety is the issue, with partners who anticipate potentially feeling embarrassed, humiliated, or mortified if they reveal core aspects of self-experience, the therapist needs first to engage their partners to help them reduce their sense of shame by soothing or even celebrating the person in their more vulnerable states. Ultimately, however, withdrawers who feel inadequate need to be helped to face their own shame and be able to self-soothe so that they are able to be present to their partners' pain of abandonment.

"I Withdraw Because I Feel Inadequate"

Jen and Dean came to therapy because they felt their problems had become intolerable, and although they did not want to split up, they were afraid things were headed in that direction. They had a 2-year-old daughter and both were feeling overwhelmed by the responsibility and that the other was not doing enough. They were fighting often and felt very hopeless about things changing. When they fought, they described how Jen often got angry and exploded and Dean would withdraw. In fact, they had developed nicknames for each other. He was "robot man" and she was "volcano head." As they told their story, it was revealed that she had had an affair 7 years ago while in their relationship. Although Dean said he had felt hurt and betrayed by this, he did not describe it as an unresolved injury that he could not get past and said it was in the past. She talked about how lonely and deserted she had felt at the time, and they both agreed her affair was a call for attention from him. In the fourth session, she was describing how impossible she felt it was for her to get access to him emotionally and although she loved him very much, he was just a "man with walls." When she began to repeat this, the therapist turned to Dean and asked him how he felt about her saying that "he is just a man with walls." With some empathic conjecturing, the therapist was able to help him identify that he in fact felt inadequate. The therapist asked him to turn to his partner and say this. He did, saying that when she talked about him like that, he felt frozen and somehow inadequate, as if he had failed her.

In the following excerpt, Dean, after being guided to attend to his immediate response to Jen's pursuit and criticism of his availability, reveals that he feels he is letting her down and feels inadequate. This is a mixed cycle in which Jen is lonely and pursuing for closeness but also is dominant, defining reality, whereas Dean feels inadequate and is engaged in protecting his identity. The excerpt begins with Jen talking about her frustration.

Jen: I just want a loving and close relationship, we have never had that in our marriage, ever, there were times when we almost attained it and then lost it again. He, as much as I love him dearly, he has walls all around him, and he is very difficult to get close to.

Therapist: That touches this deep place in you, which is "I feel lonely, I want you, and I need you to be closer." [*Attempts to help Jen focus on her primary attachment feeling.*]

Jen: I know that I need certain things from him. I know that he is able to give it to me because in the past he has been able to periodically give it to me. [*Follows the focus.*]

Therapist: So what happens to you when she says she is lonely and she needs closeness and she says you have all kinds of walls? So what happens to you inside? [*Turns to her husband to get his reaction. Focuses him internally.*]

Dean: How do I feel?

Therapist: Yes. What happens inside in your body as you sit and listen to that? What do you feel, and what does this make you think? [*Focuses on his amygdala-based immediate response.*]

Dean: When she tells me that at that time, I feel that she wants, that I have let her down because I haven't been good enough.

Therapist: You feel you have failed, that you are inadequate. [*Reflects his primary identity feeling.*]

Dean: Right, that she is now demanding more from me, and I don't know whether I can give.

Therapist: Tell her what you feel, that you feel inadequate, or like a failure? [*Puts his primary feeling in contact with her.*]

Dean: When you tell me that you are lonely and tell me that you want more closeness, it makes me feel like I have let you down and that I, that I failed, and then I feel inadequate.

Jen: I feel that I can't express anything without him going, without him feeling that I am criticizing him, but I am just . . . [*Feels unresponded to, and reacts with a counterdefense.*]

Therapist: So now we got to the real dilemma, what we have got is two very different people with very different needs, and each one actually is legitimate and valid. How do you not invalidate each other? And somehow his withdrawal invalidates you by not giving you what you need, and he says that you overreact, and you are very sensitive when he says that. And when you say that he has walls around him and "You don't give me what I want," this invalidates him, makes him feel inadequate, and he is very sensitive to that. How do we resolve it? How do you two resolve this? [*States the dilemma.*]

The distancer in a mixed identity–attachment cycle can also be experiencing core shame in the form of unresolved trauma at violation or denigration. In fact, when one member has been humiliated, severely abused, or scorned in denigrating ways in the past, it is typical to feel defective and to be afraid of intimacy. As we discussed in the chapter on fear (chap. 12), when one member of the couple has been severely traumatized in the past, he or she tends to withdraw, hiding or covering him- or herself in an attempt to hide the felt deficit. In addition, having body shame; feeling one is ugly, unattractive, or disgusting; or having been treated like garbage or having felt rotten inside because of sickness, such as cancer or infertility, all lead to withdrawal. A partner may have such internalized shame that he or she cannot bear the possibility of coming out, of being open and vulnerable, and of again being found defective or unacceptable. This is a highly stressful mode of functioning for both the individual and the partner. Pursuing partners, as they feel more rejected, inevitably begin to be critical, and this then produces further shame in the withdrawer. Thus, increasing awareness of how the pursuer's criticism or blame pushes the partner away is important. The major work with the shamed person, however, involves identifying the shame and its source and helping the person face it, express it to the partner, and receive a corrective emotional experience from the empathic responsiveness of the partner.

Shame also can appear as a secondary emotion in the withdrawer that prevents or defends against a more primary emotion such as sadness or fear. Distancers may, for example, feel sad or lonely or fear rejection but feel ashamed of what they see as their weakness and, feeling they should be strong, may hide their need for connection. Here, secondary shame related to identity prevents attachment needs from being met. Often, it is only the naming of this powerful source of shame-based avoidance and the fear of destabilization that gets men to begin talking about their feelings and needs, rather than reacting to them by hiding, clamping down, or acting out, and fleeing treatment. For example, Ben, whose brother had been sexually abused as a child by a hockey coach and had recently committed suicide, came to therapy with his wife. He had reacted to his brother's suicide with anxiety, depression, and grief, and the couple separated, at his request, for him to get his head sorted out. He viewed himself as a tough, athletic man and had strong values that he should be strong and provide and protect his family. He could not handle his reaction to his brother's suicide and saw himself as falling apart. He reported that he was depressed and anxious and felt he could not cope and said he just felt numb and did not know whether he loved his wife any more.

It soon became clear that Ben's brother's suicide precipitated in him a memory of his own sexual abuse as a child by a neighbor, and he was extremely anxious that this would drive him crazy and, like his brother, he would commit suicide. He could not tell his wife what was going on inside, as he felt ashamed that the abuse might mean he was contaminated or gay and not a man, and he began to withdraw and feel numb. His shame about his anxiety and about his not being able to cope was preventing him from talking about both his fear that he would go crazy and his more primary shame about the abuse. Helping him in some individual sessions to talk about the abuse incident and, more important, his fear that it would make him crazy was followed by having him reveal the abuse to his wife, whose soothing responses helped unfreeze him, and he began to again reconnect with his wife.

CONCLUSION

In working with shame, the EFT-C therapist needs to do different things at different times, depending on the nature of the shame and what the therapist deems necessary in the moment. When one partner is avoiding his or her own internalized shame, the therapist will help this person face the shame so that he or she can begin to process and transform it. When, however, the shame is due to humiliation by the partner, then the shame and the shaming process needs to be named and the interaction changed to reduce the invalidation and shaming. Transformation of shame is dependent on two factors, the empathic affirmation of another person who disconfirms pathogenic beliefs about the self and the ability of the self to access internal emotional resources to counteract the shame. In couples therapy, transformation of maladaptive shame occurs both through work on the couples relationship and through work with the individual to develop self-soothing and to transform shame. To overcome shame that interferes with self-acceptance, people first have to come out of hiding. However, one of the difficulties in changing shame is the difficulty in accessing the emotion scheme generating it, because of the powerful tendency to hide. Emotion-focused interventions are needed to help clients acknowledge and fully experience shame, humiliation, and embarrassment in the session, rather than avoid it, so that the shame can be exposed to belief-disconfirming experiences with their partners. Clients will learn that if they reveal their self-viewed flaws and shortcomings, they will not be judged as fundamentally worthless or defective, as they had feared they would be. Many clients report that the most helpful and healing aspect of treatment involved revealing their vulnerable, disorganized, and hidden aspects of self and having these received by their partner, most important, and then by the therapist. The experience of simply being seen, heard, and accepted, despite one's feelings of unworthiness and desperation, is highly affirming. The partner has a new interpersonal learning and internalizes the partner's acceptance, which enhances his or her capacity to accept him- or herself. In addition, regrettable behaviors can be acknowledged as mistakes without treating these as destroying the person's entire self-worth.

In addition to discussing shaming experiences from the past, explorations focus on how the partner or the therapist may have shamed the client in the session by misunderstanding or missing something important. Thus, immediacy in attending to how shame may be generated by the partner's or therapist's action is another important aspect of shame work. Inquiries into whether a partner or the therapist has unwittingly shamed the client by not being attuned to the client's feelings or by failing to support when support was needed are important. Healing these types of ruptures in the relationship and correcting current misunderstandings can be highly therapeutic and, again, can provide a new interpersonal learning. In these situations, an understanding, supportive relationship is not a precondition to further work with shame but is the essence of the treatment itself.

14

POSITIVE EMOTION
IN COUPLES THERAPY

Hope is the thing with feathers
That perches in the soul
And sings the song—without the words
And never stops—at all.
                                    —Emily Dickinson

Recently, there has been a groundswell of interest in positive emotions and a growing awareness of their importance in promoting psychological health and well-being (Frederickson, 1998; Seligman, 2002). The pleasant emotions play a unique, enlivening role in human experience and coupling and have been crucial in the struggle to survive and grow. They have often been overlooked or underemphasized in relation to the unpleasant or negative emotions because of the latter's more evident and powerful impact on survival and adaptation. The pleasant emotions, particularly those emotions related to curiosity, affection, and social connection, are crucial, however, for survival and adaptation in that they connect the organism with the world and with others. Pleasant emotions, in addition, are rewarding and have motivational effects that are independent of both drive reduction and the relief from reduction of negative emotions. They also enhance relationships, problem solving, and learning. People connect more easily, get along better with each other, and perform better on tasks when they feel interested and happy. Positive emotions can also be helpful in transforming negative emotions. For example, the positive emotions of interest–excitement and happiness–joy help people transform sadness.

A frequent complaint among couples seeking therapy is the absence, or diminishment, of joy and interest in their relationship, leaving them feeling flat, alone, and alienated. The pleasant emotions act as a type of barometer of the strength of the couples bond. As Gottman (1999) showed, in satisfying relationships, partners experience 5 times more positive than negative emotions. Therapy needs to support and nurture the development of more frequent good-quality positive emotions.

Therapists need constantly to recognize, support, and nurture the development and expression of positive emotions for several reasons. Positive emotional experiences such as love and joy and interest are independent sources of affiliative motivation that help relationships flourish. The importance of love in coupling is obvious; love involves openness to, and concern for, the other. Joy and interest promote connection; they activate and guide approach and exploratory behavior to seek out the new and assimilate it into the familiar. With their exploratory, stimulus-seeking functions, joy and interest therefore are an engine of growth and development and lead to paying attention to, and involvement with, one's partner. The experience of positive emotions builds a reservoir of good feeling that helps people deal with negative feelings, as a storehouse of positive feelings helps override and transform negative feelings when they do arise.

The building of positive experience between couples is very helpful, and a reservoir of positive experience with one's partner is one of the best forms of insurance against negative feelings escalating into conflict. A backlog of positive feelings helps one attenuate negative feelings when they arise. This backlog is like having money in the bank in that when negative feelings such as anger, sadness, shame, or fear arise, it is like making a withdrawal that does not leave one in a deficit situation. One then still has a positive sentiment toward one's partner, and conflict is easier to resolve because one feels more loving, compassionate, and forgiving. If, however, one has no positive feelings in the bank, a withdrawal takes one into a negative state, and conflict is much harder to resolve.

The positive emotions, however, often appear as the result of other changes. Once people connect with and validate each other, they begin to feel more positive. Given that the pleasant emotions are often the sought-after goals of treatment, when they emerge on a consistent basis, it is often a sign that therapy is drawing to a close.

In this chapter, we first review the emotions of love and then look at the emotions of happiness–joy and excitement–interest. The last of these, excitement–interest, is often not thought of as an emotion but rather simply as an index of arousal associated with a variety of emotional states. Along with other emotion theorists (e.g., Tomkins, 1963),we argue that interest is in fact one of the most fundamental emotions, that it is highly prevalent in human relationships, and that it is most necessary in helping these relationships thrive. It is also important to note that there is a very strong reciprocal relationship between excitement and joy in that a person can enjoy excitement and be excited by enjoyment. The interrelatedness of these two emotions is so prevalent that we treat them together when looking at therapeutic intervention to activate them for their effects on curiosity and connectedness.

LOVE, AFFECTION, AND CARING

Love is fundamental to human nature. It definitely appears as though it is a part of human's biological heritage. It appears universally in some form, and romantic love—although it is claimed by some historians to be a recent social invention of the French court—has been documented since the time of Adam and Eve. Love and marriage, however, have not always gone together like a horse and carriage, and it was only in the 1700s and 1800s that they became associated (Coontz, 2005). There are a number of ways in which love differs from the other discrete emotions. Some see it as a drive rather than an emotion (Fisher, 2004). Although love appears to be basic and fundamental, it differs from sadness or joy, which have identifiable expressions, more specific feeling states, and patterns of actions. Love is more complex than the other basic emotions and may involve patterns of emotions, cognitions, and drives rather than being a unitary phenomenon. There is no single definition of love, probably because there are several types of love, each with different types of connotations. As we have seen, a distinction is readily made among romantic or passionate love, companionate or attachment love and lust (Fisher, 2004). Then, there is mother love, father love, sibling love, friendship love, and platonic love. All differ and are unique in their own way.

Love, in the most general sense, is an emotion that connects people to others and is a response to what people value most highly. To a large degree, love derives from the experience of joyous excitement in interaction or involvement with another. It is, however, a special type of joy. It involves taking delight in the person whom one loves and finding fulfillment and pleasure in being in contact with the other. Love also seems to involve an expansion of the self. In making contact with another, people become not only more whole and more integrated but also expand, incorporating aspects of the other into the self and developing new skills, attitudes, and resources and a greater ability to survive and grow. People experience the loved person as a source of fulfillment for important psychological needs. Aron and colleagues (2005) argued that this expansion of the self in love happens very rapidly and appears to be one of the most exhilarating experiences people have. Receptive affective experiences of feeling seen, loved, or understood also arise as a result of the intersubjective experiences of feeling known. Having the sense of existing in the heart and mind of the other as one's self and of being the recipient of the other's empathy, care, help, or compassion makes one feel loved.

Love also commonly refers to an enduring feeling in a complex relationship rather than a momentary emotional state. Perhaps the feelings of love arise from affective intermixtures of strivings for sexual gratifications, maternal nurturance, alleviation of separation distress, and friendly playfulness, embedded in and combined with the specifics of unique lives. However, *love*, as a momentary experience, also refers to a fleeting feeling, such as momentary affection that comes and goes. When people feel loved, they experience momentary states of bliss and joy, generally feel accepted and understood, and enjoy a sense of union; they also feel safe; secure; and, often, more self-confident. Passionate love involves an intense longing for connection or union with the loved person and often results in joy and fulfilment; as well as being filled with excitement and longing, it is also fraught with anxiety, despair, loneliness, and intense fear. Companionate love is far less intense than passionate love but involves commitment and closeness. Love has been viewed as a form of adult attachment, rooted in childhood experiences of attachment, and therefore as subject to some of the same processes that occur in childhood experiences of attachment, separation, and loss. In our view, however, attachment is based on security and fear and is not the same as the emotion of love. Without attachment, however, people would not feel the safety needed to maintain a loving relationship.

The first neuroscientists to study passionate love (using functional magnetic resonance imaging [fMRI] brain imaging techniques) concluded that passionate love was mental chaos (Birbaumer & Öhman, 1993). More recently, Bartels and Zeki (2000, 2004) also used fMRI techniques to determine what brain regions were associated with passionate love. They put up posters that advertised for men and women who were "truly, deeply, and madly in love." Seventy young men and women from 11 countries and several ethnic groups responded; all scored high on a scale measuring passionate love. Bartels and Zeki gave each of 17 subjects a photograph of the beloved to gaze at, alternating the beloved's picture with friends with whom the subject was not in love. They found that passion sparked increased activity in the brain areas associated with euphoria and reward, and decreased levels of activity in the areas associated with sadness, anxiety, and fear. Most of the regions that were activated during the experience of romantic love had previously been shown to be active while people were under the influence of euphoria-inducing drugs such as opiates or cocaine. Apparently, both passionate love and those drugs activate a "blissed-out" state in the brain, as well as an area that becomes active when people view sexually arousing material. The authors thus found passionate love and sexual arousal to be tightly linked. This makes sense because passionate love and sexual desire are generally thought to be closely related.

Bartels and Zeki (2004) also found that the regions in which activity decreased during the experience of love were areas of the brain controlling critical thought and the experience of painful emotions. They thus argued that once people get close to someone, there is less likelihood that they will critically assess the loved one's character and personality. In this sense, then, love may indeed be blind. They concluded that love uses a push–pull mechanism that overcomes social distance by deactivating networks used for critical social assessment and negative emotions, while it bonds individuals through the involvement of the reward circuitry, providing love with the power to motivate and exhilarate.

Romantic love involves having an emotional bond to someone for whom one yearns, as well as having sensory stimulation that one desires (Komisaruk & Whipple, 1998). The word *love* derives etymologically from words meaning "desire," "yearning," and "satisfaction" and shares a common root with *libido* (Onions, 1966). Thus, the psychological sense of love can be interpreted as referring to the satisfaction of a yearning, which may be associated with the obtaining of certain sensory stimulation. Love, therefore, possesses a close connection not only with reward and pleasure phenomena but also with appetitive and addictive behaviors. However, as a relationship deepens, the brain scans in the previously mentioned studies suggest the neural activity associated with romantic love alters slightly and in some cases primes areas deep in the primitive brain that are involved in long-term attachment. The research on the brain in love helps explain why love produces such disparate emotions, from euphoria to anger to anxiety, and why it seems to become even more intense when it is withdrawn. People in the throes of romantic love often are overwhelmed, out of control, and irrational, and when rejected, some people contemplate stalking, homicide, and suicide. This drive for romantic love can be stronger than the will to live.

In another study of students who were in the 1st weeks or months of new love, Fisher Aron, Mashek, and Brown (2002) used magnetic resonance imaging to scan these participants' brains while they looked at a picture of their beloved and found that a passion-related region was activated in the brain. This area was found to be on the opposite side of the brain from the area that registers physical attractiveness. The passion-related area appeared to be involved in longing, desire, and the inexplicable tug that people feel toward one person among many attractive alternative partners. This distinction between finding someone attractive and desiring him or her, between liking and wanting, is all happening in an area of the mammalian brain that takes care of most basic functions, such as eating, drinking, and eye movements. This is all at an unconscious level, so it is very basic and not under rational control. They also found that the intoxication of new love mellows and changes with time. Differences were found in the group of smitten lovers and were based on how long the participants had been in the relationships. Compared with the students who were in the 1st weeks of a new love, those who had been paired off for a year or more showed significantly more activity in an area of the brain linked to long-term commitment than to passion.

Social constructivism advocates emphasize, however, that love, like all emotions, still is a cultural construct. Russell (1997) gave the example of different cultures defining different types of love and regarding them as different emotions. For example, the Utku (indigenous Canadian Inuit) distinguish *niviuq* (i.e., the romantic feeling between lovers) from *naklik* (i.e., love for a baby or a small animal, or God's love for humanity). Some cultures do not even have a concept of "love." There thus clearly are love concepts (i.e., social constructions) as well as natural social-emotional types of love (based on basic processes), and love involves many component psychological processes. In a series of social psychological studies, Aron and Aron (1997), for example, found that among other processes, new love involves psychologically internalizing a lover; absorbing elements of the other person's opinions, hobbies, expressions, and character; and sharing one's own.

ACTION TENDENCY

The emotion of love entails the action tendency to make some form of contact with the loved one and a disposition to evaluate the other positively and as profoundly important for one's well-being. In romantic love, the tendency is an urge for intimacy and physical affection from the loved one, including concern, warmth, tenderness, and sexual contact. There is a strong desire to touch and be touched. This is also the case in parent–child relationships, and clients often feel profoundly sad and doubt that their parents love them when they have been deprived of physical contact, including hugs. Common complaints are "He never hugged me" or "She never liked to cuddle with me." It seems it is difficult to truly feel loved without this physical contact. In platonic love or liking, there is a desire for social and personal intimacy, and although it is nonsexual, it still involves interest, warmth, and concern for the other.

Researchers have attempted, with some success, to pinpoint facial expressions involved with love and have found that people may be able to distinguish them from those of other primary emotions (Ekman & Davidson, 1994). Exactly how people do this is not yet clear, but it may be that the face takes on the look of mothers happily, tenderly gazing at their infants. As they gaze downward at the infant, the face softens with a slight tender smile on the lips. Love, in addition, has characteristic postural and auditory features. The postures and gestures involve kissing, caressing, embracing, cradling, rocking, and nuzzling infants and adults alike, as well as making cooing or crooning sounds. In tenderness, breathing is regular and slow, whereas in erotic passion, it is uneven and more intense, with the mouth being relaxed and open.

ACCESSING LOVE IN COUPLES THERAPY

Working with the process of accessing love differs from the process of accessing the negative emotions. The goal, however, is similar: to access the adaptive striving associated with the primary emotion. The experience of love will motivate contact and caring actions. Accessing love for one's partner is commonly a part of resolving couples conflict. As the positive emotion of love increases, distance and anger decrease. For example, we describe the process in a client who, in anger, had cut herself off from her husband, and the process in couples therapy had reached an impasse. Each of the partners was seen alone or in a number of individual sessions interspersed with monthly couples sessions. In the individual sessions, the wife's anger was worked on in an empty-chair dialogue in which she faced her husband in imagination, and after dealing with her anger and what she missed, she accessed her love for him. This, in turn, accessed intentions to seek more contact with him and to maintain contact. Then, in couples therapy, she began to be able to open herself to his overtures.

Love is evoked to access the positive affiliative tendencies toward others and for the intrinsic meaning that this emotion gives to life. It is helpful in sessions to have partners symbolize loving feeling toward each other in words because these feelings so often are taken for granted or overlooked, and yet they are one of the prime motivating forces in making intimate relationships work. It is important in therapy to have the partners turn to each other and make visual contact when they express their love for each other. This provides a contactful experience of feeling love for and loved by another. Clients often feel embarrassed to express love or are frightened of the intensity of their feelings of love. In addition, clients often fear expressing love for their partner for fear of being devastated if their love is not reciprocated. These are blocks to the expression of love that need to be worked through in therapy to access and express the motivating aspects and the meanings of love.

Problem states in therapy related to love, however, are most generally addressed by working on other unresolved emotional issues that prevent love from being experienced. The emotions most implicated in the demise of love are shame and anger at feeling unvalued and fear in response to separation. Feelings of alienation, deadness, or inability to love also result from other complex processes of resignation and self-protection. Accessing love in couples therapy is often a result of therapeutically resolving the issues that block love rather than working directly on promoting love—Although, as we have said, working to promote love is also important, at the right time. This can be done by suggesting such things as having so-called caring days and positive expressions of affection.

JOY AND HAPPINESS

When the predominant affect felt by both partners in a relationship is enjoyment, the relationship almost certainly will be governed by continuity and commitment. Enjoyment affects motivate partners to invest in maintaining the relationship over time because they enjoy reexperiencing each other each day, over months and years. If one likes one's partner, then one looks forward to seeing that same person, day after day. Continuity in a relationship thus is fostered by enjoyment, whereas the ability to sustain commitment to another person is greatly enhanced by liking him or her.

Happiness is one of the most desirable emotional states to experience. Happiness or joy, felt as a broad or global state in a relationship, typically signifies that the partners feel that all is right with them, their partner, and the relationship. Happiness and joy, although close to excitement and interest, discussed next, can be distinguished from them, in both response pattern and experienced quality. Although interest is associated with attention and learning and is experienced as absorption, happiness is associated with laughing and smiling and is experienced as highly pleasurable.

Happiness and joy involves smiling with the lips widening and the corners moving up and out. It narrows the eye opening and may cause wrinkles at the outer corner of the eyes. The experience of happiness–joy, involves expansiveness and outgoingness. Laughter is a more primitive, as well as an earlier, form of enjoyment, which then became differentiated into the smile and the laugh. Laughter is characterized by the emission of a repetitive sound, the jaw or lips vibrating, the air streaming out the mouth, the corners of which draw back and upwards. The cheeks wrinkle, and the eyes brighten and outer corners may wrinkle. With increasing intensity of laughter, movements of the trunk and limbs may occur, with people describing doubling over from laughter and laughing so hard their stomach hurts.

The evolutionary significance of the affect of joy is apparent by how important it is in social communication. Expressing pleasure in actively engaging others has adaptive significance. It attracts the care of the caretaker and enhances mutual responsiveness by both infant and caretaker being continually rewarded by each other's presence. Thus, it is easy to see how the absence of joy and emotional flatness associated with adult depression or withdrawal in relationships can interfere with responsiveness from others, disrupt emotional bonds, and exacerbate depressions. Smiling in response to the human face is the root of much human connectedness, independent of feeding and touching. In infants, smiling facilitates bonding in the loving relationship, adds feelings of warmth and pleasure, and provides the caregiver with feedback as to what is pleasing to the child. Among adults, smiling has the capacity to operate as a universally recognizable signal of readiness for friendly interaction. In addition to the positive role of smiling in bonding, the sharing of positive affect, positive emotion communication, and caregiver affirmations all provide crucial encouragement for growth and development of the self.

Enjoyment arises from diverse causes. The smiling response is clearly activated early in life by the face of the caretaker as well as by the sudden appearance of something familiar; the appearance of distortions of the familiar; and by mastery, the achievement of the somewhat expected effects of one's own efforts, that is, of getting it right. As we have said, the smiling response and the experience of joy in response to the human face makes it highly probable that people will bond. It is both enjoyable to see a human face and rewarding for one's face to be responded to with a smile. Joy, then, complements fear and sadness in guaranteeing that people are social creatures. The experience of pleasure at goal attainment also leads to joy in relation to achievement. It feels good to be effective, and this keeps people engaged in projects. Joy, then, compliments pride and shame in developing identities. Play is another area in which we feel the adaptive organizing effects of the positive emotions of joy. Joy is achieved by the repetition of behaviors that provide mastery and the attainment of a shared goal with another person, as in games. The presence of a sense of humor in a couple about their conflicts and the ability to laugh at themselves has been found to be helpful in resolving conflict (Levenson & Gottman, 1985). Laughing at each other's jokes is a strong form of affection and enjoyment. When asked what they look for in a partner, people often cite a good sense of humor. People's ability to make their partners laugh helps them feel good, and people feel good when their partner's laugh at their quips or antics.

INTEREST–EXCITEMENT

Interest is one of the more frequently experienced positive emotions in relationship. In close relationships, partners show lots of interest in each other. Interest as an emotion is an important motivator of many actions and is important in guiding perception and attention. Interest is present in ordinary consciousness at most times, and changes or novelty are the key determinants of interest.

The distinction between joy and interest–excitement appears relatively late in evolutionary development. The action tendencies of the positive emotions are less clearly differentiated from each other than they are in the negative emotions. Whereas negative emotion is associated with increased tension and fleeing or defending boundaries, joy and interest both open people up physiologically, and tension is released. With intense interest, people look with a full gaze, or the eyebrows are down, and people track, look, and listen. In excitement, there may be, as in fear, a breathless moment of anticipation followed by rapid, shallow breathing. Interest and excitement both involve opening the individual up to the other. In therapy, encouraging partners to look at each other as they communicate vulnerable emotions or positive feelings often generates positive emotional experience.

There appear to be two distinct forms of responses to interest–excitement—passive and active. In the first type, a person can be passively fascinated by one's partner. *Interest* means "to be among or to dwell in something." It is an experience in which attention is fully absorbed, the partner is breathless, and the gaze is full. In the active type of response, a partner is excited, rapidly explores the other, is breathing rapidly, and is actively trying to maximize information about the other. Excitement can thus be sufficiently intense to motivate motor action and amplify sexual stimulation, as well as being sufficiently graded so as to support subtle cognitive activity and maintain long-term effort and commitment.

Interest is one of the primary forces that keeps people actively engaged in making contact with each other. Without interest, partners no longer engage with the other, no longer explore possibilities, and no longer are curious about the other. Interest in the other is validating and flattering for the other. To voluntarily do something and to engage in much activity, one must be excited, one must be interested. Natural curiosity to novelty is thus a key, and helping couples access their curiosity about the other can help them feel more connected and willing to engage in problem solving.

Interest and excitement are central, too, in sexual experience and striving. Without these emotions, sex would be dull and boring and not nearly as motivationally charged. This emotion is therefore evolutionarily crucial, not only in keeping people active in contacting each other but also in keeping them pursuing sexual contact. The sexual drive derives its power from the affect system. The drive must be amplified by excitement affect for people to experience complete sexual pleasure. This means that what usually is referred to as "sexual arousal" is not really a property of the drive at all but is a consequence of the amplifying nature of affect (Tomkins, 1963). What people are actually experiencing when they feel sexually aroused is the affect of excitement.

During sex, people experience excitement in the face and nostrils. Physical changes—such as erections, tight nipples, and moistening vaginas—occur, but the changes, even when they are in the genital areas, are not the same thing as excitement itself, which is an affect. The requirement that the sex be coupled with excitement affect to function optimally has far-reaching implications. For example, sexual desire can readily be disrupted by negative affect, such as fear and shame. Imagine that if suddenly during sex, a partner realizes that the door is unlocked or the curtain is open. Excitement is cut short by a negative affect of fear or shame. Disgust, too, will cut off excitement. For example, a conventional man, seeing hair on a woman's face or breasts, might feel sudden disgust and will lose his erection as that unexpected sight swamps his excitement. He simply is no longer aroused.

Excitement, although a positive emotion, can create problems if it is the only emotion motivating sexual connection. People who are principally motivated by needs for excitement to the exclusion of intimacy will be likely to seek out novelty through affairs. It is natural for partners' excitement level to decrease from its initial level over time, but enjoyment of one's partner cannot only persist but can intensify over time. For example, shared participation in novel and challenging activities has been shown to enhance each partner's excitement and positive affect (Aron et al., 2005). Aron and colleagues (2005) offered a self-expansion model of love in which engaging in novel and challenging activities creates a rapid experience of self-expansion, and this leads to enhanced relationship quality.

PROBLEMS

Most problems related to positive emotion in relationships have to do with their diminished presence or their total absence; it is these types of problems that we concentrate on in emotion-focused couples therapy. However, pathologies of excess in this domain may relate to mania and addiction (Tomkins, 1962).

The problems therapists deal with most frequently in relation to these emotions are, of course, related to the absence of joy and inhibited exploratory behavior and mastery experiences. Another pathology involving absence of positive emotion is the emotional numbing associated with traumatic experiences and posttraumatic stress symptomatology. The defensive shutting down of painful memories and experience, as a strategy for coping with overwhelming intrusion of these experiences, can generalize to numbing of all emotional experience. Clients who have experienced trauma report that their overall capacity for emotion, including positive emotion, is diminished.

Clients also may experience difficulty in expressing these positive emotions in their relationships. They may themselves not trust their positive experience of feelings such as hope, happiness, or excitement. They might believe that talking about them will affect them or make them disappear. Most important, they might fear that their partner may not pay these experiences the attention they deserve and, in not doing so, will invalidate these experiences. Recognition and support of the emergence of positive emotions in partners by the therapist is thus crucial to confirm and strengthen them, and their expression to their partners needs to be encouraged.

ACCESSING INTEREST, EXCITEMENT, AND JOY

Clearly, working with the process of accessing the positive emotions of interest–excitement and joy, as with love, is different in many ways from working with accessing the more painful or problematic feelings. The goal, as with other primary adaptive emotions, is to attend to or access these emotions to inform action. In the early stages of therapy, where absence of positive emotion is a problem, attending to this absence can evoke a kind of longing for this lost part of self. Interventions that direct attention to and heighten this longing enhance motivation to access this hidden essential self. Once positive emotions are experienced, it is helpful to have partners turn to each other and make contact with each other while experiencing these emotions. This intensifies the positive feeling and connection.

Intervention needs to respond to, direct attention to, and facilitate exploration of the emotions of interest, joy, and excitement and focus on both their self- and relationship-growth-enhancing potential. These experiences are acknowledged to heighten awareness, clarify what is valued, strengthen a sense of self, and promote healthy relationship development. Interventions need to be aimed at directing attention to positive emotions as they emerge in therapy or accessing them through memory evocation, for example, asking the partners to remember what it was like when they were first in love or to remember the most positive time in their relationship. The experience of mutuality is both deepened and renewed by the shared enjoyment felt when partners periodically relive shared events from the past. Spending time together remembering doing things together and looking at old love letters, gifts, or photos can all play a key role in nurturing intimacy between partners.

Therapeutic work often focuses more on overcoming the manner of blocking the emotions of joy or interest than on evoking the emotions themselves. The pleasant emotions are generally blocked by other unresolved emotions or by complex interruptive process such as fear of disappointment or resignation, alienation, and emptiness. Once the anger or sadness that is blocking connection and valuing of the other is overcome, the positive emotions emerge. These positive emotions need to be confirmed by the therapist, who needs to have the couple elaborate them often, with an aim of translating them into positive action, such as complements, and doing special things for the other. Once joys emerge, they are acknowledged and sustained, and generally their emergence represents a marker for helping the partners move into appropriate action or contact, on the basis of this emotion. In therapy, they are expressed and enjoyed in the present, and finally, when arousal has decreased, they are reflected on for their significance to the couple's past and future. When joy emerges, it is symbolized and appreciated and is a clear marker for promoting positive contact both in the session and at home.

For example, a therapist was working with a woman who was depressed, experienced life as flat and joyless, and felt stuck in an unhappy marriage. As the client discussed parenting, she began to explore a memory of the time soon after her first child was born when she felt very much loved and happy. The therapist picked up on the joyful affect that suddenly emerged and drew her attention to that emotion. Further exploration of times in which she felt love and joy led her to experience how much she wanted and needed to feel loved and led her to realize the effect this had had on her life, providing confidence and a sense of well-being. Accessing these positive emotions and her healthy needs and desires helped motivate her to find ways to seek them out in her marriage again. Feeling these also helped her overcome her fear of leaving if she could not find these feelings in her marriage rather than continuing to sacrifice herself to a loveless marriage.

Finally, in discussing positive emotions, the creation of hope is of crucial importance. To write a book on emotion in couples therapy without even commenting about hope would be a serious omission, as it is such a central ingredient of overcoming discouragement and producing change. Although hope is a complex emotion and beyond the scope of this book, involving as it does expectations about the future, positive affect, and motivation, hope is also related to joy and excitement.

Positive emotional states thus need to be symbolized, and the direction for action, goals, and intentions that they embody need to be articulated. Establishing intentions and setting goals in these states is important, for this sets up a hopeful view of possibilities and a sense of what to aim toward. Detailed planning of how to implement these hoped-for goals should not be emphasized while people are in an expansive state because it will dampen the feeling. This should be done later, when emotional arousal has decreased but a clear general vision or goal should be symbolized, along with deep experiences of how good it feels.

CALMNESS

Calmness, although more of a complex state than an emotion, is highly desired and is greatly facilitated in the context of couples by learning self-soothing. Self-soothing can be achieved by a process of mindful somatic focusing that grounds experience in the adaptive, healing-oriented, self-reparative tendencies of the body. Positive somatic affective experiences result from the moment-to-moment tracking of bodily sensations and responses, as there is a shift from in-the-head thinking to in-the-body sensing. It also is important to note another paradoxical positive feeling: Sometimes feeling bad can feel good. This occurs when one acknowledges a painful feeling, long avoided. This change feels good even when it involves dealing with excruciating experiences. By *good*, we do not mean that the individual feels happy. Rather, a feeling of relief and a relaxation of tension accompany the process of therapeutic transformation. In addition, when a felt sense of what is happening is correctly identified, even if this is a painful feeling, a positive feeling of discovery and sureness results. Something inside the person says, "Yes, that's it, *that's* what I've been feeling!" A moment of transformation thus is bathed in positive emotion because it feels deeply right. *Positive feeling* here thus refers to calm, to contact, and to having access to a vibrant, embodied, flowing, bodily felt experience.

CONCLUSION

When interaction becomes locked in negative interactional cycles, love and positive feelings take a back seat to the struggle for connectedness and identity. This, too, is when the sexual relationship is affected, and without the bolstering effect of this primal merging and connection involving touch, pleasure, and soothing, there is no positive emotional buffer to the inevitable differences and disagreements in a relationship. The positive feelings act to undo some of the negative emotions that arise in a relationship, and they keep the emotional bond strong.

Therapists need to amplify positive feelings when they emerge as the result of resolving conflict, and when virtuous cycles replace vicious ones, the positive feelings need to be expressed. Therapists also need to intervene to activate and promote expressions of love, joy, excitement, interest, and self-soothing. This is done both in the session and by assigning homework. Positive feelings, in addition to strengthening the relational connection, also build up a reservoir of good will and good feeling that help ameliorate any conflict and promote creative problem solving.

REFERENCES

Abu-Lughod, L. (1986). *Veiled sentiments: Honor and poetry in a Bedouin society*. Berkeley: University of California Press.

Ackerman, D. (1995). *A natural history of love*. New York: Vintage.

Ahmed, S. (2006). *Contextualizing selves of South Asian Canadian couples: A grounded theory analysis*. Unpublished master's thesis, York University, Toronto, Ontario, Canada.

Ainsworth, M. D. S. (1967). *Infancy in Uganda: Infant care and the growth of love*. Baltimore: John Hopkins University Press.

Angus, L. E., & McLeod, J. (2004). *The handbook of narrative and psychotherapy: Practice, theory, and research*. Thousand Oaks, CA: Sage.

Aron, A., & Aron, E. (1997). Self-expansion motivation and including other in the self. In S. Duck (Ed.), *Handbook of personal relationships: Theory, research and interventions* (2nd ed., pp. 251–270). Chichester, England: Wiley.

Aron, A., Fisher, H., Mashek, D., Strong, G., Haifang, L., & Brown, L. (2005). Reward, motivation, and emotion systems associated with early-stage intense romantic love. *Journal of Neurophysiology, 94*, 327–337.

Atkinson, B. (2005). *Emotional intelligence in couples therapy*. New York: Norton.

Averill, J. R. (1980). A constructivist view of emotion. In R. Plutchik & H. Kellerman (Eds.), *Emotion: Theory, research, and experience: Vol. I. Theories of emotion* (pp. 305–339). New York: Academic Press.

Averill, J. R. (1983). Studies on anger and aggression: Implications for theories of emotion. *American Psychologist, 38*, 1145–1160.

Bakan, D. (1966). *The duality of human existence*. Boston: Beacon Press.

Bando, M. (1992). *Data bank of Japanese women*. Tokyo: Ministry of Finance.

Bartels, A., & Zeki, S. (2000). The neural basis of romantic love. *NeuroReport, 11*, 3829–3834.

Bartels, A., & Zeki, S. (2004). The neural correlates of maternal and romantic love. *NeuroImage, 21*, 1155–1166.

Bartholomew, K., & Horowitz, L. (1991). Attachment styles among young adults. *Journal of Personality and Social Psychology, 61*, 226–244.

Beebe, B., & Lachmann, F. M. (1998). Co-constructing inner and relational processes: Self and mutual regulation in infant research and adult treatment. *Psychoanalytic Psychology, 15*, 480–516.

Benjamin, J. (1988). *The bonds of love*. New York: Pantheon Books.

Benjamin, J. (1990). An outline of intersubjectivity: The development of recognition. *Psychoanalytic Psychology, 7*, 33–46.

Benjamin, L. S. (1993). *Interpersonal diagnosis and treatment of personality disorders*. New York: Guilford Press.

Benjamin, L. S. (1996). Introduction to the special section on structural analysis of social behavior. *Journal of Consulting and Clinical Psychology, 64*, 1203–1212.

Benjamin, L. S., Rothweiler, J., & Critchfield, K. (2006). The use of structural analysis of social behavior (SASB) as an assessment tool. *Annual Review of Clinical Psychology, 2*, 83–109.

Berzon, B. (1988). *Permanent partners: Building gay and lesbian relationships that last.* New York: Dutton.

Betcher, W., & Pollack, W. (1993). *In a time of fallen heroes: The re-creation of masculinity.* New York: Atheneum.

Bierman, R. (1997). Focusing in therapy with incarcerated domestically violent men. *The Folio: A Journal for Focusing and Experiential Therapy, 15*, 47–58.

Birbaumer, N., & Ohman, A. (1993). *The structure of emotion: Psychophysiological, cognitive, and clinical aspects.* Seattle, WA: Hogrefe & Huber.

Blank, G., & Blank, R. (1974). *Ego psychology: Theory and practice.* New York: Columbia University Press.

Bly, R. (1990). *Iron John.* Reading, MA: Addison Wesley.

Bowen, M. (1978). *Family theory in clinical practice.* New York: Jason Aronson.

Bowlby, J. (1962). *Separation anxiety: A critical review of the literature.* New York: Child Welfare League of America.

Bowlby, J. (1969). *Attachment and loss: Vol. I. Attachment.* London: Hogarth Press.

Bowlby, J. (1973). *Attachment and loss: Vol. II. Separation: Anxiety and anger.* New York: Basic Books.

Bowlby, J. (1980). *Attachment and loss: Volume III. Loss: Sadness and depression.* New York: Basic Books.

Bradley, B., & Furrow, J. (2004). Toward a mini-theory of the blamer softening event: Tracking the moment-by-moment process. *Journal of Marital and Family Therapy, 30*, 233–246.

Bray, T. C. (2002). Intimacy, attachment styles, and shame in married couples. *Dissertation Abstracts International, 62*(09), 4210B.

Brown, J. A. (1987). Casework contacts with Black–White couples. *Social Casework: The Journal of Contemporary Social Work, 6*, 24–29.

Buber, M. (1958). *I and thou.* New York: Scribner.

Burgoon, J., & Dunbar, N. (2000). An interactionist perspective on dominance–submission: Interpersonal dominance as a dynamic, situationally contingent social skill. *Communication Monographs, 67*(1), 91–121.

Burgoon, J., & Dunbar, N. (2005). Perceptions of power and interactional dominance in interpersonal relationships. *Journal of Social and Personal Relationships, 22*, 207–233.

Buss, D. M. (1992). Mate preference mechanisms: Consequences for partner choice and intrasexual competition. In J. H. Barkow, L. Cosmides, & J. Tooby (Eds.), *The adapted mind* (pp. 267–288). New York: Oxford University Press.

Cacioppo, J. T. (2002). Social neuroscience: Understanding the pieces fosters understanding the whole and vice versa. *American Psychologist, 57,* 819–827.

Carr, A., Malouf, M., Altman, A., Kaduvettoor, A., Inman, A., & Walker, J. A. (2006, June). *Reflections and experiences of Asian Indian–White interracial couples.* Paper presented at the Society for Psychotherapy Research Conference, Edinburgh, Scotland.

Cassidy, J. (1999). The nature of the child's ties. In J. Cassidy & P. R. Shaver (Eds.), *Handbook of attachment: Theory, research, and clinical applications* (pp. 3–20). New York: Guilford Press.

Cherlin, A. J. (1992). *Marriage, divorce, and remarriage.* Cambridge, MA: Harvard University Press.

Christensen, A., & Heavey, C. L. (1990). Gender and social structure in the demand/withdraw pattern of marital conflict. *Journal of Personality and Social Psychology, 59,* 73–81.

Cicchetti, D., & Toth, S. L. (Eds.). (1991). *Rochester Symposium on Developmental Psychopathology: Vol. 2. Internalizing and externalizing expressions of dysfunction.* Hillsdale, NJ: Erlbaum.

Clancy, P. M. (1986). The acquisition of communicative style in Japanese. In B. B. Schieffelin & E. Ochs (Eds.), *Language of socialization across cultures* (pp. 213–250). New York: Cambridge University Press.

Cloninger, C. R., Svrakic, D. M., & Przybeck, T. R. (1993). A psychobiological model of temperament and character. *Archives of General Psychiatry, 50,* 975–990.

Coontz, S. (2005). *Marriage, a history: From obedience to intimacy, or how love conquered marriage.* New York: Viking Press.

Cowan, G., Drinkard, J., & MacGavin, L. (1984). The effects of target, age, and gender on use of power strategies. *Journal of Personality and Social Psychology, 47,* 1391–1398.

Cozolino, L. (2002). *The neuroscience of psychotherapy.* New York: Norton.

Damasio, A. (1994). *Descartes' error: Emotion, reason, and the human brain.* New York: Putnam.

Damasio, A. (1999). *The feeling of what happens.* New York: Harcourt.

Damasio, A. (2003). *Looking for Spinoza: Joy, sorrow, and the feeling brain.* London: Vintage.

Daneshpour, M. (2003). Lives together, worlds apart? The lives of multicultural Muslim couples. In V. Thomas, T. A. Karis, & J. L. Wetchler (Eds.), *Clinical issues with interracial couples: Theories and research* (pp. 57–72). New York: Haworth Press.

Davidson, R. J. (2000a). Affective style, psychopathology, and resilience: Brain mechanisms and plasticity. *American Psychologist, 5,* 1193–1196.

Davidson, R. J. (2000b). The neuroscience of affective style. In M. S. Gazzaniga (Ed.), *The new cognitive neurosciences* (2nd ed., pp. 1149–1159). Cambridge, MA: MIT Press.

Denenberg, V. H. (1999). Commentary: Is maternal stimulation the mediator of the handling effect in infancy? *Developmental Psychobiology, 34,* 1–3.

Denenberg, V. H. (2000). Evolution proposes and ontogeny disposes. *Brain and Language, 73,* 274–296.

DeVos, G. (1985). Dimensions of the self in Japanese culture. In A. Marsella, G. DeVos, & F. Hsu (Eds.), *Culture and self: Asian and Western perspectives* (pp. 149–184). New York: Tavistock.

de Waal, F. B. M. (1986). The integration of dominance and social bonding in primates. *The Quarterly Review of Biology, 61,* 459–479.

de Waal, F. B. M. (1996). *Good natured: The origins of right and wrong in humans and other animals.* Cambridge, MA: Harvard University Press.

Dion, K. K., & Dion. K. L. (1993). Individualistic and collectivist perspectives on gender and the cultural context of love and intimacy. *Journal of Social Issues, 49,* 53–69.

Dutton, D. (1995). *The batterer: A psychological profile.* New York: Basic Books.

Eibl-Eibesfeldt, I. (1980). Strategies of social interaction. In R. Plutchik (Ed.), *Emotion: Theory, research, and experience. Vol. 1: Theories of emotion* (pp. 57–80). New York: Academic Press.

Eibl-Eibesfeldt, I., & Sütterlin, C. (1990). Fear, defense, and aggression in animals and man: Some ethological perspectives. In P. F. Brain & S. Parmigiani (Eds.), *Fear and defense* (pp. 381–408). London: Harwood.

Ekman, P. (1984). Expression and the nature of emotion. In K. Scherer & P. Ekman (Eds.), *Approaches to emotion* (pp. 319–343). Hillsdale, NJ: Erlbaum.

Ekman, P. (1992). An argument for basic emotions. *Cognition & Emotion, 6,* 169–200.

Ekman, P. (1993). Facial expression of emotion. *American Psychologist, 48,* 384–392.

Ekman, P., & Davidson, R. J. (1994). *The nature of emotion: Fundamental questions.* New York: Oxford University Press.

Ekman, P., & Friesen, W. V. (1975). *Unmasking the face: A guide to recognizing emotions from facial clues.* Oxford, England: Prentice Hall.

Elliott, R., Watson, J., Goldman, R. N., & Greenberg, L. S. (2004). *Learning emotion-focused therapy.* Washington, DC: American Psychological Association.

Ellis, B. (1992). The evolution of sexual attraction: Evaluative mechanisms in women. In J. H. Barkow, L. Cosmides, & J. Tooby (Eds.), *The adapted mind* (pp. 267–288). New York: Oxford University Press.

Epstein, N. B., Chen, F., & Beyder-Kamjou, I. (2005). Relationship standards and marital satisfaction in Chinese and American couples. *Journal of Marital and Family Therapy, 31,* 59–74.

Fairbairn, W. R. D. (1954). *An object-relations theory of the personality.* New York: Basic Books.

Falbo, T., & Peplau, L. A. (1980). Power strategies in intimate relationships. *Journal of Personality and Social Psychology, 38,* 618–628.

Felmlee, D. H. (1994). Who's on top? Power in romantic relationships. *Sex Roles, 31,* 275–295.

Fergus, K., & Reid, D. (2001). The couple's mutual identity and reflexivity: A systematic–constructivist approach to the integration of persons and systems. *Journal of Psychotherapy Integration, 11,* 385–410.

Firestone, R., & Catlett, J. (2002). *Fear of intimacy.* Washington, DC: American Psychological Association.

Fisch, R., Weakland, J., & Segal, L. (1984). *The tactics of change: Doing therapy briefly.* San Francisco: Jossey-Bass.

Fisher, H. (1992). *The anatomy of love: The natural history of monogamy, adultery, and divorce.* New York: Norton.

Fisher, H. (2004). *Why we love: The nature and chemistry of romantic love.* New York: Holt.

Fisher, H., Aron, A., Mashek, H., & Brown, L. (2002). Defining the brain systems of lust, romantic attraction, and attachment. *Archives of Sexual Behavior, 31,* 413–419.

Fiske, A. P. (1991). *Structures of social life.* New York: Free Press.

Fosha, D. (2001). The dyadic regulation of affect. *Journal of Clinical Psychology, 57,* 227–242.

Fox, N. A., & Davidson, R. J. (1987). Electroencephalogram asymmetry in response to the approach of a stranger and maternal separation in 10-month-old infants. *Developmental Psychology, 23,* 233–240.

Fraley, R. C., & Waller, N. G. (1998). Adult attachment patterns: A test of the typological model. In J. A. Simpson & W. S. Rholes (Eds.), *Attachment theory and close relationships* (pp. 77–114). New York: Guilford Press.

Frank, R. H. (1988). *Passions within reason.* New York: Norton.

Fredrickson, B. L. (1998). What good are positive emotions? *Review of General Psychology, 2,* 300–319.

Frederickson, B. L., & Losada, M. F. (2005). Positive affect and the complex dynamics of human flourishing. *American Psychologist, 60,* 678–691.

Freud, S. (1961). The ego and the id. In J. Strachey (Ed. & Trans.), *The standard edition of the complete psychological works of Sigmund Freud* (Vol. 19, pp. 3–66). London: Hogarth Press. (Original work published 1923)

Friedman, S. L. (2000). Spoken pleasures and dangerous desires: Sexuality, marriage, and the state in rural southeastern China. *East Asia: An International Quarterly, 18*(4), 13–39.

Frijda, N. H. (1986). *The emotions.* Cambridge, England: Cambridge University Press.

Gallese, V., Fadiga, L., Fogassi, L., & Rizzolatti, G. (1996). Action recognition in the premotor cortex. *Brain, 119,* 593–609.

Gao, G., Ting-Toomey, S., & Gudykunst, W. B. (1996). Chinese communication processes. In M. H. Bond (Ed.), *The handbook of Chinese psychology* (pp. 294–308). Oxford, England: Oxford University Press.

Gendlin, E. (1981). *Focusing*. New York: Bantam Books.

Gendlin, E. (1996). *Focusing-oriented psychotherapy: A manual of the experiential method*. New York: Guilford Press.

George, K. D., & Behrendt, E. S. (1987). Therapy for male couples experiencing relationship and sexual problems. *Journal of Homosexuality, 14*, 77–88.

Gergen, K. J. (2001). *Social construction in context*. London: Sage.

Gilbert, P. (1989). *Human nature and suffering*. Hove, England: Erlbaum.

Gilbert, P. (1997). The evolution of social attractiveness and its role in shame, humiliation, guilt, and therapy. *British Journal of Medical Psychology, 70*, 113–147.

Gilbert, P. (2001). Evolution and social anxiety: The role of attraction, social competition, and social hierarchies. *The Psychiatric Clinics of North America, 24*, 723–751.

Gilbert, P. (2003). Evolution, social roles, and the differences in shame and guilt. *Social Research, 70*, 205–230.

Gilbert, P., & McGuire, M. (1998). Shame, social roles, and status: The psychobiological continuum from monkey to human. In P. Gilbert & B. Andrews (Eds.), *Shame: Interpersonal behavior, psychopathology, and culture* (pp. 99–125). New York: Oxford University Press.

Gilligan, C. (1982). *In a different voice*. Cambridge, MA: Harvard University Press.

Glass, S. (2003). *Not "just friends": Protect your relationship from infidelity and heal the trauma of betrayal*. New York: Free Press.

Goldenberg, J. L., McCoy, S. K., Pyszczynski, T., Greenberg, J., & Solomon, S. (2000). The body as a source of self-esteem: The effect of mortality salience on identification with one's body, interest in sex, and appearance monitoring. *Journal of Personality and Social Psychology, 79*, 118–130.

Goldman, A., & Greenberg, L. S. (1992). Comparison of an integrated systemic and emotionally focused approach to couples therapy. *Journal of Consulting and Clinical Psychology, 60*, 962–969.

Goldman, R. N. (1992). *The validation of the experiential therapy adherence measure*. Unpublished master's thesis, York University, Toronto, Ontario, Canada.

Goldman, R. N., & Greenberg, L. S. (1995). A process experiential approach to case formulation. *In Session, 1*(2), 35–51.

Goldman, R. N., & Greenberg, L. S. (1997). Case formulation in experiential therapy. In T. Ells (Ed.), *Handbook of psychotherapy case formulation* (pp. 402–429). New York: Guilford Press.

Goldman, R. N., Greenberg, L. S., & Angus, L. (2006). The effects of adding emotion-focused interventions to the therapeutic relationship in the treatment of depression. *Psychotherapy Research, 16*, 537–549.

Goldman, R. N., & Keating, E. (2003, July). *Processing shame and vulnerability: A rational–empirical study*. Paper presented at the 34th International Conference of Client-Centered and Experiential Psychotherapy, Amsterdam, the Netherlands.

Goldstein, K. (1995). *The organism*. Cambridge MA: MIT Press.

Goodwin, R., & Cramer, D. (2000). Marriage and social support in a British–Asian community. *Journal of Community and Applied Social Psychology, 10,* 49–62.

Goodwin, R., & Findlay, C. (1997). "We were just fated together": Chinese love and the concept of *yuan* in England and Hong Kong. *Personal Relationships, 4,* 85–92.

Gottman, J. M. (1994). *What predicts divorce? The relationship between marital processes and marital outcomes*. Hillsdale, NJ: Erlbaum.

Gottman, J. M. (1999). *The marriage clinic: A scientifically based marital therapy*. New York: Norton.

Gottman, J. M., Coan, J., Carrère, S., & Swanson, C. (1998). Predicting marital happiness and stability from newlywed interactions. *Journal of Marriage and the Family, 60,* 5–22.

Gottman, J. M., Gortner, E., Berns, S. B., & Jacobson, N. S. (1997). When women leave violent relationships: Dispelling clinical myths. *Psychotherapy: Theory, research, practice, training. 34,* 343–352.

Gottman, J. M., & Silver, N. (1999). *The seven principles for making marriage work*. New York: Three Rivers Press.

Green, G. D., & Clunis, D. M. (1989). Married lesbians. *Women and Therapy, 8,* 41–49.

Greenberg, L. S. (1979). Resolving splits: Use of the two-chair technique. *Psychotherapy: Theory, Research & Practice, 16,* 310–318.

Greenberg, L. S. (1980). The intensive analysis of recurring events from the practice of gestalt therapy. *Psychotherapy: Theory, Research & Practice, 17,* 143–152.

Greenberg, L. S. (1983). Toward a task analysis of conflict resolution. *Psychotherapy: Theory, Research & Practice, 20,* 190–201.

Greenberg, L. S. (1984). Task analysis of intrapersonal conflict. In L. Rice & L. S. Greenberg (Eds.), *Patterns of change: Intensive analysis of psychotherapy* (pp. 66–123). New York: Guilford Press.

Greenberg, L. S. (1986). Change process research. *Journal of Consulting and Clinical Psychology, 54,* 4–9.

Greenberg, L. S. (2002a). *Emotion-focused therapy: Coaching clients to work through their feelings*. Washington, DC: American Psychological Association.

Greenberg, L. S. (2002b). Integrating an emotion-focused approach to treatment into psychotherapy integration. *Psychotherapy Integration, 12,* 154–190.

Greenberg, L. S. (2007). A guide to conducting a task analysis of psychotherapeutic change. *Psychotherapy Research, 17,* 15–30.

Greenberg, L. S., & Angus, L. (2004). The contributions of emotion processes to narrative change in psychotherapy: A dialectical constructivist approach. In L. Angus & J. McLeod (Eds.), *The handbook of narrative and psychotherapy: Practice, theory, and research* (pp. 331–350). Thousand Oaks, CA: Sage.

Greenberg, L. S., & Bolger, E. (2001). An emotion-focused approach to the over-regulation of emotion and emotional pain. *Journal of Clinical Psychology, 57,* 197–211.

Greenberg, L. S., Ford, C., Alden, L., & Johnson, S. (1993). In-session change processes in emotionally focused therapy for couples. *Journal of Consulting and Clinical Psychology, 61,* 68–84.

Greenberg, L. S., & Goldman, R. N. (2007). Case formulation in emotion-focused therapy. In T. Ells (Ed.), *Handbook of psychotherapy case formulation* (pp. 379–412). New York: Guilford Press.

Greenberg, L. S., Heatherington, L., & Friedlander, M. (1996). The events-based approach to couple and family therapy research. In D. Sprenkle & S. Moon (Eds.), *Research methods in family therapy* (pp. 411–428). New York: Guilford Press.

Greenberg, L. S., James, P., & Conry, R. (1988). Perceived change processes in emotionally focused couples therapy. *Journal of Family Psychology, 2,* 1–12.

Greenberg, L. S., & Johnson, S. (1986a). Affect in marital therapy. *Journal of Marital and Family Therapy, 12,* 1–10.

Greenberg, L. S., & Johnson, S. (1986b). Emotionally focused couples treatment: An integrated affective systemic approach. In N. Jacobson & A. Gurman (Eds.), *Clinical handbook of marital therapy* (pp. 253–276). New York: Guilford Press.

Greenberg, L. S., & Johnson, S. (1988). *Emotionally focused couples therapy.* New York: Guilford Press.

Greenberg, L. S., & Johnson, S. (1990). Emotional change processes in couples therapy. In E. Blechman & M. McEnroe (Eds.), *Emotions and the family: For better or worse* (pp. 137–153). Hillsdale, NJ: Erlbaum.

Greenberg, L. S., & Mateu-Marques, C. (1998). Emotions in couples systems. *Journal of Systemic Therapies, 17,* 93–107.

Greenberg, L. S., & Paivio, S. C. (1997a). Varieties of shame experience in psychotherapy. *Gestalt Review, 1,* 205–220.

Greenberg, L. S., & Paivio, S. C. (1997b). *Working with emotions in psychotherapy.* New York: Guilford Press.

Greenberg, L. S., & Pascual-Leone, J. (1995). A dialectical constructivist approach to experiential change. In R. A. Neimeyer & M. J. Mahoney (Eds.), *Constructivism in psychotherapy* (pp. 169–191). Washington, DC: American Psychological Association.

Greenberg, L. S., & Pascual-Leone, J. (1997). Emotion in the creation of personal meaning. In M. Power & C. Brewin (Eds.), *Transformation of meaning* (pp. 157–174). London: Wiley.

Greenberg, L. S., & Pascual-Leone, J. (2001). A dialectical constructivist view of the creation of personal meaning. *Journal of Constructivist Psychology, 14,* 165–186.

Greenberg, L. S., Rice, L., & Elliot, R. (1993). *Facilitating emotional change: The moment-by-moment process.* New York: Guilford Press.

Greenberg, L. S., & Rosenberg, R. (2002). Therapist's experience of empathy. In J. C. Watson, R. N. Goldman, & M. Warner (Eds.), *Client-centered and experiential psychotherapy in the 21st century: Advances in theory, research, and practice* (pp. 204–220). Ross-on-Wye, England: PCCS Books.

Greenberg, L. S., & Safran, J. (1981). Encoding and cognitive therapy: Changing what clients attend to. *Psychotherapy: Theory, Research & Practice, 8,* 163–169.

Greenberg, L. S., & Safran, J. (1984). Integrating affect and cognition: A perspective on the process of therapeutic change. *Cognitive Therapy and Research, 8,* 559–578.

Greenberg, L. S., & Safran, J. (1986). Hot cognition—Emotion coming in from the cold: A reply to Rachman and Mahoney. *Cognitive Therapy and Research, 8,* 591–598.

Greenberg, L. S., & Safran, J. (1987). *Emotion in psychotherapy: Affect, cognition, and the process of change.* New York: Guilford Press.

Greenberg, L. S., Warwar, S., & Malcolm, W. (in press). Emotion-focused couples therapy and the facilitation of forgiveness. *Journal of Marital and Family Therapy.*

Greenberg, L. S., & Watson, J. (1998). Experiential therapy of depression: Differential effects of client-centered relationship conditions and process experiential interventions. *Psychotherapy Research, 8,* 210–224.

Greenberg, L. S., & Watson, J. C. (2006). *Emotion-focused therapy for depression.* Washington, DC: American Psychological Association.

Greenspan, S. I., & Shanker, S. G. (2004). *The first idea: How symbols, language, and intelligence evolved from our primate ancestors to modern humans.* Cambridge, MA: Da Capo Press.

Guerrero, L. K., Andersen, P. A., & Afifi, W. A. (2001). *Close encounters: Communication in relationships.* New York: McGraw-Hill.

Guidano, V. (1991). *The self in process: Toward a postrationalist cognitive therapy.* New York: Guilford Press.

Halloran, E. C. (1998). The role of marital power in depression and marital distress. *American Journal of Family Therapy, 26,* 3–14.

Harlow, H. (1958). The nature of love. *American Psychologist, 13,* 673–685.

Harré, R. (1984). *Personal being.* Cambridge, MA: Harvard University Press.

Harris, J. R. (1999). *The nurture assumption: Why children turn out the way they do.* New York: Touchstone.

Hazan, C., & Shaver, P. R. (1987). Romantic love conceptualized as an attachment process. *Journal of Personality and Social Psychology, 52,* 511–524.

Hazan, C., & Shaver, P. R. (1990). Love and work: An attachment theoretical perspective. *Journal of Personality and Social Psychology, 59,* 270–280.

Heatherington, L., Friedlander, M., & Greenberg, L. (2005). Change process research in couples and families: Methodological challenges and opportunities. *Journal of Family Psychology, 19,* 18–27.

Hendrick, C., & Hendrick, S. (1986). A theory and method of love. *Journal of Personality and Social Psychology, 50,* 392–402.

Hendrix, L. (1997). Quality and equality in marriage: A cross-cultural view. *Cross-Cultural Research: The Journal of Comparative Social Science, 31,* 201–225.

Herman, J. L. (1992). *Trauma and recovery.* New York: Basic Books.

Hirsch, J. (2003). *A courtship after marriage: Sexuality and love in Mexican transnational families*. Berkeley: University of California Press.

Holtzworth-Munroe, A., Smutzler, N., & Stuart, G. L. (1998). Demand and withdraw communication among couples experiencing husband violence. *Journal of Consulting and Clinical Psychology, 66*, 731–743.

Horak, J. J. H. (2003). Factors predicting distress at marital therapy onset. *Dissertation Abstracts International, 63*, 4373.

Horowitz, L. M. (2004). *Interpersonal foundations of psychopathology*. Washington, DC: American Psychological Association.

Ibrahim, F. A., & Schroeder, D. G. (1990). Cross-cultural couples counseling: A developmental, psychoeducational intervention. *Journal of Comparative Family Studies, 21*, 193–205.

Isaac, R., & Shah, A. (2004). Sex roles and marital adjustment in Indian couples. *International Journal of Social Psychiatry, 50*, 129–141.

Iwao, S. (1993). *The Japanese woman: Traditional image and changing reality*. Cambridge, MA: Harvard University Press.

Izard, C. E. (1991). *The psychology of emotions*. New York: Plenum Press.

Jacobson, N., & Whisman, M. A. (1990). Power, marital satisfaction, and response to marital therapy. *Journal of Family Psychology, 4*, 202–212.

James, P. (1985). *Couples perception of change in psychotherapy*. Unpublished master's thesis, University of British Columbia, Vancouver, Canada.

James, P. (1991). The effects of a communication training component added to an emotionally focused couples therapy. *Journal of Marital and Family Therapy, 17*, 268–275.

James, W. (1902). *The varieties of religious experience: A study in human nature*. New York: Long.

Johnson, S. (1986). Bonds or bargains: Relationship paradigms and their significance for marital therapy. *Journal of Marital and Family Therapy, 12*, 259–267.

Johnson, S. (1996). *The practice of emotionally focused couples therapy: Creating connections*. New York: Bruner-Routledge.

Johnson, S. (2002). *Emotionally focused couples therapy with trauma survivors*. New York: Guilford Press.

Johnson, S. (2004). Attachment theory: A guide for healing couple relationships. In W. S. Rholes & J. A. Simpson (Eds.), *Adult attachment: Theory, research, and clinical implications* (pp. 367–387). New York: Guilford Press.

Johnson, S., Bradley B., Furrow, J., Lee, A., Palmer, G., Tilley, D., & Wooley, S. (2005). *Becoming an emotionally focused couple therapist*. New York: Routledge.

Johnson, S., & Greenberg, L. S. (1985a). Differential effects of experiential and problem-solving interventions in resolving marital conflict. *Journal of Consulting and Clinical Psychology, 53*, 175–184.

Johnson, S., & Greenberg, L. S. (1985b). Emotionally focused marital therapy: An outcome study. *Journal of Marital and Family Therapy, 11*, 313–317.

Johnson, S., & Greenberg, L. S. (1988). Relating process to outcome in marital therapy. *Journal of Marital and Family Therapy, 14*, 175–183.

Johnson, S., Hunsley, J., Greenberg, G., & Schindler, D. (1999). Emotionally focused couples therapy: Status and challenges. *Clinical Psychology: Science and Practice, 6*, 67–79.

Johnson, S., Makinen, J. A., & Millikin, J. (2001). Attachment injuries in couples relationships: A new perspective on impasses in couple therapy. *Journal of Marital and Family Therapy, 27*, 145–156.

Johnson, S., & Whiffen, V. E. (2003). *Attachment processes in couple and family therapy*. New York: Guilford Press.

Kaufman, G. (1989). *The psychology of shame: Theory and treatment of shame-based syndromes*. New York: Springer Publishing Company.

Keenan, J. (1977). Power and wealth are cousins: Descent, class, and marital strategies among the Kel Ahaggar (Tuareg-Sahara). *Africa, 47*, 333–343.

Keltner, D., & Buswell, B. (1996). Evidence for the distinctness of embarrassment, shame, and guilt: A study of recalled antecedents and facial expressions of emotion. *Cognition and Emotion, 10*, 155–172.

Keltner, D., Ellsworth, P., & Edwards, K. (1993). Beyond simple pessimism: Effects of sadness and anger on social perception. *Journal of Personality and Social Psychology, 64*, 740–752.

Keltner, D., & Harter, L. (1998). The forms and functions of the nonverbal signal of shame. In P. Gilbert & B. Andrews (Eds.), *Shame: Interpersonal behavior, psychopathology, and culture* (pp. 78–98). New York: Oxford Press.

Kerr, M. E., & Bowen, M. (1988). *Family evaluation: An approach based on Bowen theory*. New York: Norton.

Khantzian, E., Halliday, K., & McAuliffe, W. (1990). *Addiction and the vulnerable self: Modified dynamic group therapy for substance abusers*. New York: Guilford Press.

Kiesler, D. (1996). *Contemporary interpersonal theory and research: Personality, psychopathology, and psychotherapy*. New York: Wiley.

Kitayama, S., Markus, H. R., & Matsumoto, H. (1995). Culture, self, and emotion: A cultural perspective on "self-conscious" emotions. In J. P. Tangney & C. W. Fischer (Eds.), *Self-conscious emotions: The psychology of shame, guilt, embarrassment, and pride* (pp. 439–464). New York: Guilford Press.

Kohut, H. (1977). *The restoration of the self*. New York: International Universities Press.

Kohut, H. (1984). *How does analysis cure?* Chicago: University of Chicago Press.

Komisaruk, B., & Whipple, B. (1998). Love as sensory stimulation: Physiological consequences of its deprivation and expression. *Psychoneuroendocrinology, 23*, 927–944.

Krugman, S. (1995). Male development and the transformation of shame. In R. F. Levant & W. S. Pollack (Eds.), *A new psychology of men* (pp. 91–126). New York: Basic Books.

L'Abate, L. (1977). Intimacy is sharing hurt feelings: A reply to David Mace. *Journal of Marital and Family Therapy, 3*, 13–16.

Larsen, R., & Diener, E. (1992). Problems and promises with the circumplex model of emotion. *Review of Personality and Social Psychology, 13,* 25–59.

Leach, E. (1972). The influence of cultural context on nonverbal communication in man. In R. A. Hinde (Ed.), *Nonverbal communication* (pp. 315–347). Cambridge, England: Cambridge University Press.

Leary, T. (1957). *Interpersonal diagnosis in personality.* New York: Ronald Press.

LeDoux, J. (1996). *The emotional brain: The mysterious underpinnings of emotional life.* New York: Simon & Schuster.

Levenson, R. (1992). Autonomic nervous system differences among emotions. *Psychological Science, 3,* 23–27.

Levenson, R., & Gottman, J. (1985). Physiological and affective predictors of change in relationship satisfaction. *Journal of Personality and Social Psychology, 49,* 85–94.

Levinas, E. (1998). *Otherwise than being: Or beyond essence.* Pittsburgh, PA: Duquesne University Press.

LeVine, R. A., & LeVine, B. B. (1967). *Nyansongo: A Gusii community in Kenya.* New York: Wiley.

Lewis, H. B. (1971). *Shame and guilt in neurosis.* Hillsdale, NJ: Erlbaum.

Locke, D. C. (1992). *Increasing multicultural understanding.* Newbury Park, CA: Sage.

Lutz, C., & White, G. (1986). The anthropology of emotions. *Annual Review of Anthropology, 15,* 405–436.

MacDonald, K. (1992). Warmth as a developmental construct: An evolutionary analysis. *Child Development, 63,* 753–773.

Mahoney, M. (1991). *Human change processes.* New York: Basic Books.

Malcom, W., Warwar, S., & Greenberg, L. S. (2005). Facilitating forgiveness in individual therapy as an approach to resolving interpersonal injuries. In E. L. Worthington Jr. (Ed.), *The handbook of forgiveness* (pp. 379–393). New York. Routledge.

Markus, H., & Kitayama, S. (1991). Culture and the self: Implications for cognition, emotion, and motivation. *Psychological Review, 98,* 224–253.

Maslow, A. (1958). *Understanding human motivation.* Cleveland, OH: Howard Allen.

Masten, A. S. (2001). Ordinary magic: Resilience processes in development. *American Psychologist, 56,* 227–238.

McGinn, N. (1966). Marriage and family in middle-class Mexico. *Journal of Marriage and the Family, 28,* 305–313.

McRoy, R., & Freeman, E. (1986). Racial-identity issues among mixed-race children. *Social Work in Education, 8,* 164–174.

Mehrabian, A. (1995). Relationships among three general approaches to personality description. *Journal of Psychology, 129,* 565–581.

Menon, U., & Shweder, R. (1994). Kali's tongue: Cultural psychology and the power of "shame"in Orissa. In S. Kitayama & H. Markus (Eds.), *Emotion and culture:*

Empirical studies of mutual influence (pp. 241–282). Washington, DC: American Psychological Association.

Mesquita, B. (2000). Emotions in collectivist and individualist contexts. *Journal of Personality and Social Psychology, 80,* 68–74.

Mikulincer, M., & Goodman, G. (Eds.). (2006). *Dynamics of romantic love: Attachment, care, giving, and sex.* New York: Guilford Press.

Miller, J. B. (1976). *Toward a new psychology of women.* Boston: Beacon Press.

Miller, J. B., & Stiver, I. (1997). *The healing connection: How women form relationships in therapy and in life.* Boston: Beacon Press.

Miller, R. S., & Leary, M. R. (1992). Social sources and interactive functions of embarrassment. In M. Clark (Ed.), *Emotion and social behavior* (pp. 202–221). New York: Sage.

Minuchin, S., & Fishman, H. C. (1981). *Family therapy technique.* Cambridge, MA: Harvard University Press.

Morgan, R. L., & Heise, D. (1988). Structure of emotions. *Social Psychology Quarterly, 51,* 19–31.

Murray, H. A. (1938). *Explorations in personality.* New York: Oxford University Press.

Murray, S. L., Holmes, J. G., & Griffin, D. W. (2000). Self-esteem and the quest for felt security: How perceived regard regulates attachment processes. *Journal of Personality and Social Psychology, 78,* 478–498.

Murray, S. L., Holmes, J. G., Griffin, D. W., Bellavia, G., & Rose, P. (2001). The mismeasure of love: How self-doubt contaminates relationship beliefs. *Personality and Social Psychology Bulletin, 27,* 423–436.

Nath, R., & Craig, J. (1999). Practicing family therapy in India: How many people are there in a marital subsystem? *Journal of Family Therapy, 21,* 390–406.

Neimeyer, R., & Mahoney, M. (1995). *Constructivism in psychotherapy.* Washington, DC: American Psychological Association.

Nesse, R. (1990). Evolutionary explanations of emotions. *Human Nature, 1,* 261–289.

Nichols, M. (Director). (1966). *Who's Afraid of Virginia Woolf?* [Motion picture]. United States: Chenault Productions.

Nwoye, A. (2000). Building on the indigenous: Theory and method of marriage therapy in contemporary Eastern and Western Africa. *Journal of Family Therapy, 22,* 347–359.

Oatley, K. (1992). Human emotions: Function and dysfunction. *Annual Review of Psychology, 43,* 55–85.

Oatley, K. (2004). *Emotions: A brief history.* Malden, MA: Blackwell.

Oatley, K., Keltner, D., & Jenkins, J. M. (2006). *Understanding emotions* (2nd ed.). Malden, MA: Blackwell Publishers.

Obbo, C. (1976). Dominant male ideology and female options: Three East African case studies. *Africa, 46,* 371–389.

Öhman, A. (1986). Face the beast and fear the face: Animal and social fears as prototypes for evolutionary analysis of emotion. *Psychophysiology, 23*, 123–145.

Okun, B. F. (1996). *Understanding diverse families*. New York: Guilford Press.

Olsen, D. H., & DeFrain, J. (1994). *Marriage and the family: Diversity and strengths*. Mountain View, CA: Mayfield.

Onions, C. T. (1966). *The Oxford dictionary of English etymology*. NewYork: Oxford University Press.

Panksepp, J. (1998). *Affective neuroscience: The foundations of human and animal emotions*. Oxford, England: Oxford University Press.

Panksepp, J. (2002). On the animalian values of the human spirit: The foundational role of affect in psychotherapy and the evolution of consciousness. *European Journal of Psychotherapy, Counseling, and Health, 5*, 225–245.

Panksepp, J., Siviy, S. M., & Normansell, L. A. (1985). Brain opioids and social emotions. In M. Reite & T. Field (Eds.), *The psychobiology of attachment and separation* (pp. 3–49). New York: Academic Press.

Pascual-Leone, J. (1987). Organismic processes for neo-Piagetian theories: A dialectical causal account of cognitive development. *International Journal of Psychology, 22*, 531–570.

Pascual-Leone, J. (1990a). An essay on wisdom: Toward organismic processes that make it possible. In R. J. Sternberg (Ed.), *Wisdom: Its nature, origins, and development* (pp. 244–278). New York: Cambridge University Press.

Pascual-Leone, J. (1990b). Reflections on life-span intelligence, consciousness, and ego development. In C. Alexander & E. Langer (Eds.), *Higher stages of human development: Perspectives on adult growth* (pp. 258–285). New York: Oxford University Press.

Pascual-Leone, J. (1991). Emotions, development, and psychotherapy: A dialectical constructivist perspective. In J. Safran & L. S. Greenberg (Eds.), *Emotion, psychotherapy, and change* (pp. 302–335). New York: Guilford Press.

Pearlman, S. (1989). Distancing and connectedness: Impact of couple formation in lesbian relationships. In E. D. Rothblum & E. Cole (Eds.), *Loving boldly: Issues facing lesbians* (pp. 77–88). New York: Huntington Park Press.

Perls, F. (1969). *Gestalt therapy verbatim*. Lafayette, CA: Real People Press.

Pietromonaco, P. R., & Feldman Barrett, L. (2000). The internal working models concept: What do we really know about the self in relation to others? *Review of General Psychology, 4*, 155–175.

Pimentel, E. E. (2000). Just how do I love thee? Marital relations in urban China. *Journal of Marriage and Family, 62*, 32–47.

Pinsof, W. (2002). The death of "till death us do part": The transformation of pair-bonding in the 20th century. *Family Process, 41*, 135–157.

Pittman, F. (1989). *Private lies: Infidelity and the betrayal of intimacy*. New York: Norton.

Plutchik, R. (1980). A general psychoevolutionary theory of emotion. In R. Plutchik & H. Kellerman (Eds.), *Emotion: Theory, research, and experience: Vol. 1. Theories of emotion* (pp. 3–33). New York: Academic Press.

Plysiuk, M. (1985). *A process study of marital conflict resolution*. Unpublished master's thesis, University of British Columbia, Vancouver, British Columbia, Canada.

Porges, S. (1995). Orienting in a defensive world: Mammalian modifications of our evolutionary heritage: A polyvagal theory. *Psychophysiology, 32*, 301–318.

Porges, S. (1996). Vagal tone: An autonomic mediator of affect. In J. Garber & K. Dodge (Eds.), *The development of affect regulation and dysregulation* (pp. 11–128). New York: Cambridge University Press.

Rajecki, D. W., Lamb, M. E., & Obsmacher, P. (1978). Toward a general theory of infantile attachment: A comparative review of aspects of the social bond. *The Behavioral and Brain Sciences, 1*, 417–464.

Rampage, C. (2002). Marriage in the 20th century: A feminist's perspective. *Family Process, 41*, 61–69.

Ramu, G. (1988). Marital roles and power: Perceptions and reality in the urban setting. *Journal of Comparative Family Studies, 19*, 207–227.

Real, T. (1997). *I don't want to talk about it: Overcoming the secret legacy of male depression*. New York: Scribner.

Rehman, U., & Holtzworth-Munroe, A. (2006). A cross-cultural analysis of the demand–withdraw marital interaction: Observing couples from a developing country. *Journal of Consulting and Clinical Psychology, 74*, 755–766.

Reid, D. W., Dalton, E. J., Laderoute, K., Doell, F., & Nguyen, T. (2006). Therapeutically induced changes in couple identity: The role of "we-ness" and interpersonal processing in relationship satisfaction. *Genetic, Social, and General Psychology Monographs, 132*(3), 121–143.

Reis, H., & Patrick, B. (1996). Attachment and intimacy: Component processes. In E. T. Higgins & A. W. Kruglanski (Eds.), *Social psychology: Handbook of basic principles* (pp. 523–563). New York: Guilford Press.

Rice, F. (1990). *Intimate relationships, marriages, and families*. Mountain View, CA: Mayfield Publishing.

Rice, L., & Greenberg, L. S. (Eds.). (1984). *Patterns of change: An intensive analysis of psychotherapeutic process*. New York: Guilford Press.

Rilke, R. (1934). *Letters to a young poet*. London: Norton.

Roberts, L. (2000). Fire and ice in marital communication: Hostile and distancing behaviors as predictors of marital distress. *Journal of Marriage and the Family, 62*, 693–707.

Rogers, C. (1951). *Client-centered therapy: Its current practice, implication, and theory*. Boston: Houghton Mifflin.

Rogers, C. (1959). A theory of therapy, personality, and interpersonal relationships, as developed in the client-centered framework. In S. Koch (Ed.), *Psychology: A study of a science* (Vol. 3, pp. 184–256). New York: McGraw-Hill.

Rogers, C. (1975). Empathic: An unappreciated way of being. *The Counseling Psychologist, 5*, 2–10.

Rogers-Millar, E. L., & Millar, F. E. (1979). Domineeringness and dominance: A transactional view. *Human Communication Research, 5*, 238–246.

Rosenblatt, P. C. (1996). Grief that does not end. In D. Klass, P. R. Silverman, & S. L. Nickman (Eds.), *Continuing bonds: New understandings of grief* (pp. 45–58). Washington, DC: Taylor & Francis.

Rothbaum, F., Pott, M., Azuma, H., Miyake, K., & Weisz, J. (2000). The development of close relationships in Japan and the United States: Paths of symbiotic harmony and generative tension. *Child Development, 7,* 1121–1142.

Rozin, R., Haidt, J., & McCauley, C. R. (2000). Disgust. In M. Lewis & J. M. Haviland-Jones (Eds.), *Handbook of emotions* (2nd ed., pp. 637–653). New York: Guilford Press.

Rusbult, C. E., Van Lange, P. A. M., Wildschut, T., Yovetich, N. A., & Verette, J. (2000). Perceived superiority in close relationships: Why it exists and persists. *Journal of Personality and Social Psychology, 79,* 521–545.

Russell, J. A. (1997). Reading emotions from and into faces: Resurrecting a dimensional–contextual perspective. In J. A. Russell & J. M Fernández-Dols (Eds.), *The psychology of facial expression* (pp. 295–320). New York: Cambridge University Press.

Russell, J. A., & Mehrabian, A. (1977). Evidence for a three-factor theory of emotions. *Journal of Research in Personality, 11,* 273–294.

Ryan, R. M., & Deci, D. C. (2000). Self-determination theory and the facilitation of intrinsic motivation, social development, and well-being. *American Psychologist, 55,* 68–78.

Safdar, S. (2006, October). *Emotional display rules: A comparison between Canada, the USA, and Japan.* Paper presented at York University Brown Bag Series, York University, Toronto, Ontario, Canada.

Satir, V. (1988). *The new peoplemaking.* Palo Alto, CA: Science and Behavior Books.

Scherer, K. R., Wallbott, H. G., & Summerfield, A. B. (Eds.). (1986). *Experiencing emotion: A cross-cultural study.* Cambridge, England: Cambridge University Press.

Schnarch, D. (1991). *Constructing the sexual crucible: An integration of sexual and marital therapy.* New York: Norton.

Schnarch, D. (1997). *Passionate marriage: Love, sex, and intimacy in emotionally committed relationships.* New York: Holt.

Schore, A. N. (1994). *Affect regulation and the origin of the self: The neurobiology of emotional development.* Hillsdale, NJ: Erlbaum.

Schore, A. N. (2003). *Affect dysregulation and disorders of the self.* New York: Norton.

Schwartz, B., Tesser, A., & Powell, E. (1982). Dominance cues in nonverbal behavior. *Social Psychology Quarterly, 45,* 114–120.

Searight, H. R. (1997). *Family-of-origin therapy and diversity.* Washington, DC: Taylor & Francis.

Seay, B., Alexander, B. K., & Harlow, H. H. (1964). Maternal behavior of socially deprived rhesus monkeys. *Journal of Abnormal and Social Psychology, 69,* 345–354.

Seligman, M. (2002). *Authentic happiness: Using the new positive psychology to realize your potential for lasting fulfillment.* New York: Free Press.

Sharma, R. (2007). *A task analytic examination of dominance in emotion-focused couples therapy*. Unpublished master's thesis. York University, Toronto, Ontario, Canada.

Shaver, P. R., & Hazan, C. (1988). A biased overview of the study of love. *Journal of Social and Personal Relationships, 5*, 473–501.

Shaver, P. R., Hazan, C., & Bradshaw, D. (1988). Love as attachment: The integration of three behavior systems. In R. J. Sternberg & M. L. Barnes (Eds.), *The psychology of love* (pp. 68–99). New Haven, CT: Yale University Press.

Shen, T. (1996). The process and achievements of the study on marriage and family in China. *Marriage and Family Review, 22*, 19–53.

Shweder, R. A., & Haidt, J. (2000). The cultural psychology of the emotions: Ancient and new. In M. Lewis & J. M. Haviland-Jones (Eds.), *Handbook of emotions* (2nd ed., pp. 116–134). New York: Guilford Press.

Siddizi, M. U., & Reeves, E. Y. (1986). A comparative study of mate selection criteria among Indians in India and the United States. *International Journal of Comparative Sociology, 27*, 226–233.

Silverstein, O., & Roshbaum, B. (1994). *The courage to raise good men*. New York: Viking.

Singer, I. (1984). *The nature of love*. Chicago: University of Chicago Press.

Singh, R. N., & Kanjirathinkal, M. (1999). Levels and styles of commitment in marriage: The case of Asian Indian immigrants. In J. M. Adams & W. H. Jones (Eds.), *Handbook of interpersonal commitment and relationship stability* (pp. 307–322). New York: Kluwer Academic/Plenum Publishers.

Sluzki, C. E. (1983). Process, structure, and world views: Toward an integrated view of systemic models in family therapy. *Family Process, 22*, 469–476.

Smith, K., & Greenberg, L. S. (2007). Internal multiplicity in emotion-focused psychotherapy. *Journal of Clinical Psychology, 63*, 175–186.

Snarey, J. (1993). *How fathers care for the next generation*. Cambridge, MA: Harvard University Press.

Sonpar, S. (2005). Marriage in India: Clinical issues. *Contemporary Family Therapy, 27*, 301–313.

Spiegel, J., & Machotka, P. (1974). *Messages of the body*. New York: Free Press.

Stearns, C., & Stearns, J. (1988). *Emotion and social change: Toward a new psychohistory*. New York: Holmes & Meier.

Stern, D. N. (1985). *The interpersonal world of the infant*. New York: Basic Books.

Stets, J. E., & Burke, P. J. (1994). Inconsistent self-views in the control identity model. *Social Science Research, 23*, 236–262.

Sue, D. W., & Sue, D. (1990). *Counseling the culturally different: Theory and practice* (2nd ed.). New York: Wiley.

Sullivan, H. (1955). *The interpersonal theory of psychiatry*. New York: Norton.

Surrey, J. (1991). The "self-in-relation": A theory of women's development. In J. Jordan, A. Kaplan, J. B. Miller, & I. Stiver (Eds.), *Women's growth in connection: Writings from the Stone Center* (pp. 51–66). New York: Guilford Press.

Tambashe, B. O., & Shapiro, D. (1996). Family background and early life course transitions in Kinshasa. *Journal of Marriage and the Family, 58,* 1029–1037.

Tan Tzer, E. (1998). *The decision-making process toward divorce: The perspective of woman.* Unpublished master's thesis, National University of Singapore, Singapore.

Tang, A. C. (2001). Neonatal exposure to novel environment enhanced hippocampal-dependent memory function during infancy and adulthood. *Learning and Memory, 8,* 257–264.

Tang, A. C. (2003). A hippocampal theory of cerebral lateralization. In R. Davidson & K. Hugdahl (Eds.), *The asymmetrical brain* (pp. 37–68). Cambridge, MA: MIT Press.

Tangney, J. P. (1991). Moral affect: The good, the bad, and the ugly. *Journal of Personality and Social Psychology, 61,* 598–607.

Tangney, J. P., Miller, R. S., Flicker, L., & Barlow, D. H. (1996). Are shame, guilt, and embarrassment distinct emotions? *Journal of Personality and Social Psychology, 6,* 1256–1269.

Thomas, S. P. (2003). Men's anger: A phenomenological exploration of its meaning in a middle-class sample of American men. *Psychology of Men & Masculinity, 4,* 163–175.

Thomas, V., Karis, T. A., & Wetchler, J. L. (2003). *Clinical issues with interracial couples: Theories and research.* New York: Hayworth Press.

Tomkins, S. S. (1962). *Affect, imagery, consciousness: Vol. I. The positive affects.* New York: Springer-Verlag.

Tomkins, S. S. (1963). *Affect, imagery, consciousness: Vol. III. The negative affects: Anger and fear.* New York: Springer-Verlag.

Tomkins, S. S. (1984). Affect theory. In K. R. Scherer & P. Ekman (Eds.), *Approaches to emotion* (pp. 163–195). London: Erlbaum.

Tooby, J., & Cosmides, L. (1990). On the universality of human nature and the uniqueness of the individual: The role of genetics and adaptation. *Journal of Personality, 58,* 17–67.

Trivers, R. L. (1971). The evolution of reciprocal altruism. *Quarterly Review of Biology, 46,* 35–57.

Tronick, E. (2006). *The neurobehavioral and social-development of infants and children.* New York: W. W. Norton.

Tubbs, C. Y., & Rosenblatt, P. C. (2003). Assessment and intervention with Black–White multiracial couples. In V. Thomas, T. A. Karis, & J. L. Wetchler (Eds.), *Clinical issues with interracial couples: Theories and research* (pp. 131–149). New York: Hayworth Press.

Tucker, D. M., Luu, P., Desmond, R. E., Jr., Hartry-Speiser, A., Davey, C., & Flaisch, T. (2003). Corticolimbic mechanisms in emotional decisions. *Emotion, 3,* 127–149.

Usita, P. M., & Poulsen, S. (2003). Interracial relationships in Hawaii: Issues, benefits, and therapeutic interventions. In V. Thomas, T. A. Karis, & J. L. Wetchler

(Eds.), *Clinical issues with interracial couples: Theories and research* (pp. 73–83). New York: Hayworth Press.

Vogel, S. (1996). Urban middle-class Japanese family life, 1958–1996: A personal and evolving perspective. In D. Schwalb & B. Schwalb (Eds.), *Japanese child rearing: Two generations of scholarship* (pp. 177–201). New York: Guilford Press.

Watson, D. (2000). *Mood and temperament.* New York: Guilford Press.

Watson, J., Goldman, R. N., & Vanaerschot, G. (1998). Empathic: A postmodern way of being? In L. S. Greenberg, J. Watson, & G. Lietaer (Eds.), *Handbook of experiential psychotherapy* (pp. 61–81). New York: Guilford Press.

Watson, J., & Greenberg, L. S. (1996). Emotion and cognition in experiential therapy: A dialectical-constructivist position. In H. Rosen & K. Kuelwein (Eds.), *Constructing realities: Meaning-making perspectives for psychotherapists.* (pp. 253–276). San Francisco: Jossey-Bass.

Watson, J., & Greenberg, L. S. (in press). Empatheic resonance: A neuroscience perspective. In J. Decety & W. Ickes (Eds.), *The social neuroscience empathy.* Cambridge, MA: MIT Press.

Watson, J., & Rennie, D. (1994). Qualitative analysis of clients' subjective experience of significant moments during the exploration of problematic reactions. *Journal of Counseling Psychology, 41*, 500–509.

Watzlawick, P., Beavin, J. H., & Jackson, D. D. (1967). *Pragmatics of human communication.* New York: Norton.

Weiss, R. S. (1982). Attachment in adult life. In C. M. Parkes & J. Stevenson-Hinde (Eds.), *The place of attachment in human behavior* (pp. 171–184). NewYork: Basic Books.

Whelton, W., & Greenberg, L. S. (2001). The self as a singular multiplicity: A process–experiential perspective. In J. C. Muran (Ed.), *Self-relations in the psychotherapy process* (pp. 87–110). Washington, DC: American Psychological Association.

Whelton, W., & Greenberg, L. S. (2004). From discord to dialogue: Internal voices and the reorganization of the self in process–experiential therapy. In H. Hermans & G. Di Maggio (Eds.), *The dialogical self* (pp. 108–123). London: Brunner-Routledge.

Wieling, E. (2003). Latino/a and White marriages: A pilot study investigating the experiences of interethnic couples in the United States. In V. Thomas, T. A. Karis, & J. L. Wetchler (Eds.), *Clinical issues with interracial couples: Theories and research* (pp. 41–56). New York: Hayworth Press.

Wiggins, J. (1973). *Personality and prediction.* Reading, MA: Addison-Wesley.

Wile, D. (1993). *After the fight.* New York: Guilford Press.

Wilson, M. I., & Daly, M. (1996). Male sexual proprietariness and violence against wives. *Current Directions in Psychological Science, 5*, 2–6.

Winnicott, D. (1965). *The maturational process and the facilitating environment.* New York: International Universities Press.

Yelsma, P., & Athappilly, K. (1988). Marital satisfaction and communication practices: Comparisons among Indian and American couples. *Journal of Comparative Family Studies, 19,* 37–54.

Zane, N., Sue, S., Hu, L., & Kwon, J. (1991). Asian American assertion: A social learning analysis of cultural differences. *Journal of Counseling Psychology, 38,* 63–70.

AUTHOR INDEX

Jenkins, J. M., 27
Johnson, S., ix, 4, 5, 7–11, 14, 49, 137, 138, 159, 176, 264, 288, 289, 293

Kanjirathinkal, M., 120
Karis, T. A., 122
Kaufman, G., 317
Keating, E., 218
Keenan, J., 118
Keisler, D., 96
Keltner, D., 27, 31, 318
Kerr, M. E., 47
Khantzian, E., 288
Kitayama, S., 33, 113
Kohut, H., 23, 44, 57, 61, 62, 316
Komisaruk, B., 355
Krugman, S., 129
Kwon, J., 114

L'Abate, L., 8
Lachman, F. M., 62
Laderoute, K., 77
Lamb, M. E., 86
Larsen, R., 32
Leach, E., 100
Leary, M. R., 31
Leary, T., 91, 95, 96
LeDoux, J., 21, 22, 26, 27, 30
Levenson, R., 87, 359
Levinas, E., 77
LeVine, B. B., 86
LeVine, R. A., 86
Lewis, H. B., 129, 320
Locke, D. C., 122
Losada, M. F., 98
Lutz, C., 29

MacDonald, K., 85–87
MacGavin, L., 100
Machotka, P., 100
Mahoney, M., 34
Makinen, J. A., 264
Malcolm, W., 36, 289, 318
Markus, H., 33, 113
Mashek, H., 355
Maslow, A., 60
Masten, A. S., 66
Mateu-Marques, C., 108
Matsumoto, H., 113
McAuliffe, W., 288
McCauley, L. R., 33
McCoy, S. K., 319

McGinn, N., 118
McGuire, M., 68, 69
McLeod, J., 39
McRoy, R., 122
Mehrabian, A., 31, 32
Menon, U., 34
Mesquita, B., 113
Mikulincer, M., 80
Millar, F. E., 100
Miller, J. B., 131, 287
Miller, R. S., 31, 318
Millikin, J., 264
Minuchin, S., 7
Miyake, K., 114
Morgan, R. L., 32
Murray, H. A., 62
Murray, S. L., 69, 70

Nath, R., 116
Neimeyer, R., 34
Nesse, R., 31
Nguyen, T., 77
Nichols, M., 187
Normansell, L. A., 82
Nwoye, A., 118

Oatley, K., 25, 27, 28, 81
Obbo, C., 118
Obsmacher, P., 86
Öhman, A., 30, 31, 354
Okun, B. F., 123, 131, 133, 134
Olsen, D. H., 119
Onions, C. T., 355

Paivio, S. C., 4, 150, 327, 328
Panksepp, J., 21, 26, 29, 82, 85
Pascual-Leone, J., 10, 27, 28, 34, 56
Patrick, B., 82
Pearlman, S., 131
Peplau, L. A., 100
Perls, F., 7
Pietromonaco, P. R., 82
Pimentel, E. E., 114, 119, 121
Pinsof, W., 111
Pittman, F., 289
Plutchik, R., 29
Plysiuk, M., 8, 9
Pollack, W., 287
Porges, S., 26, 29, 88
Pott, M., 114
Poulsen, S., 122
Powell, E., 100

Vogel, S., 118

Wallbott, H. G., 227, 284
Waller, N. G., 284
Warwar, S., 36, 289, 318
Watson, D., 32
Watson, J., viii, 4, 10, 21, 22, 27, 34, 35, 36, 37, 52, 57, 144, 150, 164, 165, 169, 263, 328
Watzlawick, P., 7
Weakland, J., 7, 104
Weiss, R. S., 8
Weisz, J., 114
Wetchler, J. L., 122
Whelton, W., 10, 39, 93
Whiffen, V. E., 10, 59, 288

Whipple, B., 355
Whisman, M. A., 100, 101
White, G., 29
Wieling, E., 123
Wiggins, J., 95
Wildschut, T., 69
Wile, D., 108
Wilson, M. I., 30
Winnicott, D., 57, 87

Yelsma, P., 114–116, 119, 121
Yovetich, N. A., 69

Zane, N., 114
Zeki, S., 354

SUBJECT INDEX

and power, 230
primary adaptive, 232–235
primary maladaptive, 235–236
problematic expression of, 228–229
proneness to, 231
of pursuer, 238–242
secondary, 236–237
and shame, 128–129
of submissive partner, 254
types of, 231–238
and unloved feeling, 271–272
Anglo Saxon cultures, 228
Anxiety, 69, 80, 296–297
Anxious–ambivalent attachment, 79
Appeasement, 31
Appreciation, encouraging, 168
Arranged marriages, 115, 116, 120, 121
Asian culture
companionable love in, 117
emotional expression in, 115
and status, 73–74
Assertion
evolution of, 31
of identity, 69–72
in identity cycles, 245, 254
of preference, 64
Assertiveness, 181, 230
Assessment, emotion. *See* Emotion assessment
Assimilation, 126
Ataque, 112–113
Attachment, 77–85
adult, 8, 10, 67, 79–80, 84–85
adult-intimate-relational parameters for,
84–85
and affection, 86
as affect regulating process, vii
and connection, 4–5
emotions in adult, 81–84
and fear, 30
function of, 85
and identity, 62
importance of, 60
infant, 77–78
as interactional dimension, 95
as motivation, 59
as process, 82–83
proximity/availability required for, 65
revised theory of intimate-relationship,
80–81
ruptures in, 61
and self-esteem, 66

threats to, 61
Attachment anxiety, 283–285
Attachment bonds, 77, 84
Attachment injuries, 264–265, 273–277
Attachment-related affiliation axis, 96, 97
Attachment styles, 79–80
Attachment theory, 77
Attack–attack cycles, 187
Attack system, 102
Attending to felt sense, 213
Attention, emotion and, 20
Attitudes, toward extended family, 124
Attraction, 6–7, 60, 61, 85–88
Attraction–affection system, 60
Attractiveness, physical, 355
Attunement, 67
Authority, respect for, 127–128
Autonomy, 47
Availability, 65, 78, 79
Avoidance, 53, 80, 148–150
Awareness
of anger, 228
of emotion, 53–54
of past socialization, 54
of primary adaptive emotions, 51

Bacon, Francis, 59
Bakan, David, 12
Belonging, sense of, 69
Betrayal, 233, 289
Bicultural cultures. *See* Multicultural couples
Biracial children, 124–125
Blake, William, 315
Blame, 49
and anger, 236–237
and dominance, 105
and sadness, 262
Blamer softening, 8
Blocks, overcoming, 148–150
Body shame, 319–320, 325
Bonds, emotional, 22
Borderline processes, 236
Boundary violations, 233
Bowenian approaches, 47
Brain
and anger/fear, 27
and love, 354–355
Buber, M., 3
Bullying, 68
Bypassed shame affect, 129

Calmness, 363

and love, 355–356
and marriage/identity, 116–119
and power/equality/marital satisfaction, 119–128
and relationship views, 48
and role agreements, 73–74
and romantic love, 114–115
and social emotions, 32–34
and validation, 64
Cycles, of attack and defense, 49

Davidson, R. J., 41
De-escalation, of negative cycle (old Stage 2), 139
Depression, 262–263, 288
Describing felt sense, 213–214
Describing negative cycle (Stage 2), 141–147
Desire, 30
Dialectical constructivist view, 34–39
and complexity of being, 37–39
core schemes in, 37
emotion schematic processing/scripts, 35–37
and narrative, 39
Dickinson, Emily, 351
Differences
accepting, 168
acknowledging, 75
assimilating, 76
recognizing, 84
Dimensional approaches, 31–32
Diminishment, 49, 64
Disabilities, 183
Disclosing process, 159–161
Disgust, 194
and culture, 33
and dominance, 32
evolution of, 26
and shame, 320–321
Disillusionment, 76
Dismissive avoidant attachment, 79, 80
Distance cycles, pursue–. See Pursue–distance cycles
Distancer
anger of, 242–243
fear of, 304–309
sadness of, 273–277
shame of, 345–348
Distress
evolution of, 30
and problems with automatic emotions, 36

sadness vs., 261
Divorce, 111, 116, 130, 193
Dominance
and control, 72
and differentiated identity, 76
dimensional approaches to, 32
and fear of vulnerability, 71
feelings involved in, 102–104
measuring, 99–100
in negative interactional cycles, 173–174
and power, 99–101
and primary maladaptive anger, 236
process of, 104–106
Dominance conflicts, 6
Dominance cycles, 5
Dominance hierarchy, 68
Dominance-related emotions, evolution of, 30–31
Dominant
anger of, 243–245
fear of, 310–311
sadness of, 277–280
shame of, 328–343
Dominate–submit cycles, 176–183
Dominating anger, 70
Dowries, 120
Dress, 125–126
The Duality of Human Existence (David Bakan), 12
Dyadic regulation of affect, 42–47

EFT-C. See Emotion-focused couples therapy
Egalitarian relationships, 111–112, 118, 121
Ego psychological approaches, 47
8-point scale of couples validation, 109–110
Ekman, P., 41
Elaborated emotions, 33, 34
Elevation, as dominance strategy, 100
Embarrassment, 31, 69
Emotion(s), 19–40
awareness of, 20
basic, 21–22
as communication, 19–20
and conflict, 120–121
and consciousness, 20–21
couples and transformation of, 22–23
dialectical constructivist view of, 34–39
evolution of, 25–27
fear/sadness/shame as, 23–25
generation of, 27–29
identifying types of, 50–52

and interaction/motivation/cognition, 94–95
as meaning, 20
and memories, 21
neurochemical/physiological, 19
purposes of, 26
as raw material to be accessed/changed, vii
regulation of, 12
social, 29–34
and systems, 12
Emotional dominance, 32
Emotional expression
and culture, 112–113
in gay/lesbian relationships, 132–133
in multicultural couples, 123–124
Emotionally controlling behaviors, 71
Emotional neglect, 288
Emotional reactivity, 83
Emotional regulation, 83
Emotion assessment, 156–169
and accepting difference, 168
and compassion, 167–168
confrontation in, 159
and disclosing, 159–161
and empathic conjecture, 157
and encouraging appreciation/resentment, 168
and engendering/expressing positive emotions, 168–169
individual vs. couples, 158–159
and listening, 157
and overcoming self-interruptions, 166–169
and owning vulnerability/weakness, 162–163
and self-focus, 160, 162
and self-/other-focus, 157
and self-soothing/self-compassion, 163–166
Emotion change principles, 52–57
expressing emotion, 55
increasing awareness of emotion, 53–54
reflecting on emotion, 56
regulating emotion, 54–55
transforming emotion, 56–57
Emotion coaching, 153–156
Emotion-focused couples therapy (EFT-C), 7–10
developments in, 10–11
influences on, vii–ix

intervention framework of. *See* Intervention framework
Emotion-focused therapy, x
Emotions and needs worksheet, 161
Emotion schemes, 35–37, 81–84
Empathically affirming vulnerability, 218–224
Empathic attunement, 12, 44, 55, 61
Empathic conjecture, 157, 158
Empathy, 8, 26, 321, 322, 324, 326
Empowering anger, 70, 193–194, 227
Encouraging appreciation and resentment, 168
Endorphins, 20
Entitlement, sense of, 47
Envy, 31, 33, 133
Establishing collaborative alliance (Stage 1), 141
Euphoria, 354, 355
Evocative unfolding of problematic reaction points, 200–212
facilitating broader self-exploration in, 202, 204
reevoking experience in, 203–204
sample sessions of, 205–212
stages of therapist operations in, 202–203
tracking construed personal meaning of stimulus situation in, 202, 204
Excitement, 353, 359–361
Exercise of power, 68
Experiential–systemic synthesis, 92–97
dimensions of interaction, 95–97
interaction/emotion/motivation/cognition, 94–95
Experiential Therapy Adherence Measure, ix
Explicit reflexive experience, 34
Expressing emotion, 55
Expression
of anger, 228–231
of instrumental anger, 237–238
of secondary anger, 236–237
of vulnerabilities (Stage 3), 147–150
Expressivity, rejection of, 288
Extended family
approval of, 121–122
attitudes toward, 124
in Indian culture, 118
and marital satisfaction, 120
and marriage, 116
Externalization, 129
Eye contact, 69, 100

Face-to-face encounters, 77
Facial expressions, 193, 356
Facilitating broader self-exploration, 202, 204
Family of origin, 142
Fantasies, 76
Fathers, absence of, 287
Fear, 283–313
    of abandonment, 23, 49, 60, 61
    of abuse, 102
    in affiliative cycles, 298–309
    of annihilation, 61
    and anxiety, 23
    and attachment, 85
    as attachment anxiety, 284–285
    brain's reaction to, 27
    denial of, 105
    dimensional approaches to, 31, 32
    of distancer, 304–309
    and dominance, 102–103
    of dominant partner, 310–311
    evolution of, 25, 30
    in influencing cycle, 309–313
    of intimacy, 285–288
    of loss of control, 63–64, 102
    of loss of identity, 104
    as positive or negative emotion, 194
    and power, 99
    of pursuer, 298–301
    of rejection, 49, 60
    in relational attachment, 10
    revealing, 301–304
    and shame, 24
    and submission, 32
    of submissive partner, 311–313
    and trauma, 288–296
    treating, 296–297
Fearful avoidant attachment, 79–80
Feedback loop, 107
Feelings, revealing underlying, 4
Felt sense, focusing on, 213–217
Feminism, 121
First-moment emotional experience, 27, 28
Five-stage framework, 138–140
"Fixers," 177
Flourishing cycle, 197
FMRI (functional magnetic resonance imaging), 354
Focusing intervention, 213–217
Food, 125
Forgiveness, 290, 318
Freud, Sigmund, 259

Functional magnetic resonance imaging (fMRI), 354

Gandhi, Mahatma, 111
Gay relationships. *See* Lesbian and gay relationships
Gender differences
    in anger expression, 231
    in dominance strategies, 100
    in emotional expression, 128–131
    in fear of intimacy, 286–288
    with shame, 320
Gender identity, 67
Gender role expectations, 125
Goldman, Rhonda N., ix
Goldstein, K., 91
Gratitude, 31
Greenberg, Leslie S., viii–ix
Grief, 124–125, 260
Growth tendency, 60
Guilt, 31, 316, 318
Gusii people, 86

Happiness, 25, 87–88, 357–359
Harmony, 118
Hatred, 33
Healthy dominance, 72
Healthy fear, 283
Herd animals, humans as, 96
Hierarchy, 5
    and marriage in different cultures, 118–119
    and role agreements, 73
    of status, 31
"High road" of emotion, 26, 27
Homesickness, 126–127
Homework, 154
Homophobia, 133
Hong Kong, 117
Hope, 363
Hopelessness, 182, 262, 285
Hostility, 96, 97
Humiliation, 60
Humor, 55, 87, 231, 359

Identity(-ies)
    and couples' conflicts, 5–6
    defining, 63–65
    development of sense of, 44
    evolutionary development of, 68–69
    fusion of, 84
    in gay/lesbian relationships, 132, 133

of caregiver and attachment, 78
nurturing, 12
and self-regulation, 45
Restructuring, of negative interaction (old Stage 4), 139–140
Revealing underlying feelings, 9–10
Reward systems, 85–86, 88
Rice, Laura, viii
Right (to define reality)
and culture, 73
and power/dominance, 99, 101–103
and shame, 329–330
Right frontal activation, 88
Right side of cortex, 85
Rilke, R., 137
Role agreements, 72–74
Role expectations, 125
Role-theory framework, 118
Romantic love
action tendency for, 356
and attachment, 83–84
and culture, 114–115
drive for, 355
in Japanese culture, 117
in Western culture, 111
Romantic relationships, 79, 101
Romeo and Juliet (William Shakespeare), 33
Roosevelt, Franklin D., 283

Sadness, 259–281
action tendencies with, 259–260
adaptive, 24
in affiliation cycles, 265–277
and connection, 23
of distancer, 273–277
distress vs., 261
of dominant partner, 277–280
evolution of, 25, 30
and grief, 260
importance of, 259
in influence cycles, 277–281
and loneliness, 260–261
primary adaptive vs. secondary, 261–265
of pursuer, 265–272
of submissive partner, 280–281
unresolved past loss and maladaptive, 272–273
Safe haven, 77
Satir, Virginia, viii, ix
Sawabone, 62
Scripts, 36–37, 317

Secondary anger, 229, 238–242, 293
Secondary attachment figures, 81
Secondary emotions, 50–51, 53, 106–110
Secondary rage, 55
Secondary sadness, 262–263
Secondary shame, 321
Second-moment emotional experience, 27–28
Secrecy, 287
Secure attachment, 79
Secure base, 77
Security
and affect regulation, 83
and attachment, 78
and connectedness/closeness, 43, 44
Self, love and expansion of, 353
Self-assertion, 114
Self-compassion, 163–166
Self-confidence, 65
Self-critical conflict, 8
Self-development, 60, 66–67
Self-disclosure, 287
Self-esteem, 66, 70
and dominance, 101, 103
and empathic attunement, 44
Self-exploration, facilitating broader, 202, 204
Self-focus, 22, 54, 102, 160, 162
Self-formation, 34
Self-functioning, 10
Self-inhibition, 55
Self-in-relation, 34–39
Self-interruptions, 166–169
Self narrative, 44
Self-organization, 26
and attachment, 80
and emotion schemes, 37
Self-regulation of affect, 3, 11, 43–47
and adult attachment, 84–85
and couple relationships, 45–47
emergence of, 62
importance of adult, 44–45
and self-soothing, 11
usefulness of, 11
Self-self relationship, 63
Self-soothing, 4, 43
and attachment, 81
calmness achieved with, 363
and couple relationships, 46, 47
and dominance, 5, 102
and fear, 300–301
in gay/lesbian relationships, 132, 133

Trauma
    and fear, 283
    violational vs. neglectful, 288
Trauma in relationships, 288–296
    active, 292–296
    affairs as, 290–292
    passive, 288–290
Traumatic experience
    defined, 288
    and emotional brain, 21
    and emotional numbing, 361
Trust, 71, 290–291
Twain, Mark, 199

Ugandan people, 86
Ultimatums, 230
Unclear felt sense, focusing on, 213–217
Undercontrol, of anger, 232, 236
Underfunctioning cycle, overfunctioning–.
    See Overfunctioning–underfunc-
    tioning cycle
Underlying feelings, accessing (old Stage 3),
    139
Underregulated emotions, 54
United States
    marital satisfaction in, 119–120
    marriage/divorce in, 111
Unloved feeling, 271–272
Unmet needs, 3, 4, 11, 60, 236–237
Unresolved past loss, 272–273
Utku culture, 356

Validation
    and alliance formation (old Stage 1),
        138–140
    and attachment, 80
    compensating for lack of, 64
    couples 8-point system of, 109–110
    and dominance, 103
    in gay/lesbian relationships, 132, 133
    of identity, 65–67
    from intimate partner, 44
    as motivation, 60
    of partner, 244–245
    in positive interaction cycles, 192–193
    and shame, 23–24
Values
    and culture, 115
    sharing, 117

Vasopressin (VP), 78
Violence, 68, 70
    and primary maladaptive anger, 236
    and shame, 320
    and trauma, 296
Voles, 78
VP (vasopressin), 78
Vulnerability(-ies)
    accepting (Stage 4), 150–153
    acknowledgment of, 53
    and culture, 113
    and dominance process, 105–106
    empathically affirming, 218–224
    expressing (Stage 3), 147–150
    expressions of, 55
    fear of, 71, 301–309
    identifying (Stage 2), 141–147
    as lens filters, 143
    owning, 162–163
    and primary maladaptive anger, 235
    rejection of, 288
    and shame, 316
    sharing/responding to, 49–50

Weakness, owning, 162–163
Well-being, sense of, 65
"We-ness," sense of, 77
Western culture
    marital satisfaction in, 119
    marriage in, 111
    respect in, 121
    shame in, 129, 319–320
    and status, 73, 74
    vulnerability in, 113
Whining, 262
Who's Afraid of Virginia Woolf (film), 188
Wife-demand/husband-withdraw pattern,
    100
Withdrawal, 49, 71, 194, 334–343
Withdrawer reengagement, 8
Withdraw–withdraw cycles, 187, 273–277
Women, 121. See also Gender differences
Working model, 81–83

"You" language, 53, 194

Zeno, 59
Zulu language, 62

ABOUT THE AUTHORS

Leslie S. Greenberg, PhD, is a professor of psychology and director of the Psychotherapy Research Clinic at York University in Toronto, Ontario, Canada. He is one of the leading authorities on working with emotions in psychotherapy and is an originator of emotion-focused approaches to the treatment of individuals and couples, having written the major original texts on the approach. He has trained intensively in both experiential and systemic approaches and has integrated these into the development of an emotion-focused approach to couples therapy. Dr. Greenberg also has written extensively on the theory and practice of emotion-focused therapy with individuals. He conducts a private practice for individuals and couples and offers training internationally in emotion-focused approaches to treatment.

Rhonda N. Goldman, PhD, is an associate professor at Argosy University, Schaumburg Campus, Schaumburg, Illinois, and is also affiliated as a therapist with the Family Institute at Northwestern University in Evanston, Illinois, where she works with both couples and individuals. She became active in the development of emotion-focused therapy in graduate school while working with Leslie S. Greenberg. Since then, she has coauthored two texts illustrating the approach for working with individuals. More recently, she became involved in writing about emotion-focused therapy for couples. She also practices, teaches, and conducts research on emotional processes and outcomes in emotion-focused therapy and has written on empathy, vulnerability, depression, and case formulation.